Roerich

east & *west*

Paintings

from the

Nicholas Roerich Museum

by Kenneth Archer

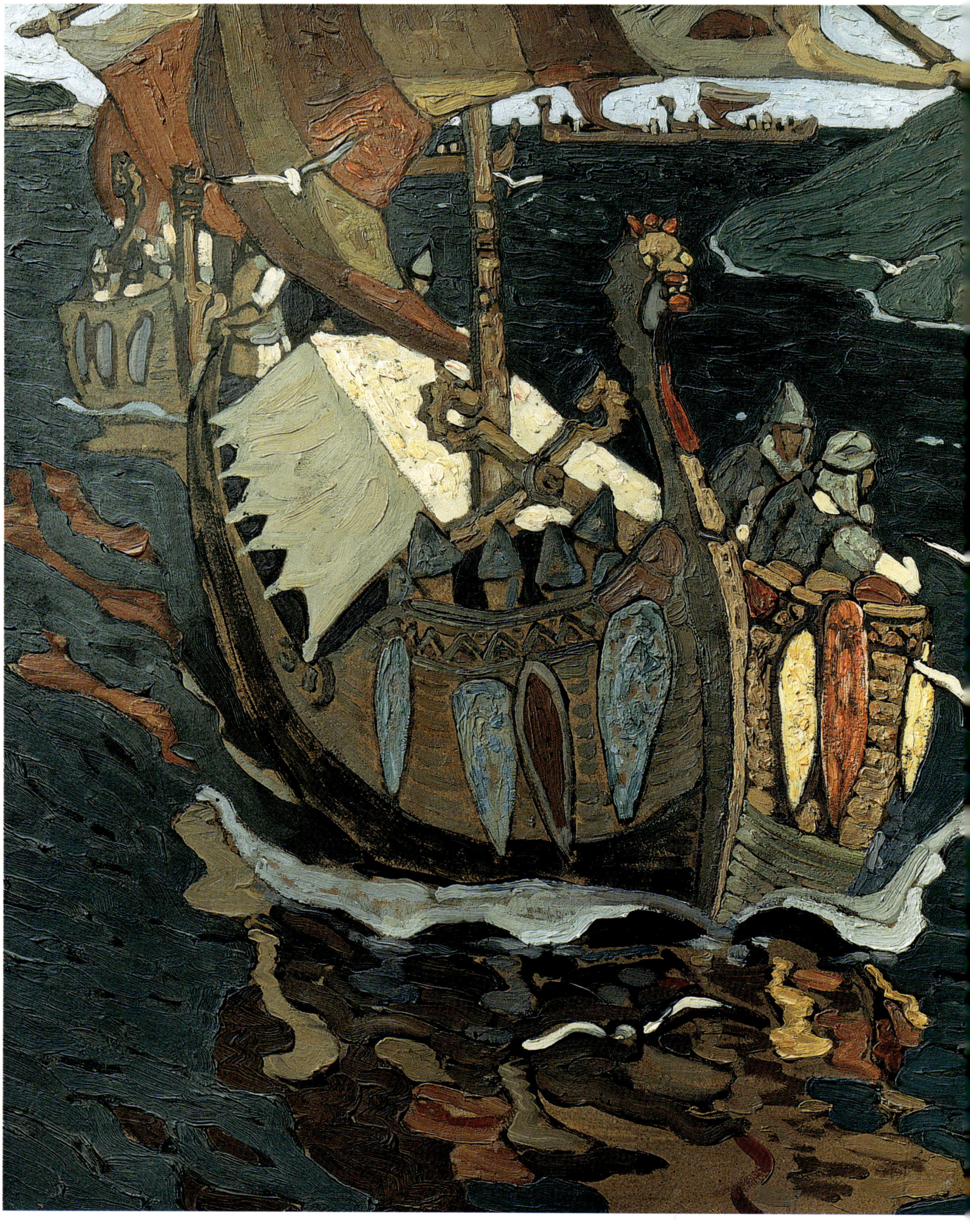

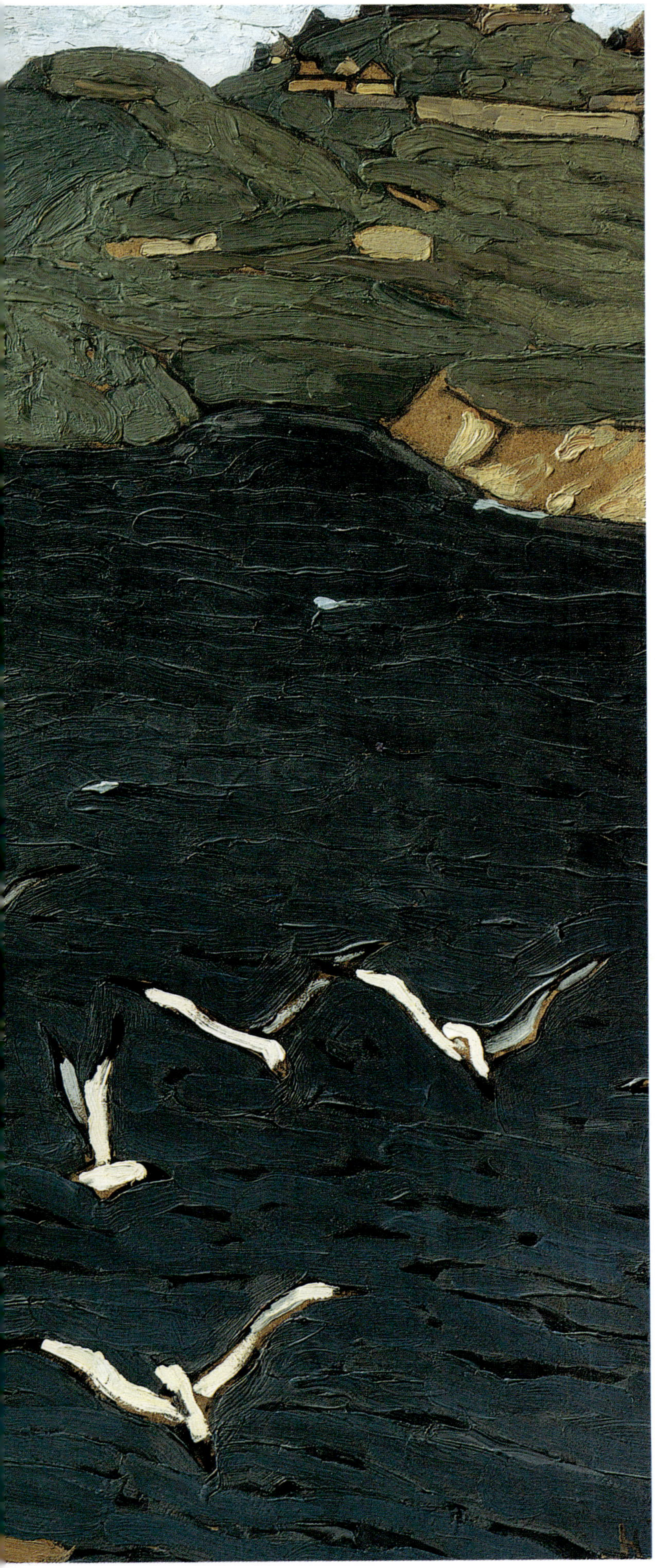

Overseas Guests: a folk painting, 1902

Oil on board, 79 x 100 cm.
Russian Museum, Saint Petersburg

Publishing editor: Jean-Paul Manzo
Publishing Associate: Cornelia Sontag
Texts by: Kenneth Archer
Design and typsetting by: Russell Stretten Consultancy

Coordination: Barbara Vignaux
Publishing assistants: Peggy Cambier, Sophie Delmar
Photographic credits:
Picture of *Remember* (pages 92 and 174-175) : Erik Landsburg
The Nicholas Roerich Museum provided most of the slides.

Printed and bound in Europe 1999

ISBN 1 85 995 483 9

We are very grateful to the Nicholas Roerich Museum for their kind help.

Roerich

east & west

by Kenneth Archer

I dedicate this book with gratitude to my wife and collaborator, Millicent, who has worked with me on the research and realization of this project and many others.

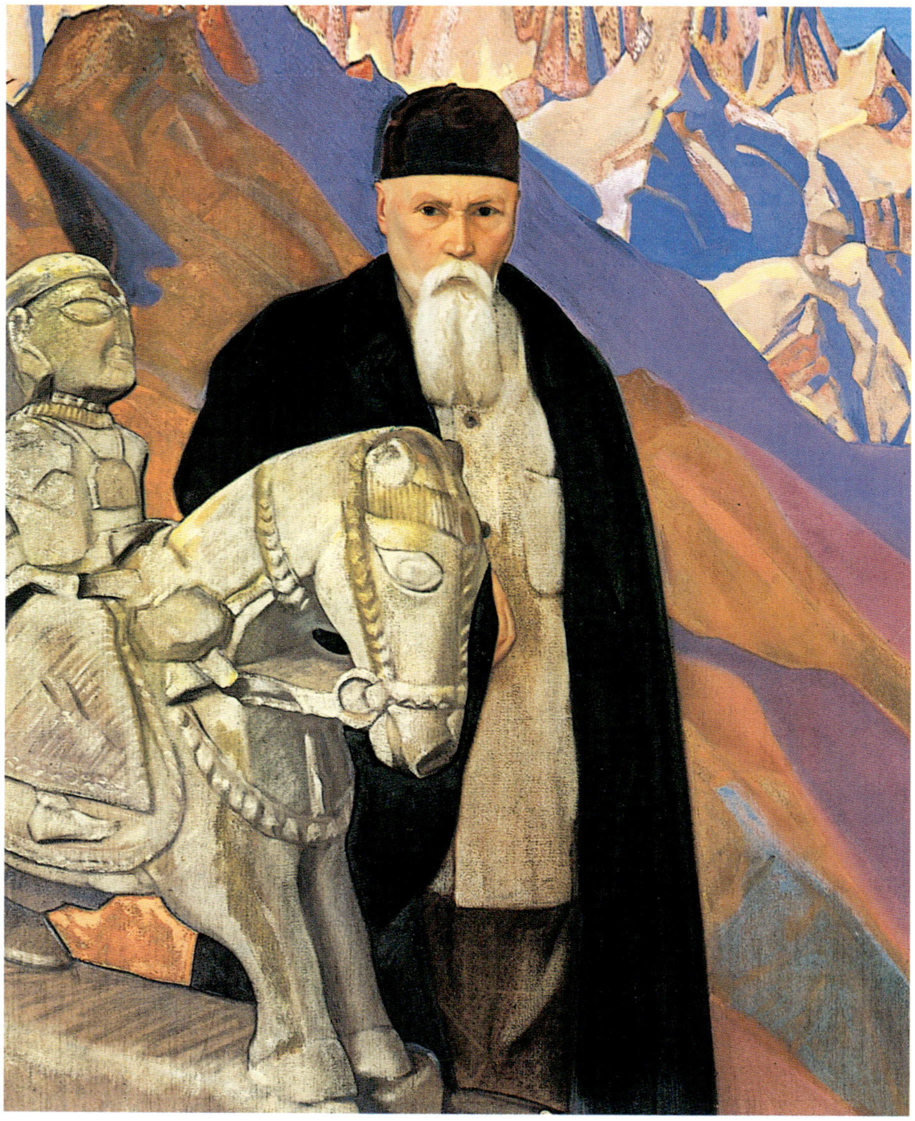

Svetoslav Roerich

Portrait of Nicholas Roerich, 1937

Oil on canvas, 137 x 150 cm
Nicholas Roerich Museum,
New York

'The idea of east and west – the idea of the twain which shall never meet – is to our mind already a fossilized idea. We are already ashamed to believe that superficial walls can exist and can divide the best impulses of humanity, this impulse of creative evolution. And now before our eyes is the so-called west and the so-called east. Piercingly they look at each other. They can be the closest friends and co-workers.'

Nicholas Roerich, New York, 1929

preface

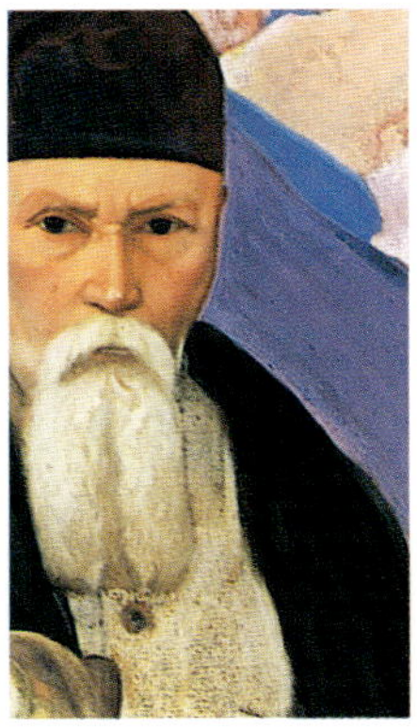

This monograph on the art of Nicholas Roerich is based on information gathered over three decades. The main thrust of the research took place, however, during a two-year period when I travelled to the Soviet Union, United States and India to see key collections of his art and interview those who knew most about it.

In 1981 I benefitted from a three-week residency at the Nicholas Roerich Museum, New York, by invitation of its executive vice-president, Sina Fosdick, who had corresponded with me for ten years. I saw the museum's collection of one-hundred-and-fifty paintings and discussed them with Mrs. Fosdick, a close friend and collaborator of the artist. During our talks I verified information acquired in the early 1970's from Roerich's former secretary, Vladimir Shibayev, based at Cardiff University, and from Roerich's younger son, Svetoslav, when he came to London.

During a second visit to the museum in 1982, I prepared a catalogue of the collection. In addition to further talks with Sina Fosdick, I interviewed Daniel Entin, the museum's archivist (now its director) and Edgar Lansbury, its curator. While in New York I traced many Roerich paintings once owned by the former Roerich Museum-a collection which had numbered over one thousand works. I also interviewed Frances Grant, who, like Mrs Fosdick, had headed Roerich institutions.

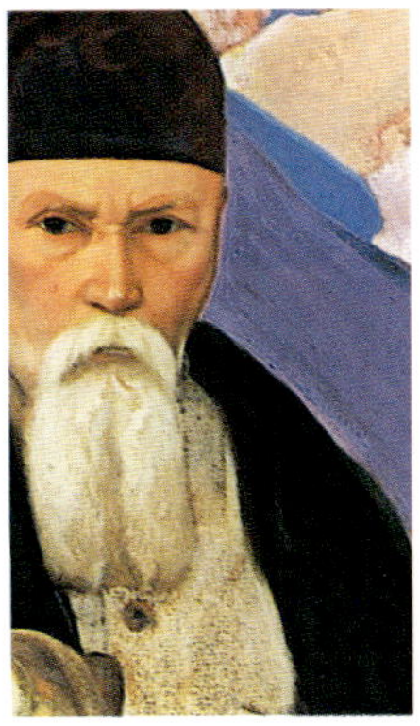

Funded by the International Research and Exchanges Board in summer 1983, I documented the largest Roerich collections in the USSR. In Moscow I conducted interviews with Olga Rumyansova, director of the Roerich Study at the State Oriental Museum, and with curators at the Tretyakov Gallery and the Bakhrushin Theatre Museum. In Leningrad I viewed Roerich materials at the Academy of Art and had a week of meetings with Valentina Knyaseva, twentieth century curator at the State Russian Museum and Roerich's leading biographer. Her collaborator, Pavel Belikov, had for years shared information with me through the post.

In autumn 1983 I toured India with a travel grant from the Indian Council for Cultural Relations. I spent three weeks in Bangalore interviewing Svetoslav Roerich, studied Roerich collections at Indian institutions and stayed for two weeks researching at Roerich's former residence, now a gallery of his art, at Naggar in the Himalayas.

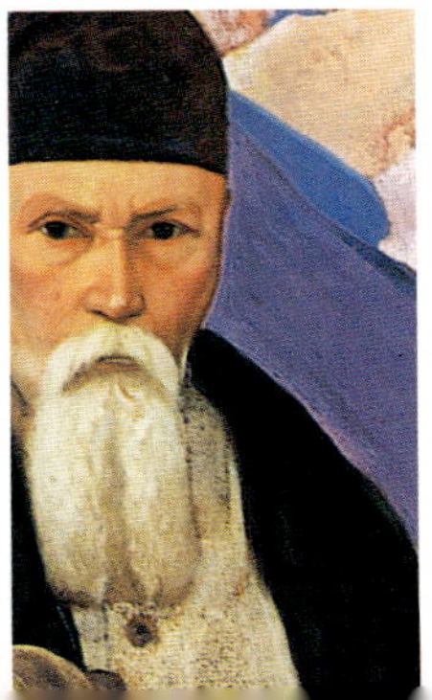

Acknowledgements

Many people and organizations have been of assistance in the course of my research on Nicholas Roerich, and I am grateful to them all. In addition to the individuals and institutions named in my preface, I should like to mention specifically Jean Archer, my foremost helper since I began the Roerich work, and Devika Rani Roerich, with whom I corresponded for two decades. Among the many institutions whose directors and staff members I should like to thank, the following are particularly relevant to this book-in London: Antioch International, India Office Library, Oriental Department of the British Museum and Victoria and Albert Museum; and elsewhere in England: Ashmolean Museum, Oxford, Department of Art History, University of Essex, and Worthing Municipal Art Gallery; in Helsinki, the Atheneum Museum and Synebrychoff Museum; in Paris: Bibliothèque Nationale, Institut Nationale des Etudes Slaves, Documentation du Musée d'Orsay, Grande Chancellerie, Légion d'Honneur, Fonds Nationale d'Art Contemporain, Bibliothèque de l'Opéra, Musée des Arts Decoratifs, Louvre, Musée National d'Art Moderne, Centre Georges Pompidou, and Service Slave, Bibliothèque Nationale; in New Delhi: Lalit Kala Academi, National Gallery of Modern Art and Pusa Institute Library; elsewhere in India: Allahabad Museum, Bhavat Kala Bhavan Museum of Art and Archaeology in Varanasi, Karnataka Chitrakala Parishath Art Complex, Bangalore, Roerich Art Gallery, Naggar, Sri Chitra Art Gallery, Trivandrum, and Theosophical Society Museum, Adyar; in Milan: Museo di Teatro alla Scala; in St Petersburg: Academy of Art, Hermitage Museum, Institute of Archaeology, Saltykov- Schedrin Library and State Theatrical Museum; and elsewhere in Russia: Lenin Library, Moscow and State Regional Museum, Novgorod; in Stockholm: Dansmuseet; in New York: Centre for Peace Through Culture, Cordier-Ekstrom Gallery, Dance Collection of the Performing Arts Library at Lincoln Center, Slavic Division, Columbia University Library and Stravinsky-Diaghilev Foundation; and elsewhere in the United States: Robert Frost Library and Slavic Studies Department, Amhurst College; Rose Art Museum at Brandeis University in Waltham; and the Library of Congress, Washington, DC.

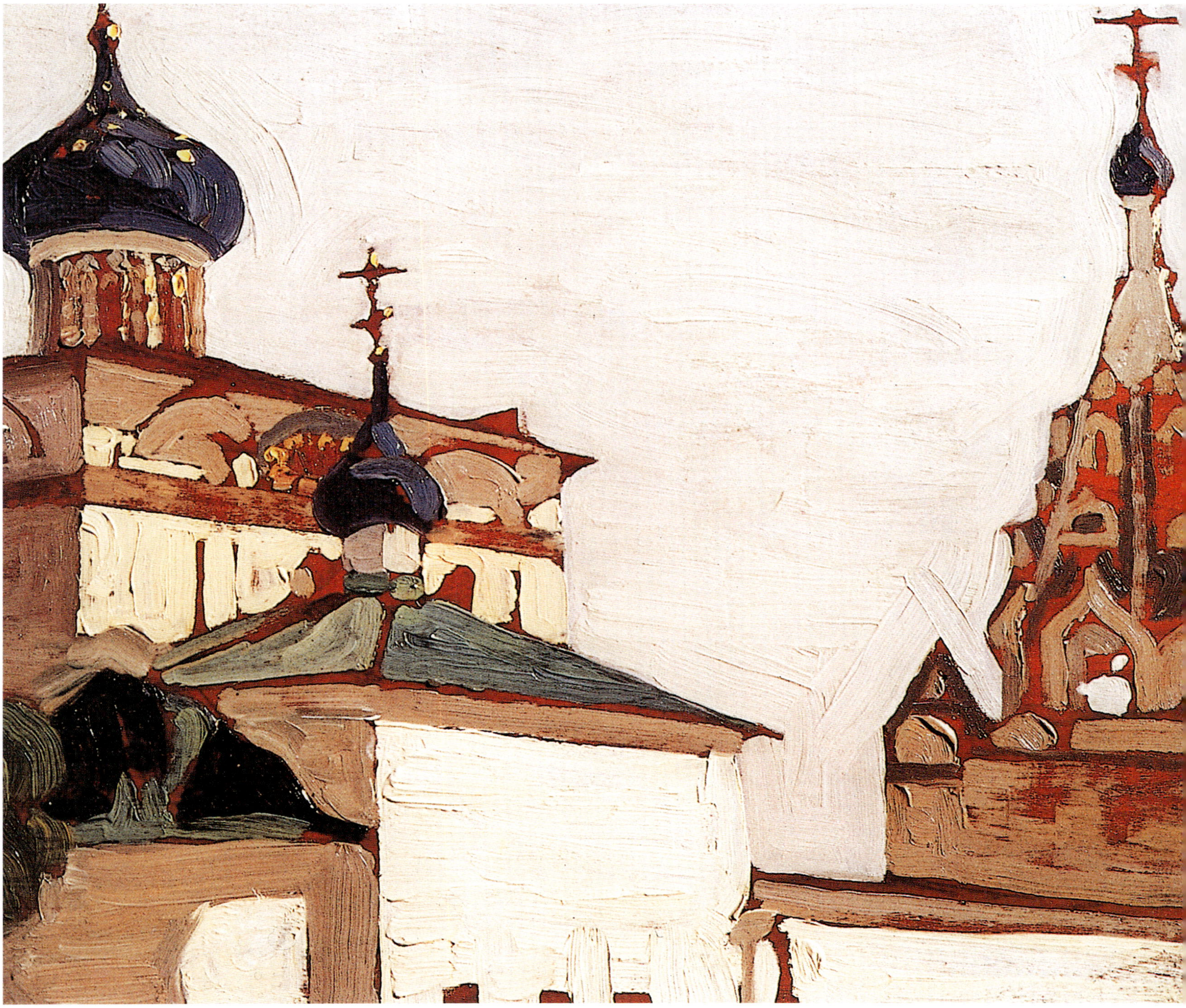

Old Russia, Yaroslav. Church of the Nativity of Our Lady, 1903

Oil on panel, 31.7 x 40 cm.
Museum of Oriental Art, Moscow

Introduction

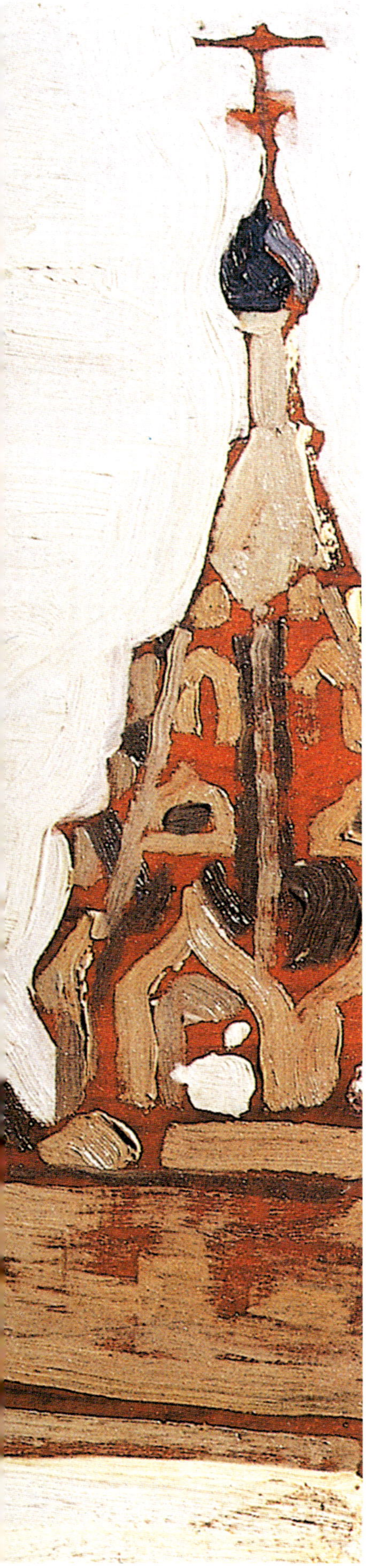

Nicholas Roerich (1874-1947) began his life in imperial Russia, on the eastern edge of western civilisation. He ended his days in the British Himalayas at an outpost of western society in the east. As a burgeoning artist and scholar, he had grown up among the intelligentsia of St Petersburg, known since its founding as Russia's 'window on the west.' Like generations of European painters, he furthered his artistic training in France and Italy. But he was always intrigued by the oriental aspects of Russia. In the World of Art circle of Sergei Diaghilev, Roerich as a young professional was identified with the Slavophile rather than the Francophile faction. (1) Designing for Diaghilev's Ballets Russes, Roerich saw Europe in the last years of the Belle Epoque, and the international exhibition of his paintings was part of the creative outburst so abruptly interrupted by World War I.

Around the time of the Russian Revolution, Roerich left his homeland- virtually for life. From 1917 until 1919 he lived in Finland and exhibited his paintings in Scandinavia. He then moved to London where he designed at Covent Garden and presented his Spells of Russia exhibition, which toured to other English cities. (2) In 1920 he took his wife and sons to the United States, becoming one of the many European artists displaced in the twentieth century by wars and revolutions. But Roerich arrived in America with considerable advantages. He had come through the prestigious invitation of the Chicago Art Institute and commissions from the Chicago Opera. New York, however, became his base, and for several years he flourished not only as a painter but as a founder of various cultural institutions. (3) At the age of forty-nine he was a successful man and a model of the western artist as the role had evolved since the Renaissance. By the time he was fifty, however, his life had undergone a total reorientation. In 1923 he sailed with his family to India and toured the subcontinent before embarking on a five-year expedition through Central Asia.

Roerich's art manifested the same polarity as his life. What first inspired his painting was the history hidden in the Russian earth, findings from his own archaeological excavations. The bones, urns, knives and other ritual objects of burial sites led the artist, even as an adolescent, to study the customs of the ancient Slavs.

Old Russia, Yaroslav. Church of the Nativity of Our Lady, detail

From this source came the master works of his early career, scenes of archaic life reimagined through myth. His fascination with subterranean clues to human development evolved over time into pure contemplation of the Himalayan peaks. There his quest culminated. In spectacular panoramas on the roof of the world he found the painterly image that linked outer reality and inner revelation. Mountains became for him the means to explore pure colour, the synthesis of visual perception and spiritual awareness. From his debut as a turn of the century Symbolist rendering archetypal visions of Russia, he eventually found his own method of abstraction- liberating the mountainscape from detail and reifying it as a medium for meditation.

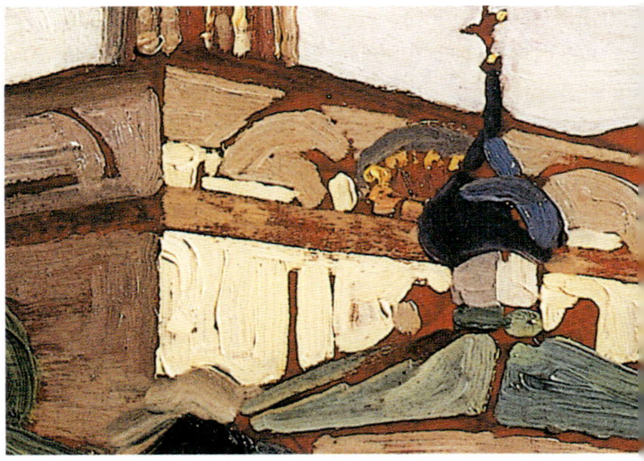

Between these points of origin and destination, Roerich was always a landscape painter, who located people within the culture they helped to build, whether that entailed ceremonial systems or architectural structures. In the course of his life the artist worked his way through figuration, shifting focus from groups to solitary human figures, which get smaller and smaller in a vast setting. Finally the figure disappears. This evolution in his art, according to Frances Grant, a New York journalist in the 1920's and an executive of his American institutions, was a process of which he was acutely aware. The change was 'not so much in subject,' she said:

His interest was in man as part of the whole cosmic process. And so youbegin with man. As far as Russia [is concerned], it began [for him] with the Stone Age- he sees the whole adventure. He once said it was wonderful to hold the end of a thread in Russia and find its beginning in Central Asia . . . .he saw this thread of mankind; always the thread; always unbroken. (4)

The geographical scope of Roerich's destiny made the wide dispersion of his paintings almost inevitable. They can be found in many countries, but the majority are located in Russia, India and the United States. Until a decade or so after Roerich died, those in Russia dated almost entirely from the years he worked there. Likewise, the Roerich paintings in India derive from the period of his residency in Asia. However, the works that are preserved in the United States cover the full span of his life- paintings from both east and west. After Roerich's death, his sons, George and Svetoslav, arranged for substantial numbers of his canvases, some early and some late, to be given to what were then Soviet museums. The paintings at the Nicholas Roerich Museum, New York, comprise the only collection on permanent view in the United States.

About two hundred works are housed there. Although the collection represents more than forty years of the artist's creativity, it is particularly strong in his Asian paintings from the 1930's.

In this monograph thirty-two works from the Nicholas Roerich Museum have been selected for interpretation. They range chronologically from 1903 to 1944. The selection starts with Roerich's years of aspiration, when as a young painter, recently married, he earned his living as the secretary of a cultural society, and it extends all the way through to his reflective last period when he was writing his memoirs. [5] Each of the selected paintings captures a specific moment, revealing the artist's present concerns, past influences and immediate sense of time and place in an unusually itinerant life. Events in the world around him make themselves felt in his painting through oblique images. This approach has roots in his early Symbolism, but it also issues quite naturally from his personality. Roerich was a contemplative whose disposition was to communicate indirectly. His paintings invite interpretation, particularly in the context of biographical facts and current affairs. The monograph provides such information about each work, together with details of subject, theme and genre, media, palette and technique, some sources, patrons and provenance.

In Russia Roerich undertook large scale works- monumental paintings, church mosaics, frescoes, murals and friezes for public buildings and private mansions. These projects were possible, Svetoslav Roerich said, because of the ateliers where his father directed 'a whole group of very talented artists, like in . . . . the Renaissance period.' [6] Such formats were not feasible for Roerich in India, where he had no assistants and where he and his son, Svetoslav- by then an accomplished painter- worked alone in studios at their home in the Himalayas. But, in Europe and America, Roerich's designs for ballet, opera and lyric theatre had been realized by scene shops for the huge proportions of the proscenium stage. Also in America he had created tall tryptics in stained glass for the multistorey Roerich Museum built in New York in 1929. The collection at the later Nicholas Roerich Museum, set up in a town house in 1958, is typical of the artist's characteristic scale- small and medium sized easel paintings and theatrical designs, providing a singular introduction to his life and work.

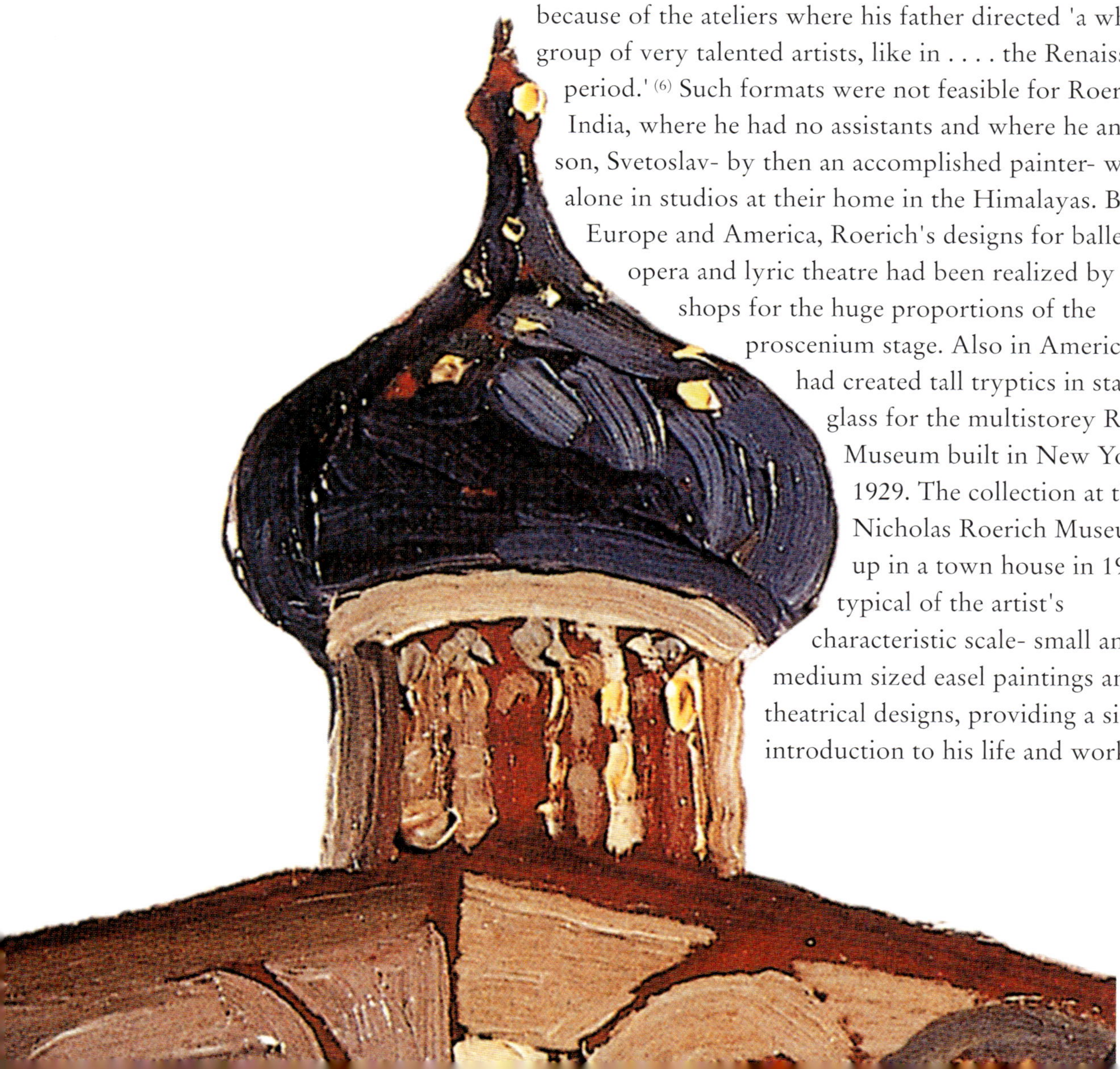

Contents

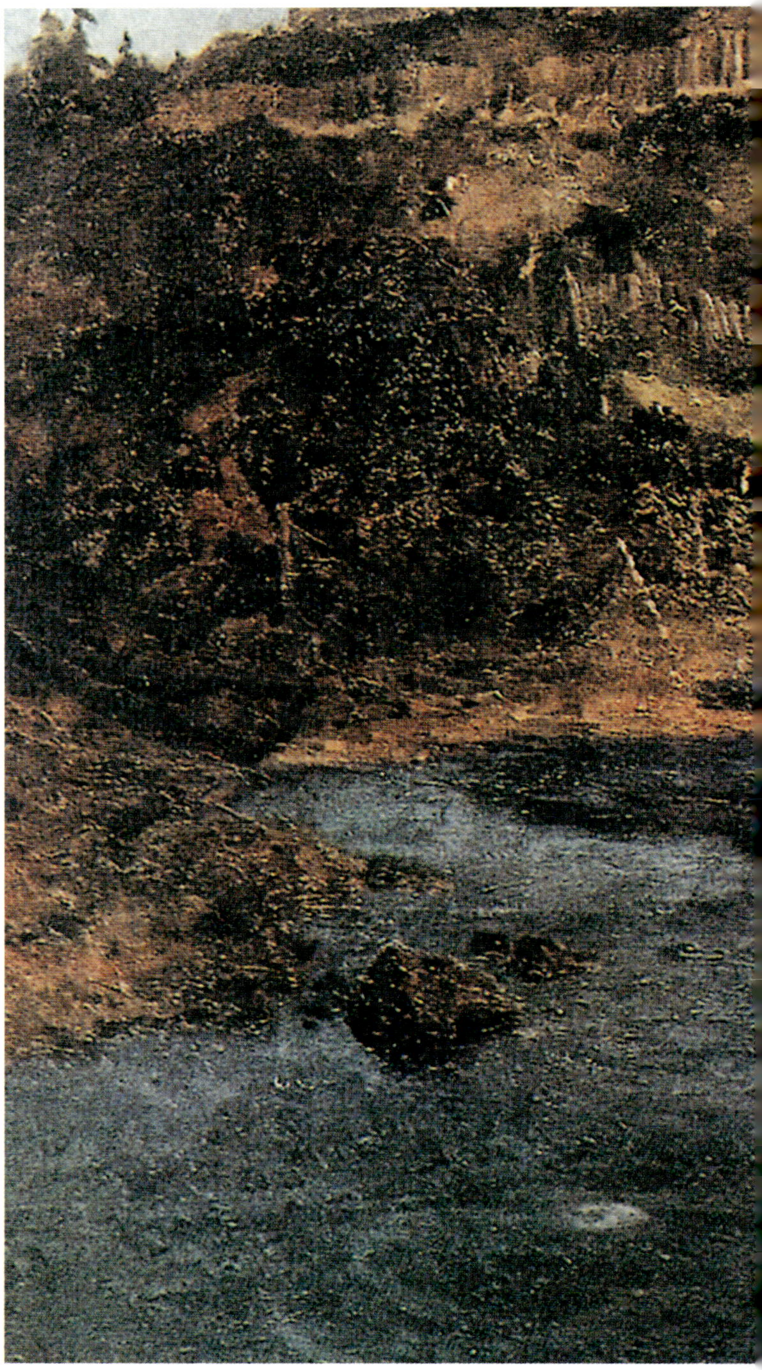

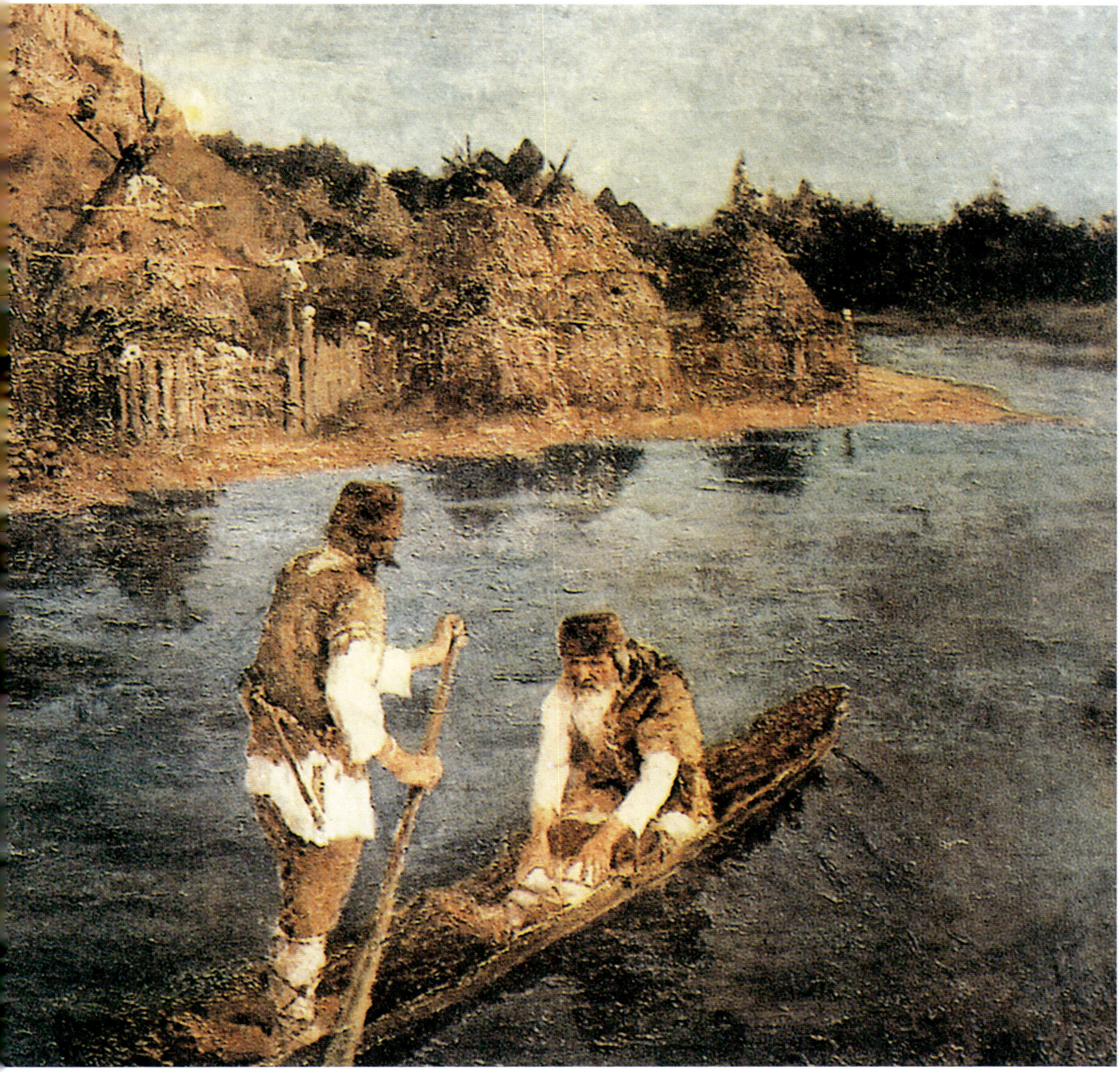

The Messenger: Tribe has risen Against Tribe, 1897

Oil on canvas, 125 x 184 cm.
Tretyakov Gallery, Moscow

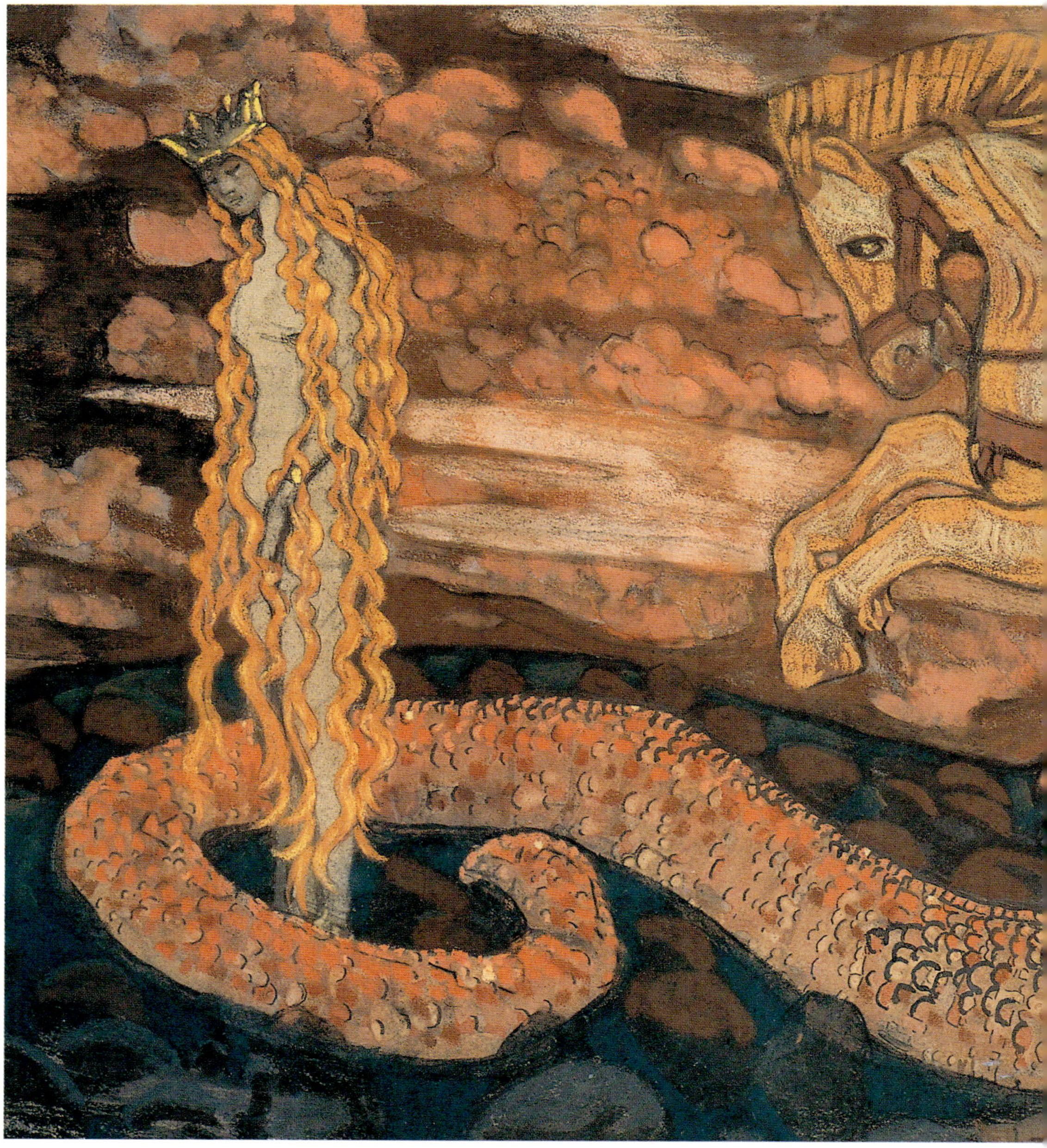

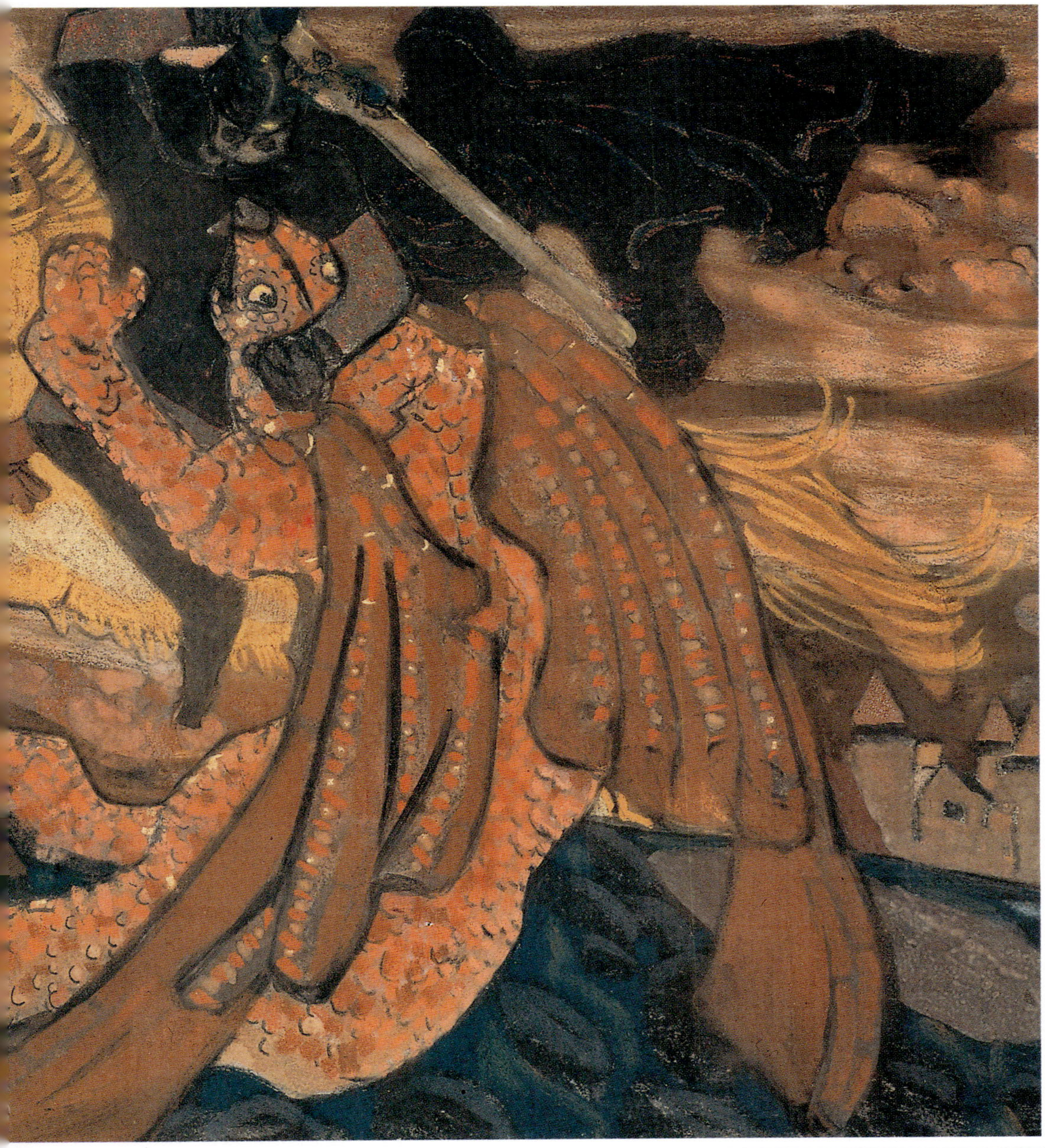

The Dragon's Daughter, 1906

Tempera on board, 50 x 48.2 cm.
Russian Museum, Saint Petersburg

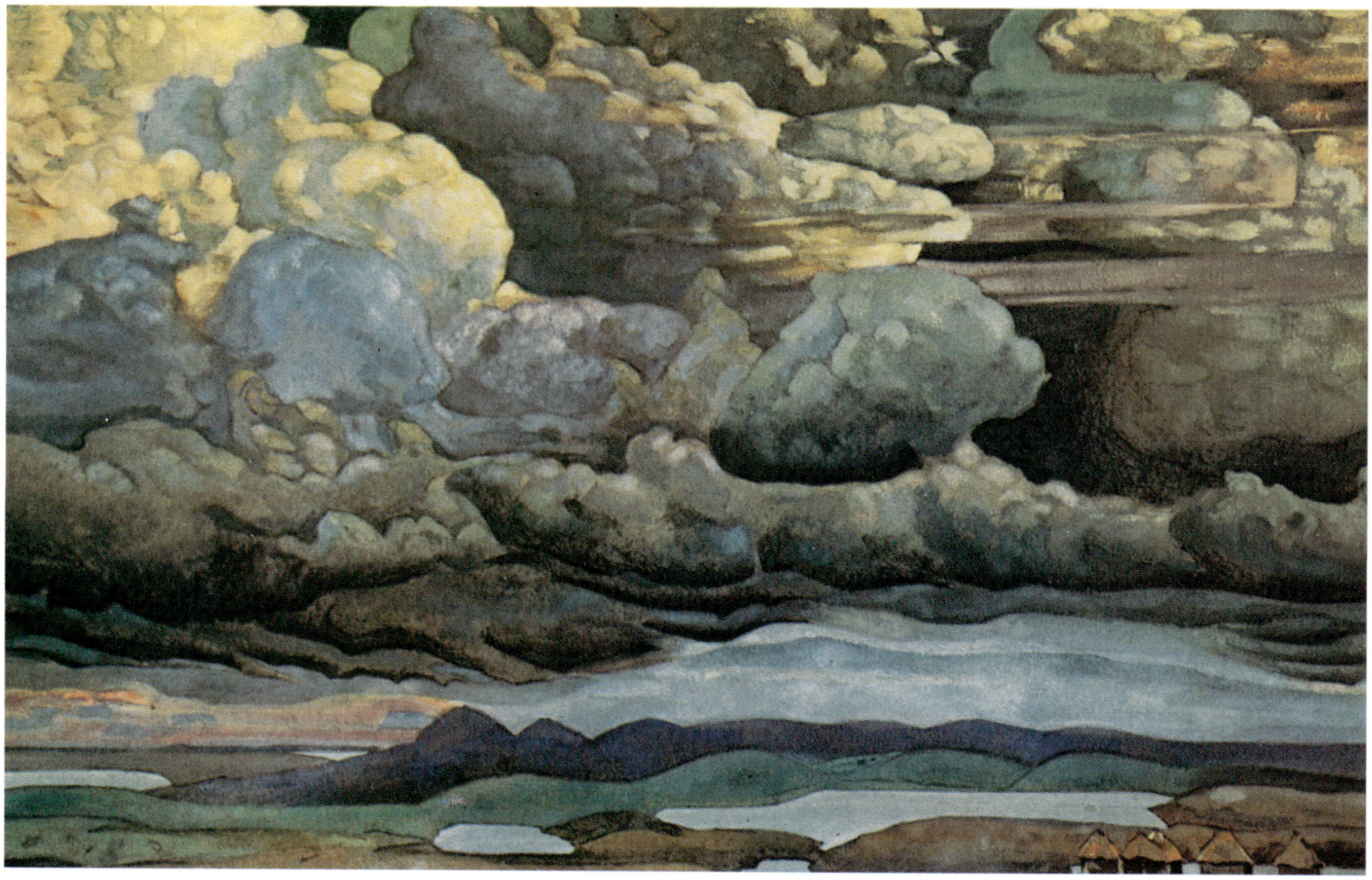

Battle in Heaven, 1912

Tempera on carboard, 66 x 95 cm.
Russian Museum, Saint Petersburg

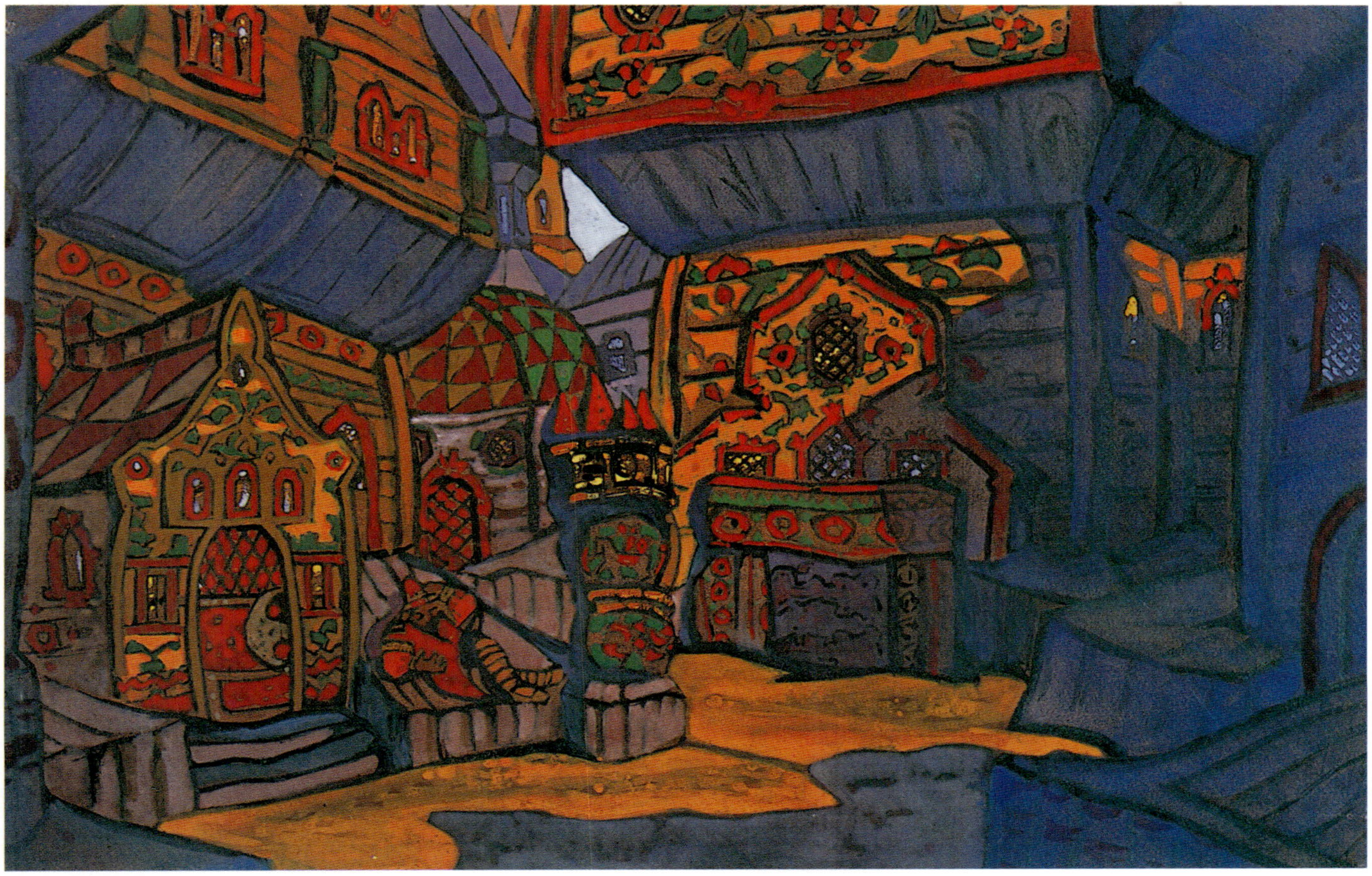

Prince Vladimir Galitsky's Courtyard, 1914

Set design for 1914 Production of Borodin's opera Prince Igor
Gouache on board, 50 x 69.2 cm.
Russian Museum, Saint Petersburg

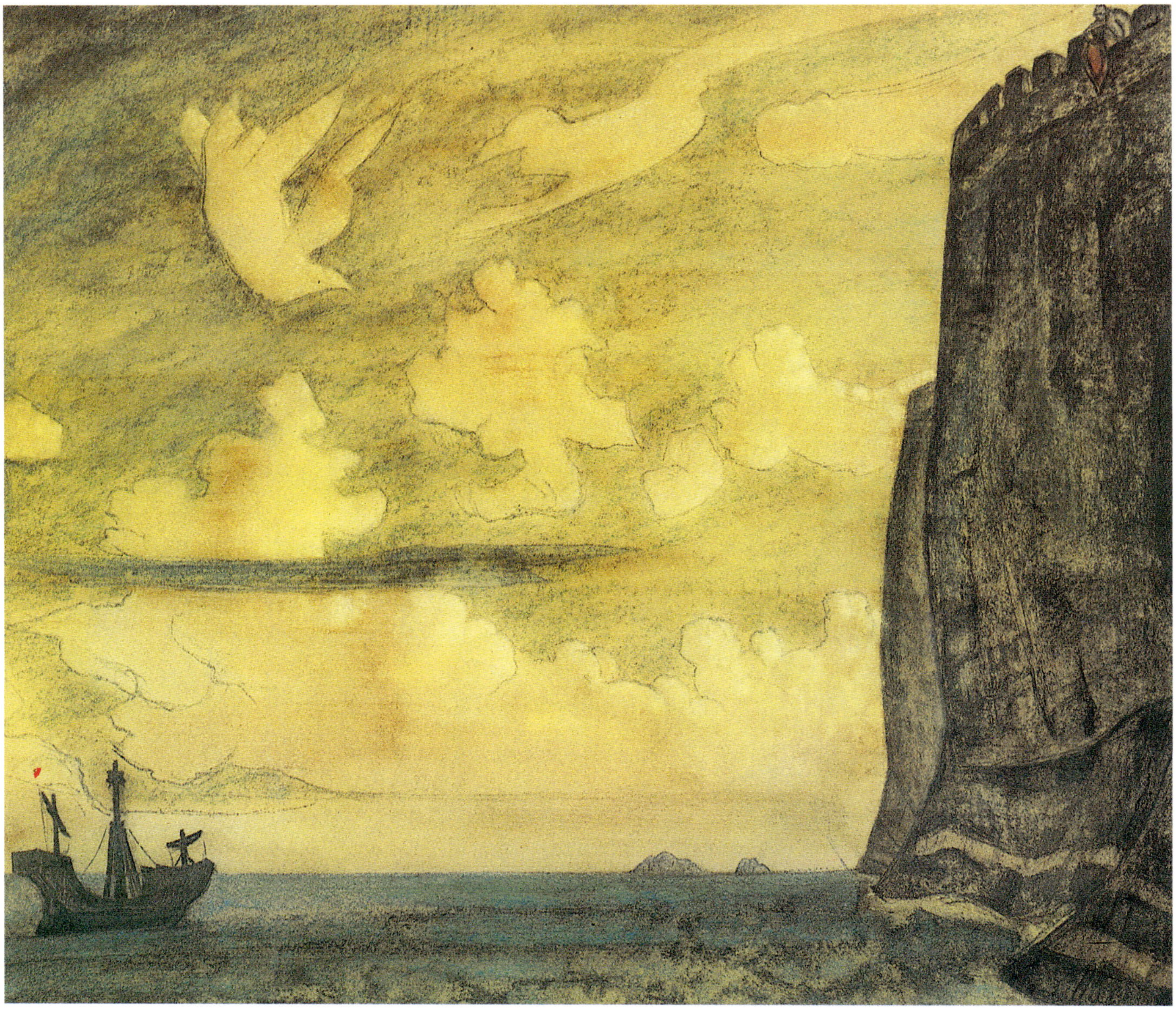

The Herald, 1914

Charcoal pastel on board, 75 x 88.9 cm.
Russian Museum, Saint Petersburg

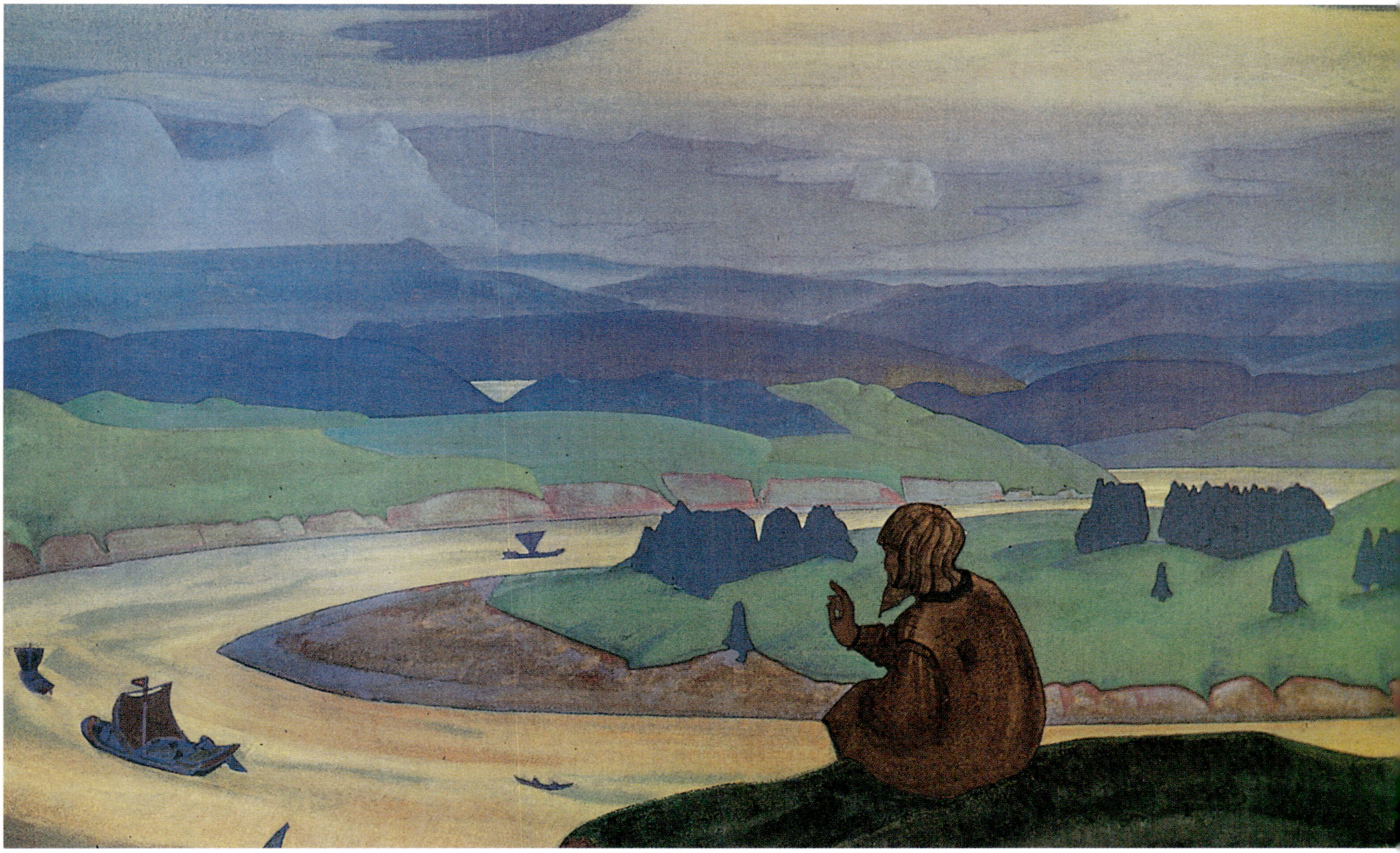

St Procopius the Righteous Prayer for Travelling People, 1914

Tempera on cardboard, 71 x 107 cm.
Russian Museum, Saint Petersburg

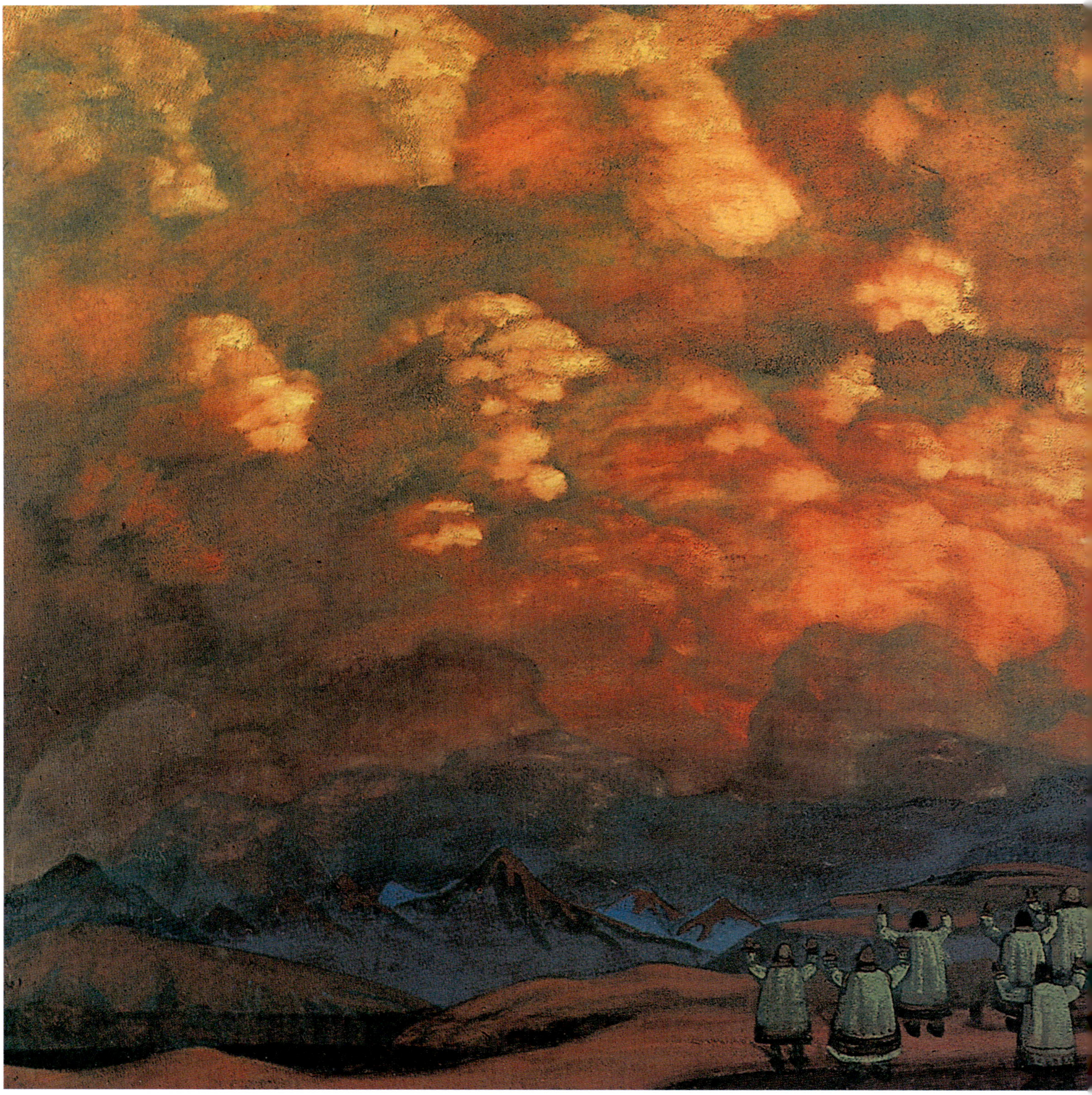

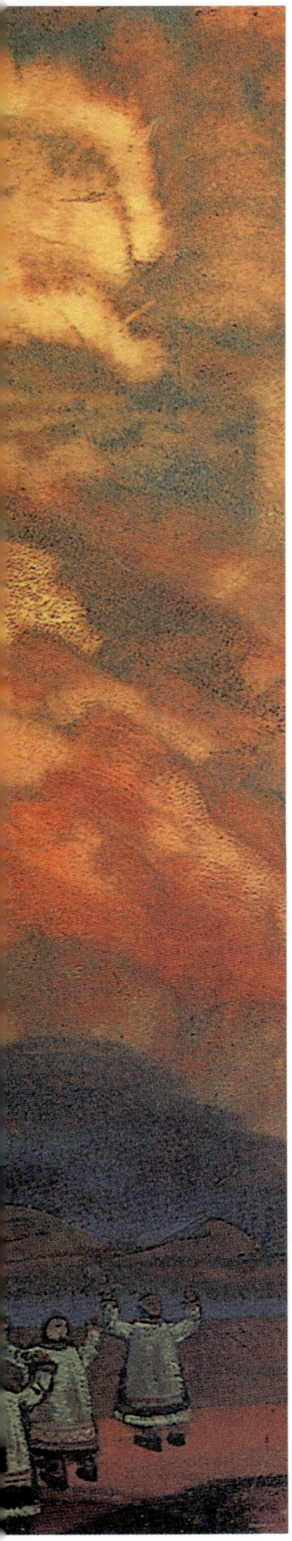

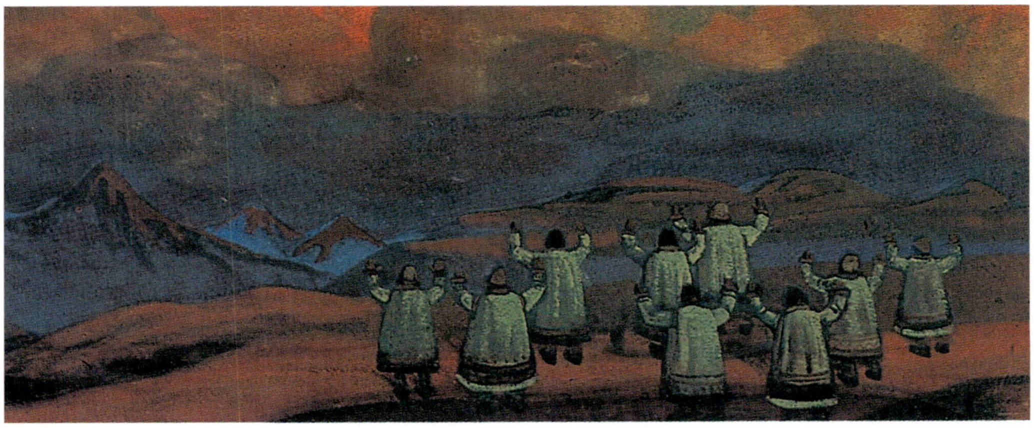

The Commands of Heaven, 1915

Tempera on cardboard, 75 x 97.5 cm.
Russian Museum, Saint Petersburg

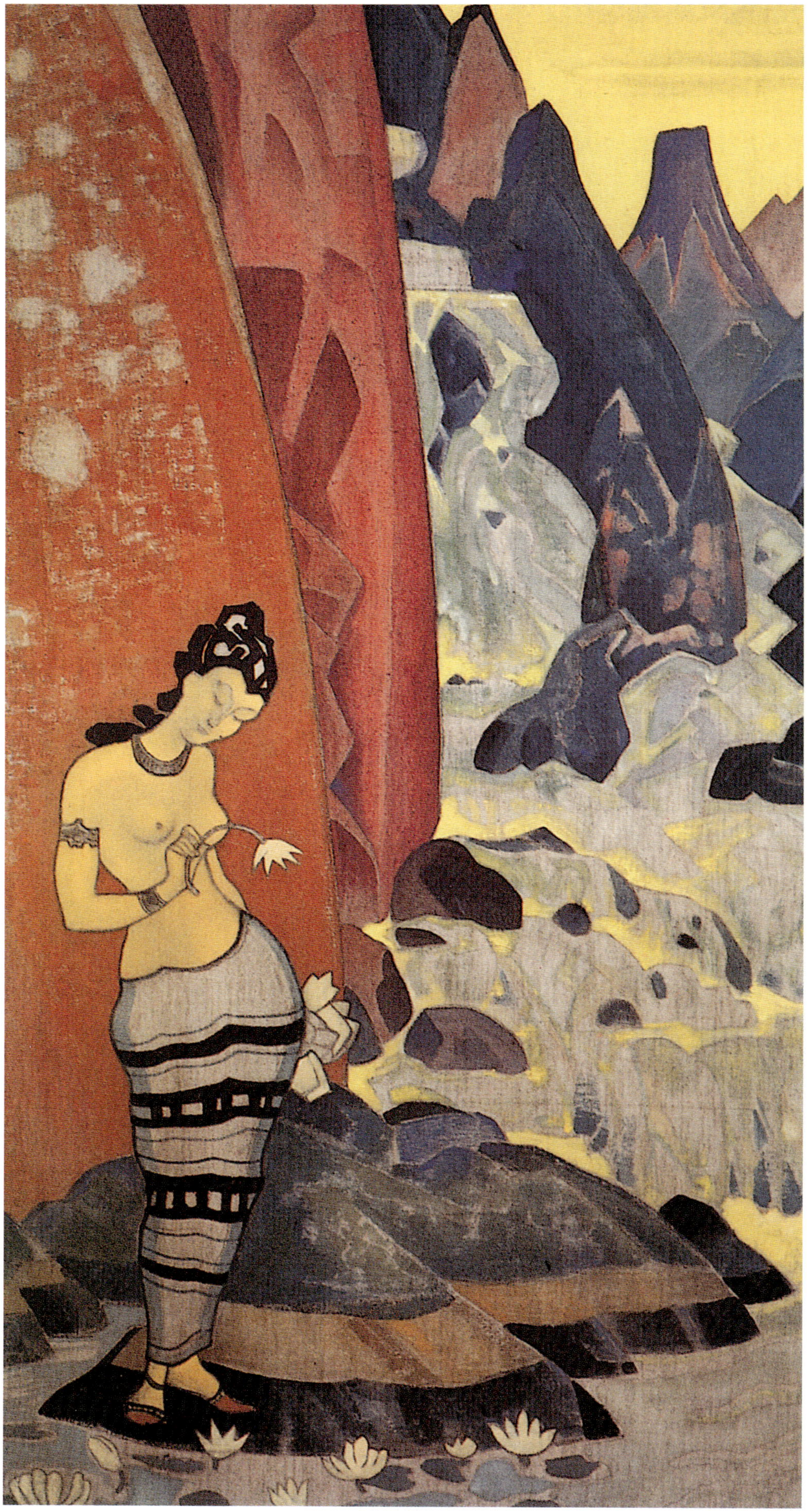

Song of the Waterfall, 1920

Tempera on canvas, 81.2 x 122 cm. Nicholas Roerich Museum, New York

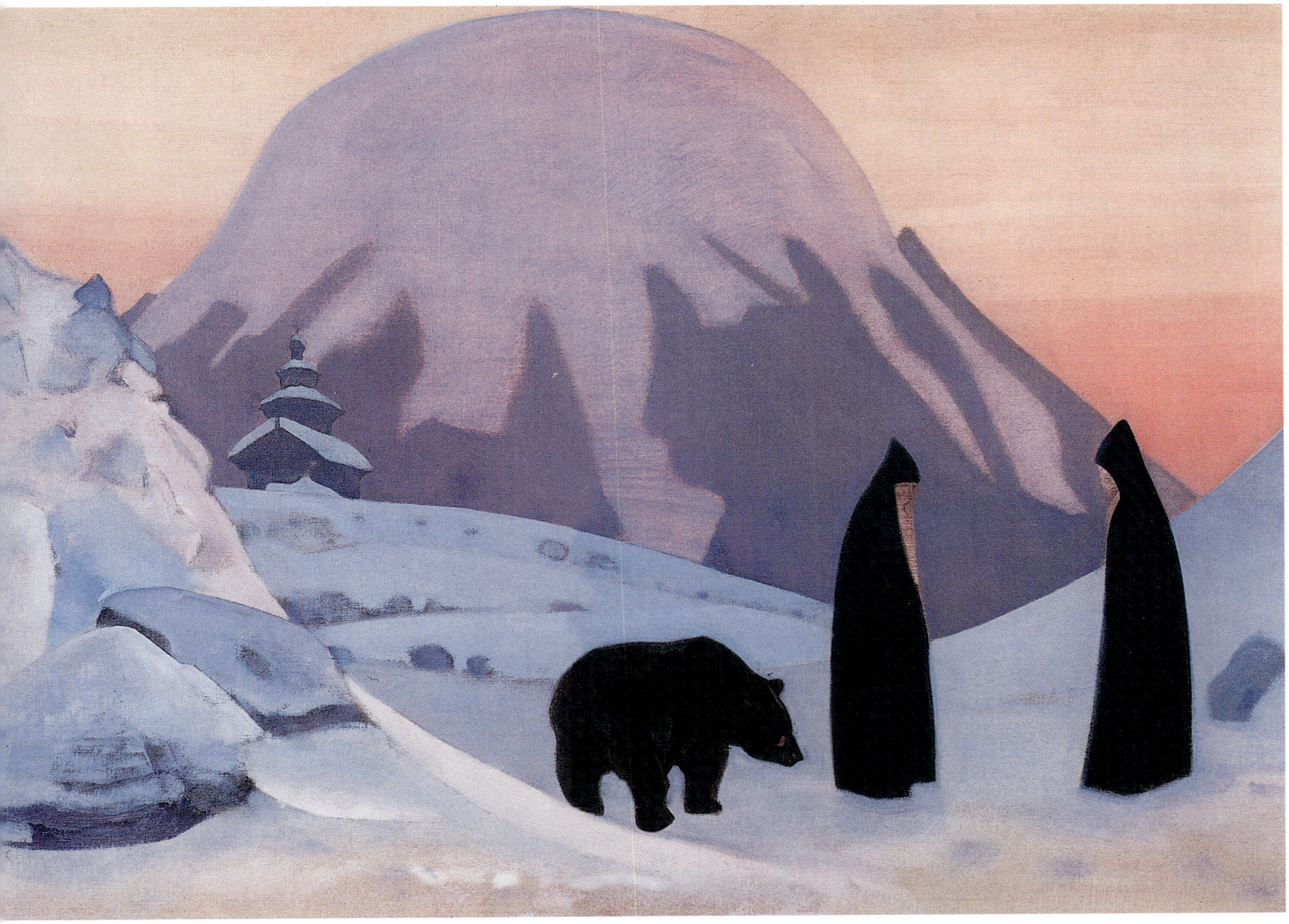

And we do not fear, 1922

Tempera on canvas, 71 x 101.6 cm.
Bolling Collection, Naples, Florida

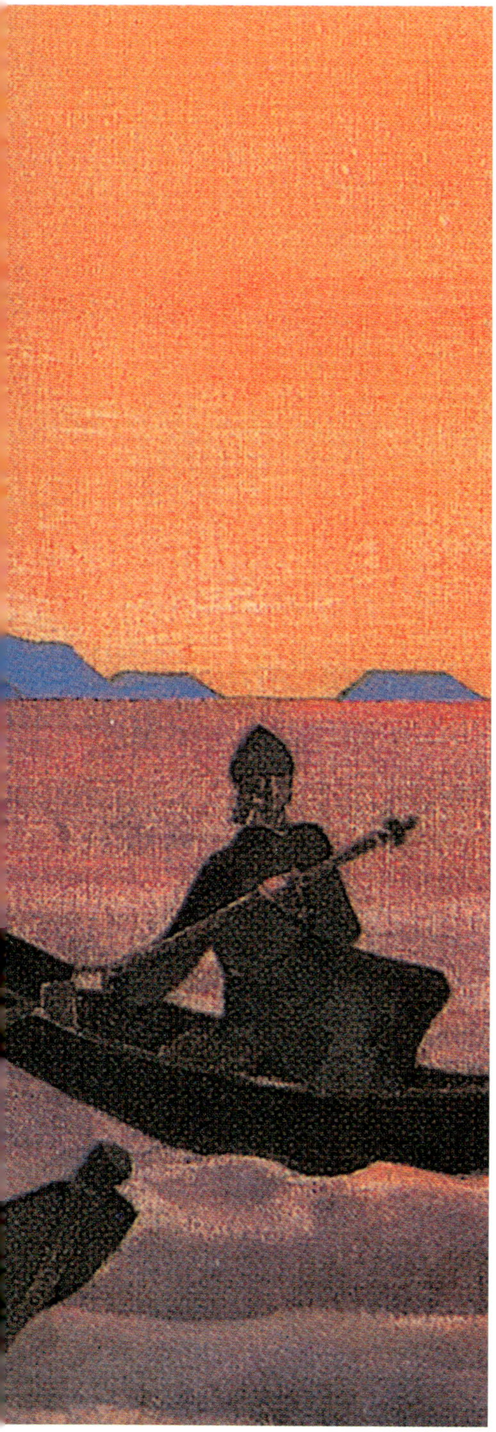

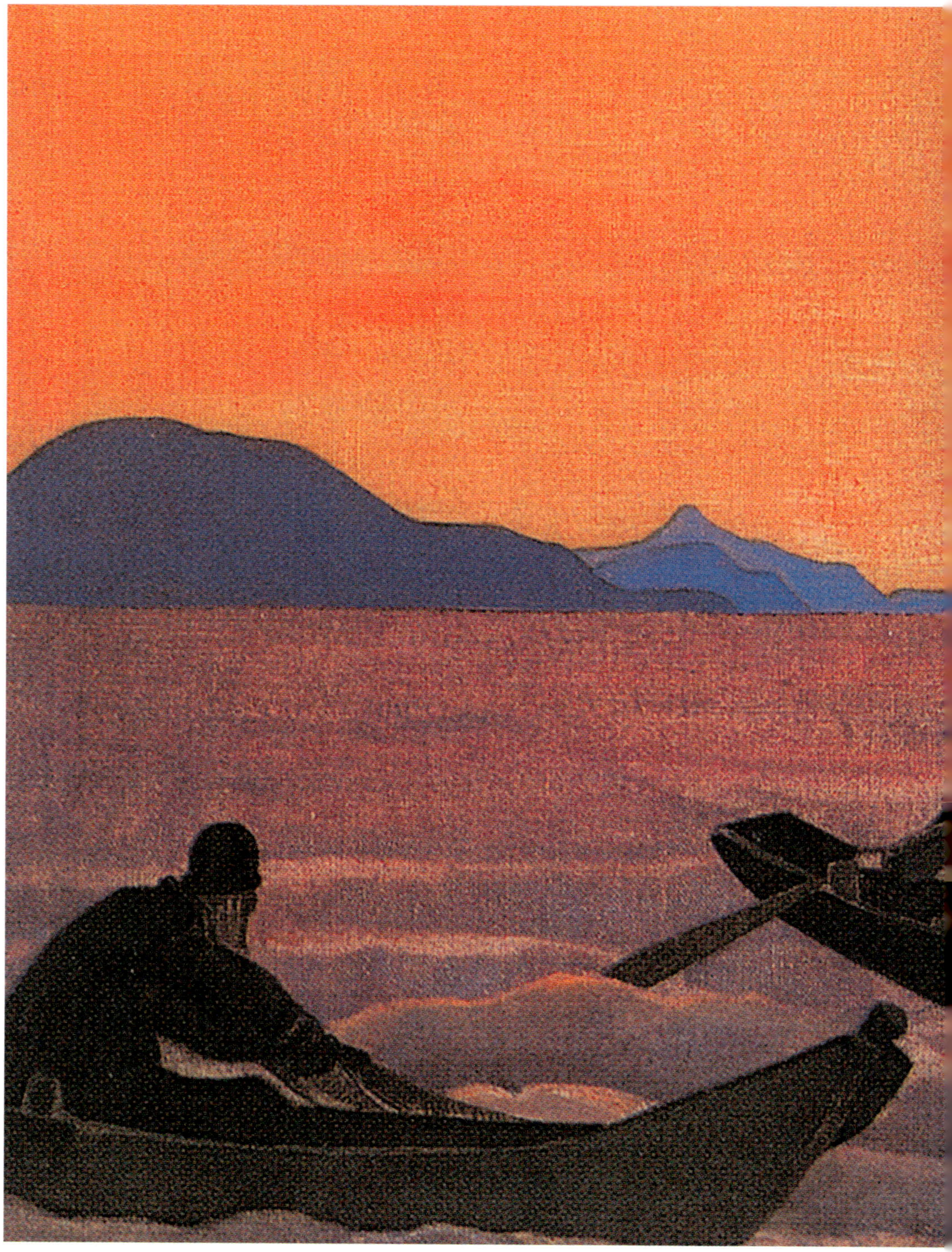

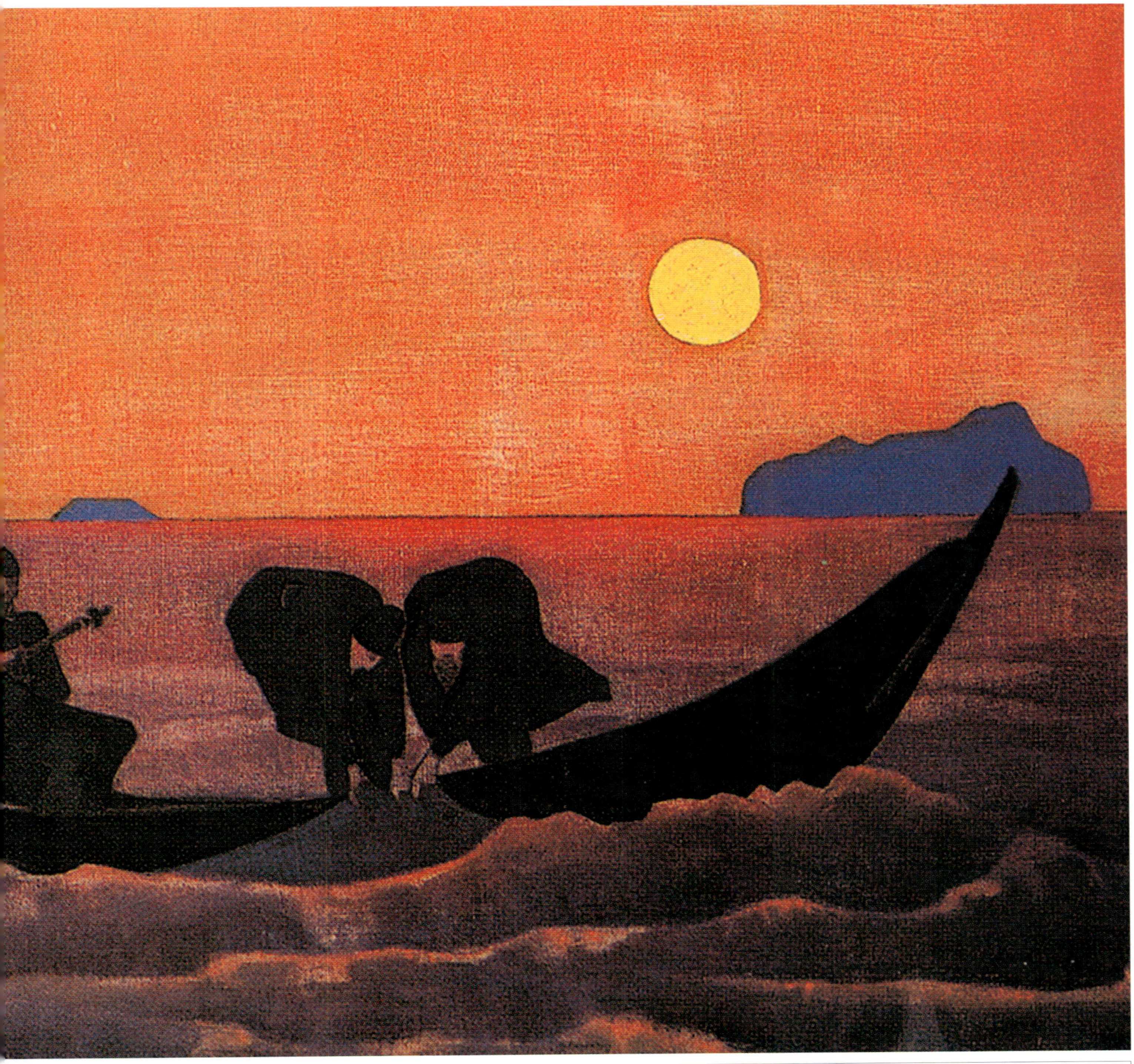

And we fish, 1922

Tempera on canvas, 71 x 101.6 cm.
Nicholas Roerich Museum, New York

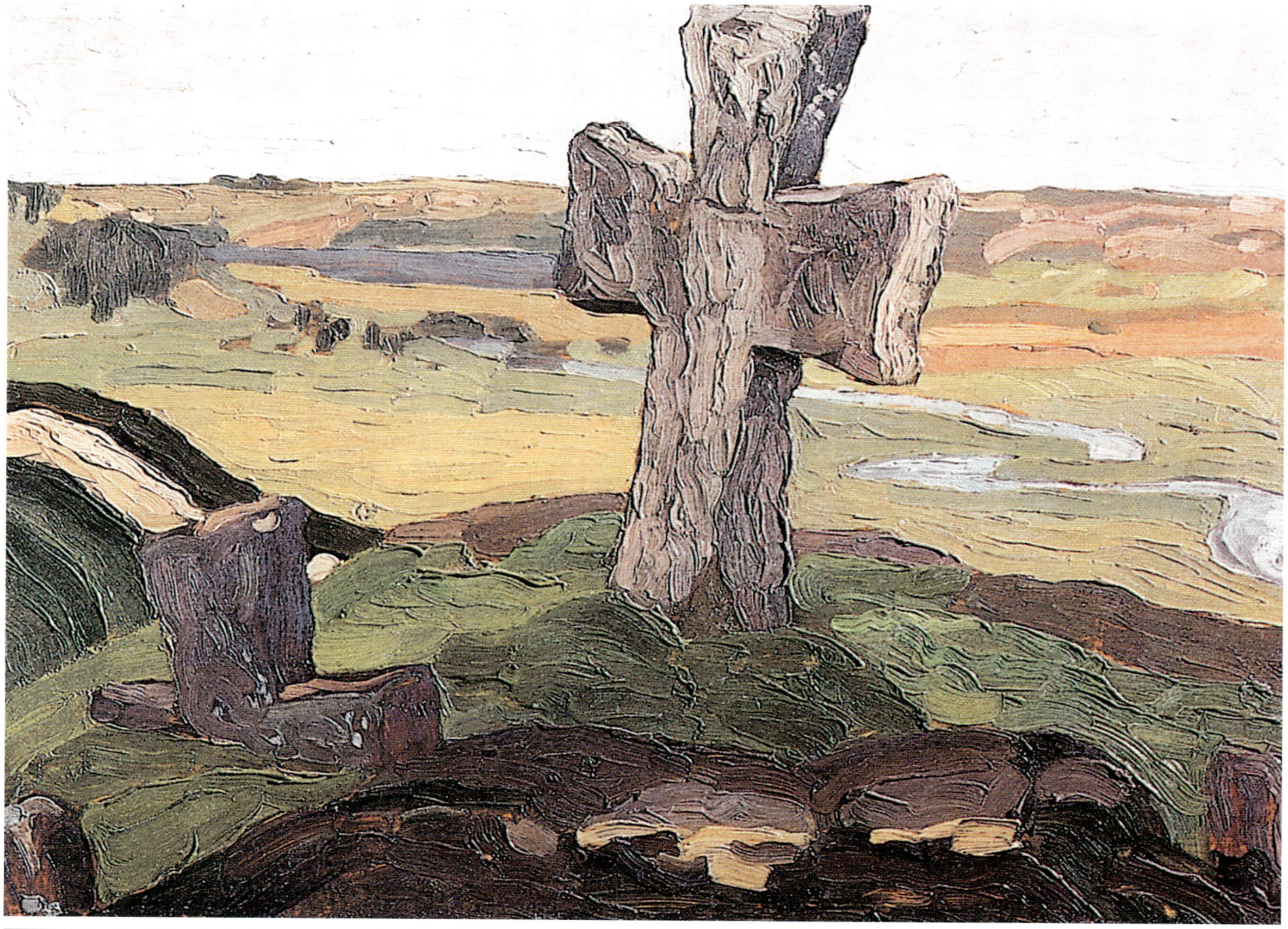

Old Russia, Izborsk. Cross for Truvor Town site, 1903

Oil on panel, 31 x 43.8 cm.
Museum of Oriental Art, Moscow

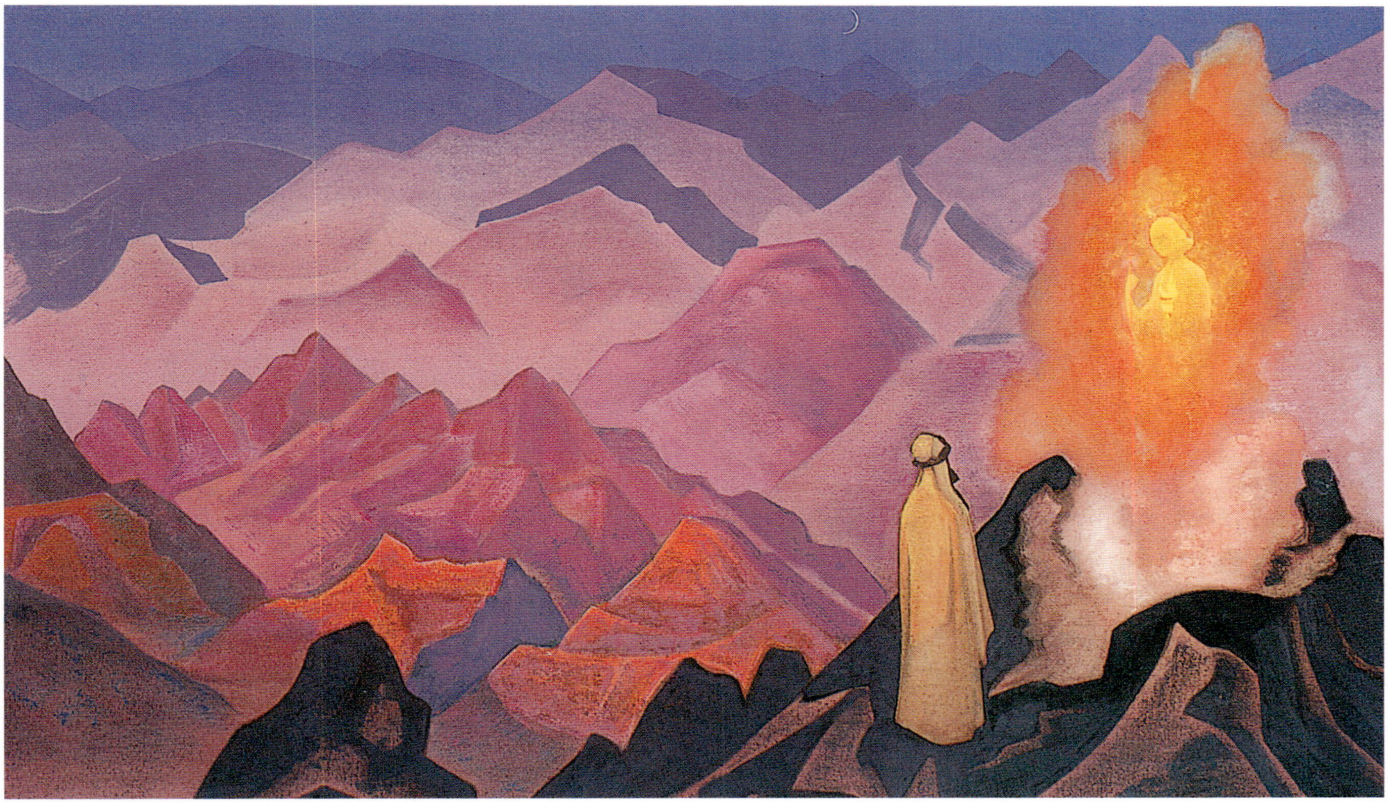

Mohammed on Mt Hira, 1925

Tempera on canvas, 73.6 x 117 cm.
Bolling Collection, Grand Haven, Michigan

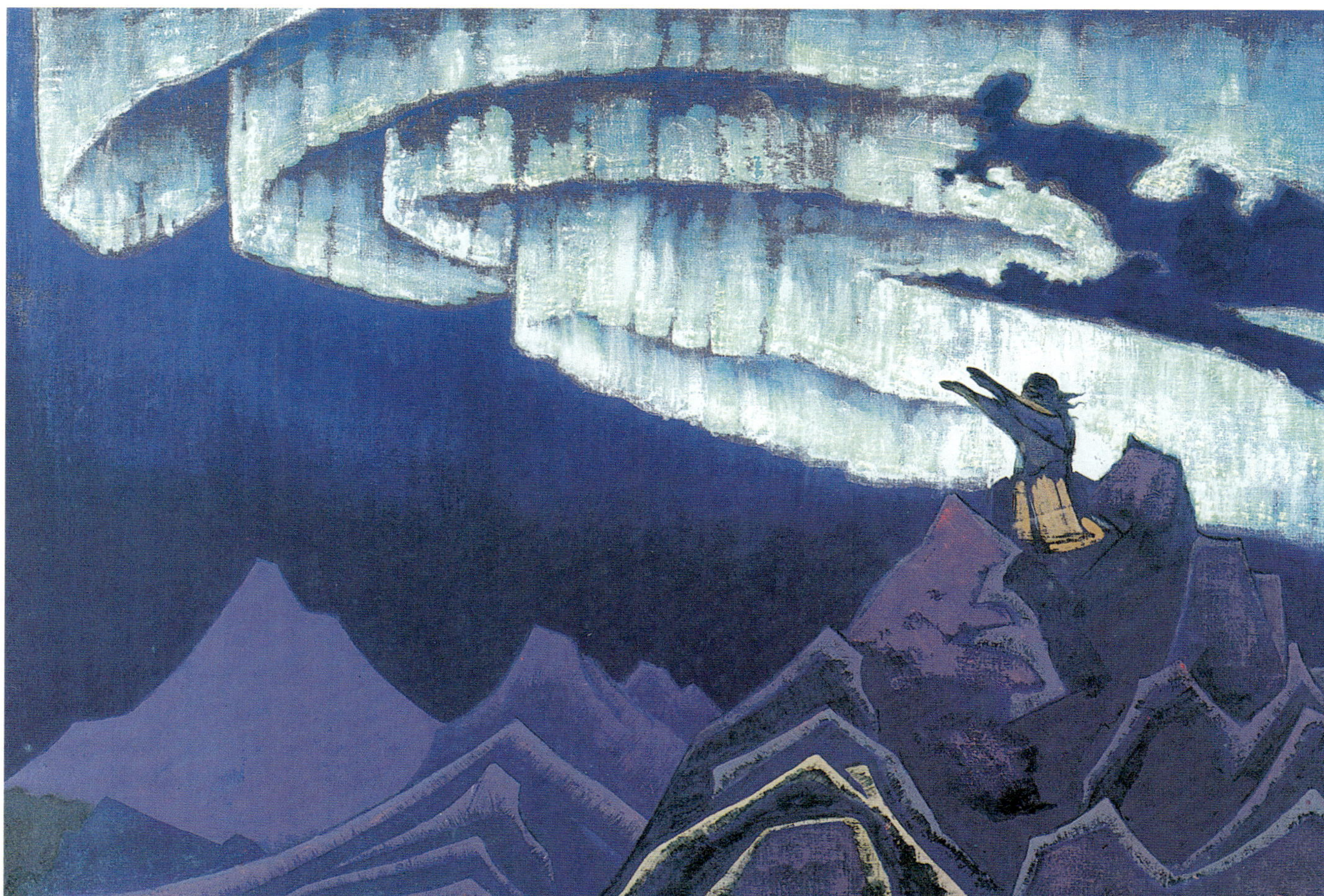

Moses the leader, 1925

Tempera on canvas, 73.6 x 117 cm.
Bolling Collection, Naples, Florida

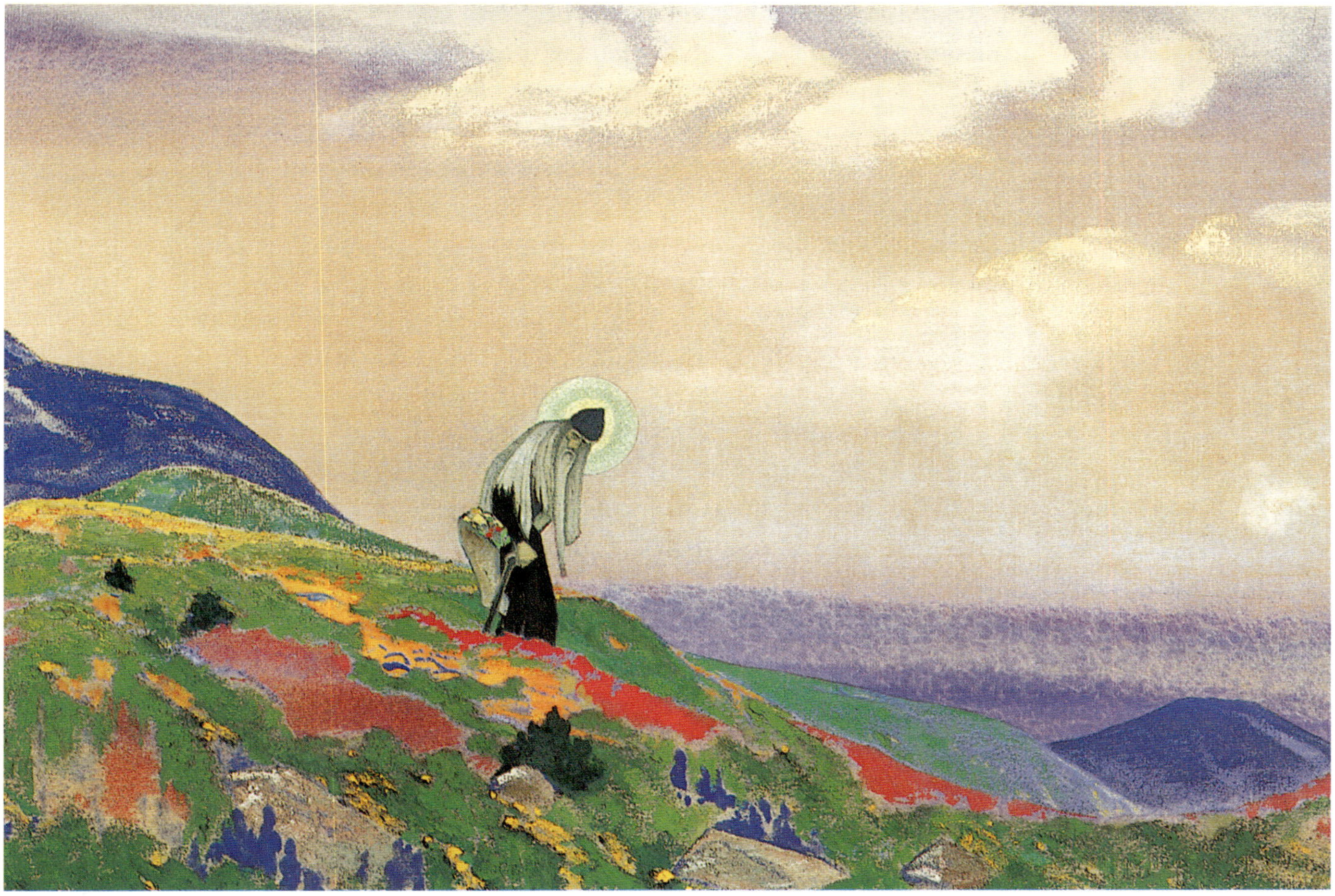

St Panteleimon, the Healer, 1931

Tempera on canvas, 53.3 x 88.2 cm.
Nicholas Roerich Museum, New York

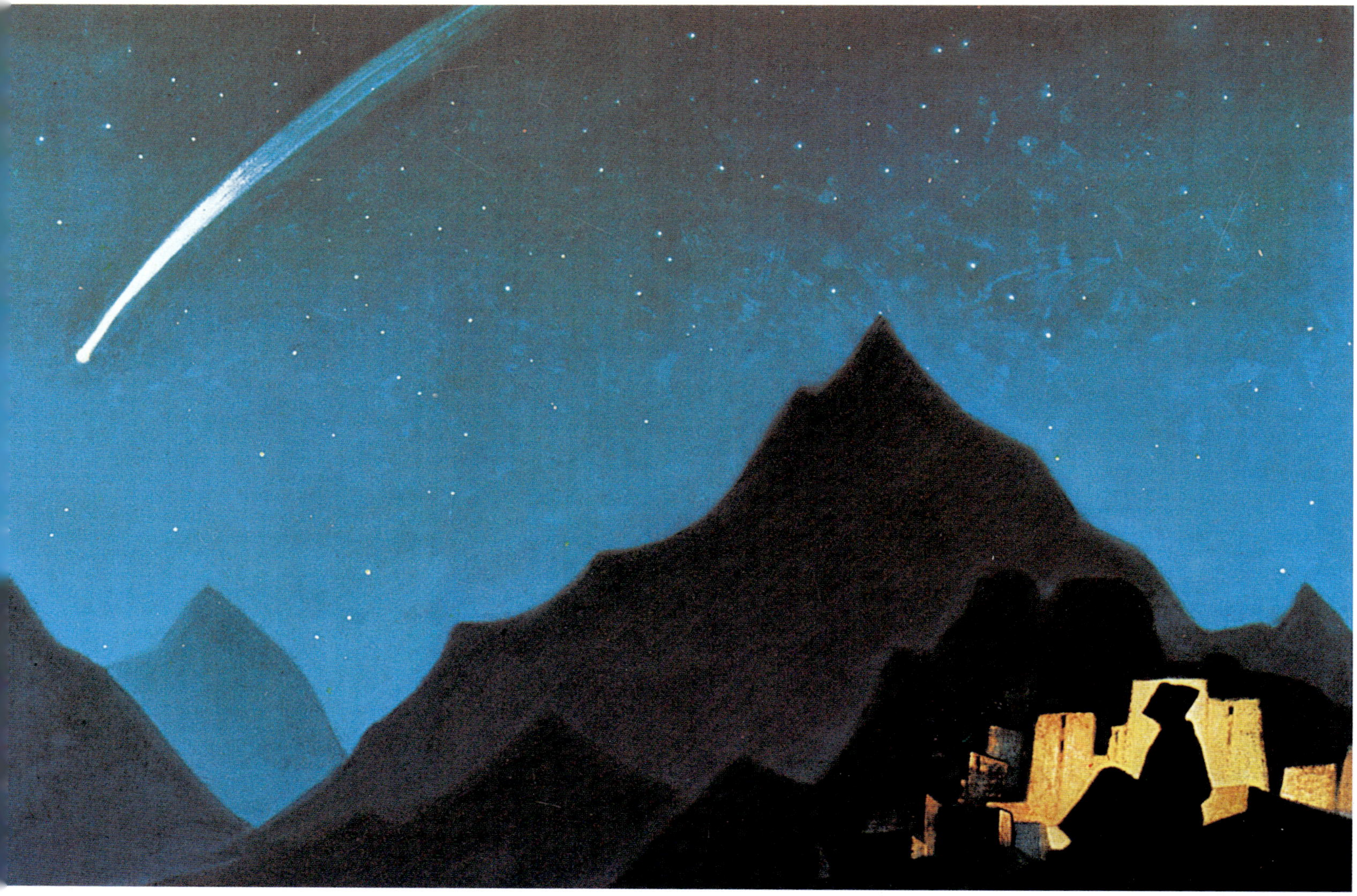

Star of the hero, 1932

Tempera on canvas, 62.8 x 96.3 cm.
Nicholas Roerich Museum, New York

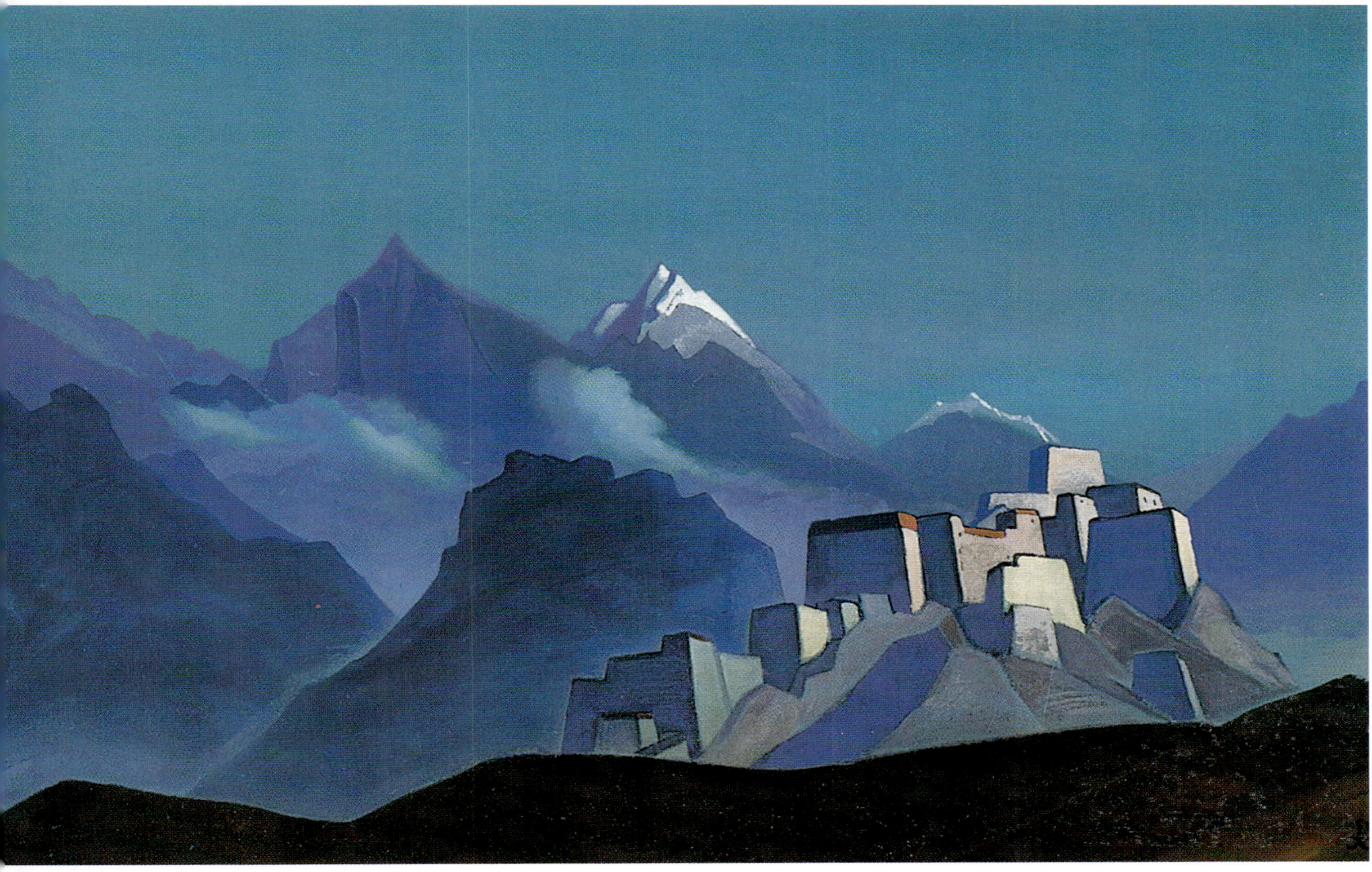

Star of the morning, 1933

Tempera on canvas, 83.8 x 104 cm.
Nicholas Roerich Museum, New York

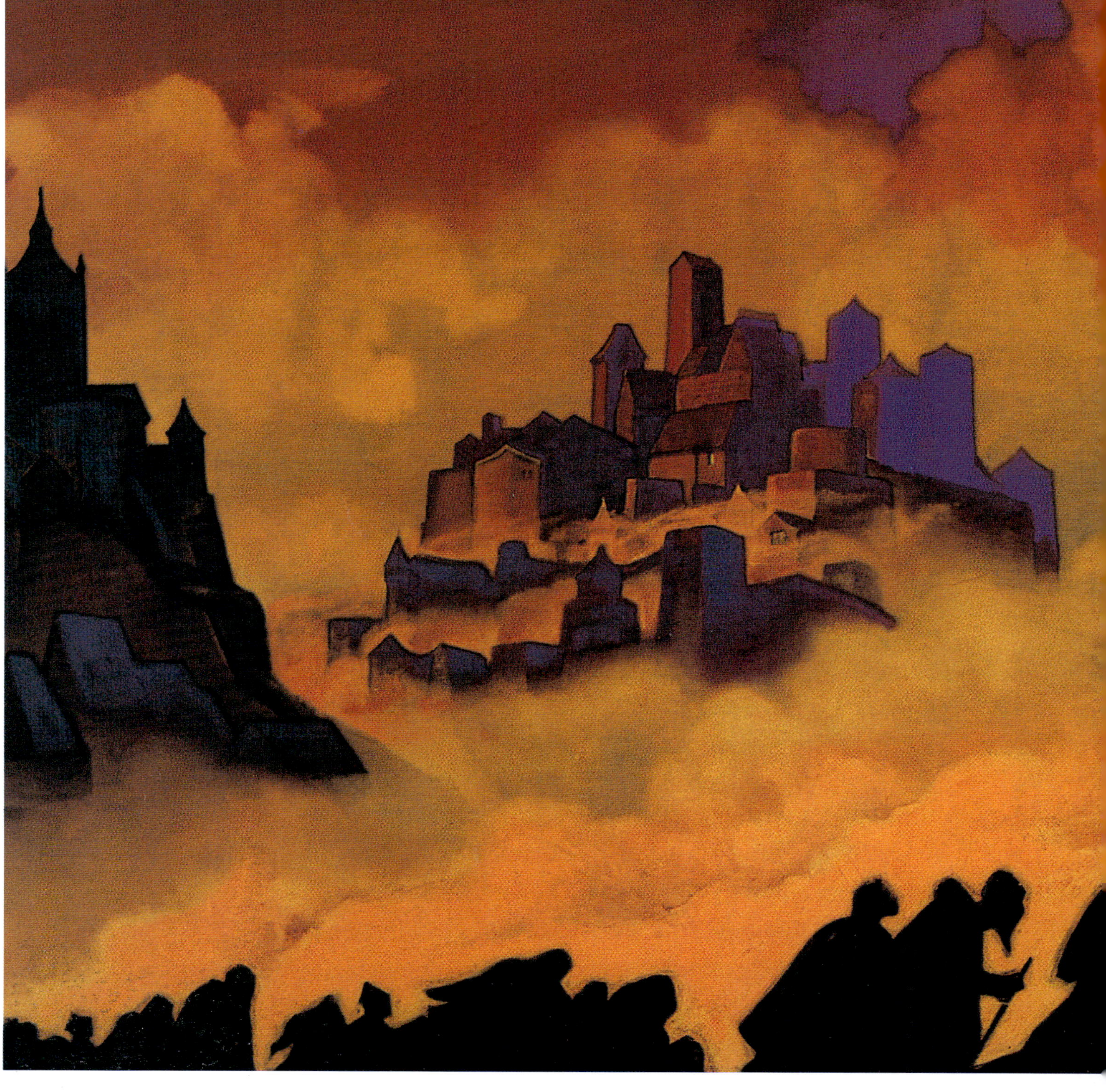

Armageddon, 1935-36

Tempera on canvas, 91.4 x 122 cm.
Svetoslav Roerich Collection, Bangalore, India

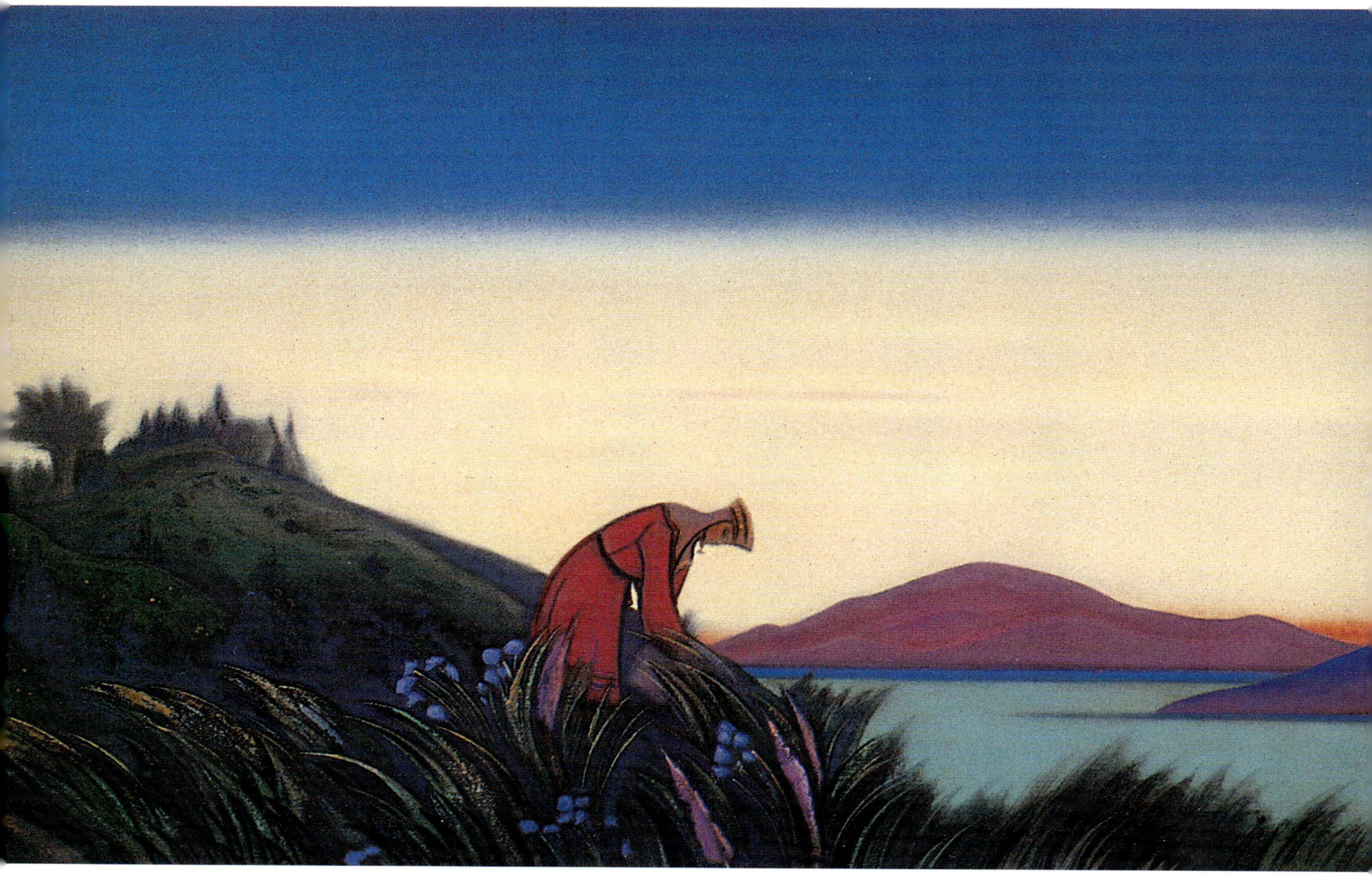

Vasilisa the Beautiful, 1941

Tempera on canvas, 73.2 x 123 cm.
Svetoslav Roerich Collection, Bangalore, India

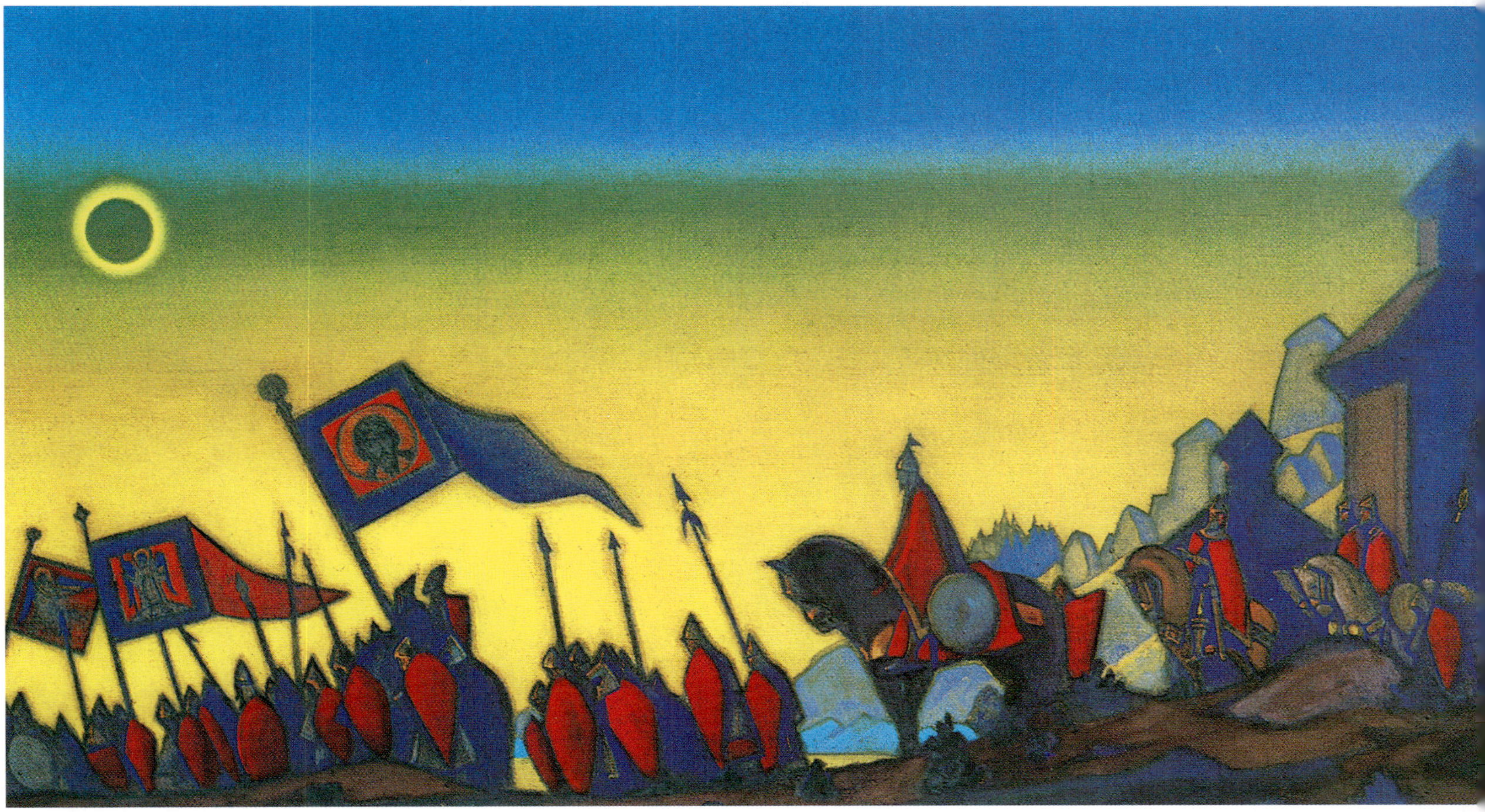

Prince Igor's campaign, 1942

Tempera on canvas, 62 x 122 cm.
Russian Museum, Saint Petersburg

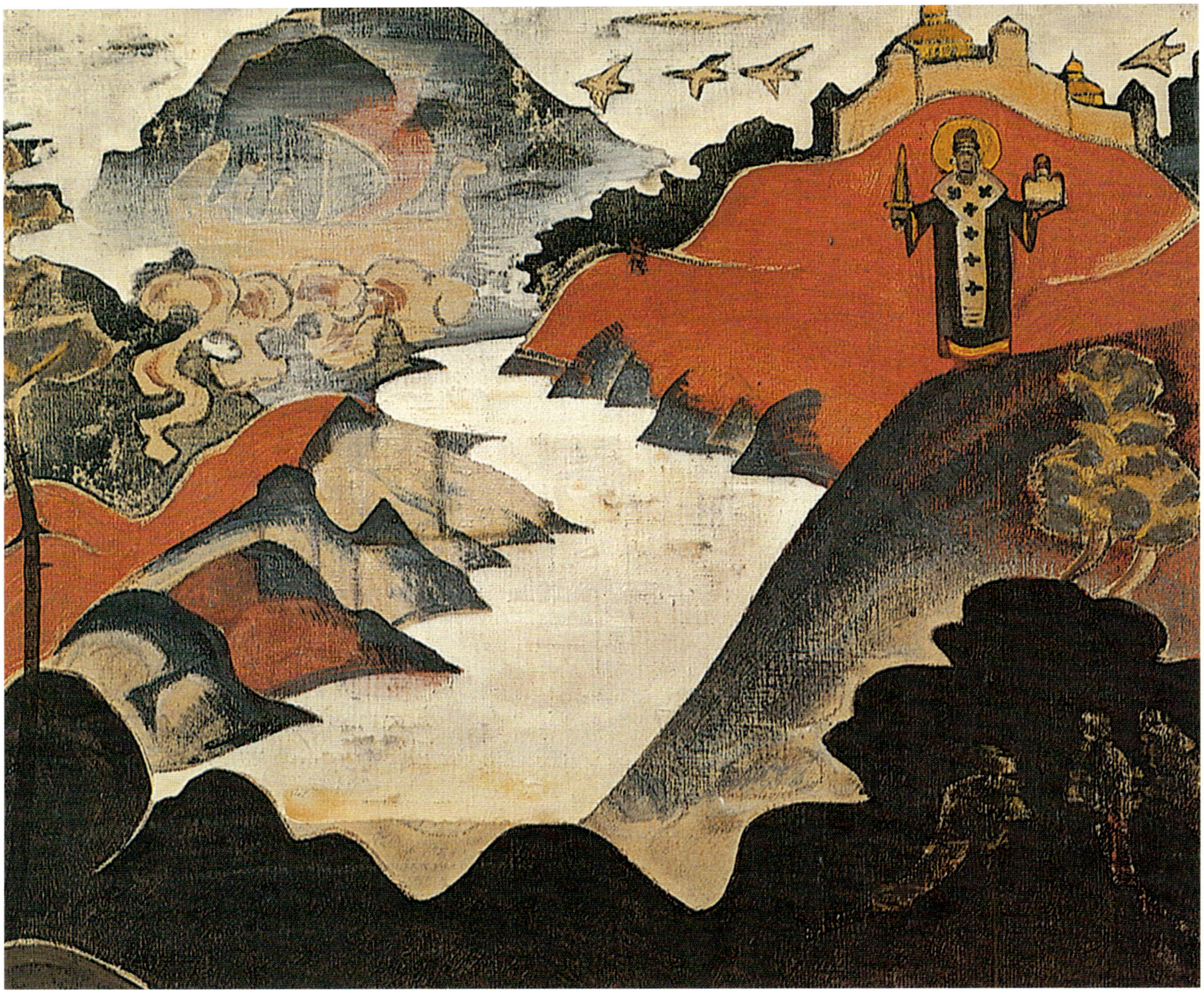

St. Nicholas

Nicholas Roerich Museum, New York

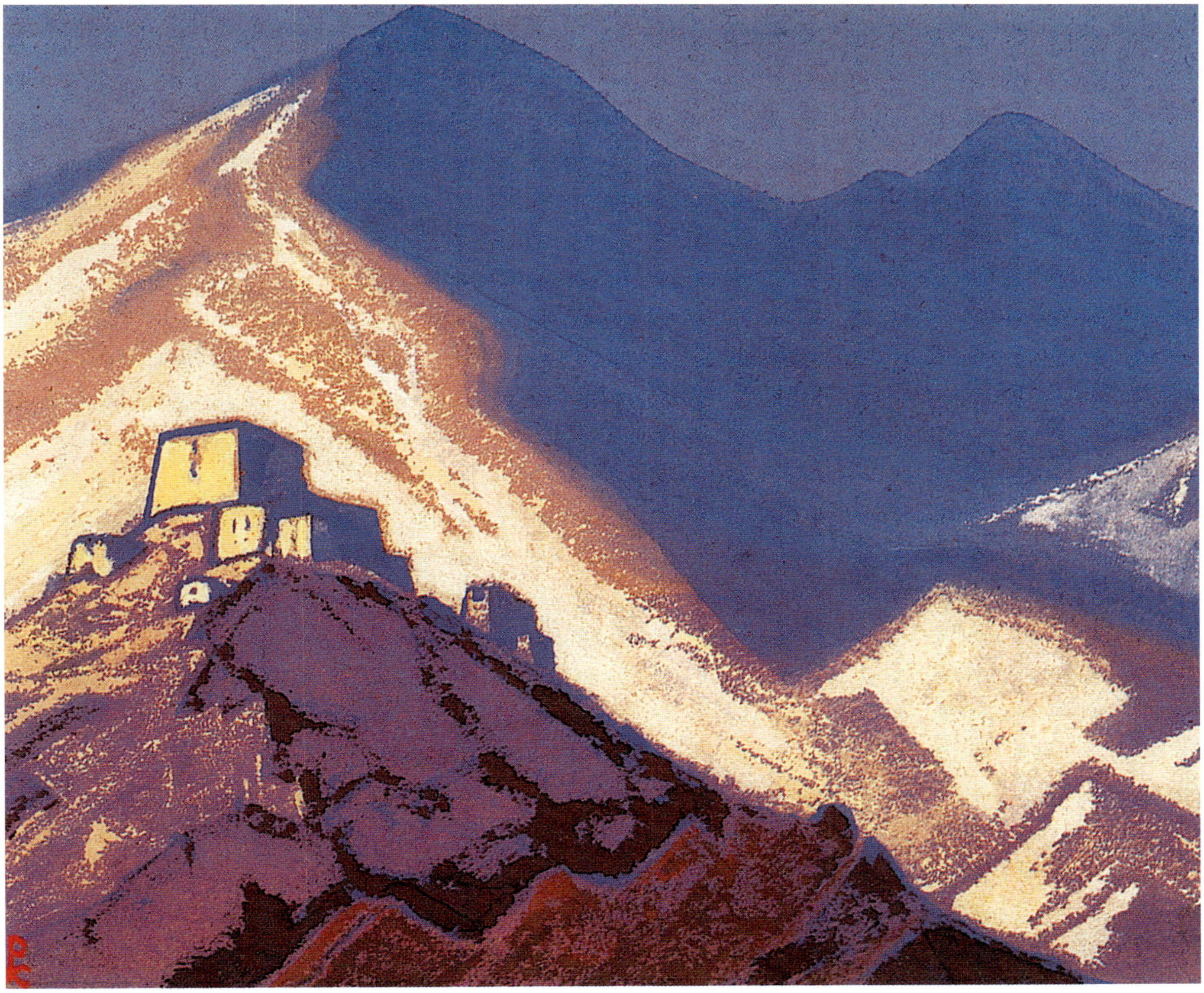

Himalayas

Nicholas Roerich Museum, New York

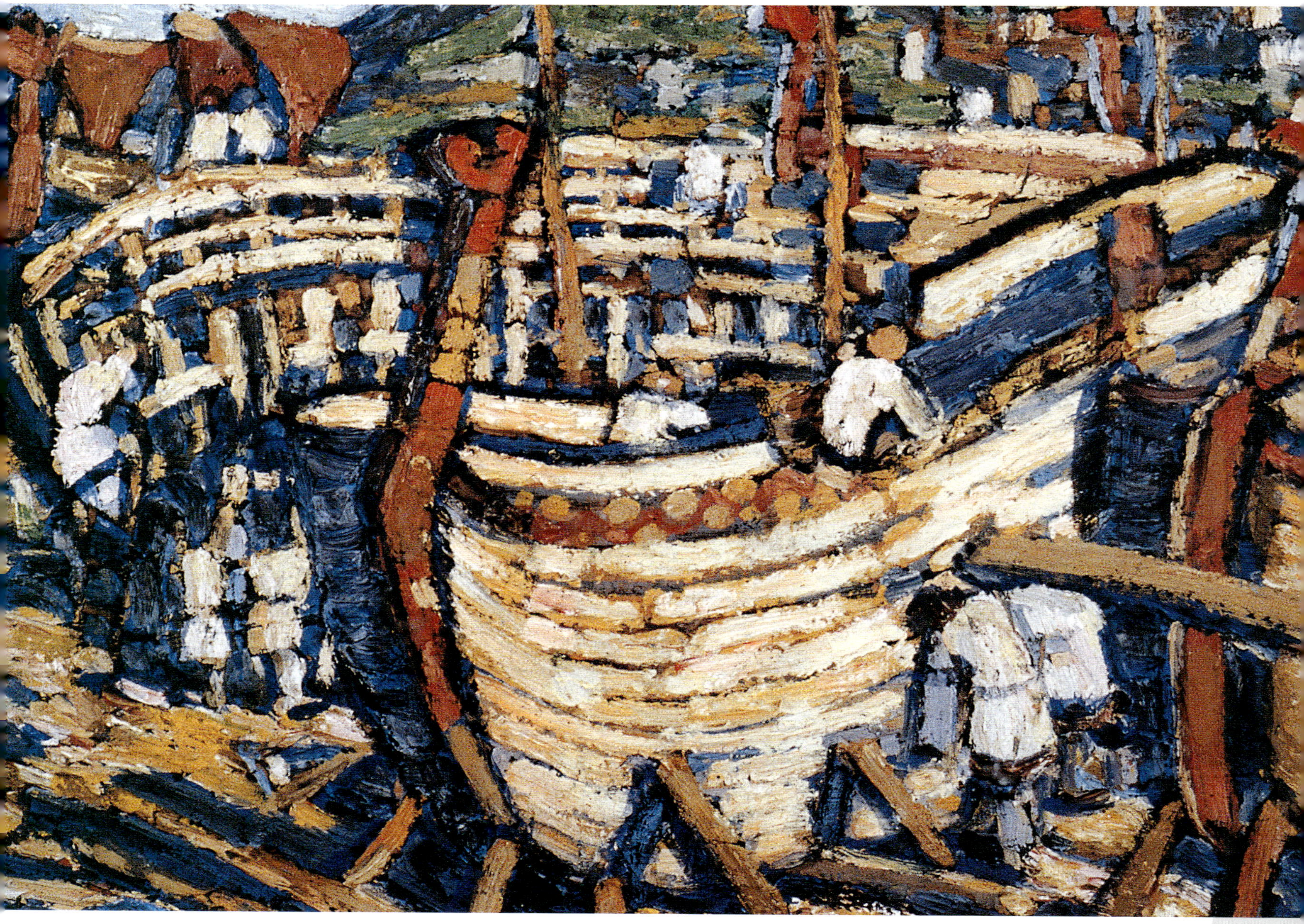

Sketch for Building the Ships, 1903

Oil on cardboard, 47.6 x 38.1 cm.
Nicholas Roerich Museum, New York

1 Sketch for *Building the Ships*

In this early painting Roerich evokes the life of the ancient Slavs, showing clusters of men busy at the task of ship construction. He depicts the vessels in varied states of completion. The one partially visible on the right appears to be fully decorated; the central one is still being painted, as indicated by the unfinished motif on its side; and one in the background is only a skeletal structure. The progressive stages create a sense of process and dailiness, making a remote epoch palpably real.

This type of historical work draws upon Roerich's passionate interest in Slavic history and archaeology. As a child he grew up overlooking the River Neva. The family lived in an apartment above his father's law office near the St Petersburg docks. From his window he could see ships being built and launched and finally disappearing toward the Gulf of Finland. So this painting depicts a scene from Roerich's own experience transposed to the ancient past that so intrigued him.

The artist's use of light and colour intensifies the innate vitality of the subject. Mythological beasts on the prows of the ships form a rhythmic pattern of reds, strong verticals in successive planes, which culminate in the vermillion sails of departing ships on the left horizon. The men in their white homespun smocks are not carefully rendered studies of physical activity but freely painted and presented as bright fields of energy. Roerich's palette, like his title *Building the Ships,* conveys notions of continuity, development and regeneration. Another sketch in his Slav series, *Building the Town* (1902), also profiles ancient man in his communal role as artisan. (7)

A number of other Russians of the period reflected upon the Slavic past in their paintings, notably Ivan Bilibin's *Princess in the Tower* (1902) and Vassily Kandinsky's *Song of the Volga* (1906). (8) But the works of such artists remain in the realm of the decorative. None had Roerich's stamp of erudition or his ability to permeate his works with such a seemingly authentic atmosphere of ancient times.

This painting is the unsigned sketch for a canvas three times the size, executed by the artist in oil the same year. (9) Once owned by Nicholas Gumilev, a Russian poet with a heroic vision of the Slavs similar to Roerich, it was acquired by Sina Fosdick, who lent it and later bequeathed it to the Nicholas Roerich Museum.

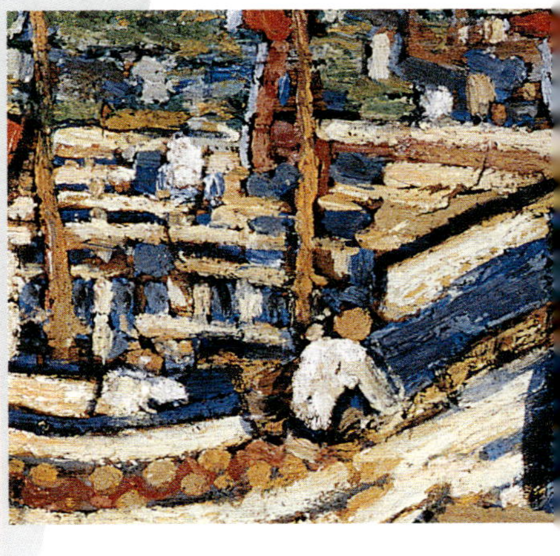

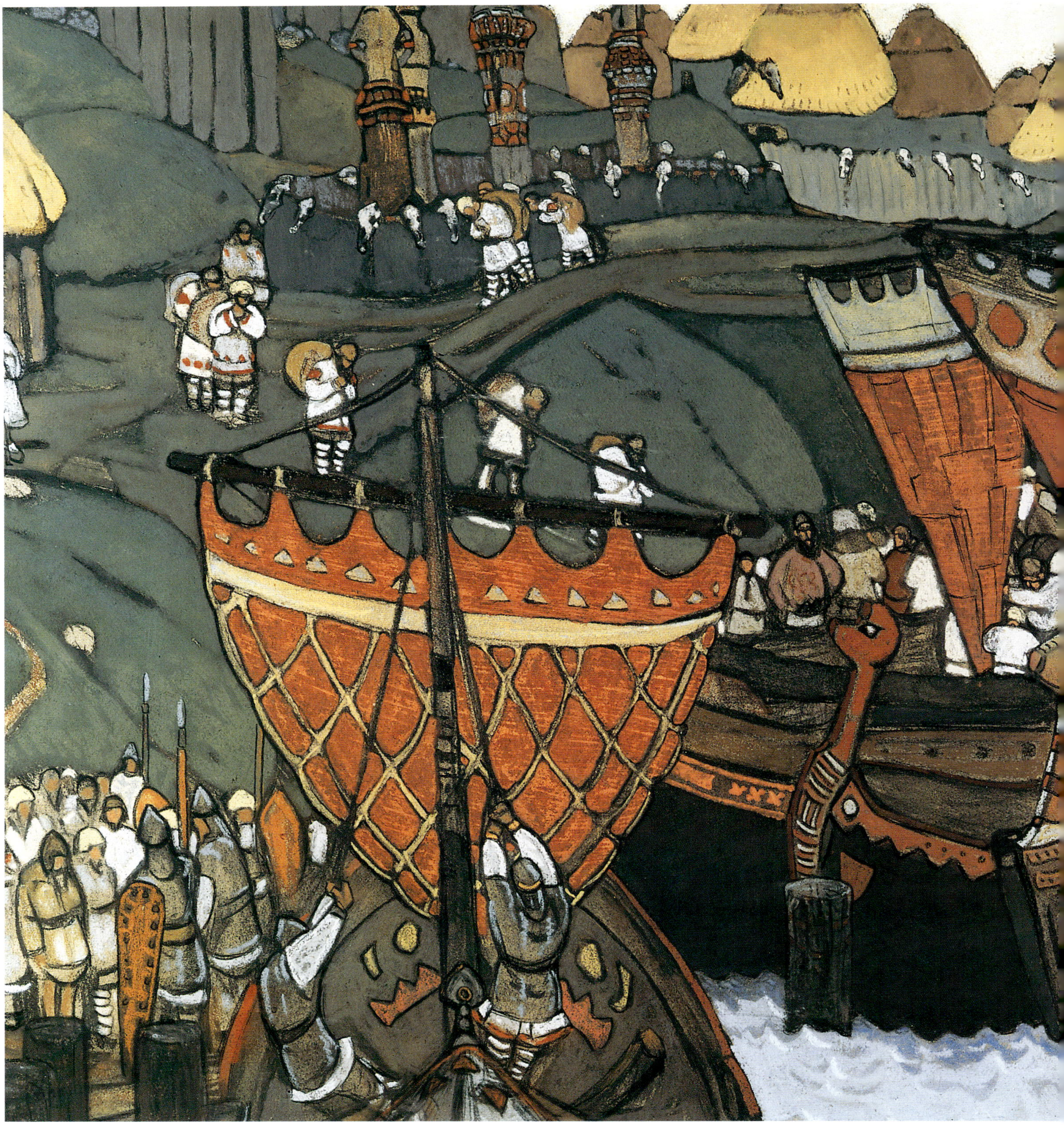

notions of continuity, development and regeneration'.

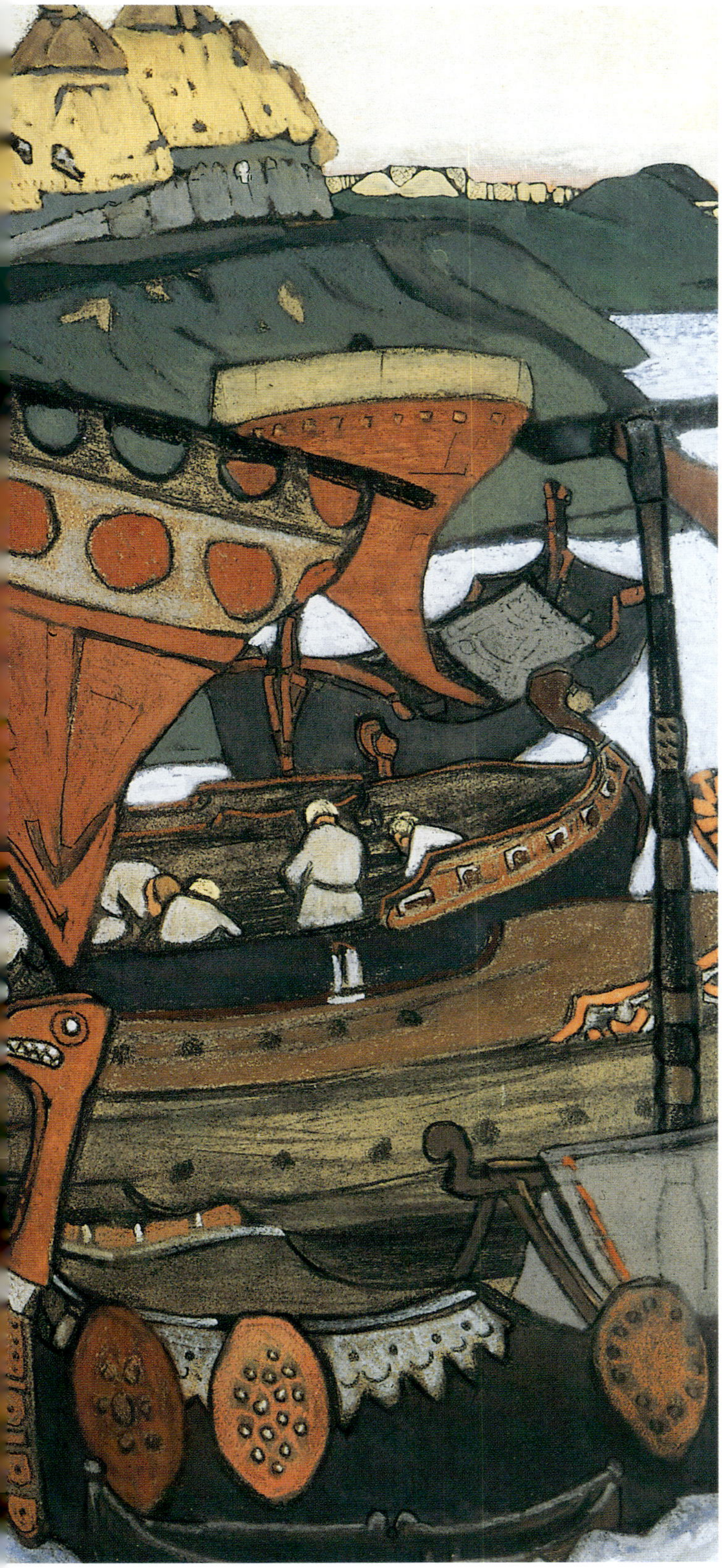

The Slavs on the Dnieper, 1905

Tempera on cardboard, 67 x 89 cm.
Russian Museum, Saint Petersburg

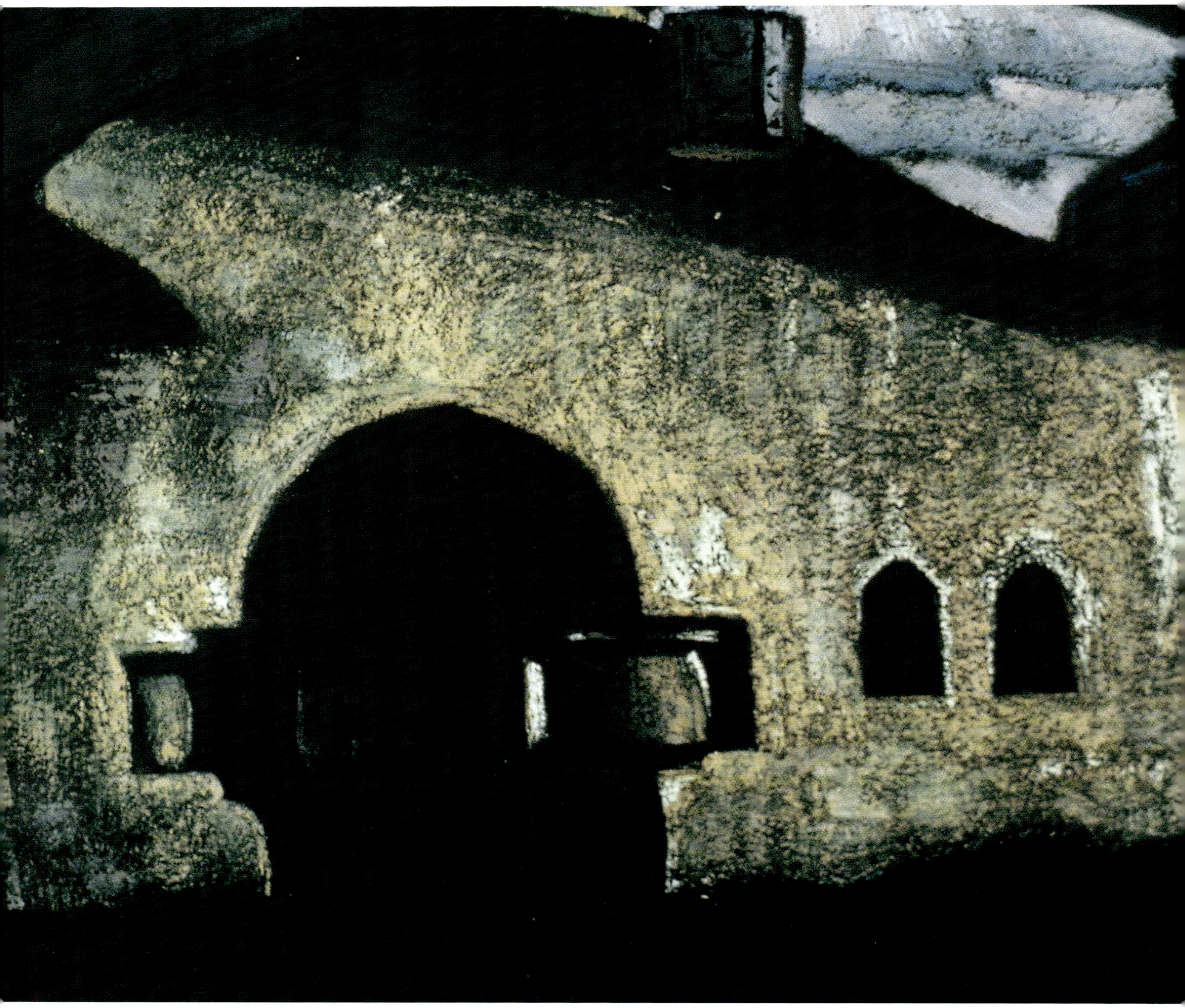

Old Monastery

Tempera on cardboard, 54.6 x 42 cm.
Nicholas Roerich Museum, New York

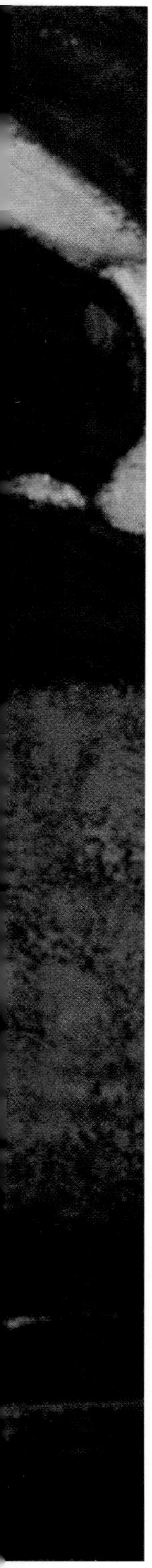

2 Old Monastery

Roerich's way of seeing the monastery makes no concession to the picturesque. He places the viewer unusually close to the subject, almost immediately beneath an arch, to confront a wall. Its stark, roughly textured surface all but fills the width of the painting. Why should so ordinary a structure impose itself with such authority? The light cast on the wall gradually draws attention to the striations of time and weather that verify its age. Accented by the adjacent cupola and distant clouds, the large flat surface of the wall conveys a sense of perseverance. Its dark recesses with glimmers of light call to mind the monastic virtues of solemnity and reflection.

The framing of a subject through arches was a signature device among World of Art painters. Alexander Benois, Konstantin Somov and Anna Ostroumova-Lebedeva were among those who used the device to create mysterious and sometimes voyeuristic situations in their work. [10] Roerich's approach encourages the viewer to look at the wall as a resident monk might do, the recessed and overhead arches focusing the eye on a whitewashed expanse for projection of images of the inner life.

Concurrent with his university studies in the 1890's, Roerich attended the Academy of Art in St Petersburg, where he worked with landscape painter, Arkhip Kuindzhi. A member of the Realist generation and part of the group called the Wanderers, Kuindzhi sometimes imbued buildings as well as natural settings with spiritual qualities through his Luminist techniques. When Roerich went to Paris in 1900, he transformed what he learned from Kuindzhi through study of the Post Impressionists and their radical simplifications, which he utilizes in this work.

On his return from France the artist married Helena Shaposhnikova, the daughter of a Moscow architect. Roerich and his wife then traveled throughout Russia doing archaeological research and documenting monuments of medieval architecture. 'He painted the churches, chapels and city walls of ancient Russia [with] Madame Roerich taking some excellent photographs on these tours of the subjects that Professor Roerich painted,' explained Sina Fosdick, their friend of later years, who eventually owned *Old Monastery.* [11] Roerich painted some ninety works on these travels to Yaroslavl, Rostov, Vladimir, Pskov, Novgorod and other cities.

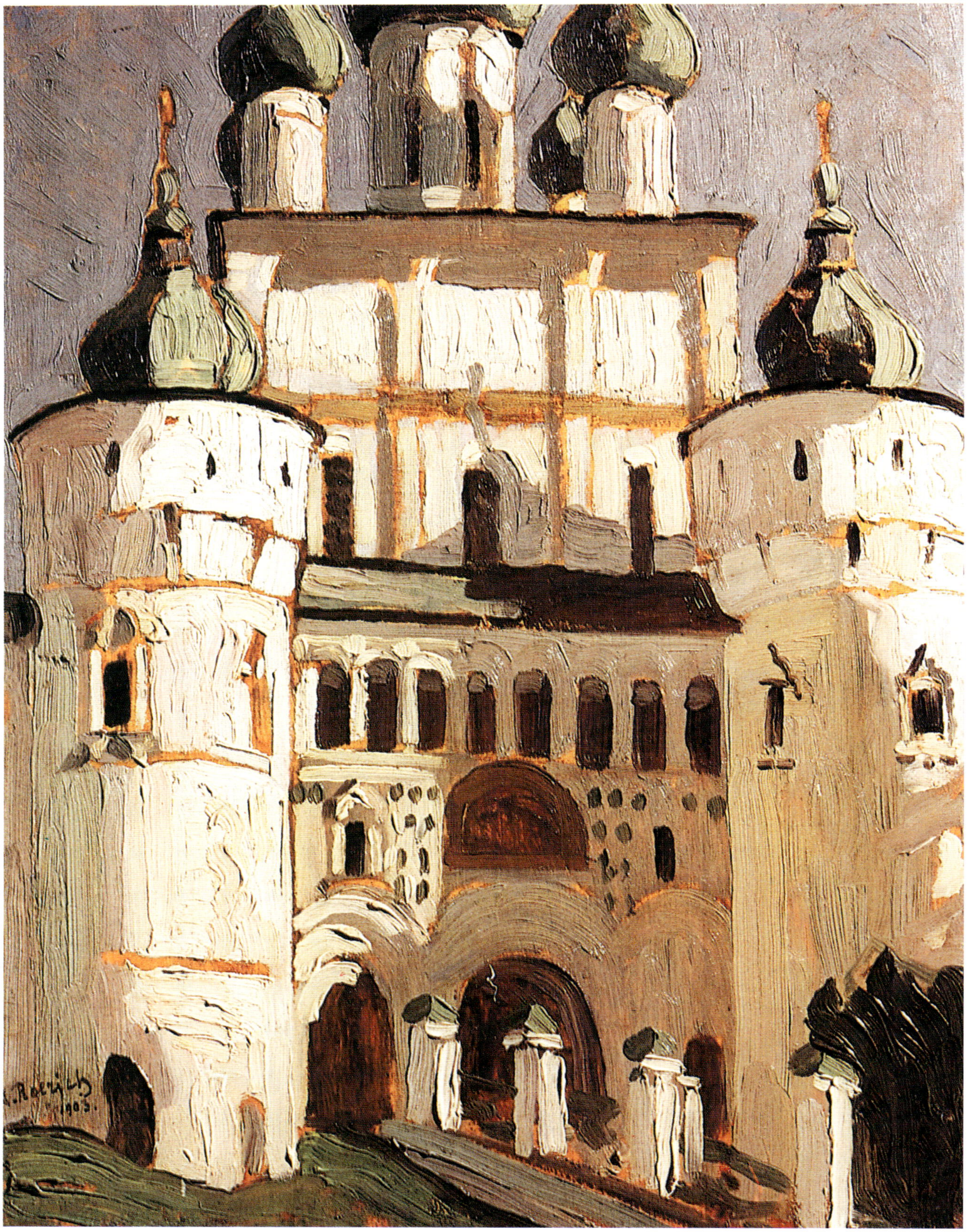

Old Russia, Rostov the Great. Entrance to the Kremlin, 1903

Oil on panel, 41 x 32 cm.
Museum of Oriental Art, Moscow

'Accented by the adjacent cupola and distant clouds, the large flat surface of the wall conveys a sense of perseverance'.

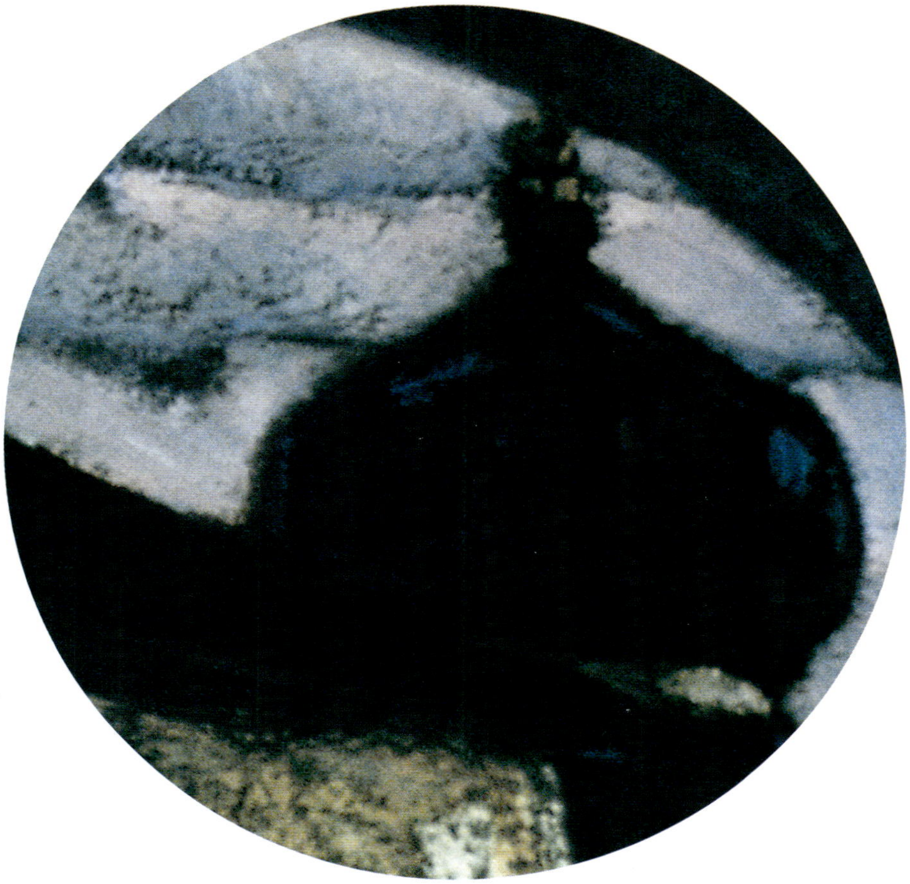

Old Monastery, detail

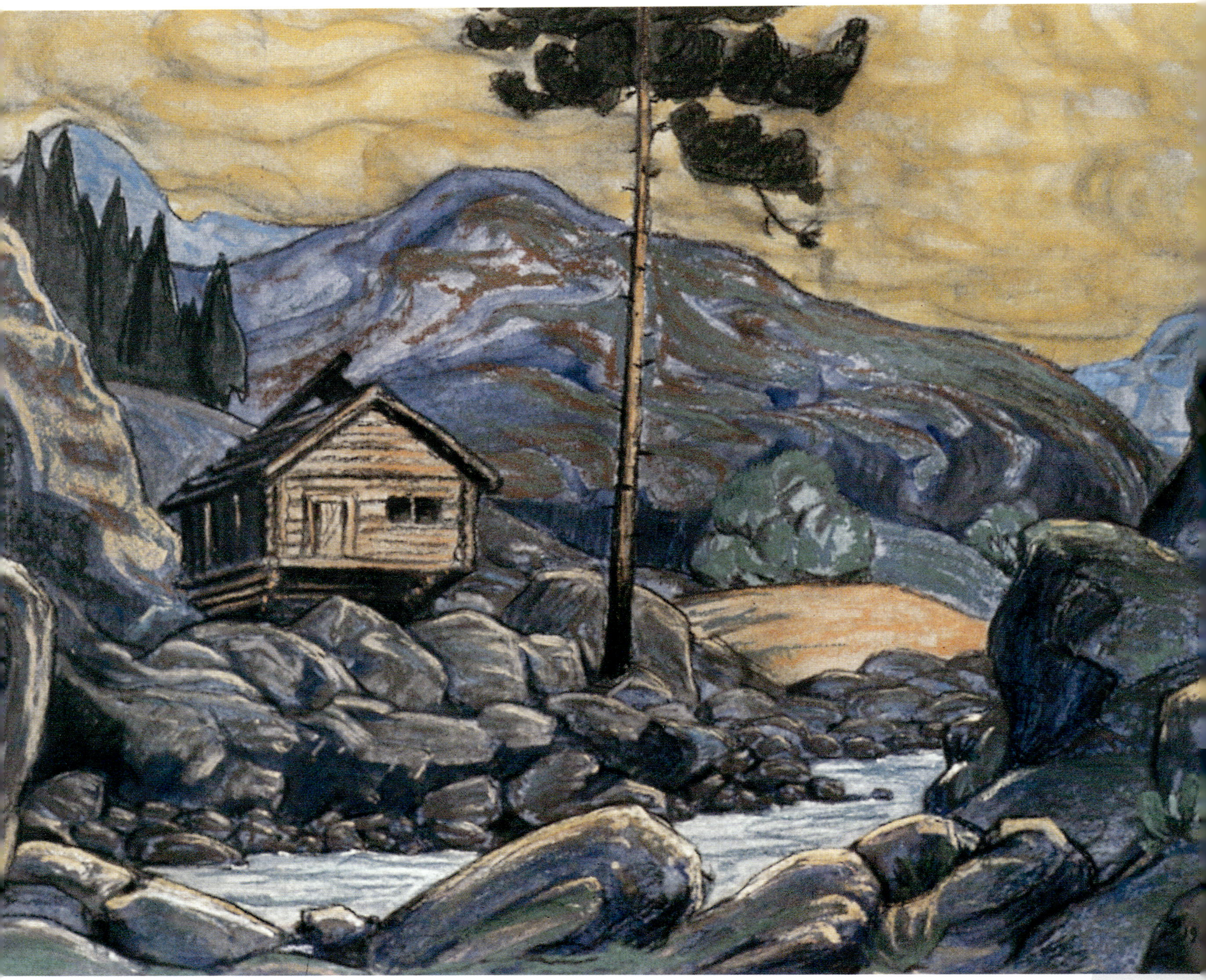

Sketch design for Peer Gynt, 1911

Pastel on cardboard, 65 x 50 cm.
Nicholas Roerich Museum, New York

Sketch design

Peer Gynt

The Nordic hut scaffolded onto rock is a solid construction that seems to balance precariously on a narrow base. By depicting the structure from a low angle, Roerich emphasizes the apparent contradiction of Solveig's hut and seems to suggest a parallel between her dwelling and her feeling for Peer Gynt, a pure love which he rejects but which survives his wanderlust. They are reunited at the hut in the climactic fifth act of Henrik Ibsen's play from 1867. The tree at the centre of the painting has lost all its sapling branches but, rooted in stone, it is sustained by this place, like the prodigal hero, who returns older and wiser after adventures in the Troll kingdom and beyond. For the Moscow Art Theatre production in 1912, Roerich created numerous settings, all full of Symbolist allusion for what he called 'that cosmic Norwegian drama.' [12] The design, executed in pastel, has a restricted palette of blues and yellows, the constituents of green, a colour used sparingly to suggest the hope and salvation that Solveig's love can provide in this Faustian tale.

Roerich was asked to design for Peer Gynt by Moscow Art Theatre directors, Konstantin Stanislavsky and Vladimir Nemirovich-Danchenko, who were mindful of his growing reputation as a designer. His first theatrical commission came when Nikolai Evreinov and Nikolai Drizen invited him to do *The Three Wise Men* for St Petersburg's Ancient (Starinny) Theatre in 1907. A second commission, *Fuente Ovejuna,* followed in 1911. Recognition by authority figures had spurred Roerich's productivity as a young man and given him confidence to take artistic risks.

Early in his career Roerich had found an adviser in Vladimir Stasov, erudite librarian, eminent critic and champion of nationalism in the arts. Svetoslav Roerich, recalling stories he had heard about that time, remarked on the encyclopedic knowledge and intellectual circle Stasov had shared with his father, introducing him to luminaries like Nikolai Rimsky-Korsakov and Leo Tolstoy. [13] Although Stasov had secured his protegé's first professional appointments, and despite the Slavophilism that linked them, the young painter was attracted to new cultural trends and particularly to Diaghilev's *World of Art.* This contact paid rich dividends when, in 1909, he was contracted to design Prince Igor for the impressario's Paris season.

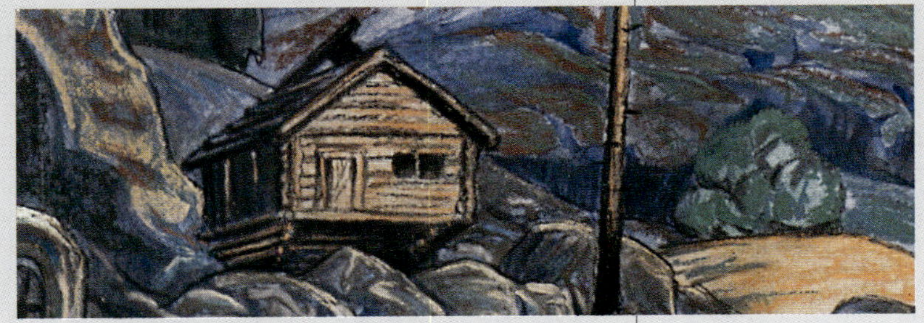

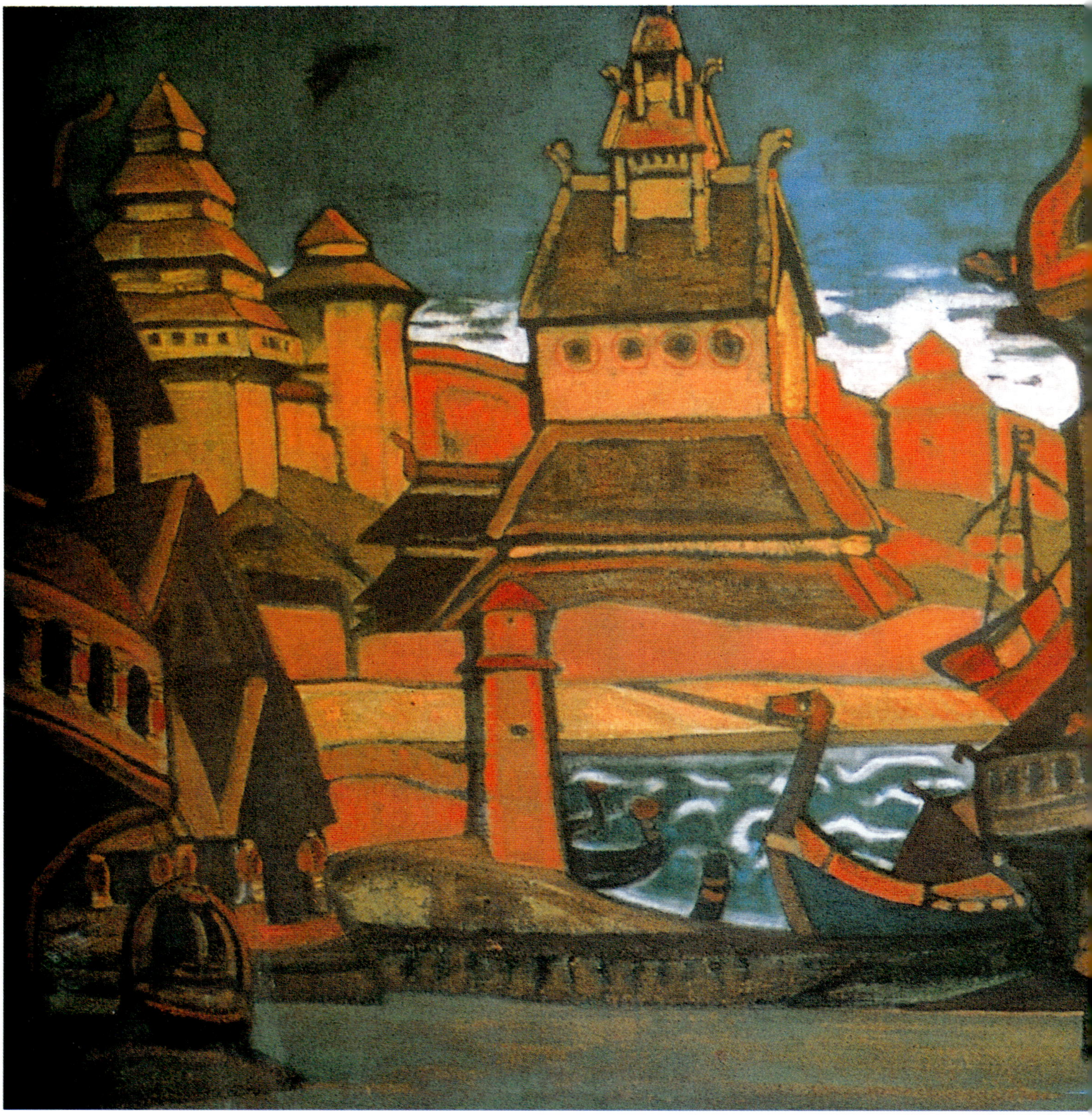

For the Moscow Art Theatre production in 1912, Roerich created numerous settings, all full of symbolist allusion for what he called "that cosmic Norwegian drama".

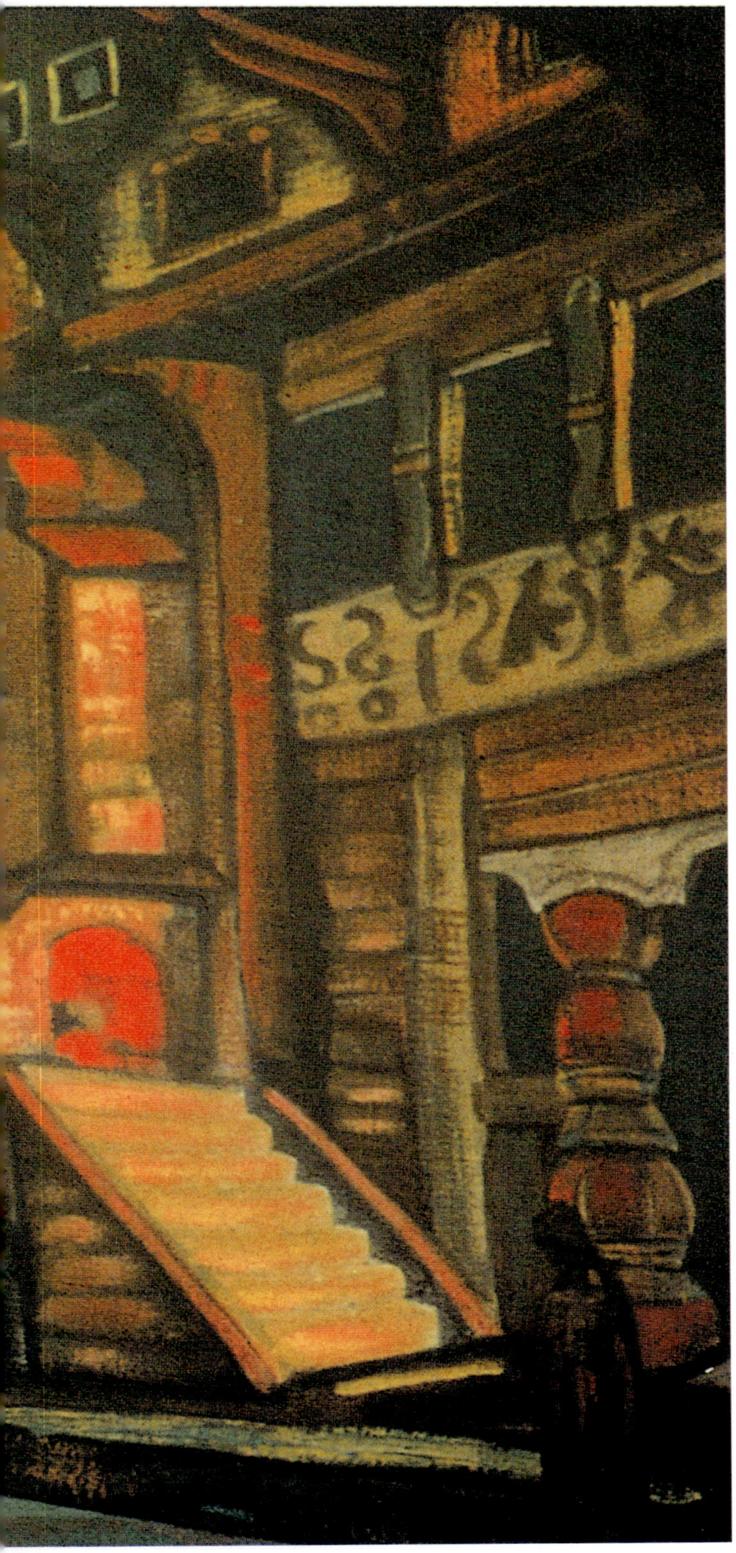

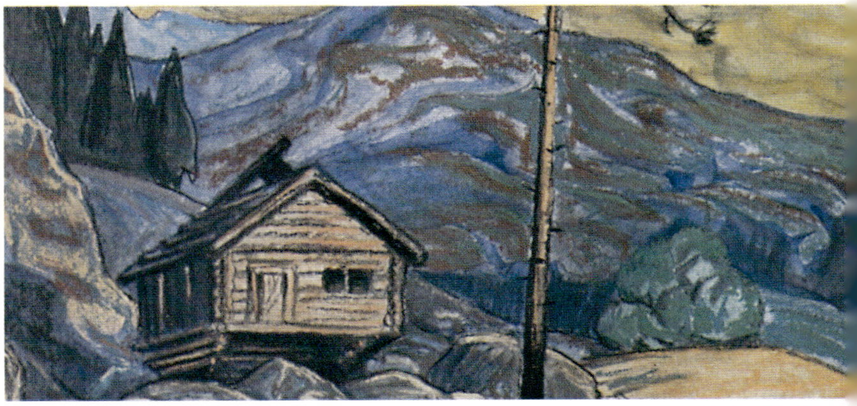

Sketch design for Peer Gynt, detail

Tmutarakan, Set design for Rimsky Korsakov's opera The Tale of Tsar Saltan, 1919

Tempera on canvas, 53.3 x 91.4 cm.
Orandeus University, Waltham, Massachusetts

Elborus, 1913

Tempera on canvas, 35.5 x 25 cm.
Nicholas Roerich Museum, New York

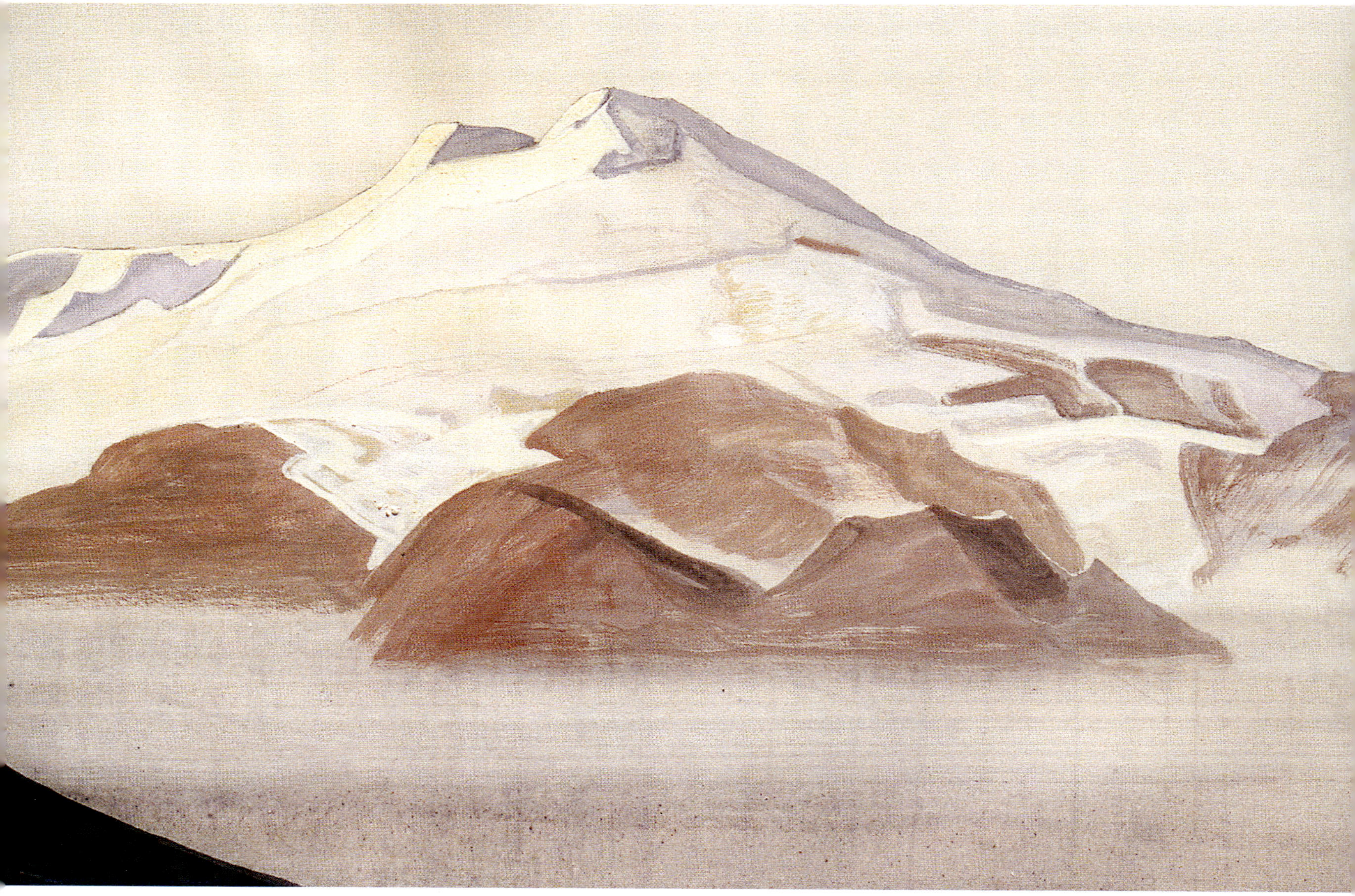

4 *Elborus*

In this rare early mountainscape from his Russian period, Roerich encounters for the first time the subject that will become identified with his name. In India later in his life he would be known as the Master of the Mountains. Unlike the intense colours and startling viewpoints of his Himalayan canvases, this portrayal of Elborus, the highest mountain in Europe, is dispassionate, even tentative. The work was probably painted in 1913 as part of the artist's Caucasian series, which included such titles as *Bugurstan, The Sunrise, Underworld Dwellers* and *Blue Mountain.* (14)

Kuindzhi took groups of his pupils from the Academy on painting excursions to the Caucases and Crimea, and his own depictions of Mount Elborus were often exhibited at the time. Svetoslav Roerich did not recall hearing that his father had taken part in these excursions, and furthermore, he felt obliged to mention that group painting situations had never been to Roerich's liking. (15) Whether it was in the studio or on location, the artist acquired valuable techniques from his teacher, particularly relating to light effects on summits covered with snow, the rendering of distance through mist and the focusing of long views through foreground details.

When Roerich visited Europe en route to India in 1923, he went to France where he painted Mont Blanc, the highest peak in the Alps. Then, shortly after reaching the Himalayas in 1924, he depicted Mount Everest, the highest peak in the world. It is intriguing that he chose to use great restraint in these works, avoiding the glamour associated with these famous sites and adopting simplicity as the method for his novitiate as a mountain painter. Yet in this period he approached lesser peaks in the Himalayan range with a certain freedom and flamboyance, as though their relative anonymity released his creative energy.

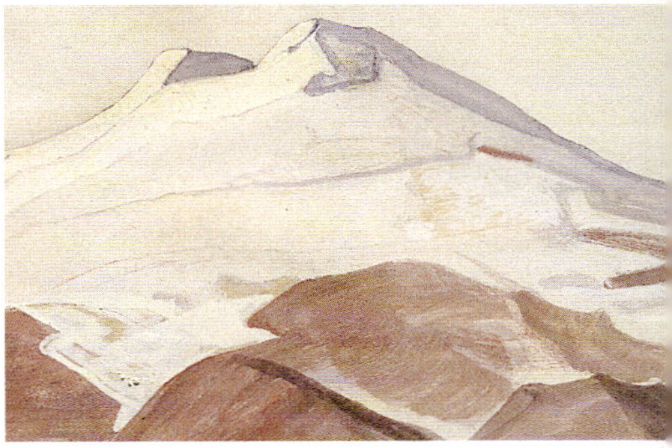

This canvas, which once belonged to Svetoslav Roerich, shows Mount Elborus towering above the clouds, which all but cover the neighbouring mountains. A dark slope on the bottom left balances the shadow on Elborus at the top right, and the peaks piercing the cloud in the middle distance accentuate the height of the mountain beyond. The composition and palette resemble Kuindzhi's *The Peak of Elborus in Sunlight* (1898-1908), but Roerich opts to economize line and purify colour. (16)

'This portrayal of Elborus is

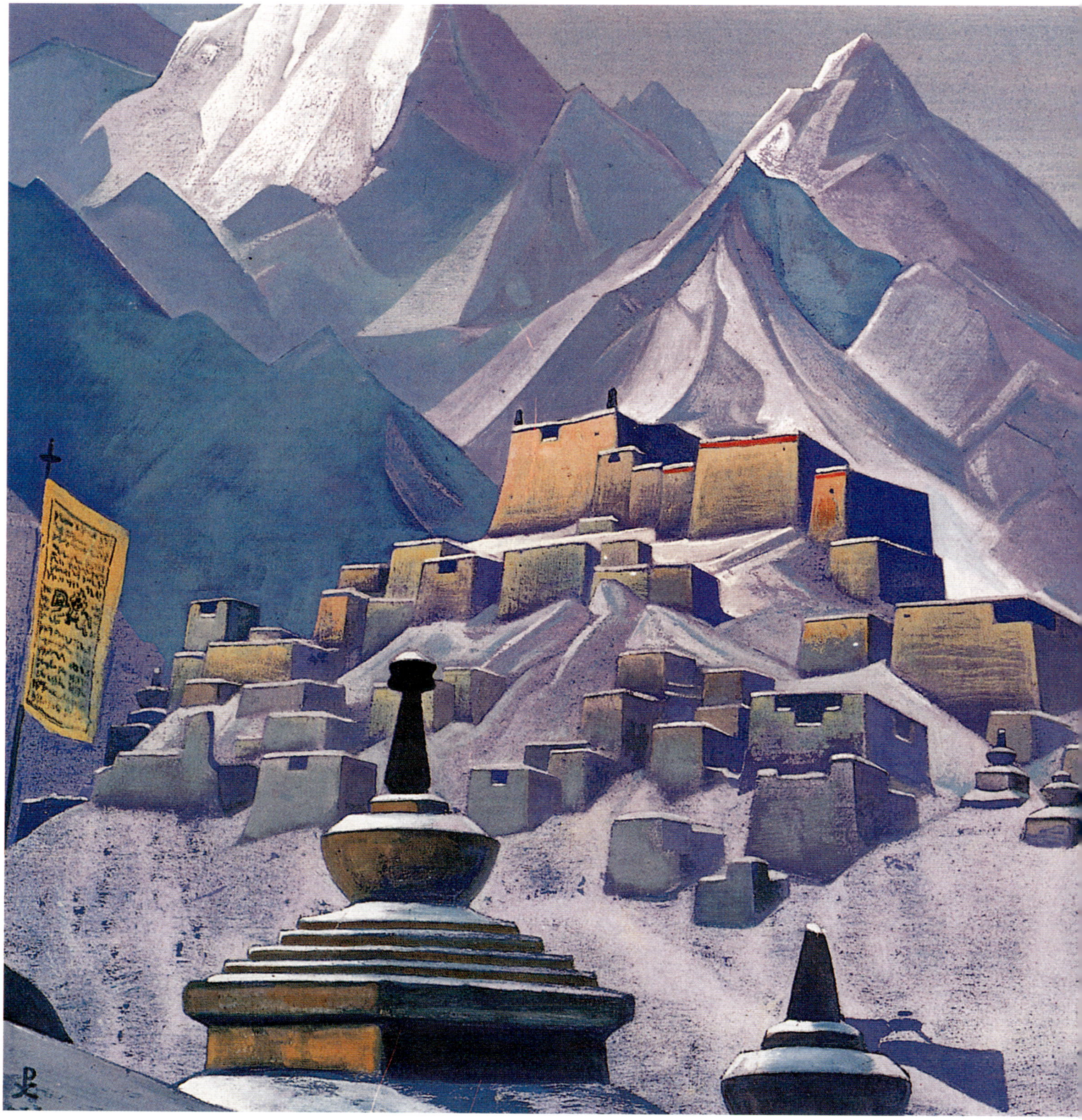

dispassionate, even tentative.'

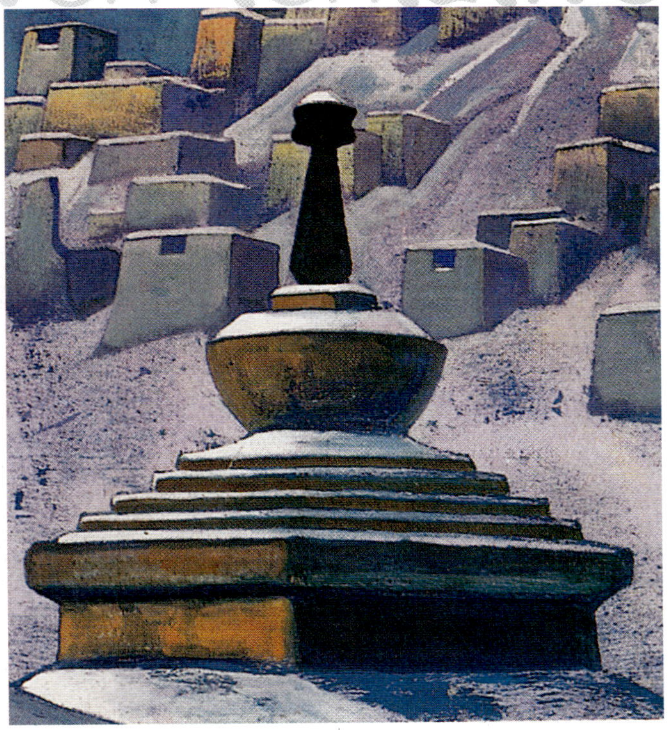

Tibet, detail

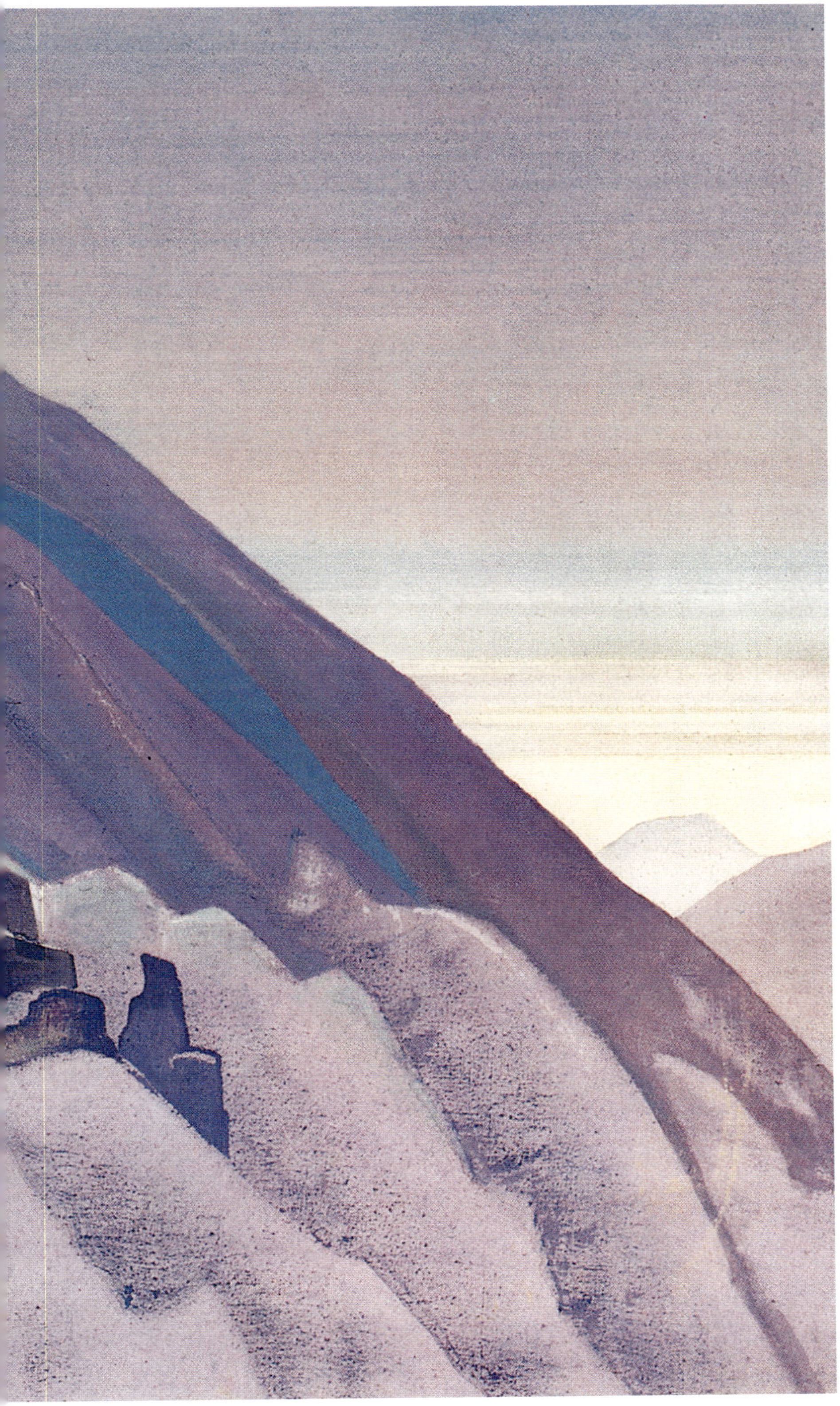

Tibet, 1933

Temperas on canvas,
75 x 118.5 cm.
Nicholas Roerich Museum, New York

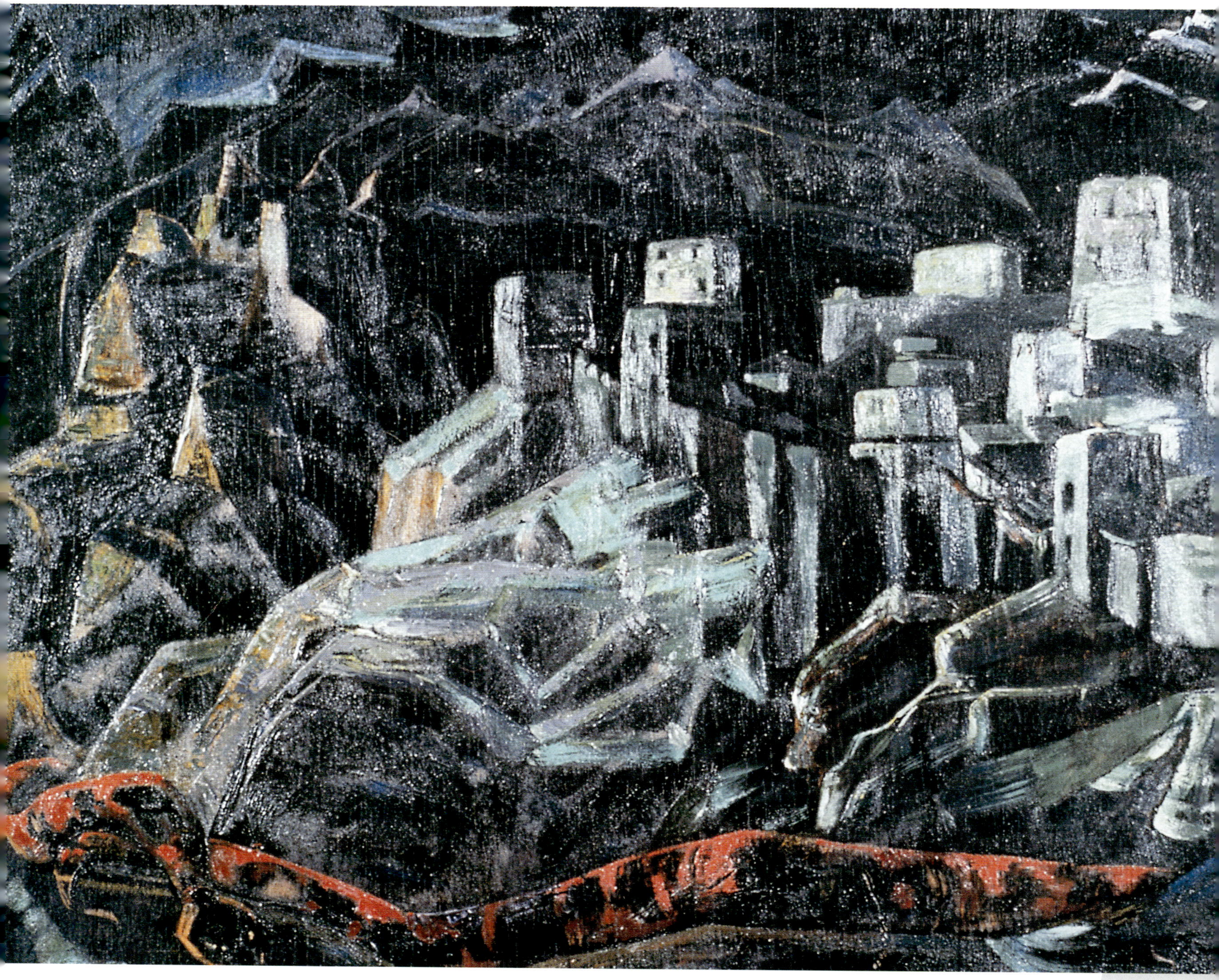

The Doomed City, 1914

Oil on cardboard, 66 x 43 cm.
Nicholas Roerich Museum, New York

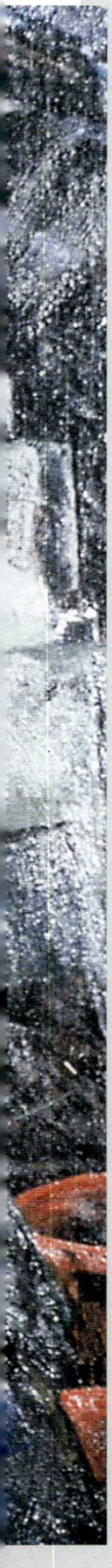

5 The Doomed City

Although there were apocalyptic elements in some of Roerich's paintings at the time of the proto-Revolution in 1905, this trait in his art becomes pronounced in 1912 and develops steadily through the outbreak of World War I in 1914. These prophetic paintings do not identify specific locations or events, although associations can be made, such as the emblematic connection of *Conflagration* (1914) with the impending German invasion of Belgium, which precipitated Britain's entry in what would be called the Great War. [17] The paintings are archetypal, demonstrating, as does *The Doomed City,* the perils of the human condition and civilization itself.

In this work Roerich presents a fortified city seemingly chiselled from the stone of the mountains that surround it. The chalk-white walls, buildings and rockface look sepulchral in the gathering shadows. An enormous serpent, scarlet and black, encircles the city, its head twisted over its tail, sealing the exits and preparing to squeeze from the citizens their last breath of life. The geometrized landscape signals the artist's appreciation of Paul Cezanne, but Roerich adapts the French painter's modelling technique to emotive ends. The blocks and facets of *The Doomed City,* a nightmare of skulls besieged by snakes, portend destruction. The tomb-like city and serpentine imagery also suggest a tribute to El Greco's *Toledo and Laocoon.* [18]

This painting prompted Alexis Remizov, a poet with Symbolist affiliations, to write a cycle of poems of the same title, putting Roerich's prophecy into words:

Doomed in the coils of the serpent stands the citadel. And yet for a long time no one knows or suspects disaster. People ate and drank, they married and sought partners in marriage. And when the hour came to sound the alarm, There was no escape. [19]

Another contemporary writer, the Realist Maxim Gorky- Roerich's good friend despite their aesthetic differences- acquired the tempera variant of this painting, which is also dated 1914. Roerich made a practice of doing a sketch or first version of his major canvases, often executing it on card in the full palette of the final work. Usually, as in this case, the initial study stands as a painting in its own right.

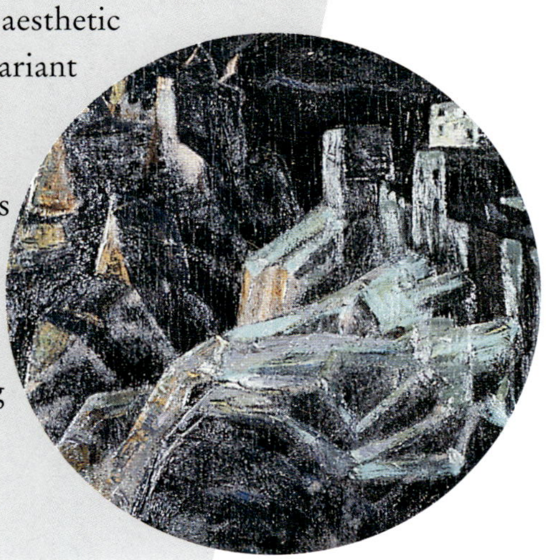

Call of the Skies, 1935-36

Tempera on canvas, 60.7 x 91 cm.
Svetoslav Roerich Collection, Bangalore, India

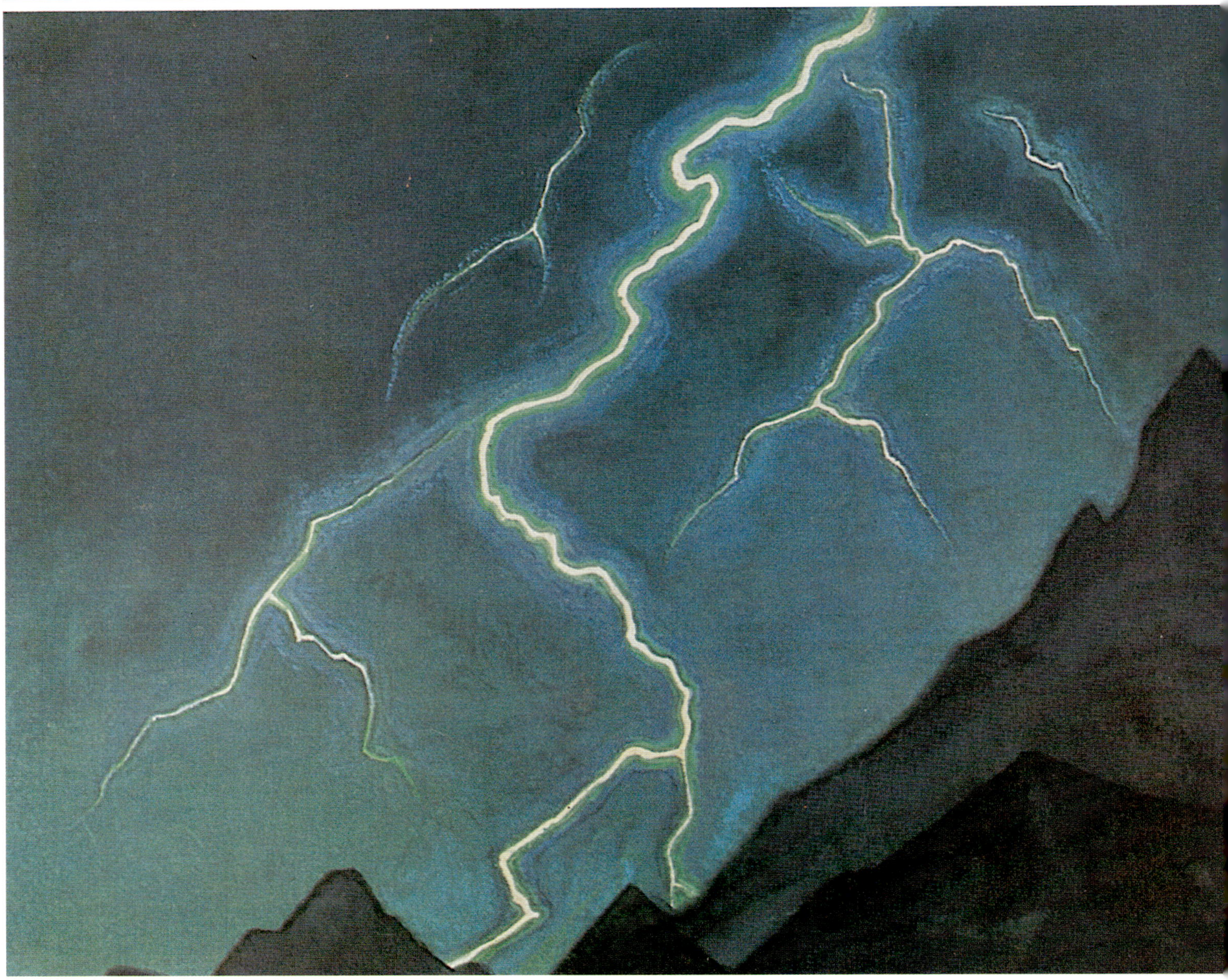

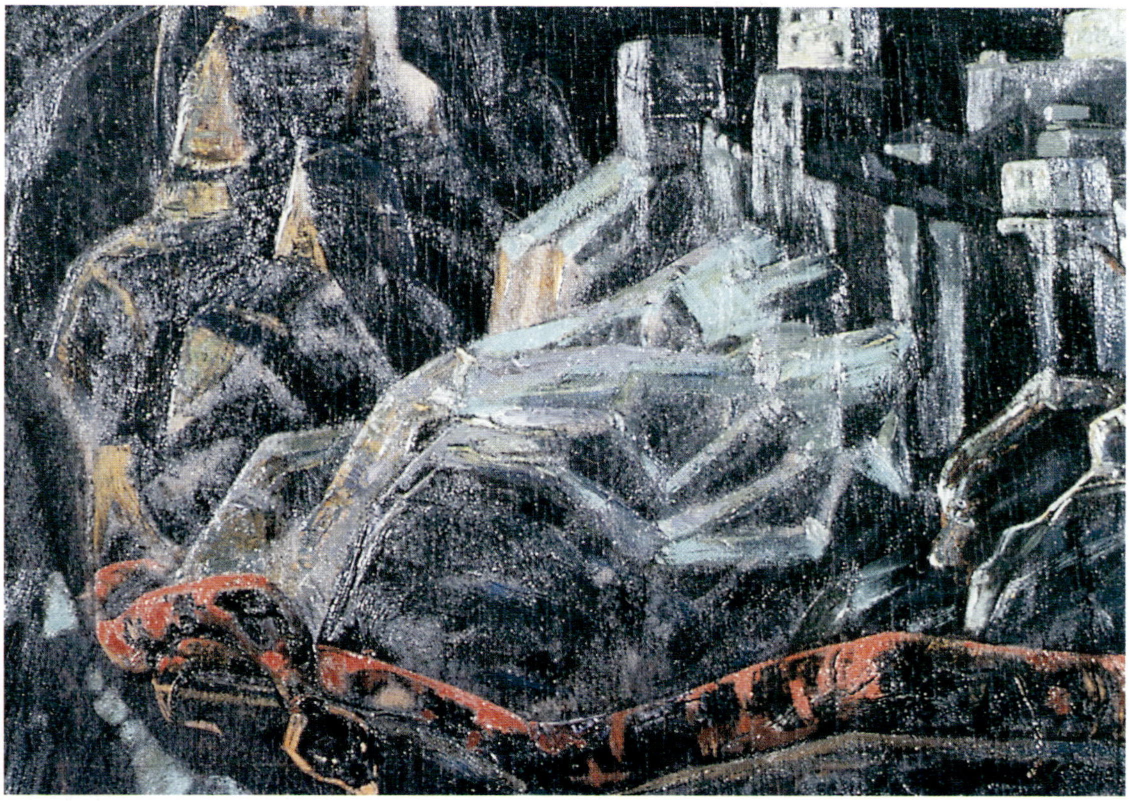

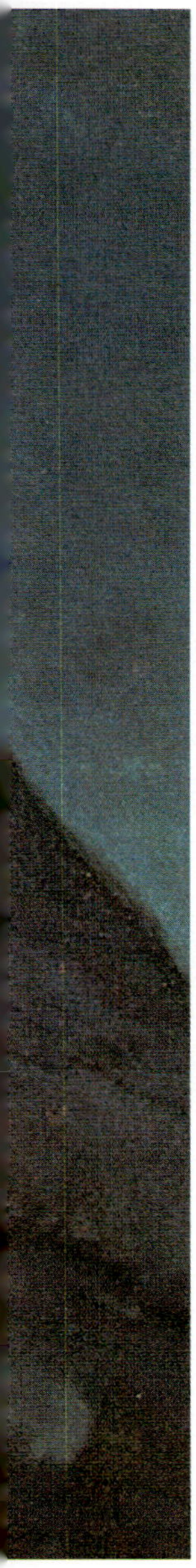

The Doomed City, detail

'The painting is demonstrating the perils of the human condition and civilization itself.'

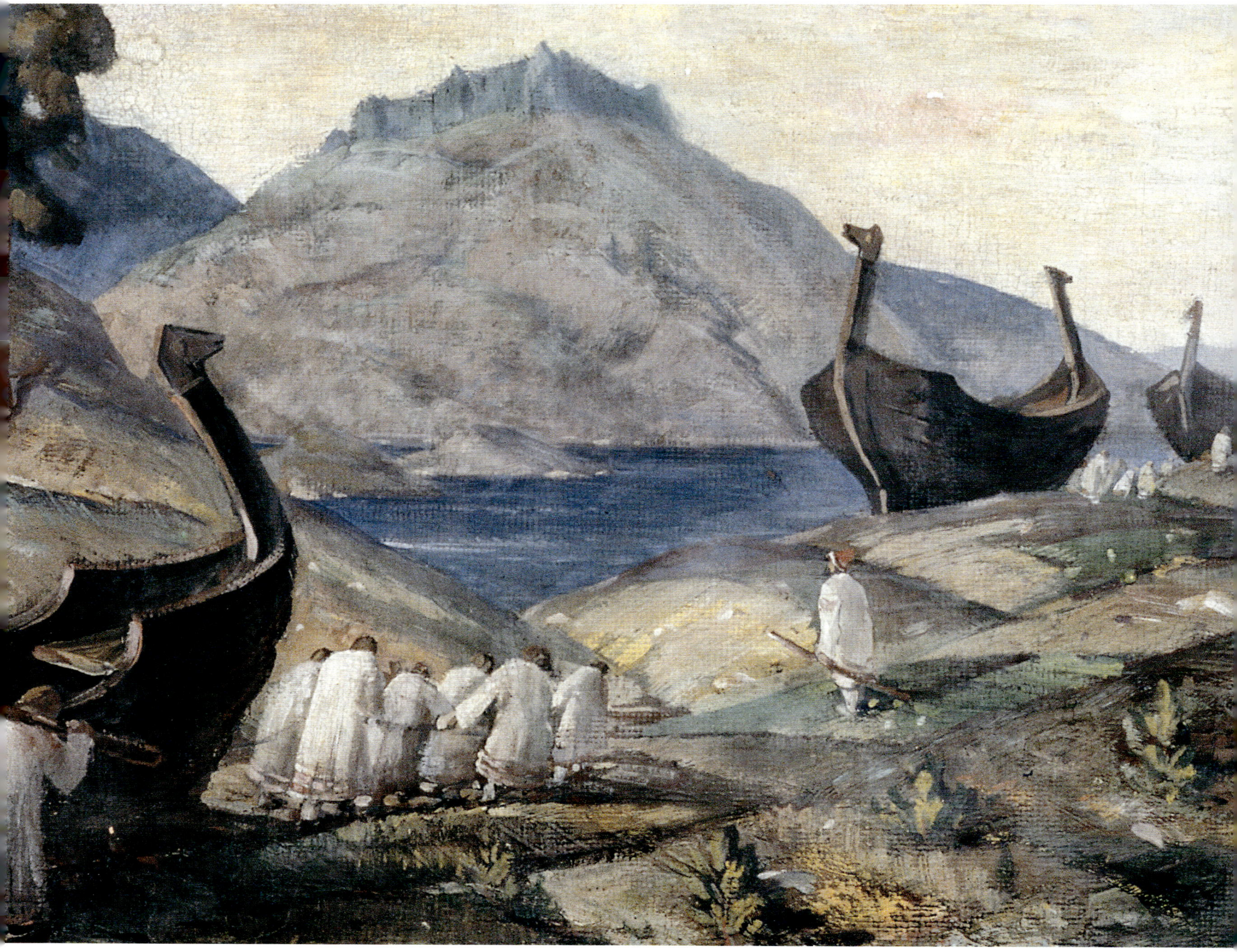

Launching the Ships, 1915

Oil on canvas, 73 x 60.3 cm.
Nicholas Roerich Museum, New York

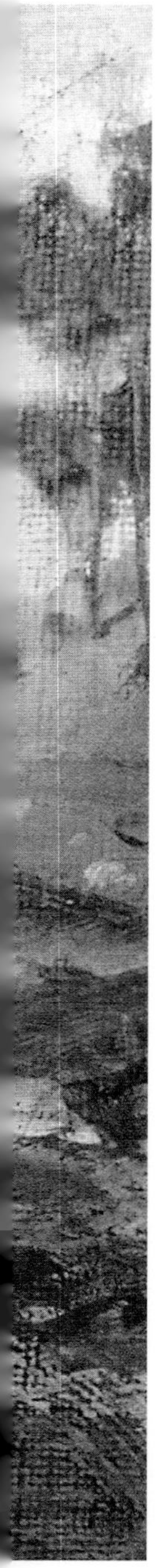

6 *Launching the Ships*

Roerich demonstrates in this painting how the ancient Slavs pulled wooden ships overland on rollers. The ships are carved at bow and prow with the heads of beasts, a motif the Slavs adopted from the Varangians who taught them the craft of ship construction. These Scandinavian warriors and traders exploited the natural system of rivers – the Dvina, Volga and Dnieper – which flowed across the plains of Russia and linked the Baltic with the Black and Caspian Seas. Their network facilitated interchange between Varangians and Greeks, linking Byzantium and points east with Scandinavia. In 1899 Roerich wrote an article for Art and Artistic Industry entitled '*On Paths from the Varangians to the Greeks,*' which was included in the first volume of his *Complete Works* published in 1914. [20] As he prepared it for the latter, the subject of the Slavs and Varangians must have been fresh in his mind.

This canvas, executed in oil, is probably a study for the tempera work of the same year, *They Drag Them Along,* still exhibited in Russia, in which Roerich maximized the sense of distance the men must pull the ships, by making their path cut a diagonal from bottom left to top right of the canvas, the longest line in a rectangle. [21] But this study in oil achieves a similar effect through breadth, the row of ships extending the width of the canvas. In the tempera painting, interestingly, the artist instead used depth, separating the ships in deeper planes. Another contrast between the two works concerns the palette: the study restricts itself to pale blues, greys, ochres and greens, the muted colours favoured by the World of Art painters at the turn of the century; the final canvas, however, shifted into the Post-Impressionist mode Roerich developed after 1900 with warmer, stronger hues broadly applied.

At the Society for the Encouragement of the Arts, where Roerich was secretary, he had by 1915 served for over a decade as head of its large school. There he introduced many reforms relating to curriculum, student enrollment and faculty, employing Bilibin, for example, and other innovative artists as well as traditional icon painters. In this period when Roerich often depicted groups of ancient Slavs involved in the common effort of nation building, he had to balance in his professional life the solitary demands of easel painting with the needs of a complex artistic community.

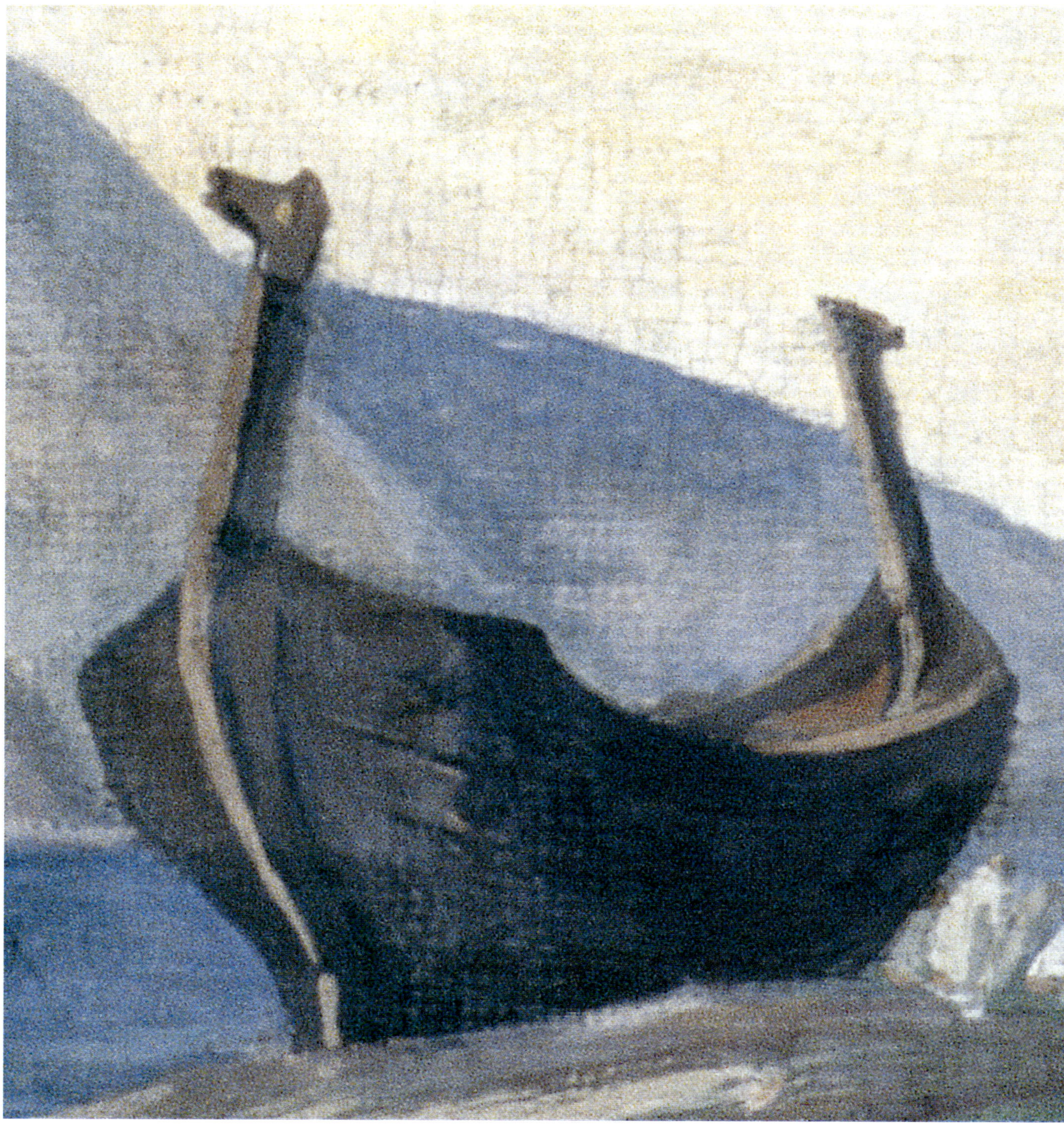

Launching the Ships, detail

'Roerich demonstrates in this painting how the ancient Slavs pulled wooden ships overland on rollers.'

Launching the Ships, detail

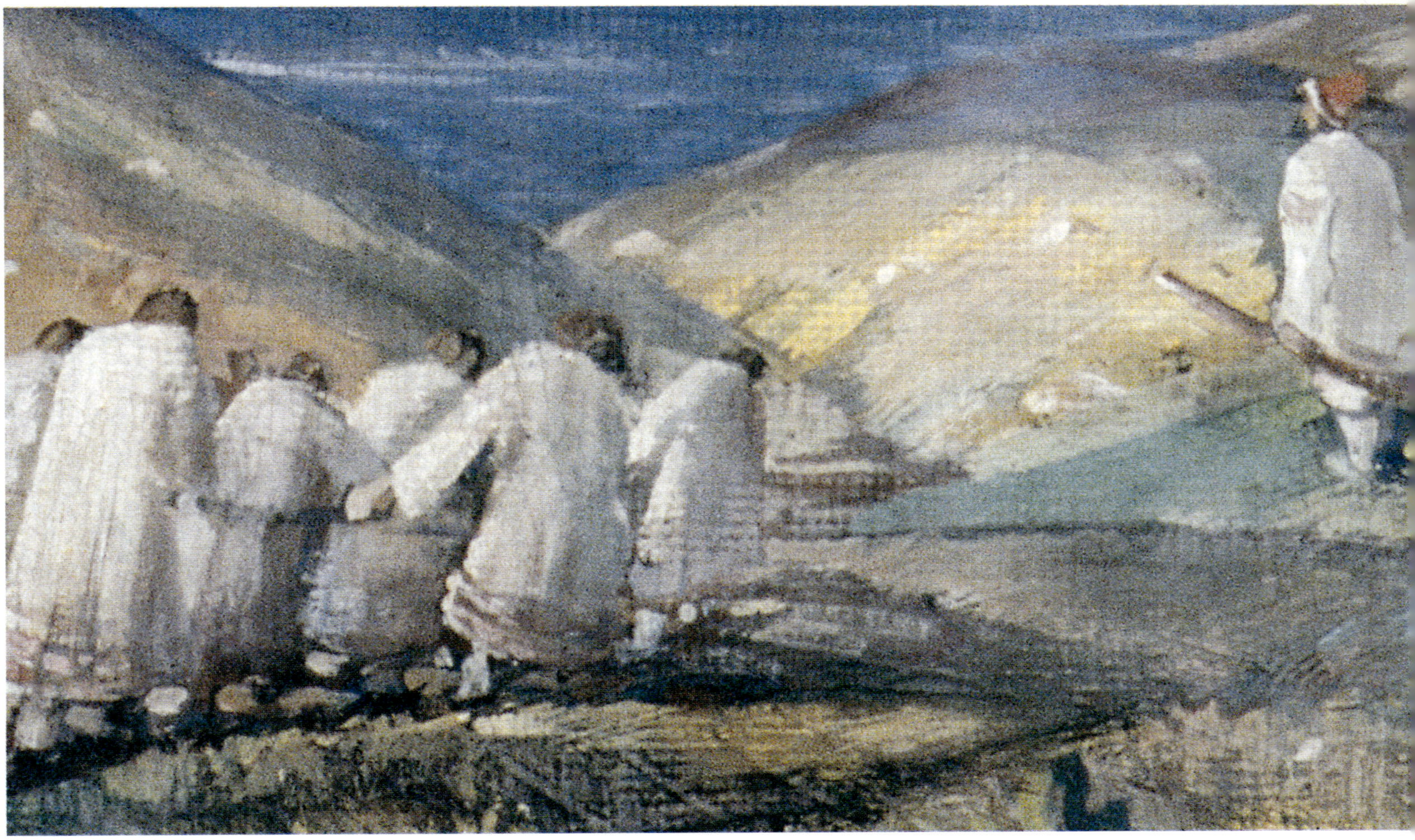

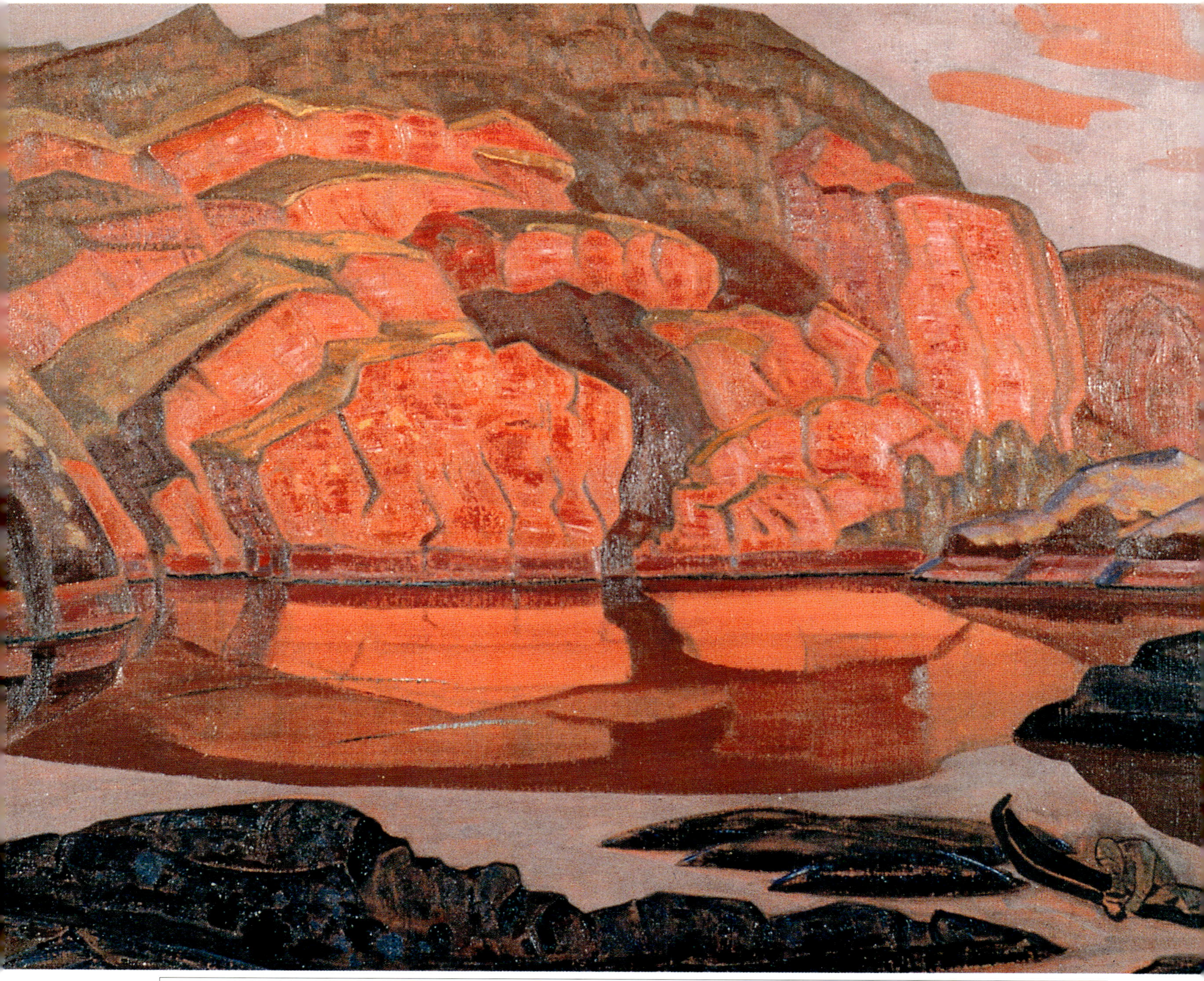

The Hidden Treasure, 1917

Oil on canvas, 76.2 x 49.5 cm.
Nicholas Roerich Museum, New York

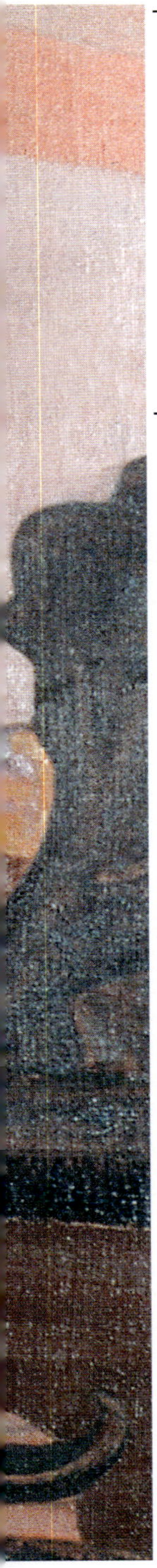

7 The Hidden Treasure

Roerich and his family left St Petersburg in the period of the Revolution in 1917 and went to Finland, which achieved its independence from Russia that same year. On the shore of vast Lake Ladoga, which separates the two countries, the artist took up residence. Compared with the administrative and academic duties of life in Russia, his Finnish interlude was fairly contemplative. Due to respiratory problems in the past, he had gone to Finland to recuperate and had developed a keen interest in its culture. Now, in the midst of all the volatile politics, he returned and focused on poetry as well as painting, turning to philosophical and religious themes in both. [22]

Landscape often served Roerich as ambience, and in his Russian and Finnish works, place was made to resonate with history and myth. *The Hidden Treasure* shows a figure in a canoe, which seems carved from the islets around it. Dwarfed by cliffs of red granite and turquoise-coloured stone that are mirrored by the lake, the figure holds a vessel on the surface of the water. This suspended gesture is full of ambiguity. The figure could be putting a treasure into the lake or lifting one from it. At the top of the steep rock on the right is a form that appears to be observing the action, unnoticed, some kind of guardian spirit that may itself be the hidden treasure. Roerich used the concept of treasure in many of his titles and created a kind of adventure for his viewers, enticing them to seek and find that which is precious.

In *The Hidden Treasure* the artist may be evoking an event from the folk literature of the Finns, perhaps from the Kalevala, their creation myth and epic saga of survival. Roerich much admired this poem of archaic origins and later wrote about it in his book *Realm of Light.* [23] His friend and contemporary, the Finnish artist Akseli Gallen-Kallela, had illustrated the Kalevala in the 1890's, providing Roerich with a model of how to use the pagan past as a spiritual resource for the present. [24] This painting is the first in the seven canvas Heroica series, all of which may refer to the Kalevala. Roerich's setting and the figure in the canoe bring to mind *The Song of Hiawatha* (1855), which the poet Henry Wadsworth Longfellow based on the Kalevala, adapting its epic structure and metrics to American Indian legend. [25] In India in 1947 Roerich did a variant of this canvas using bolder line and colour. [26]

Roerich used the concept of treasure in many of his

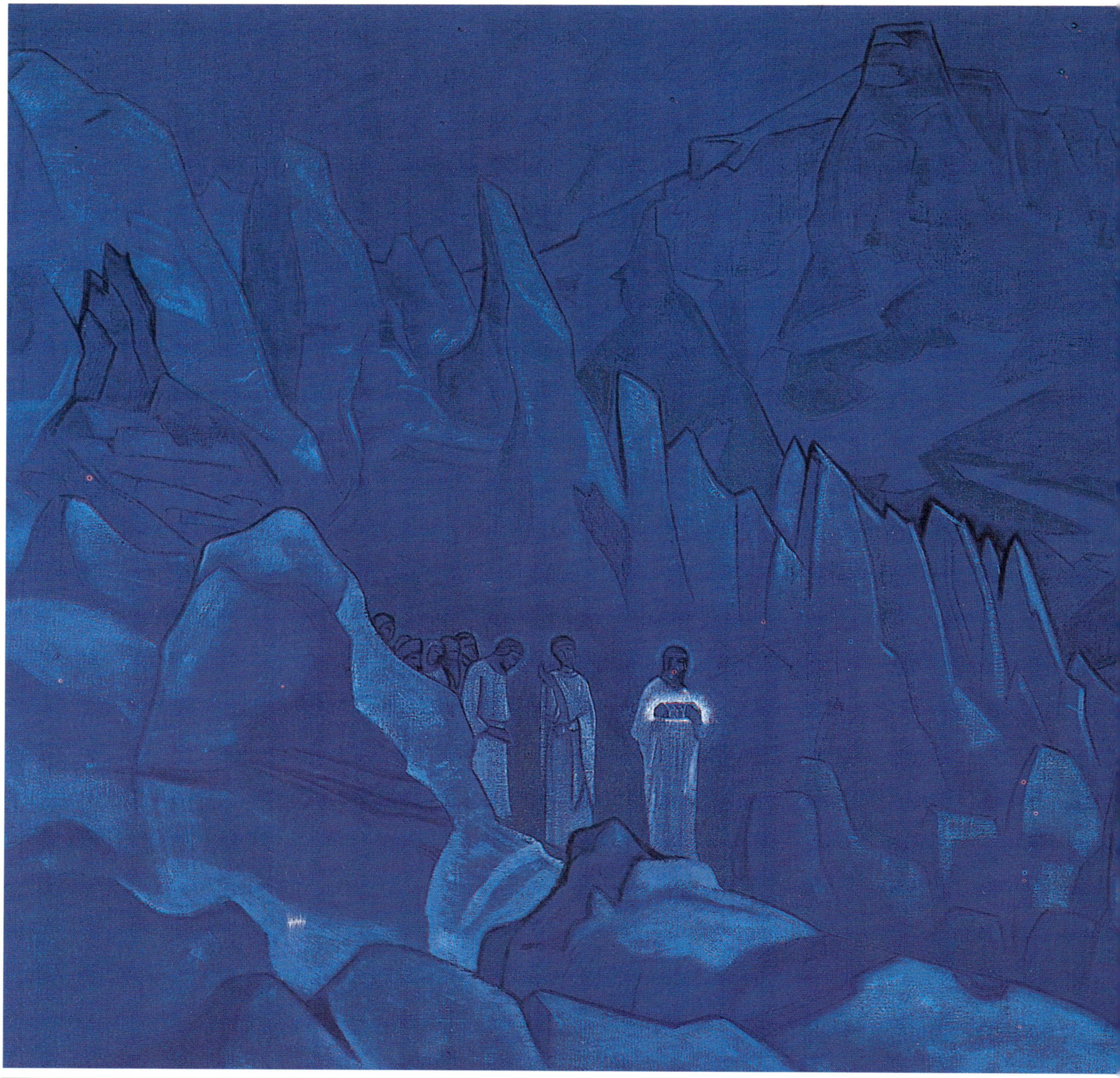

Burning of Darkness, 1924

Tempera on canvas, 76.2 x 117 cm.
Nicholas Roerich Museum, New York

titles and created a kind of adventure for his viewers.'

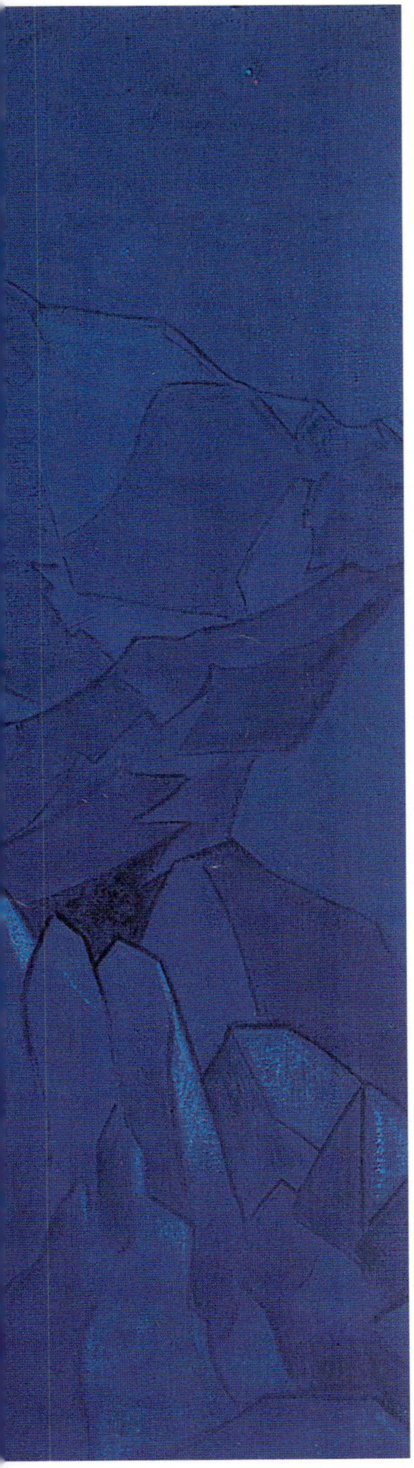

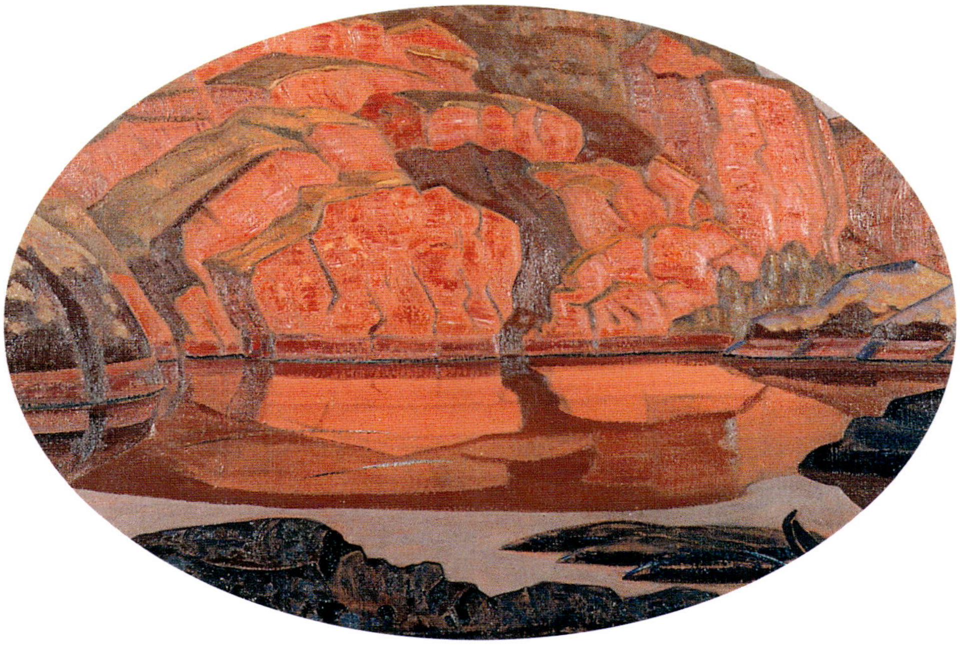

The Hidden Treasure, detail

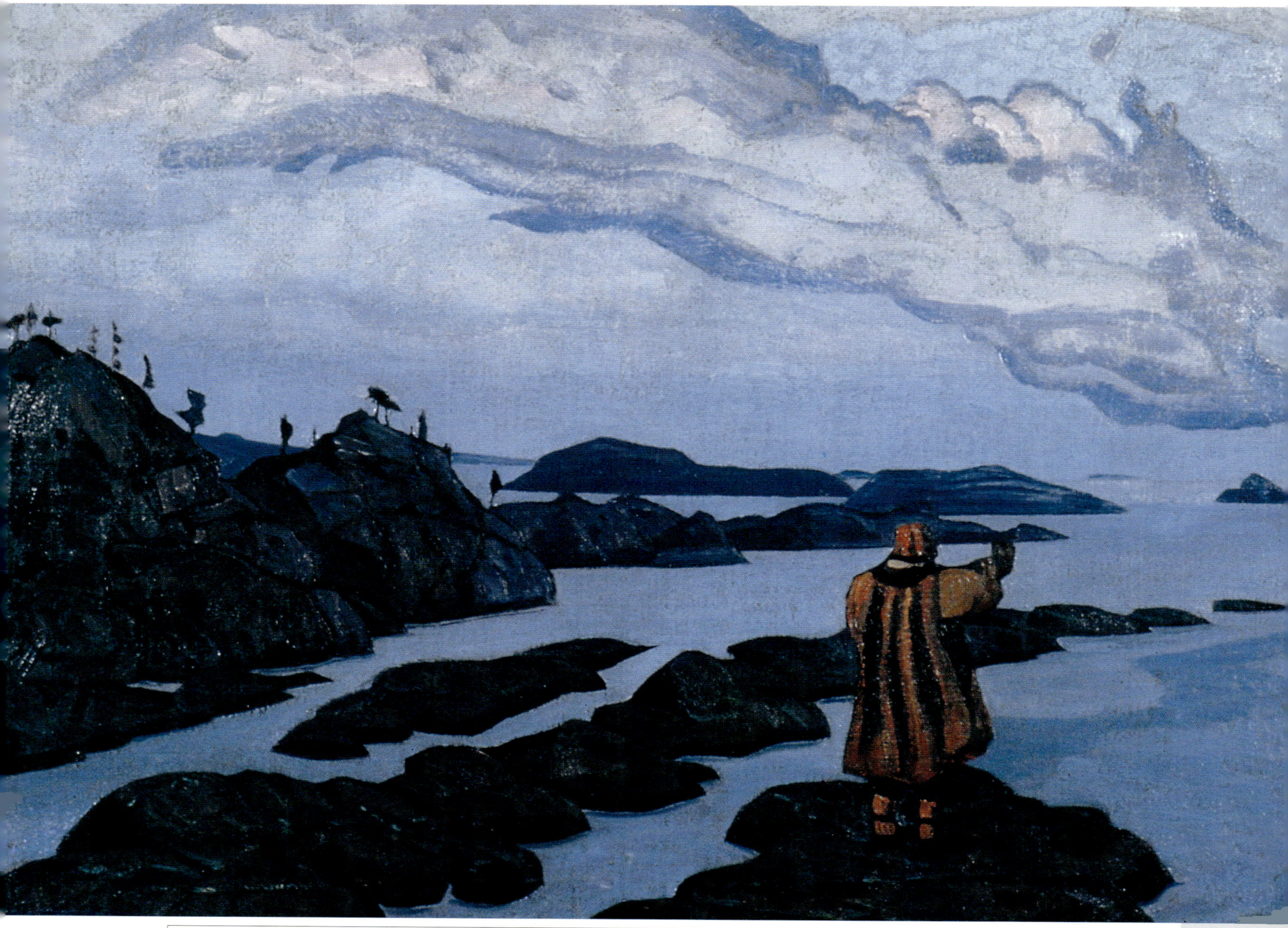

The Command, 1917

Tempera on canvas, 76.2 x 49.5 cm.
Nicholas Roerich Museum, New York

8 The Command

In *The Command* an ancient man clad in furs stands on a rock extending his arm over the water. Each of the natural features in the painting – he promontories, the long stony islands and the arrow-shaped clouds – points in the same direction, a convergence of strong diagonals toward the top right of the canvas. Is the solitary figure issuing a command to these converging elements? Or is he, together with all of them, responding to one? Above him on top of the first arrow cloud is a blue form making the same gesture of command. Characteristically, Roerich presents such enigmas for his viewers to divine and to resolve as they will.

The Command was Roerich's third canvas in the seven part Heroica series. After *The Hidden Treasure,* the first canvas, with its mysterious figure suspending a vessel over the lake, came *Brew of the Noyda – Sorcerer,* which depicted magic involving a cauldron. The four canvases that followed *The Command* were: *The Sacred Fire,* with an eternal flame burning among the stones; *They Are Waiting*, with several figures poised in expectation by a ritualistic hut; *The End of the Giants,* with demons transformed into rocks; and *The Conquerors of the Treasure,* with a group transporting something to a boat. (27)

Fire and water, magic and transformation, a human victory in a superhuman struggle – such is the stuff of the world's great mythologies, and the specific imagery is evocative of the *Finnish Kalevala.* During the campaign for national independence, Akseli Gallen-Kallela and other artists used these images to stimulate pride in the natural beauty of Finland and its imaginative culture. The Heroica series may echo this patriotic interpretation of the epic, and in *The Command* Roerich may be reflecting on the various calls to action, spiritual as well as political, which confronted every person of conscience in Russia and Finland at this time.

A collector named D S Mollo apparently bought all the Heroica paintings during Roerich's residency in Finland. But by 1940, when the artist wrote his essay entitled *Wanderers*, he no longer knew where the paintings were located. (28) In 1976 the Nicholas Roerich Museum acquired *The Command* from Jacques Garvin, and the next year acquired *The Hidden Treasure* from Alexander Garvin.

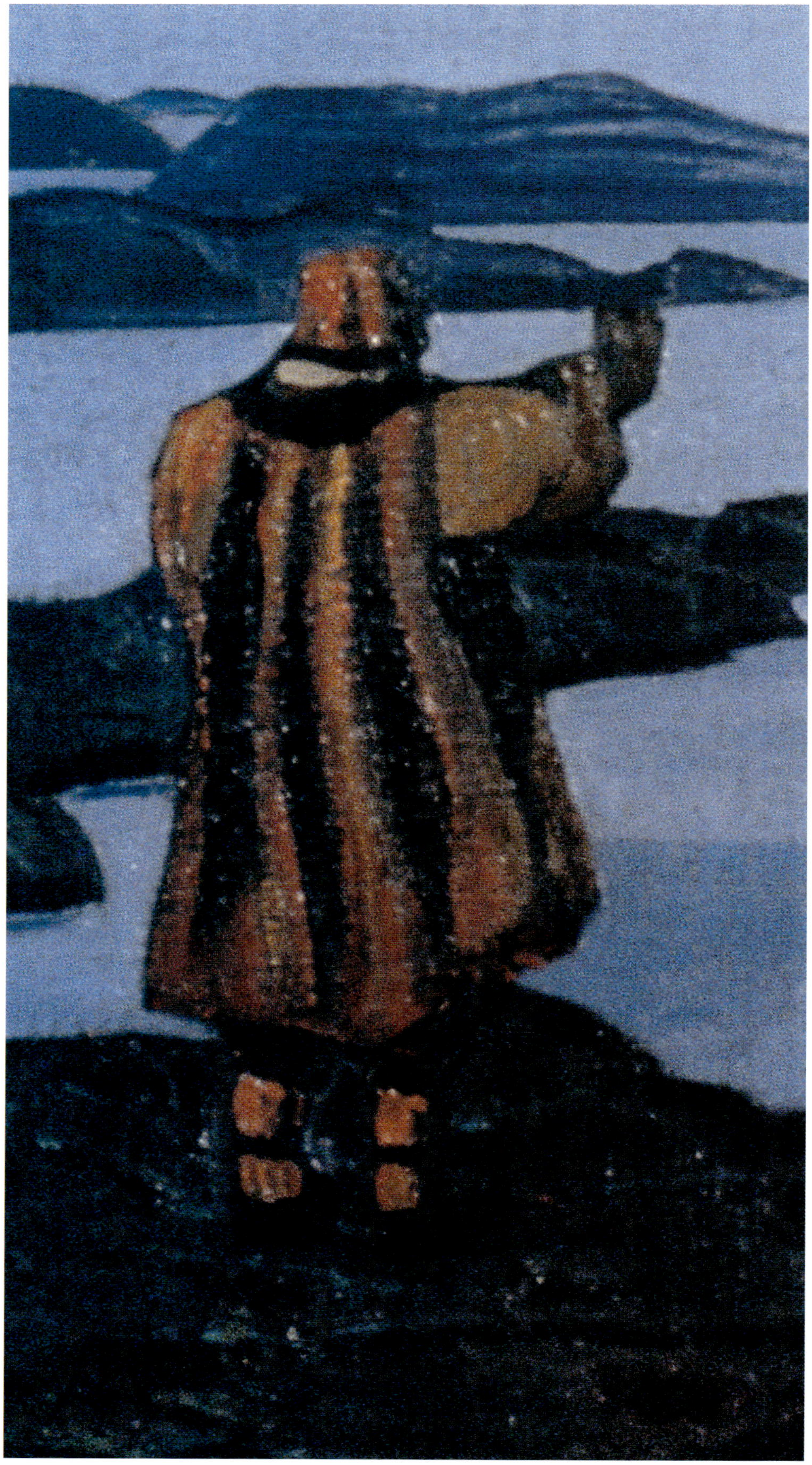

The Command, detail

'Each of the natural features in the painting points in the same direction, a convergence of strong diagonals towards the top right of the canvas.'

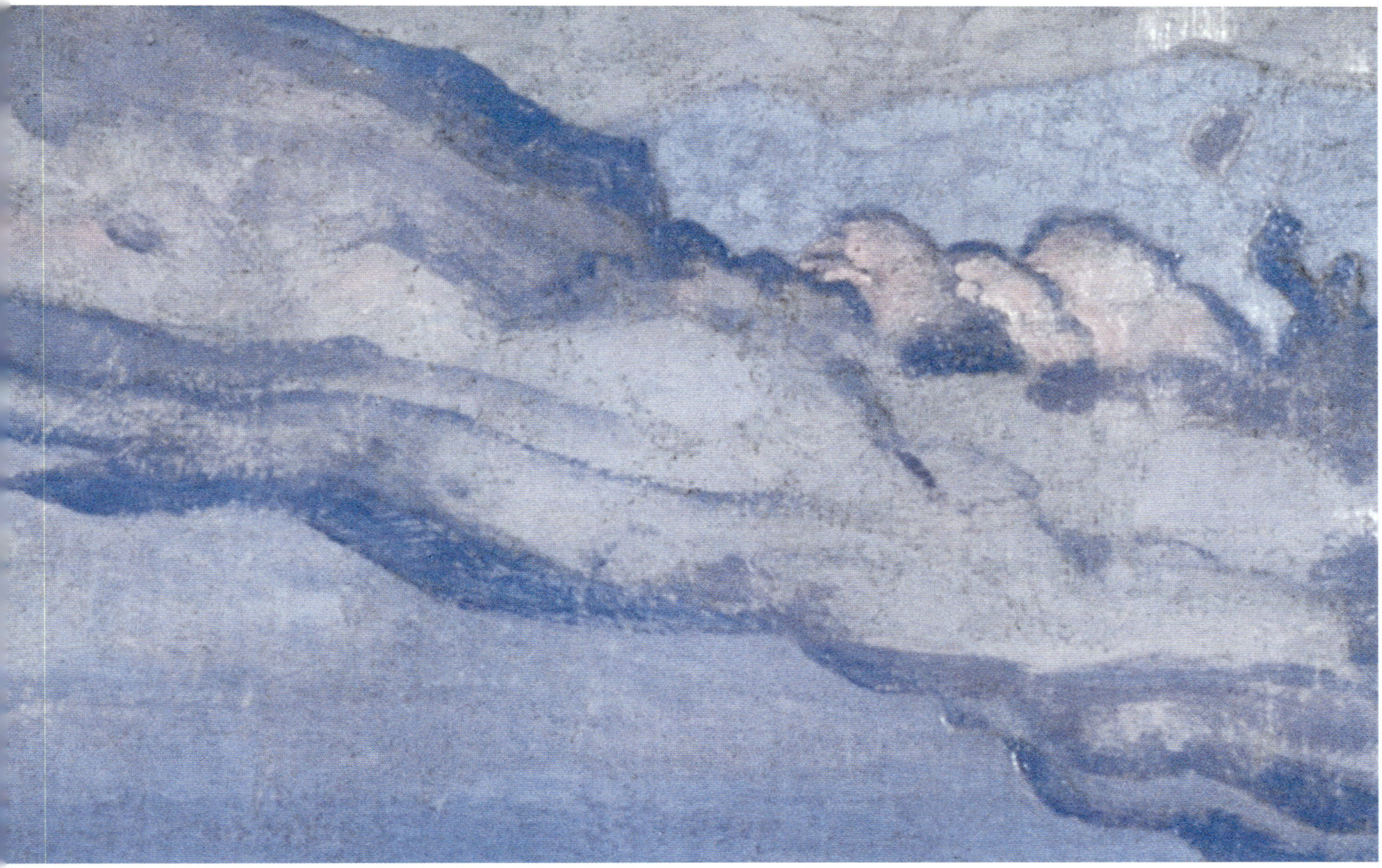

The Command, detail

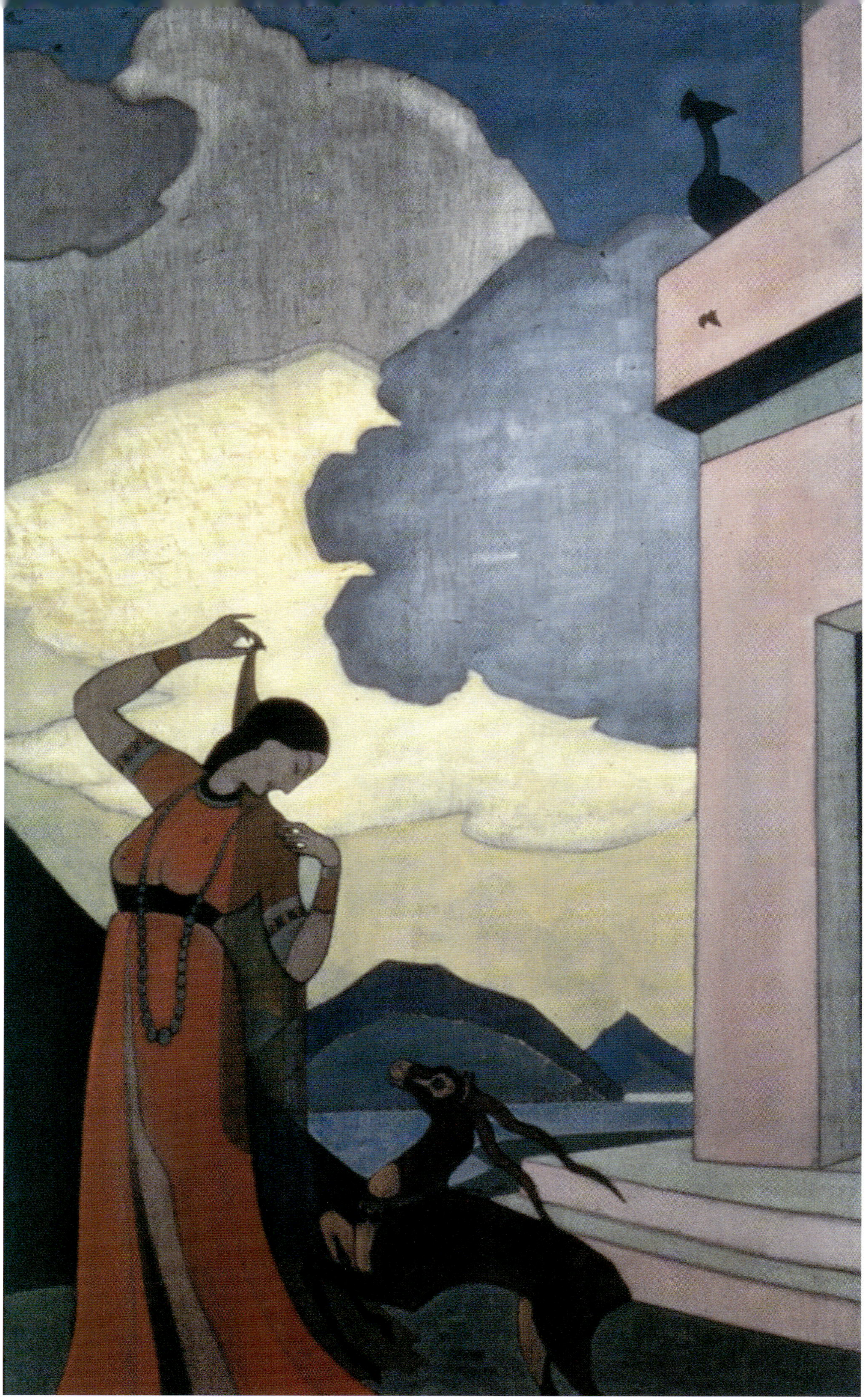

9

Song of the Morning

In 1919 Roerich left Finland with his family and travelled through Scandinavia en route to London, where he designed several Russian productions for Sir Thomas Beecham at the Royal Opera. While in England the artist was commissioned to paint a series of decorative panels for a country house planned by M L Skidelsky. Roerich conceived a suite of vertical canvases entitled, *Dreams of Wisdom.* [29] As the house was never built, Skidelsky reduced his order, buying only four panels: *Language of the Birds, Song of the Moon, Smile to a Friend* and *Sacrifice.* [30] Two other paintings from the series – this canvas, *Song of the Morning,* and a companion piece, *Song of the Waterfall* – are exhibited together at the Nicholas Roerich Museum.

Song of the Morning shows a young woman lifting her scarf as she dances with a gazelle by a pavillion, where a peacock perches on the roof. Roerich makes this genre subject from seventeenth century Indian painting contemporary through Art Deco devices, simplifying details and brightening the traditional palette of blue, green, gold, red and mauve. In this work Roerich clearly pays homage to a special type of painting from the Dekkan period, which preserved Hindu culture despite Muslim domination. *Song of the Morning* refers precisely to the genre of musical paintings that illustrated poems meant to be accompanied by Indian raga and ragini. Two famous examples of the genre were housed at the Victoria and Albert Museum, which Roerich visited during his residency in London. One of them, the Todi Ragini, depicts a girl with gazelles and the other, the Kedara Ragini, includes a peacock on a pavillion roof. [31] The dance element Roerich introduces through the gesture with the scarf is reminiscent of the Nymph's two-dimensional movement he knew so well from Vaslav Nijinsky's *L'Après-Midi d'un Faune for the Ballets Russes* in 1912.[32]

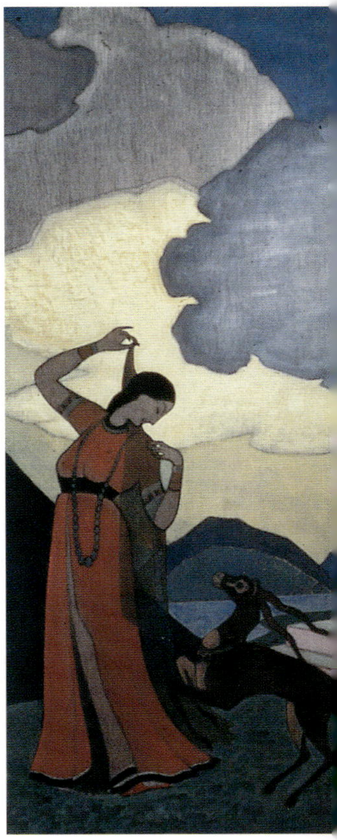

When Roerich went to New York in 1920, he took *Song of the Morning* and *Song of the Waterfall.* Later, Sina Fosdick recalled his telling her how he had shown them to a celebrated visitor at his Kensington studio near the Victoria and Albert:

Rabindranath Tagore, the Bengali poet, who saw the two panels just after they were completed, said that they were masterpieces which captured the spirit of India and that Professor Roerich should never part with them. [33]

Song of the Morning, 1920

Tempera on canvas, 122 x 233.7 cm.
Nicholas Roerich Museum, New York

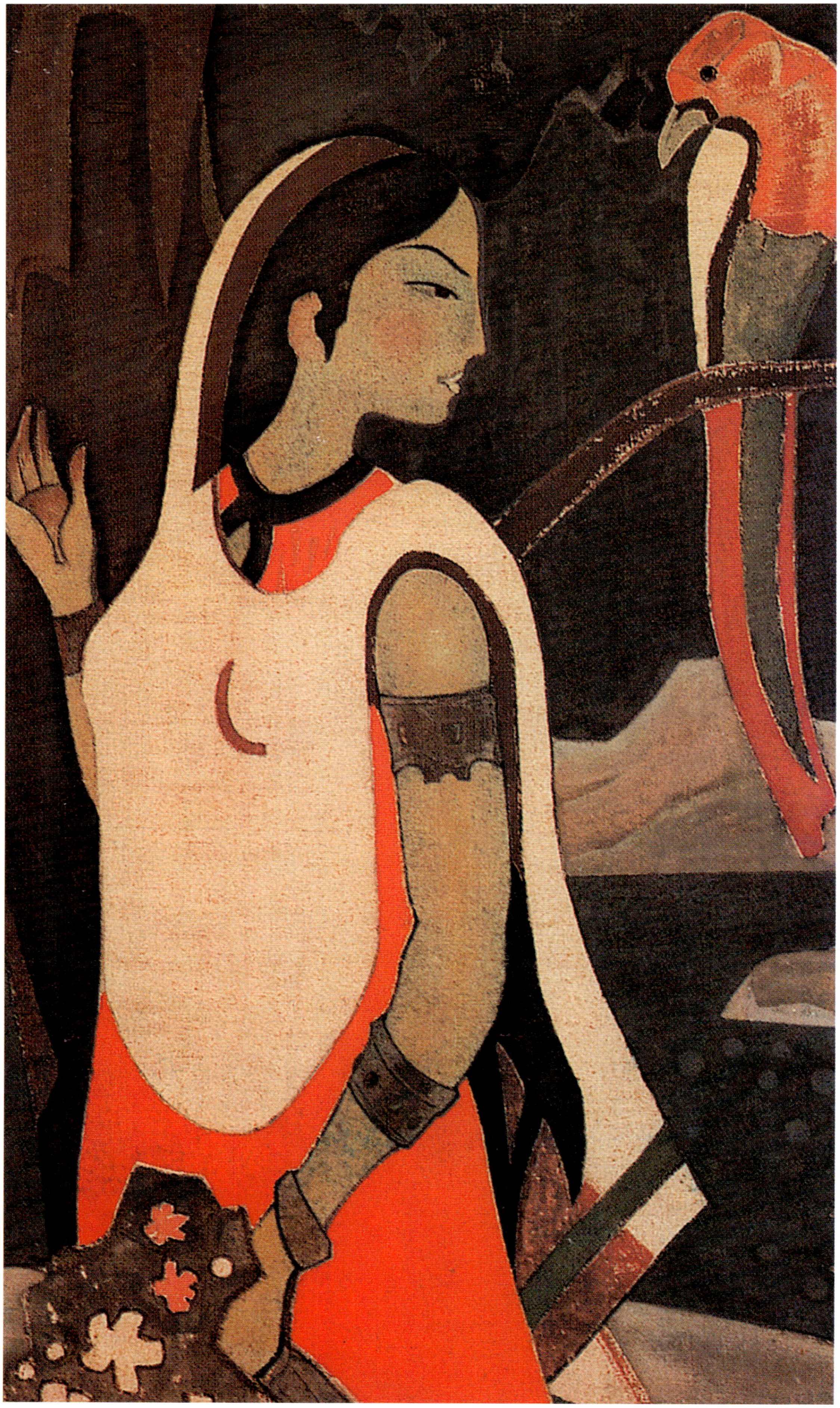

Language of the Birds, 1920

Nicholas Roerich Museum, New York

Roerich makes this genre subject contemporary, simplifying details and brightening the traditional palette of blue, green, gold, red and mauve.

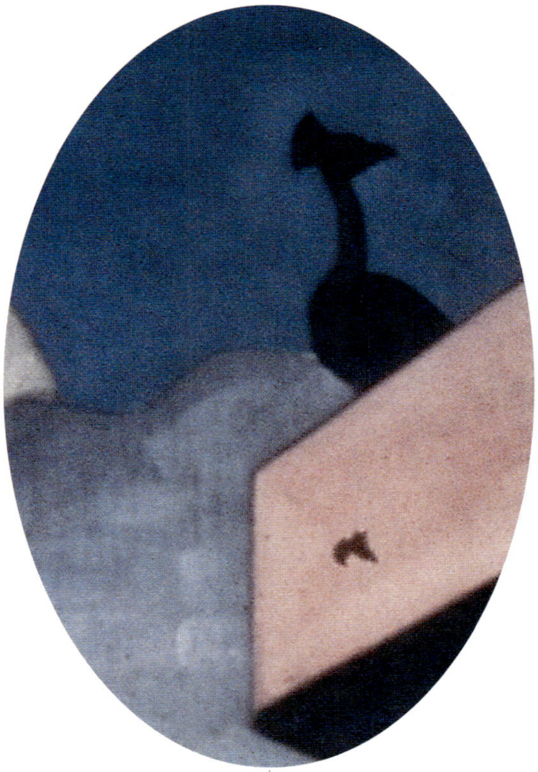

Song of the Morning, detail

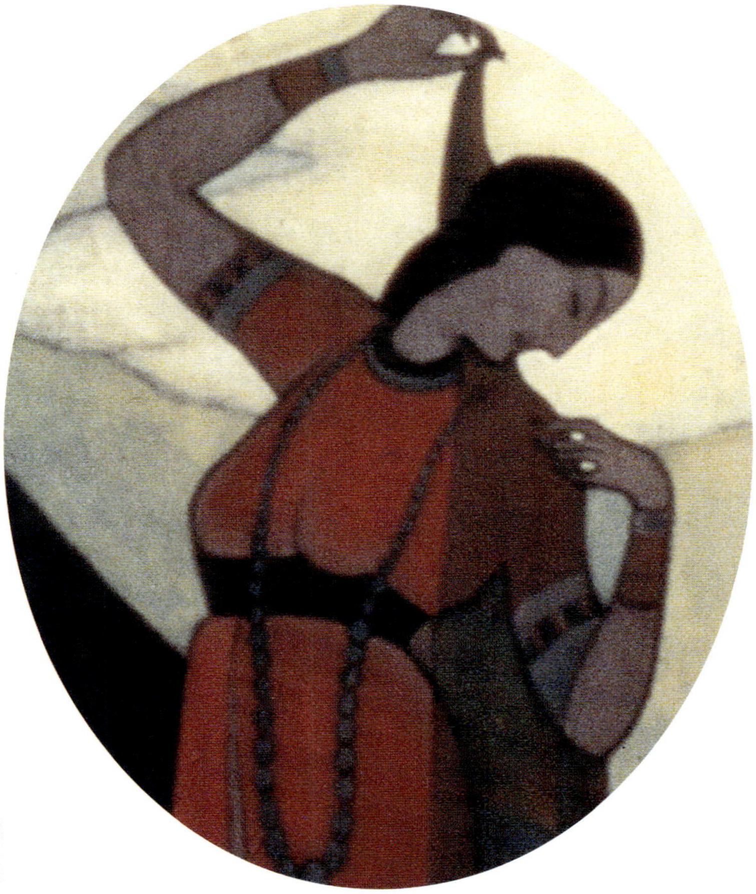

Song of the Morning, detail

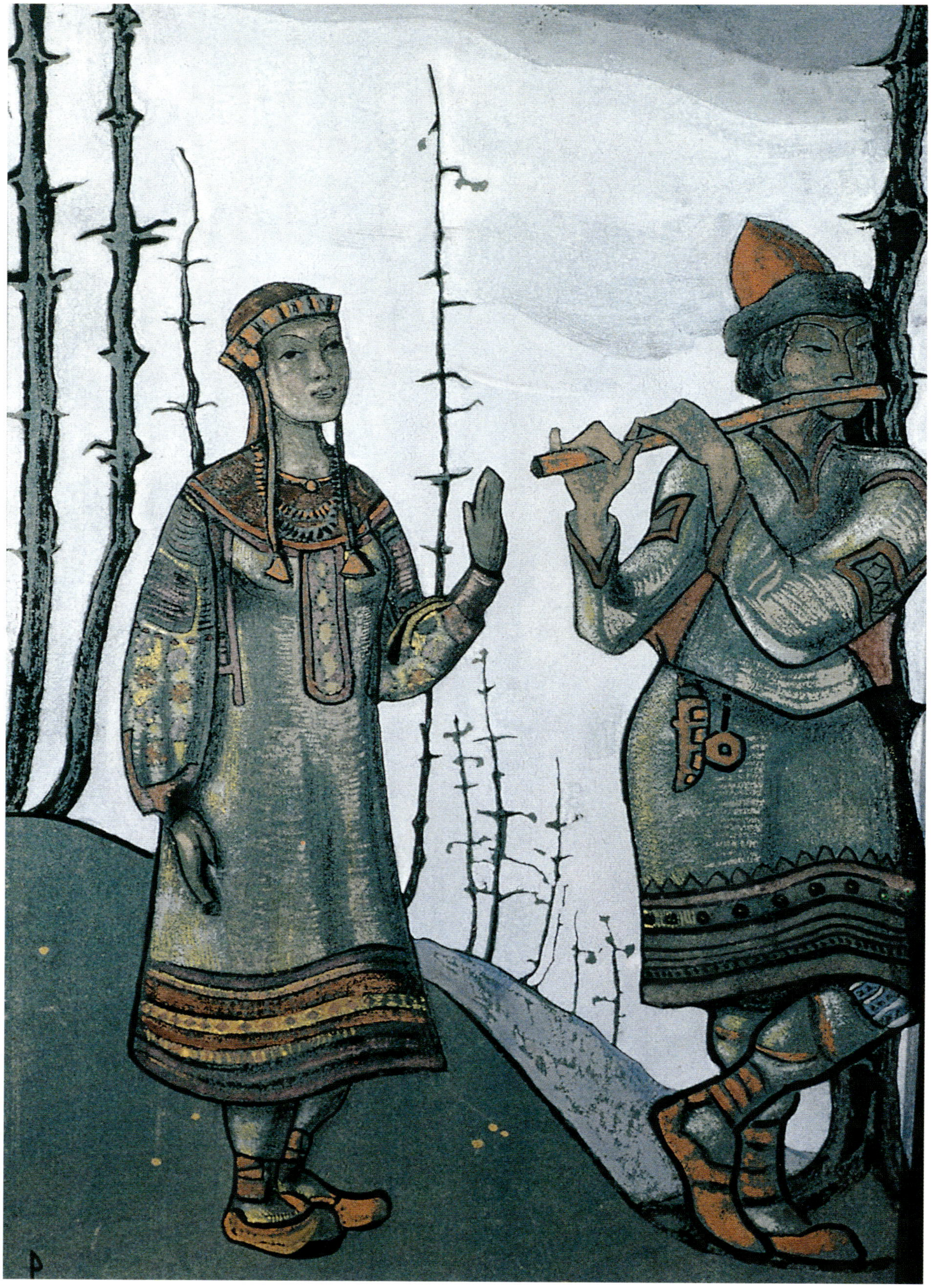

Lel and Schnegurochka - costume sketch, 1921

Tempera on cardboard, 30.5 x 40.5 cm.
Nicholas Roerich Museum, New York

10

Costume sketch

Lel and Schnegurochka

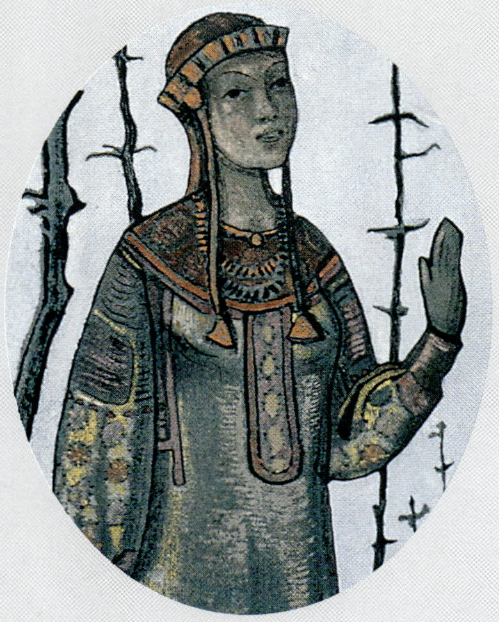

Among the attractions for Roerich in America was Mary Garden, director of the Chicago Opera, with whom he had worked when she sang for Diaghilev in Paris. In addition to Russian works, she hoped for Roerich to design Wagnerian opera, a cherished ambition of the artist. However, after submitting preliminary designs for *Tristan and Isolde* in 1921, he learned the Opera had insufficient funds to stage it.

But the Chicago production realized in 1922, Rimsky-Korsakov's *Snegurochka,* won critical acclaim for its colourful Roerich designs. His costumes presented Slavic folk decoration in a new key, stylizing the horizontal construction of patterns he had used for *Le Sacre du Printemps* in 1913 and muting the palette of primaries to pastels. The sketch captures the predicament of the *Snow Maiden,* Snegurochka, who is the daughter of King Winter and Fairy Spring, but who yearns to be a mortal so that she may love the shepherd Lel. A Russian Orpheus, Lel beguiles her with his flute but abandons her to another lover. Yet, just as she is warmed by the experience of human love, the sun shines on her, and she is melted into the torrents of spring.

Snegurochka commissions until the Chicago staging, had proved unlucky for Roerich. His first designs had been for the Opéra Comique in Paris in 1908, but his exact role is uncertain because the offically credited designer was French. The second time he treated the subject was for the original play by Alexander Ostrovsky on which Rimsky had based his opera. Produced by the Reineke Drama Theatre of St Petersburg in 1912, the work foundered. Roerich's sketches had been badly executed by the workshops, causing him to publicly dissociate himself from the production. His third effort was for Covent Garden during 1919 and 1920, but the sketches were never used, like his designs for most of the other works commissioned by Sir Thomas Beecham, whose bankruptcy forced the cancellation of many projects.

This personal history made the success of the Chicago Snegurochka especially sweet, and all the more so as Roerich had declined to do it for the Metropolitan Opera in New York in favour of Mary Garden's invitation. The artist had at last achieved his wish to emulate Viktor Vasnetsov, whose designs for Snegurochka in 1883 served the young Roerich as a touchstone for putting Slavic culture onstage. (34)

His costumes presented slavic folk decoration in a nev

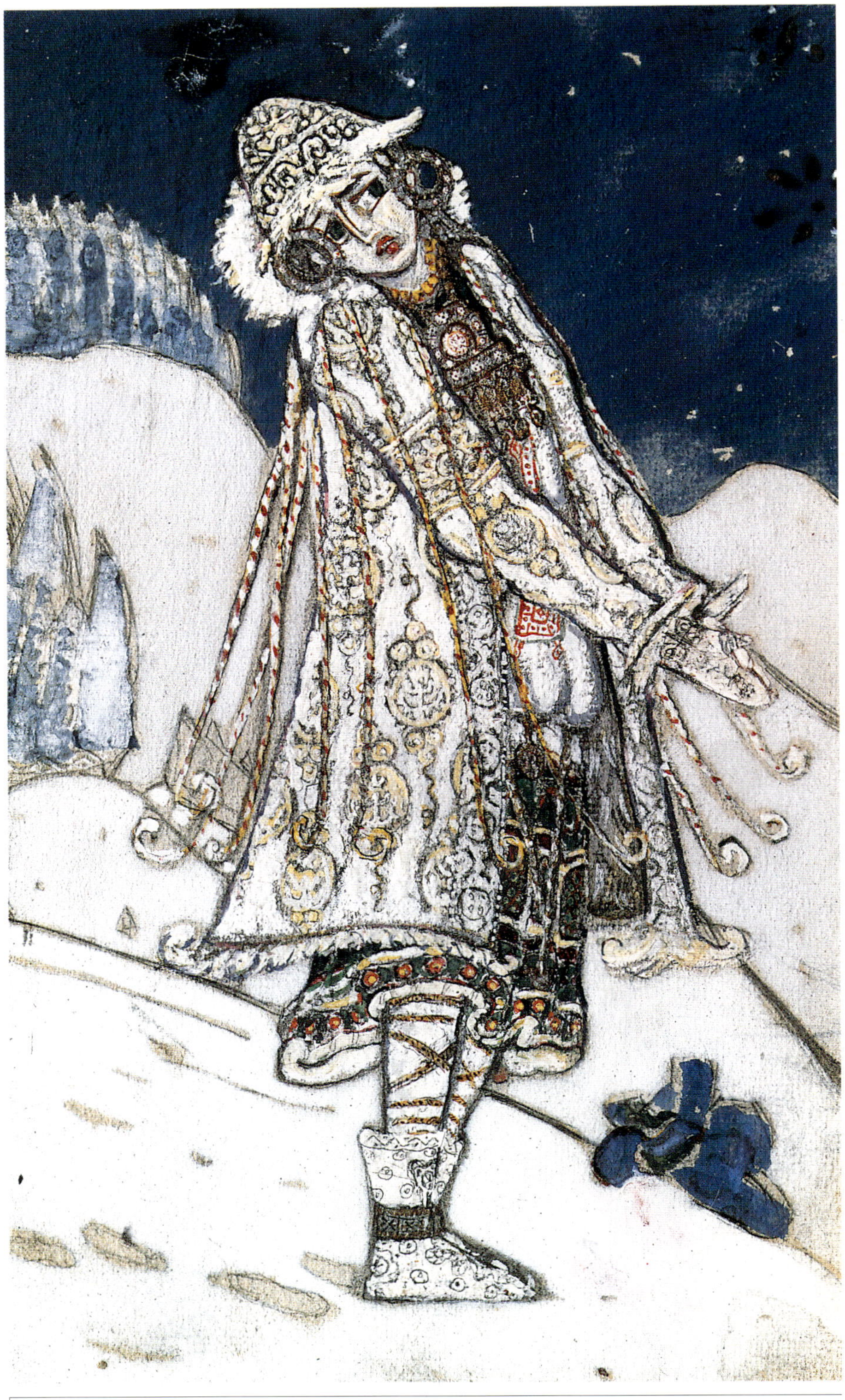

Snegurochka (the Snow Maiden)

Costume sketch for Ostrowsky's play, 1912
Russian Museum, Saint Petersburg

key, muting the palette of primaries to pastels.'

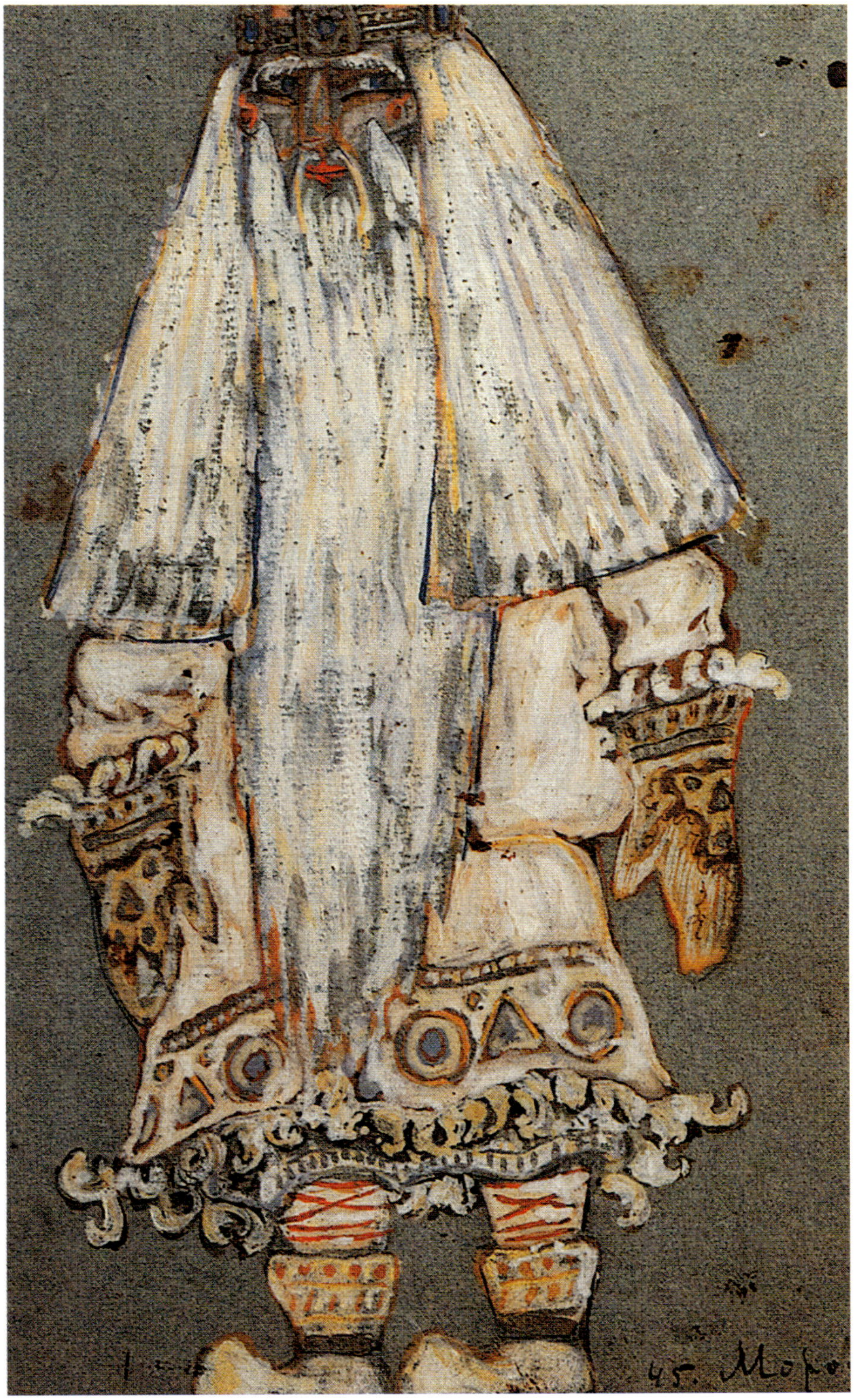

'Ded Moroz' (the Ice Man)

Costume sketch for Ostrowsky's play, 1912
Russian Museum, Saint Petersburg

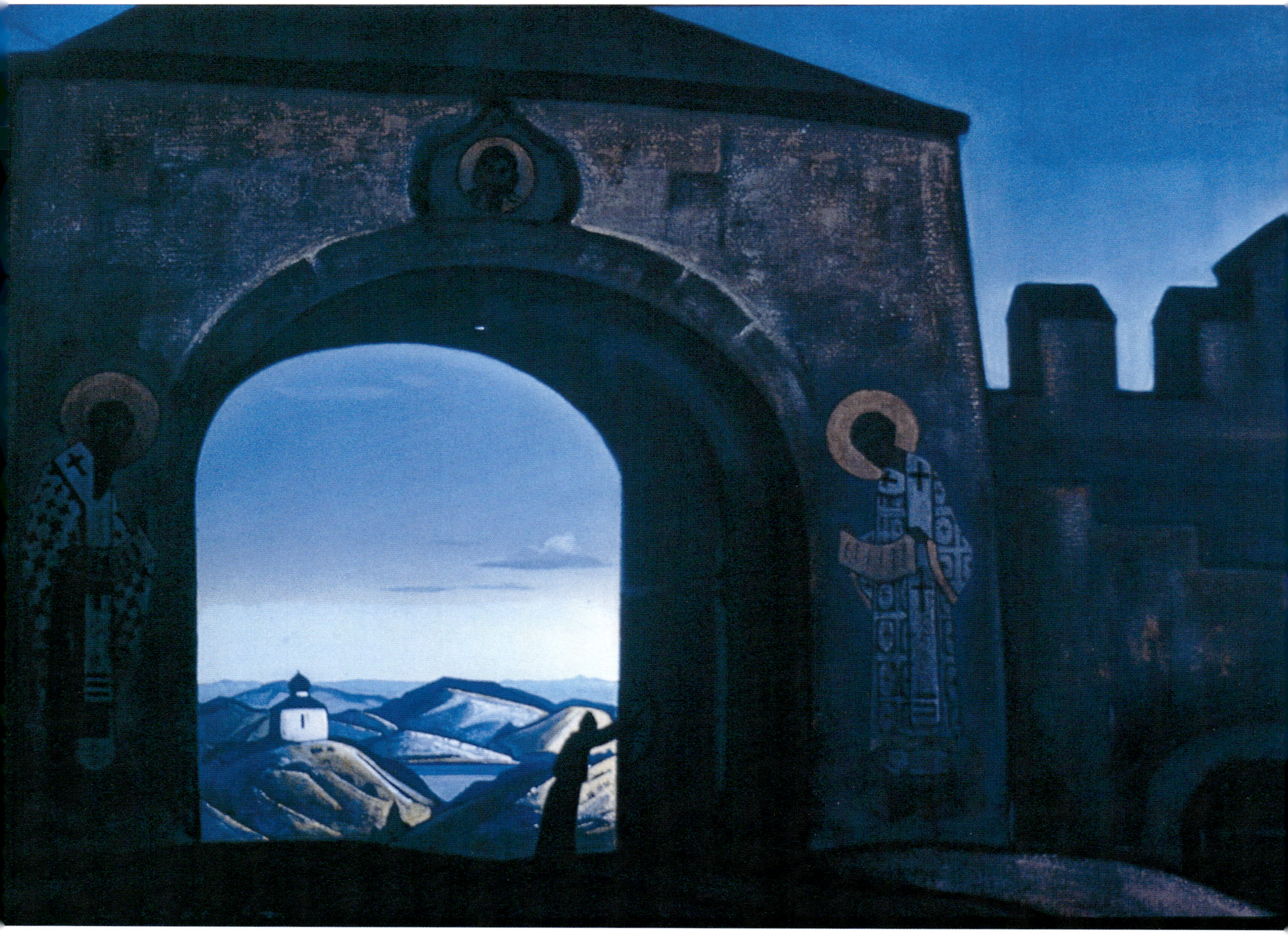

And we open the gates, 1922

Oil on canvas, 53.3 x 33 cm.
Nicholas Roerich Museum, New York

11 *And we open the gates*

In this painting a monk has just opened the gates of a great archway which almost fills the canvas. He is subsumed by the gates which are the same black and indigo as his robes. Beyond the arch is a stark whitewashed church with a cupola in the matt gold of the earth it stands upon. A small lake, which reflects the morning sky, is bordered by hills roughly indicated in cobalt and chalky blue. The scene is resolutely simple, focusing attention on the gates and the fact that they are open. Unlike the arch in Roerich's *Old Monastery* of 1903, which framed the subject, this arch and its gates comprise the subject.

And We Open the Gates is a sketch in oil for a larger tempera work which, despite similar composition, was much more detailed. (35) The arch of the larger canvas was richly coloured in violets and mauves and decorated with huge fresco figures of Orthodox saints. The scene inside its monastery walls was complete in itself but, through the arch, the bright landscape beckoned, promising new experience.

Perhaps the sketch was just an indication of the structure and basic colours for the final work. And yet it has its own power, communicating unequivocally the sense of a spiritual threshold. The sketch is an early example of Roerich's 'broken stroke,' the name Svetoslav Roerich used for his father's technique of dry brush on canvas to suggest texture and depth, encouraging the viewer to visualize and participate. (36)

And We Open the Gates, together with its sketch, began the six part work of 1922 which Roerich called the Sancta series, each canvas featuring hermitic Russian monks engaged in the ascetic discipline of inner development. The other paintings are entitled: *And We Labour, And We Do Not Fear, And We Continue Fishing, And We Are Bringing the Light, And We See.* (37)

For years Roerich and his wife Helena, like many of the literati of their generation, had been interested in the hermitic tradition within Russian Christianity and also in eastern religion and philosophy. Roerich's poetry on these subjects progressed during his initial émigré years but came to a halt in 1921, shortly after Helena Roerich began the first in a prolific series of spiritual texts. (38) However, his painting in this vein seems to have flourished in conjunction with her writing.

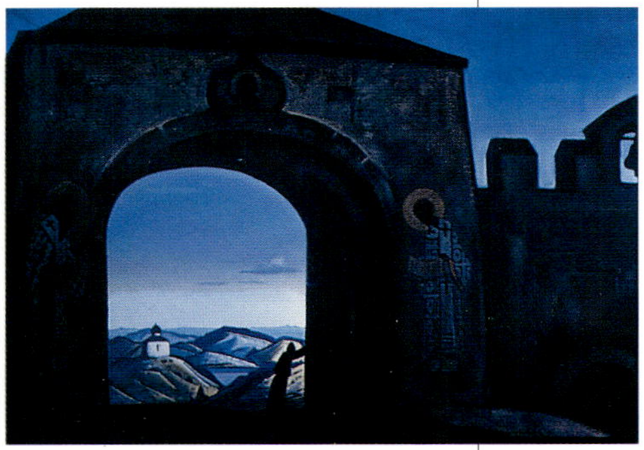

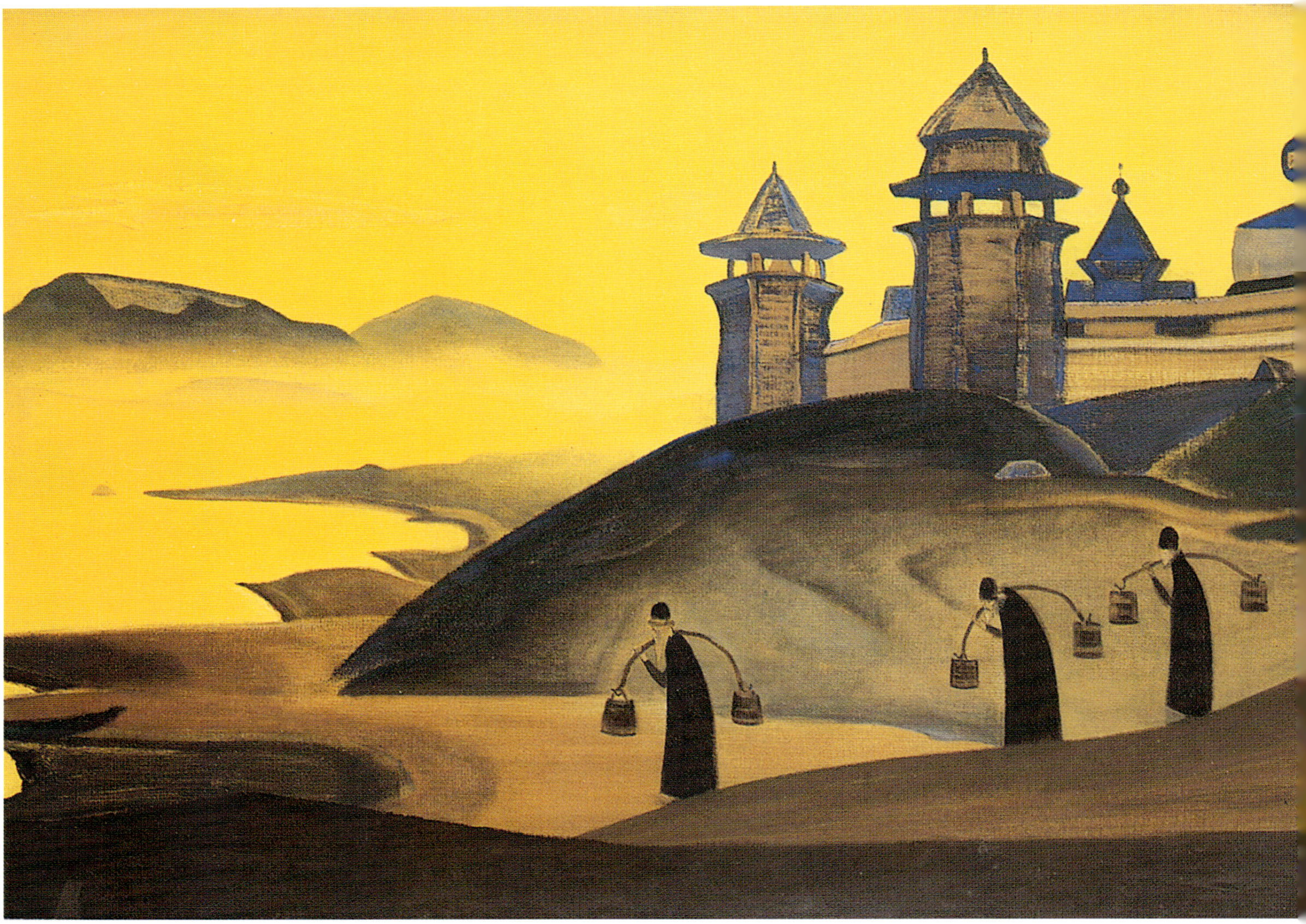

And we are trying, 1922

Tempera on canvas, 71 x 101.6 cm.
Nicholas Roerich Museum, New York

For years Roerich had been interested in the hermetic traditions within Russian Christianity and also in eastern religion and philosophy.

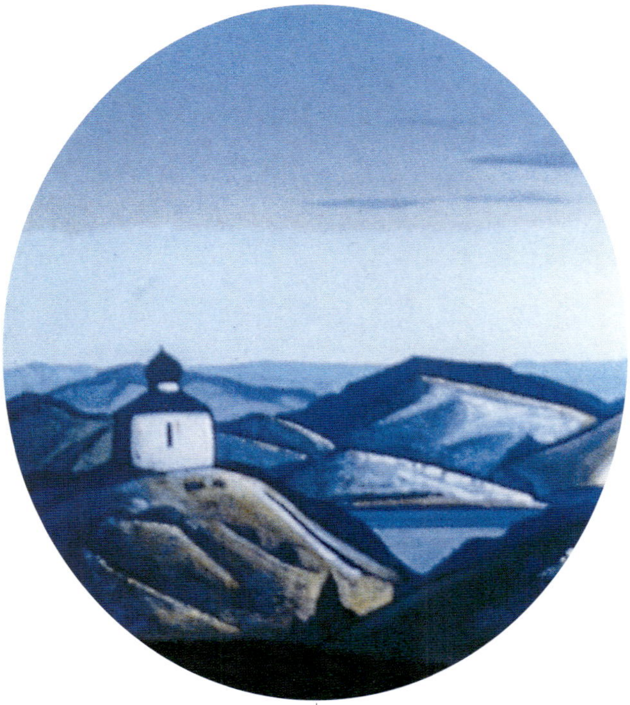

And we open the gates, detail

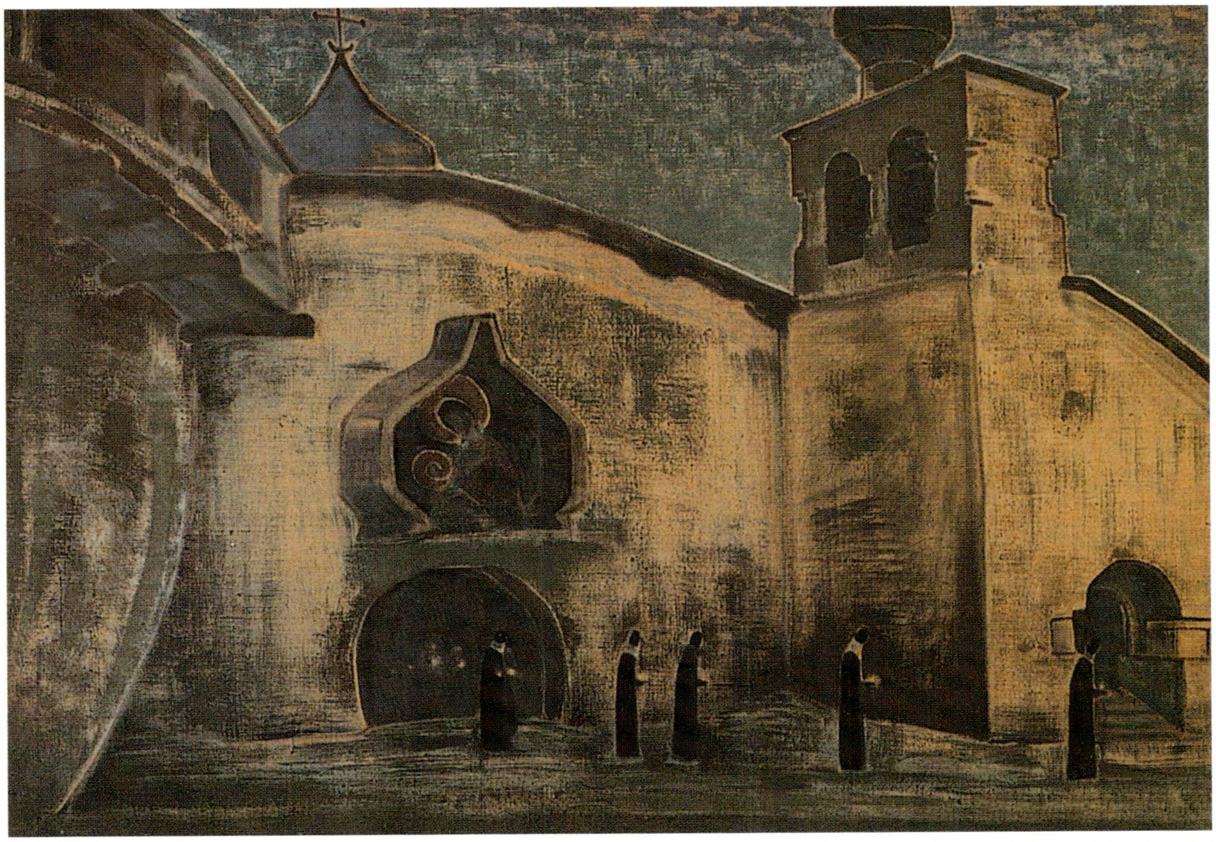

And we bring the light, 1922

Tempera on canvas, 71 x 101.6 cm.
Nicholas Roerich Museum, New York

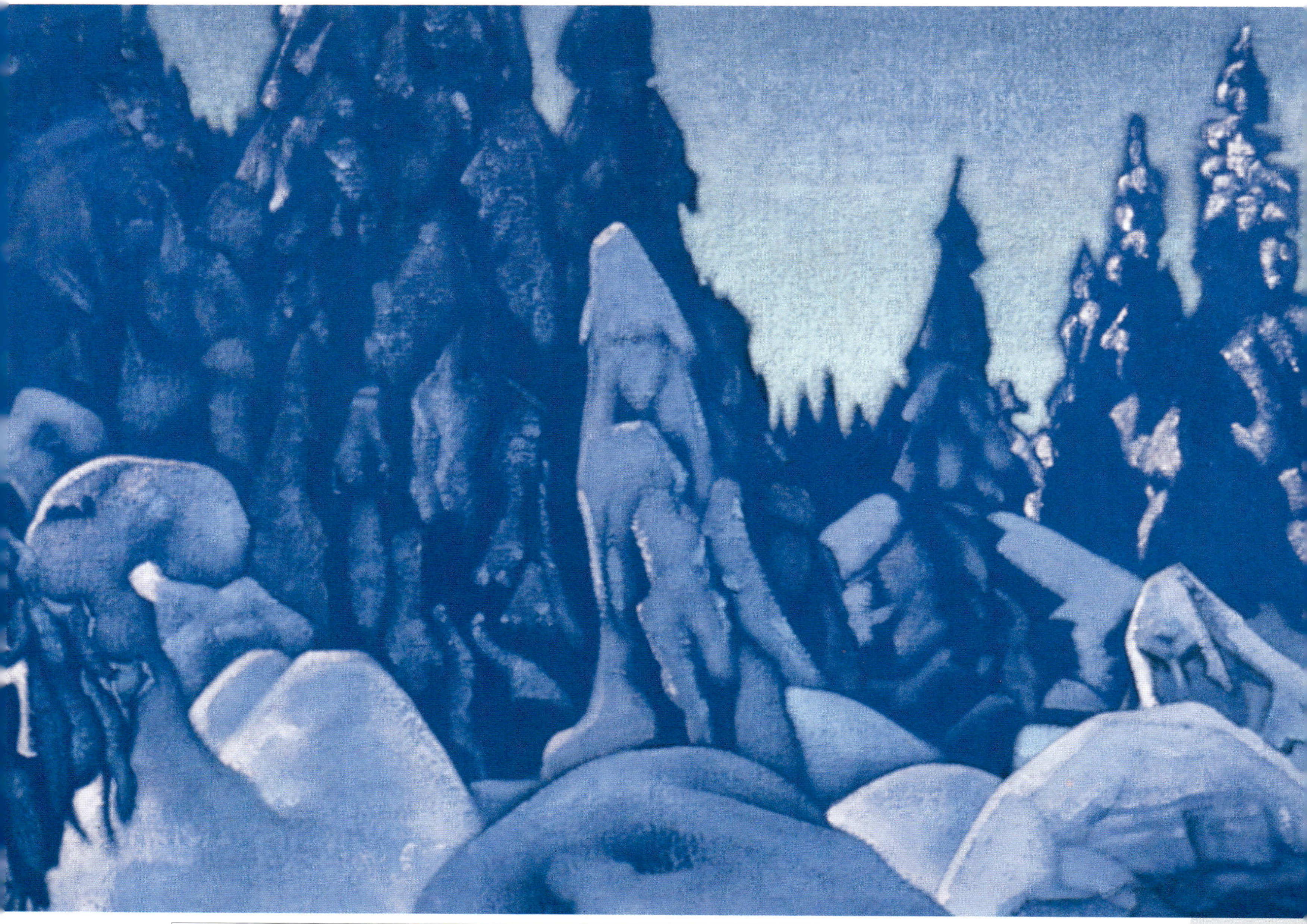

The Snow Guardians, 1922

Tempera on canvas, 75.5 x 49.5 cm.
Nicholas Roerich Museum, New York

12 The Snow Guardians

In 1920 when Roerich and his family arrived in New York on the SS Zealand, he met Frances Grant, a writer for Musical America, which, since World War I, had profiled cultural émigrés from Europe. She became a key collaborator of the artist and remembered the story of how an art critic had brought him to the United States:

Christian Brinton had been writing a great deal on Russian art. He knew about Roerich's paintings. The Chicago Art Institute knew about them and invited him through Brinton. That's how he came here. (39)

Brinton had already curated shows for Roerich's colleague from the *Ballets Russes,* Boris Anisfeld, and now he set up an exhibition of 174 Roerich paintings which toured 29 cities throughout the nation from 1920 to 1922. (40)

During the tour the artist often lectured in the exhibition cities. Despite these commitments and tasks connected with his cultural institutions, he kept up a regime of painting at his Manhattan studio. *Snow Guardians,* which Roerich did in New York toward the end of the tour, presents fir trees, bushes and boulders cloaked in snow. The painting captures the cold tranquility of winter in the northeastern United States and may even be an image of Riverside Drive or Central Park, pristine after a blizzard. But such scenery must surely have transported Roerich back to Russia and to the snowscapes of his teacher Kuindzhi – notably, *Sunlight on Hoarfrost* (1876-90), *Moonlight in the Forest* (1898-1908) and *Sunset Effects* (1885-90). (41)

Although Kuindzhi had worked as a photographic retoucher, Realism was not his goal. His painting sought to portray nature imaginatively yet render light exactly. Roerich emulated his teacher but focused on the power of suggestion and a relationship not only with his subject but also with his viewer. Perception of Roerich's work changes as multiple levels of imagery become apparent. *Snow Guardians* affirms the wonder of a scene transformed by snow. The artist taps the human reflex of seeing fantasy figures in quite familiar forms. But his gift is to prolong this play of images in the mind's eye by hinting at more. The boulder on the right may be a hooded elder crouched in a circle of peers. At the centre a woman in a pointed hat lifts her arm in a frozen moment affirming *Le Sacre du Printemps.* (42)

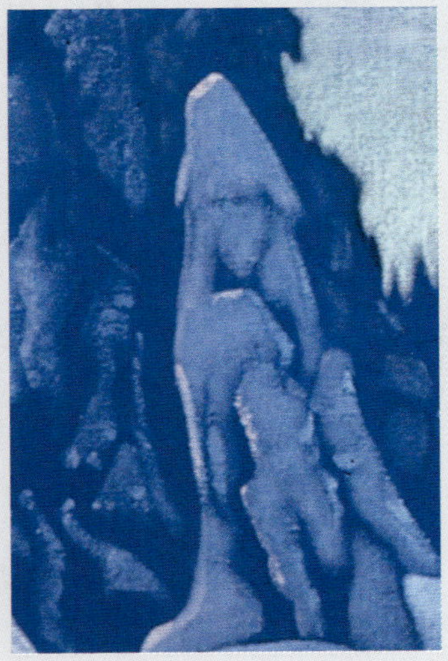

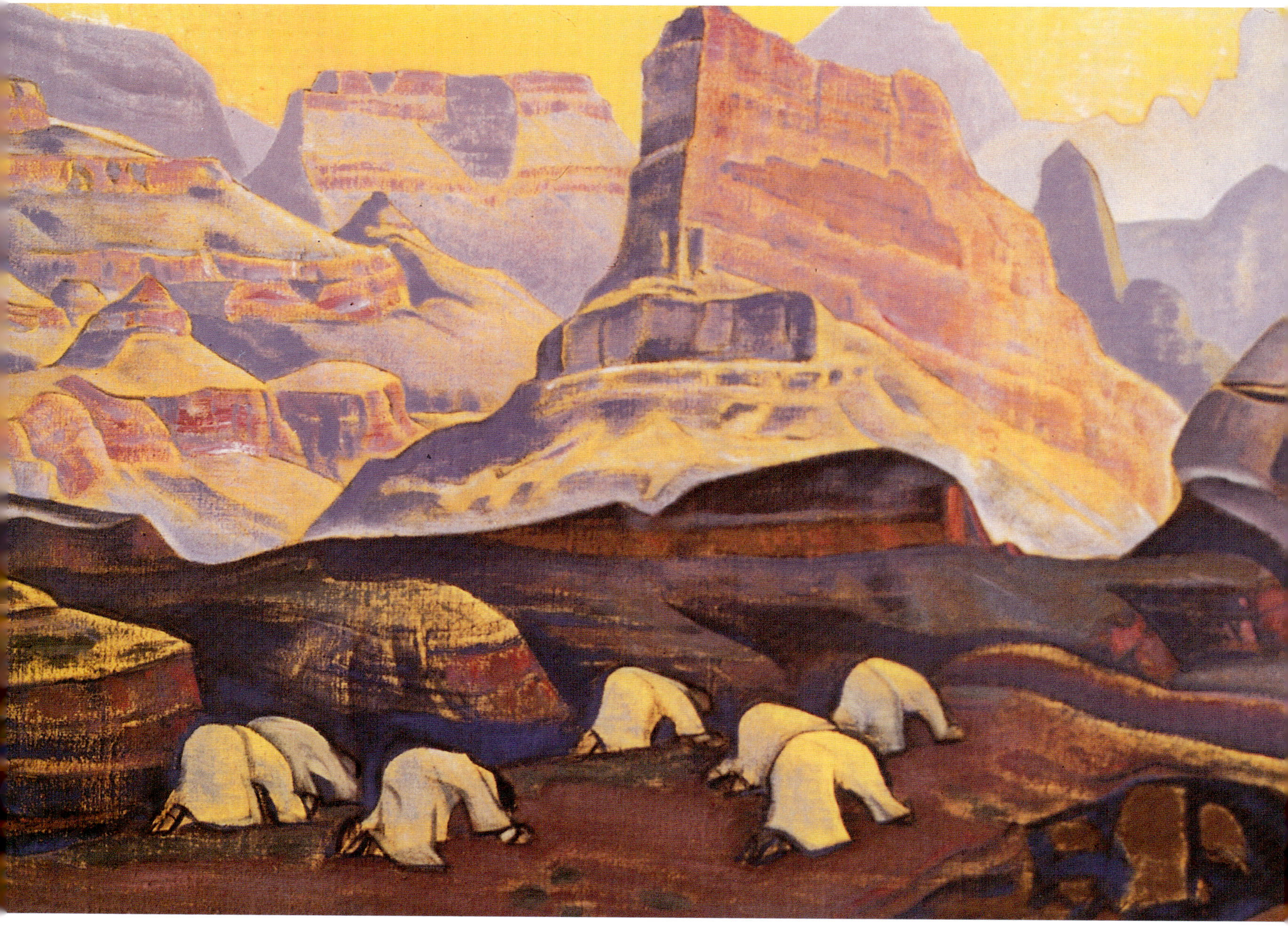

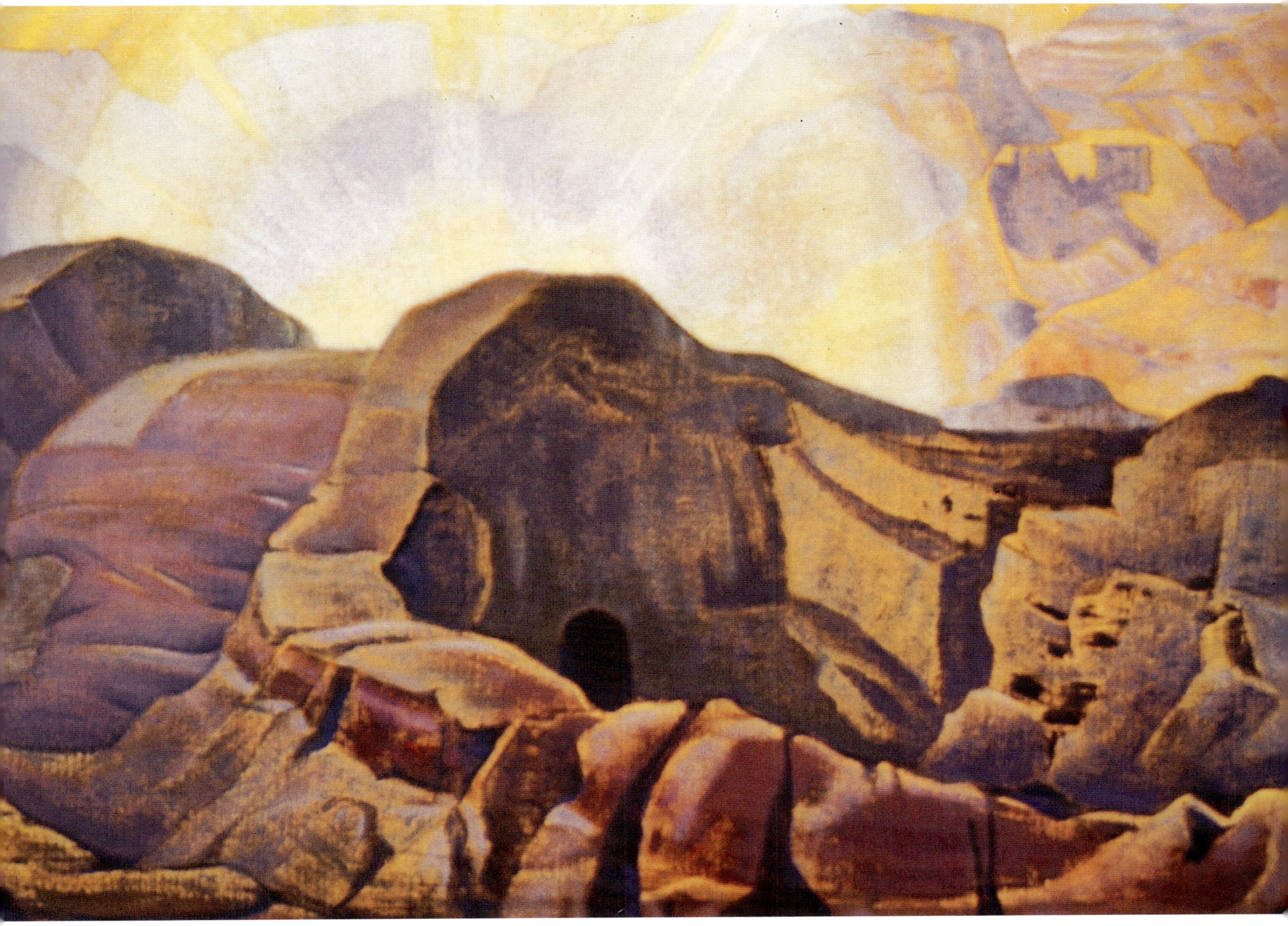

The Miracle, 1923

Tempera on canvas, 73.6 x 210 cm.
Museum of Oriental Art, Moscow

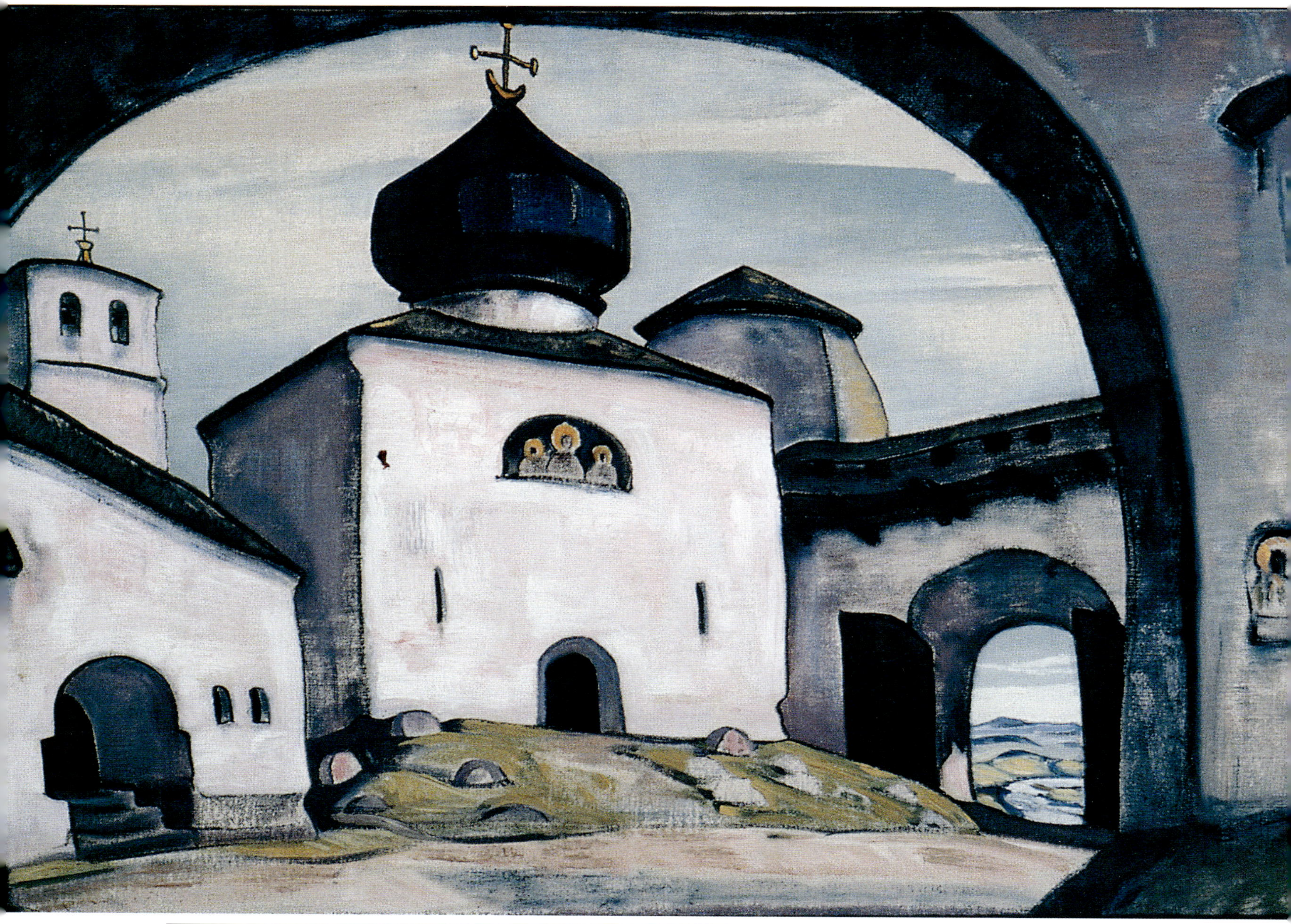

Old Pskov, 1922

Oil on canvas, 75 x 49.5 cm.
Nicholas Roerich Museum, New York

13 *Old Pskov*

Both Roerich and Alexander Golovin designed settings for Rimsky-Korsakov's opera, *The Maid of Pskov,* which Diaghilev renamed *Ivan the Terrible* when he first produced it outside Russia for his 1909 Paris season. (43) One of Roerich's settings, *Ivan's Entrance,* a quintessential World of Art decor, had an-arch-within-an-arch to frame Feodor Chaliapin's entry as the tyrant. The sketch for this backdrop has been lost and thus far no reproduction has been found. A review from the time, however, summarizes the production style, comparing it with contemporary French decor:

While our designers strive for realism and trompe l'oeil, the Russians insist on 'interpreting' . . . . Their skies are brushed in with sweeping broom-strokes, their clouds are made deliberately to look like heavy great dumplings, the pointed minarets of their palaces are splashed in without thought of detail or relief. These are huge sketches. (44)

Such Post Impressionist simplifications, learned, ironically, from the French painter Paul Gauguin, Roerich had evolved to preserve the shapes and textures of medieval Russia in his Architectural series of 1903-4, which included several depictions of Pskov. (45) No doubt the artist discussed *Ivan the Terrible* with the Chicago Opera and the Metropolitan, perhaps motivating *Old Pskov* and other 1922 canvases, unrealized theatrical designs which repeat motifs and techniques the Paris critic noted.

Parmenia Migel Ekstrom, curator of a 1974 show of Roerich's designs, recalled his contact with her parents during this period, when she was a child in New York: 'I remember that I saw him in our living room . . . . [My parents] gave money and worked voluntarily at the Roerich Museum.' She said he 'was like [Rabindranath] Tagore, with his white beard . . . . People flocked to him in thousands . . . like they did to Tagore.' Roerich's charisma facilitated his vision. 'He had a following [and] people were interested in his spiritual message,' she continued. 'He had many ideas, and people were very willing to give him money to implement them.' Among her recollections were Roerich's works at the Museum and 'a floor of old master paintings, which included El Greco, Titian and Rubens,' as well as the school of the arts and Roerich's conviction that 'it was necessary to see fine art in order to create it.' (46)

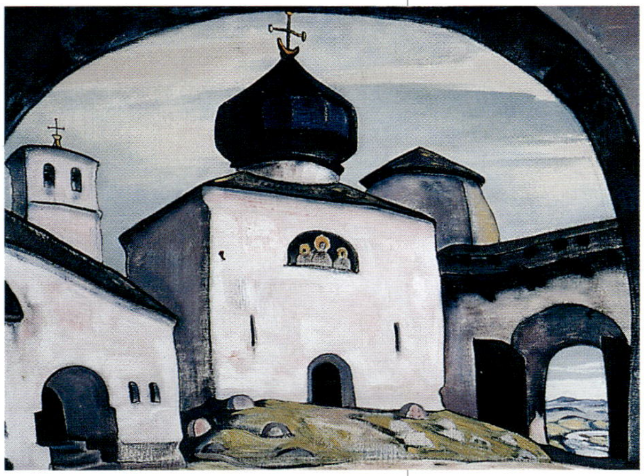

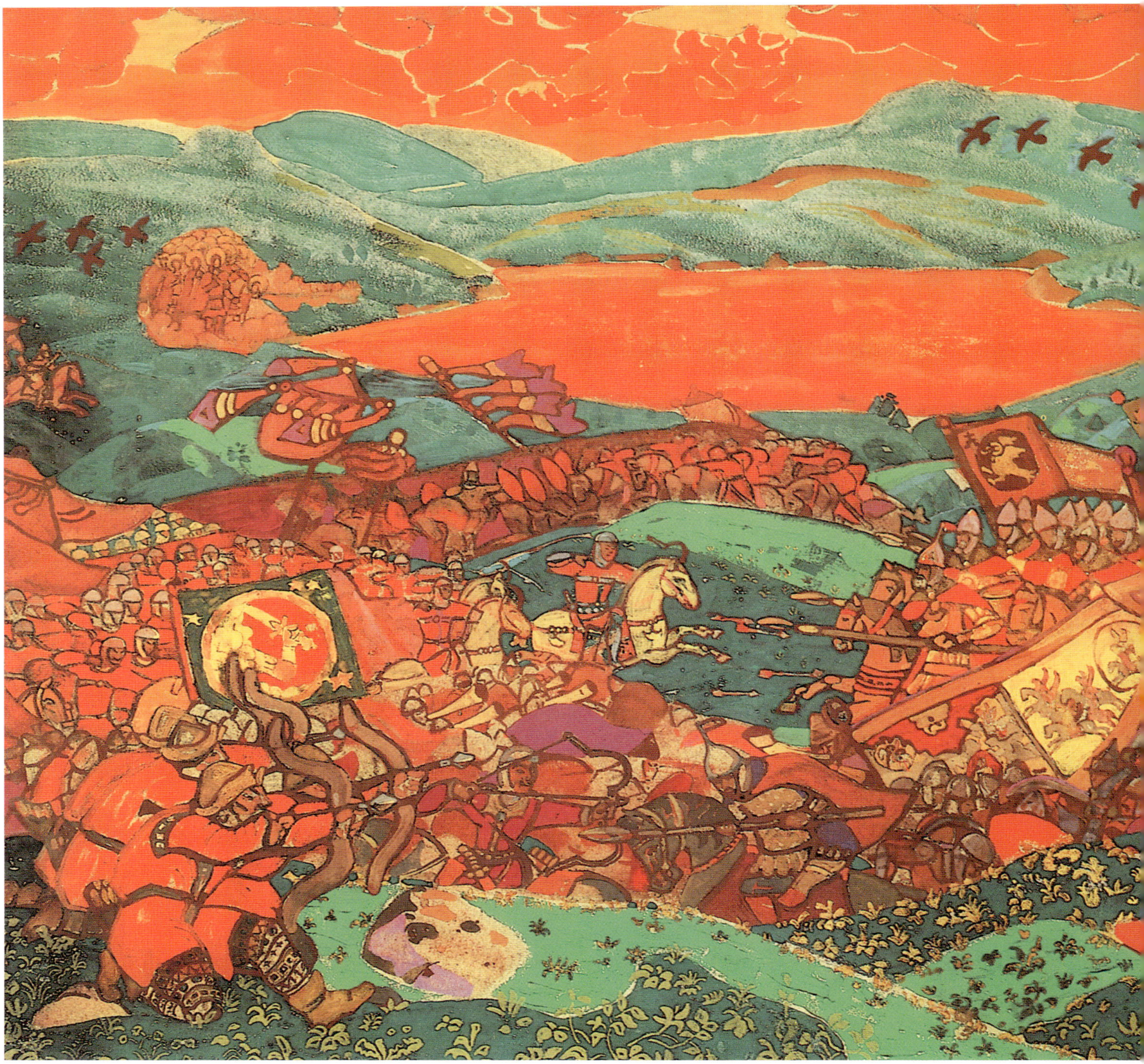

Battle of Kerzhenets, 1911

Sketch of entr'act curtain for Rimsky Korsakov's opera 'The Tale of the Invisible City Kitezh'

Tempera on canvas, 52 x 70.2 cm.
Russian Museum, Saint Petersburg

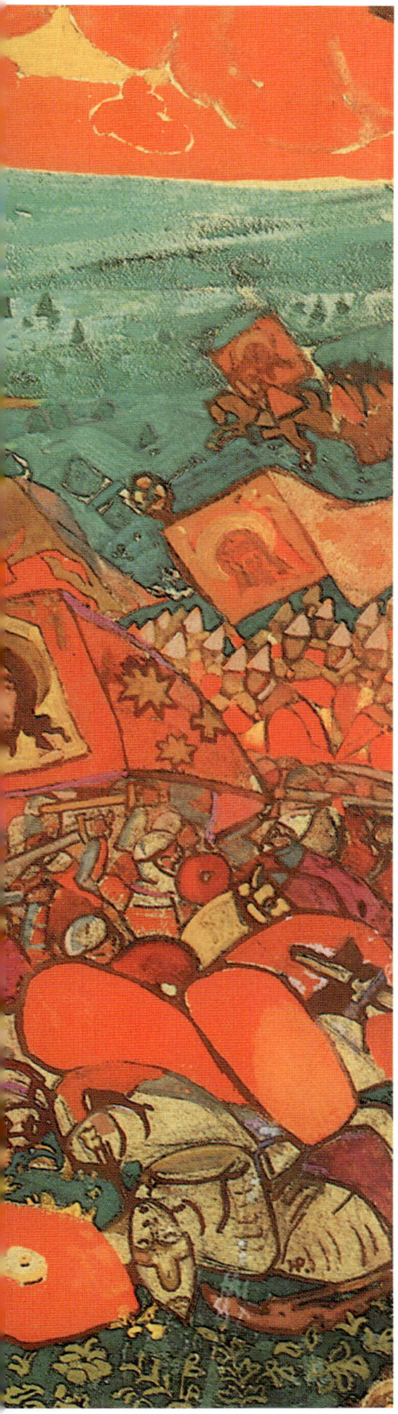

Roerich had evolved to preserve the shapes and textures of medieval Russia in his Architectural series of 1903-4.

Old Pskov, detail

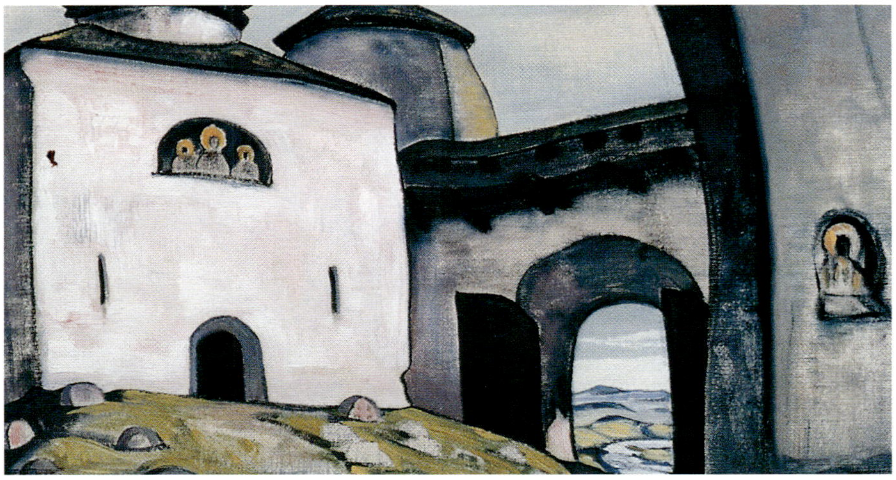

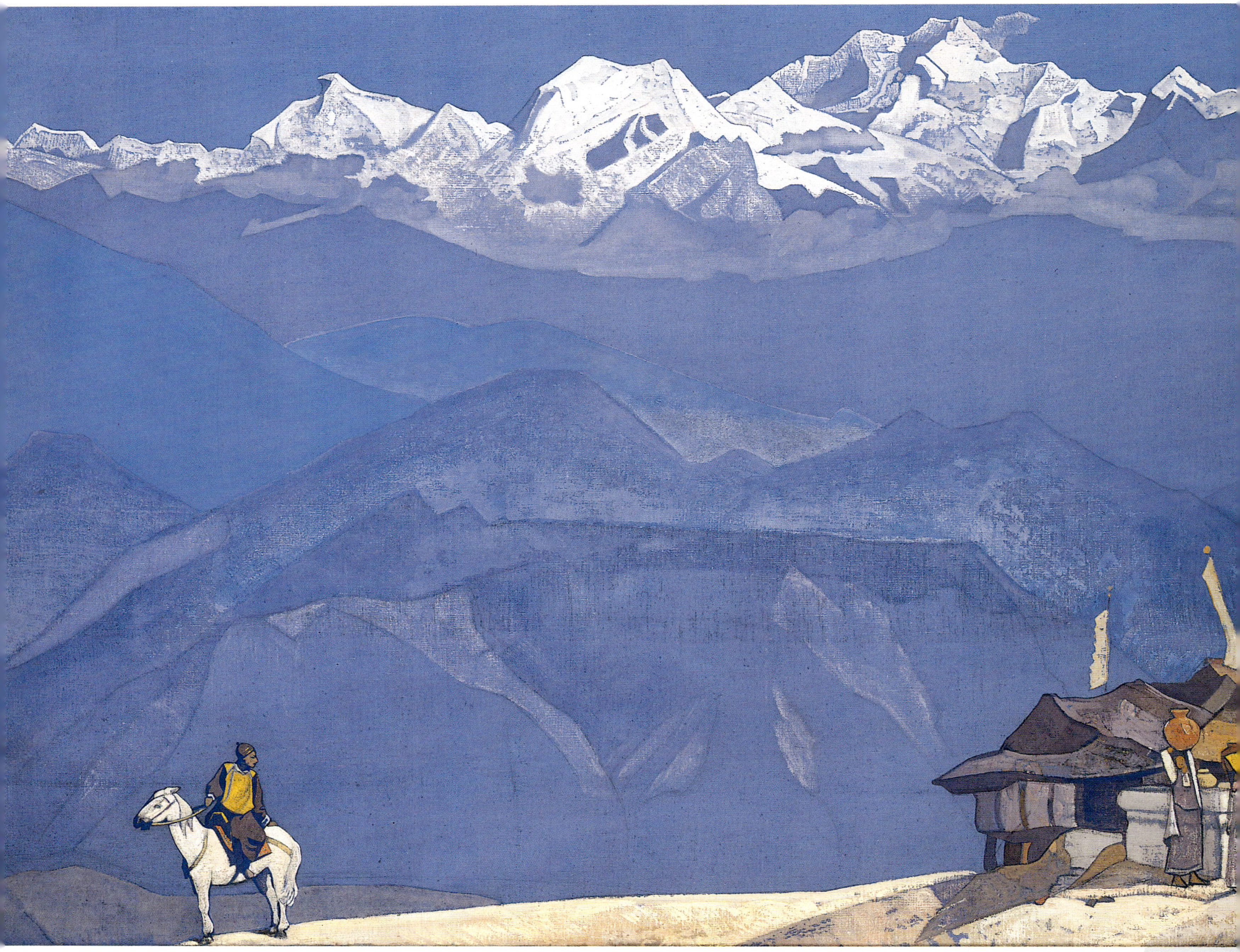

Remember, 1924

Tempera on canvas, 127 x 91.4 cm.
Nicholas Roerich Museum, New York

14 *Remember*

In May 1923, Roerich and his family went by ship to Europe, where they toured for several months before travelling on to Egypt. By November of that year they were sailing through the Red Sea and around the Arabian coast to land at Colombo, capital of Ceylon. They made their way to nothern India, arriving toward the end of December at Darjeeling. After a long search they found a suitable home in Talai-Pho-Brang. Later they discovered that it had been the residence of the Dalai Lama, who had fled from Tibet in 1910.(47) From this base the family organized excursions in Sikkim to prepare for their forthcoming Central Asian expedition. (48)

Svetoslav Roerich in his eighties could still picture the house near Darjeeling with extraordinary views of the Kanchenjunga range. (49) This location brought Roerich full circle, as Sina Fosdick explained, recounting what the artist had told her:

He was drawn to the Himalayas since his childhood – a gravure of Mount Kanchenjunga was on his wall at Isvara [the family's country estate]. He loved it and said that one day he would find the mountain and paint it. (50)

While in Darjeeling Roerich executed the twelve canvas series entitled *His Country.* His writings associate this series with one or more of the revered teachers, called in India mahatmas, who came to Sikkim on mountain horses to establish an ashram. (51)

Remember, like seven other paintings in the series, features Kanchenjunga as a setting for spiritual experience. (52) In this work a man on a white horse is about to leave a house on the plateau below the great peak. Two women stand by a well at the corner of the house, one holding a water jug, a domestic object identifying the place as their home. Observed closely, the female figures are transparent, the bevelled stone edges of the well visible through their garments. Perhaps the artist evokes the departure of a mahatma and the spirits of ashram members from the past.

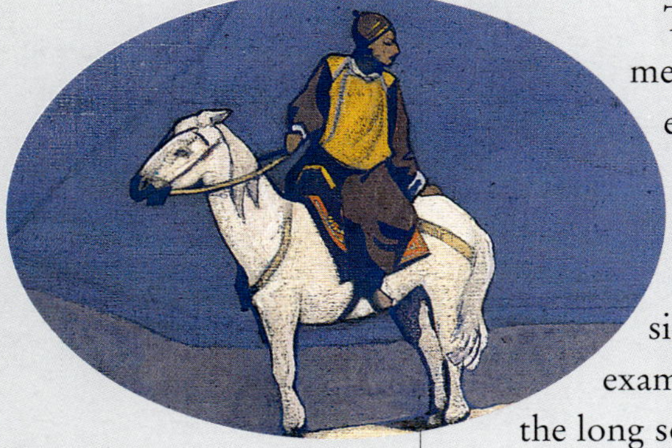

The painting may refer as well to personal memories: the Kanchenjunga gravure, the Isvara estate and the two women – Roerich's mother and sister – left behind in Russia. The Kanchenjunga setting probably also figures in the title of one other canvas in the series, *Pearl of Searching*, signifying not only to the necklace the guru examines with his pupil but also the sacred mountain as the long sought pearl.

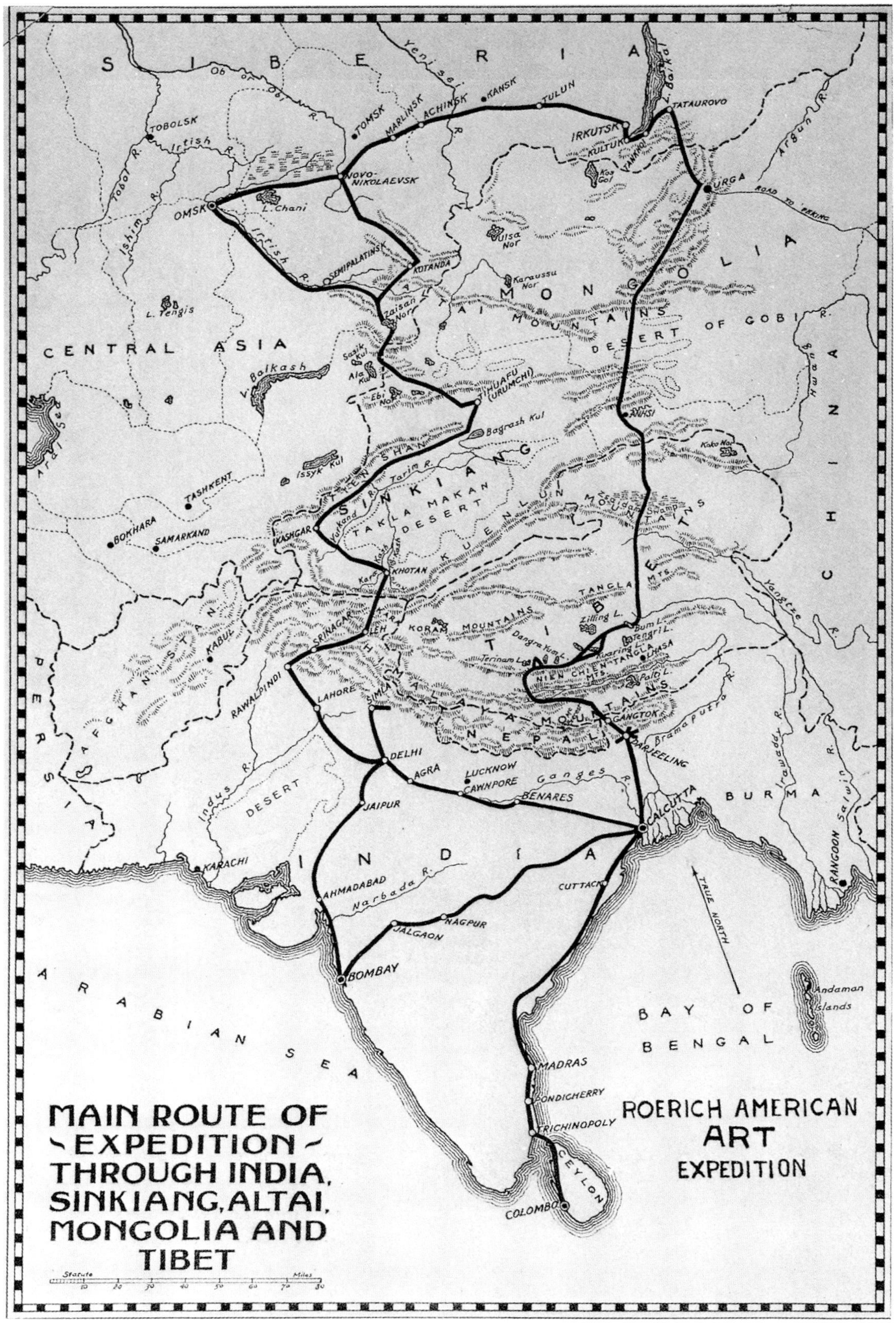

Map of Roerich's central asian expedition, 1925-1928

'Remember, like seven other paintings, features Kanchenjunga as a setting for spiritual experience'

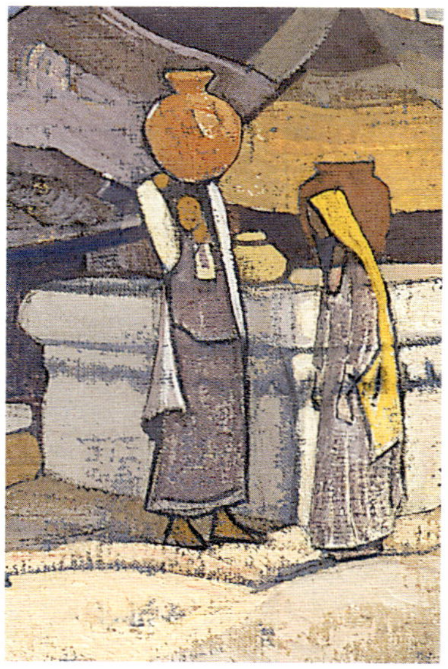

Remember, detail

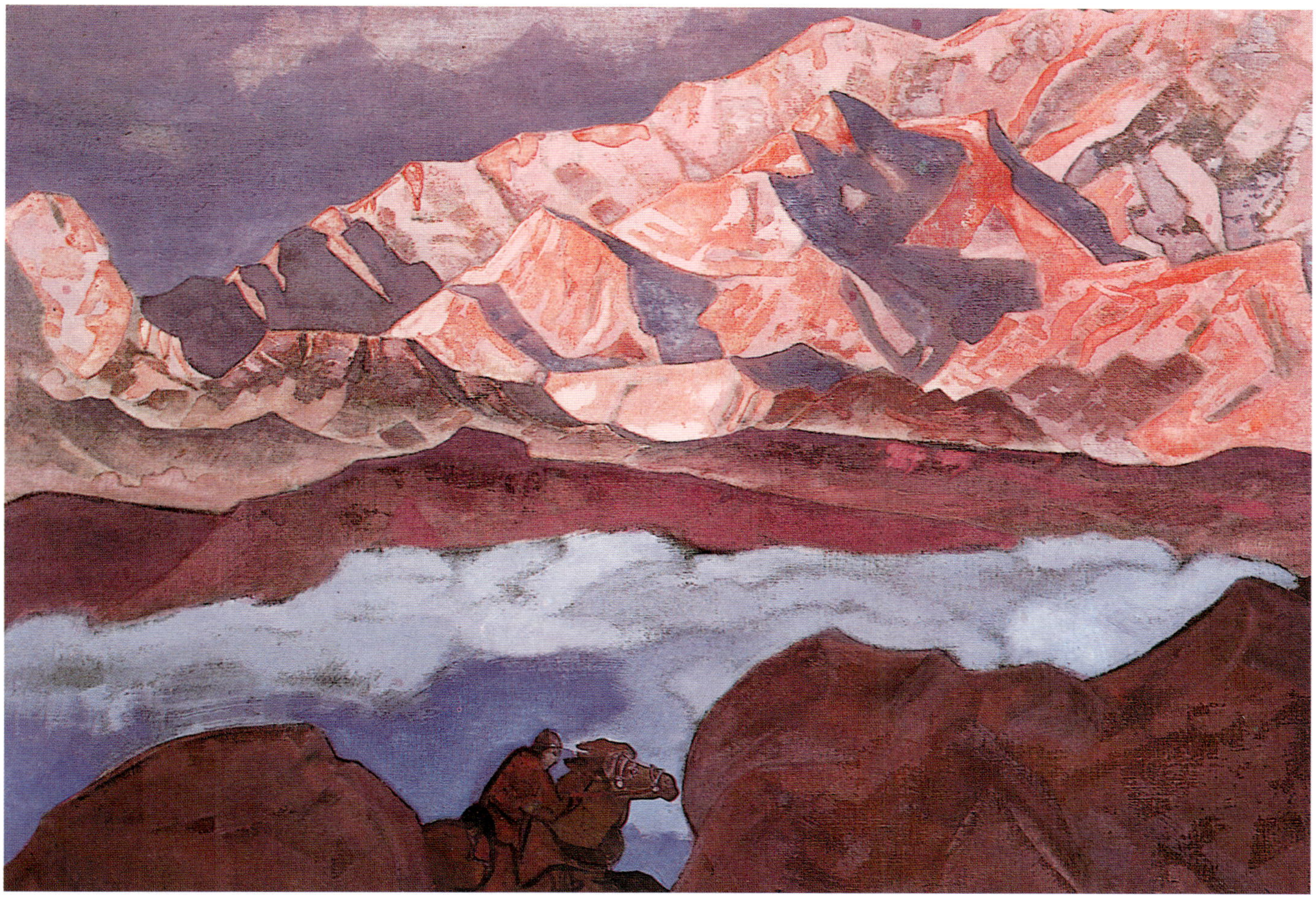

He Who Hastens, 1924

Tempera on canvas, 90.1 x 16 cm.
Nicholas Roerich Museum, New York

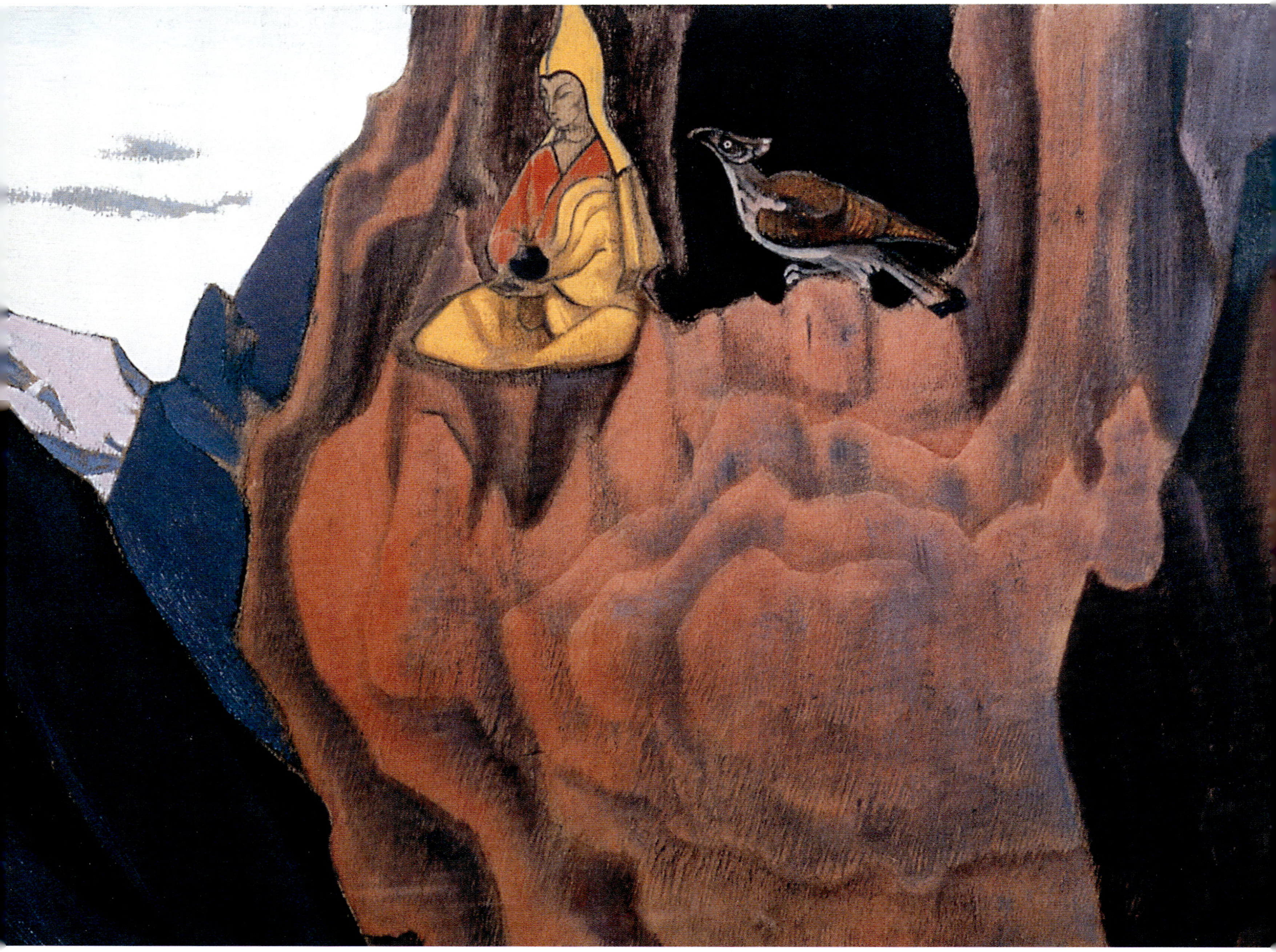

Tiding of the Eagles - Mongolia, 1927

Tempera on wood, 40.6 x 32 cm.
Nicholas Roerich Museum, New York

15

Tiding of the Eagles

Mongolia

The elder of Roerich's two sons, George, was 22 years old at the outset of the Central Asian expedition but had already completed the studies at London University, Columbia, Harvard and the Sorbonne that formed the basis of his distinguished career as an orientalist. He wrote a book on Tibetan painting in 1924 and prepared *Trails to Inmost Asia*, an account of the expedition published by Yale University Press in 1931. (53) His author's note stated the goals of the project:

In inner Asia we are able to survey one of the grandest mountain systems of the world; to journey for months across waterless deserts of sand and stone and upland plains; and to study the vestiges of a past culture that once linked ancient China with the countries of the Mediterranean basin. (54)

George Roerich also specified his father's vision for the expedition: 'to create a pictorial record of lands and peoples of inner Asia,' which he realized in 500 paintings; 'to survey the possibilities for new archaeological explorations;' and 'to secure an extensive collection of ethnographical and linguistic material.'(55)

Tidings of the Eagle shows a lama meditating by a cave high in the mountains. The eagle's presence suggests the vertiginous height of the place and the elevated consciousness of the lama who receives the bird's message. On the expedition Roerich painted lamas, monks, yogis and hermits in their austere habitats, a task never undertaken by a western artist. Alexandra David-Neel, the nineteenth century French writer initiated as a Tibetan Buddhist nun, was among the few foreigners who ever documented such phenomena. She captured in words what Roerich depicted, the tradition of 'anchorites who live in caverns or in huts generally situated at a great altitude, sometimes right up to the . . . line of perpetual snow . . . well above 10,000 feet in the Himalayas and Tibet.' (56) Helena Roerich's writings focused on the risks and challenges of the spiritual life: 'The mole is warm in his hole./The eagle is chilled before sunrise.' (57) Her family had exchanged the security of New York for this dangerous venture, with its privations and dwindling supplies, during which, Sina Fosdick said, the artist painted on packing cases, as in this work, on 'tent covering and even, at the prompting of Madame Roerich, on fabrics from her dresses.' (58)

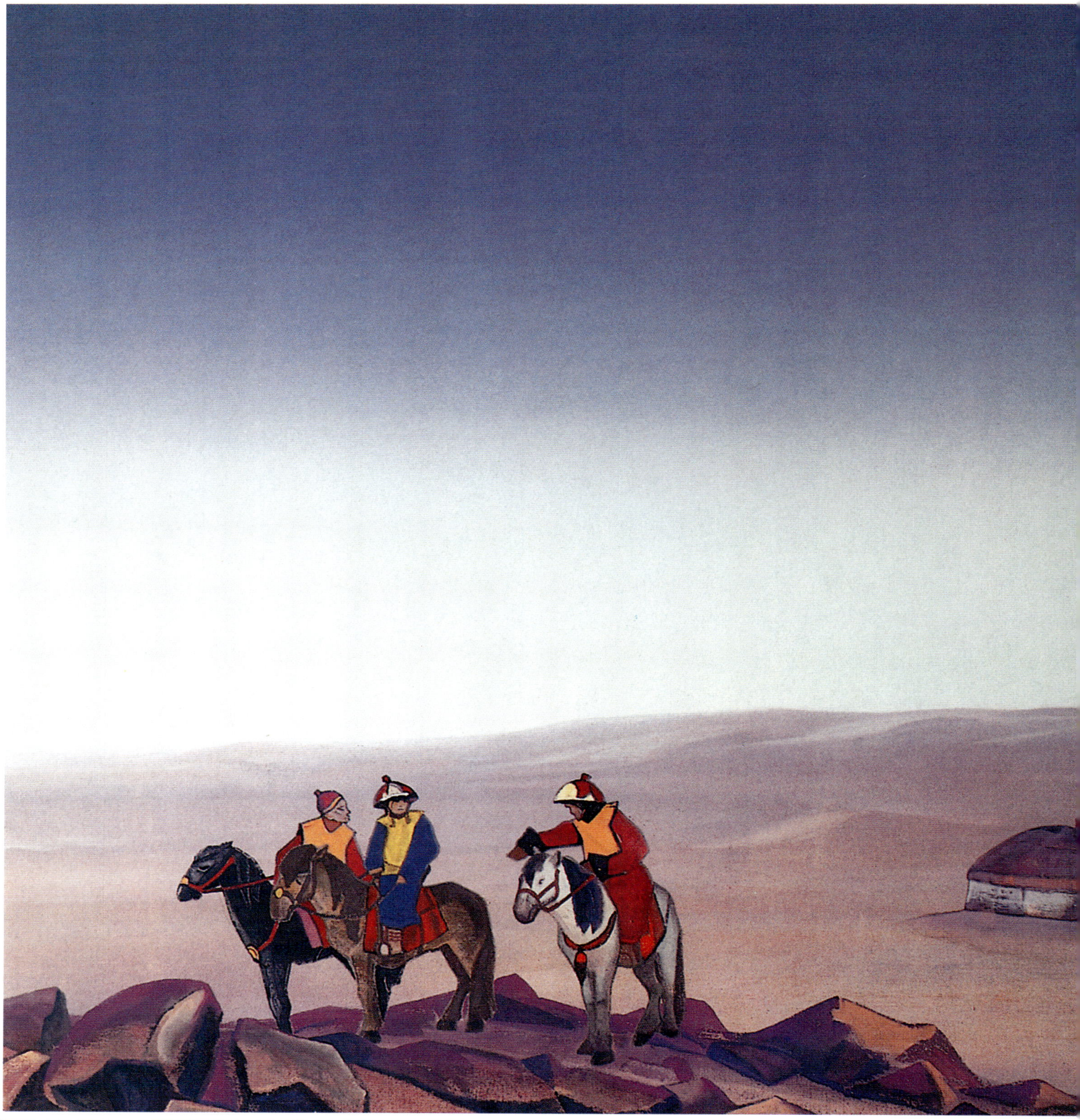

Roerich painted lamas, monks, yogis and hermits in their austere habitats, a task never undertaken by a western artist

Mongolia I, 1938

Tempera on canvas, 90.5 x 124.5 cm.
Svetoslav Roerich Collection, Bangalore, India

Tiding of the Eagles, detail

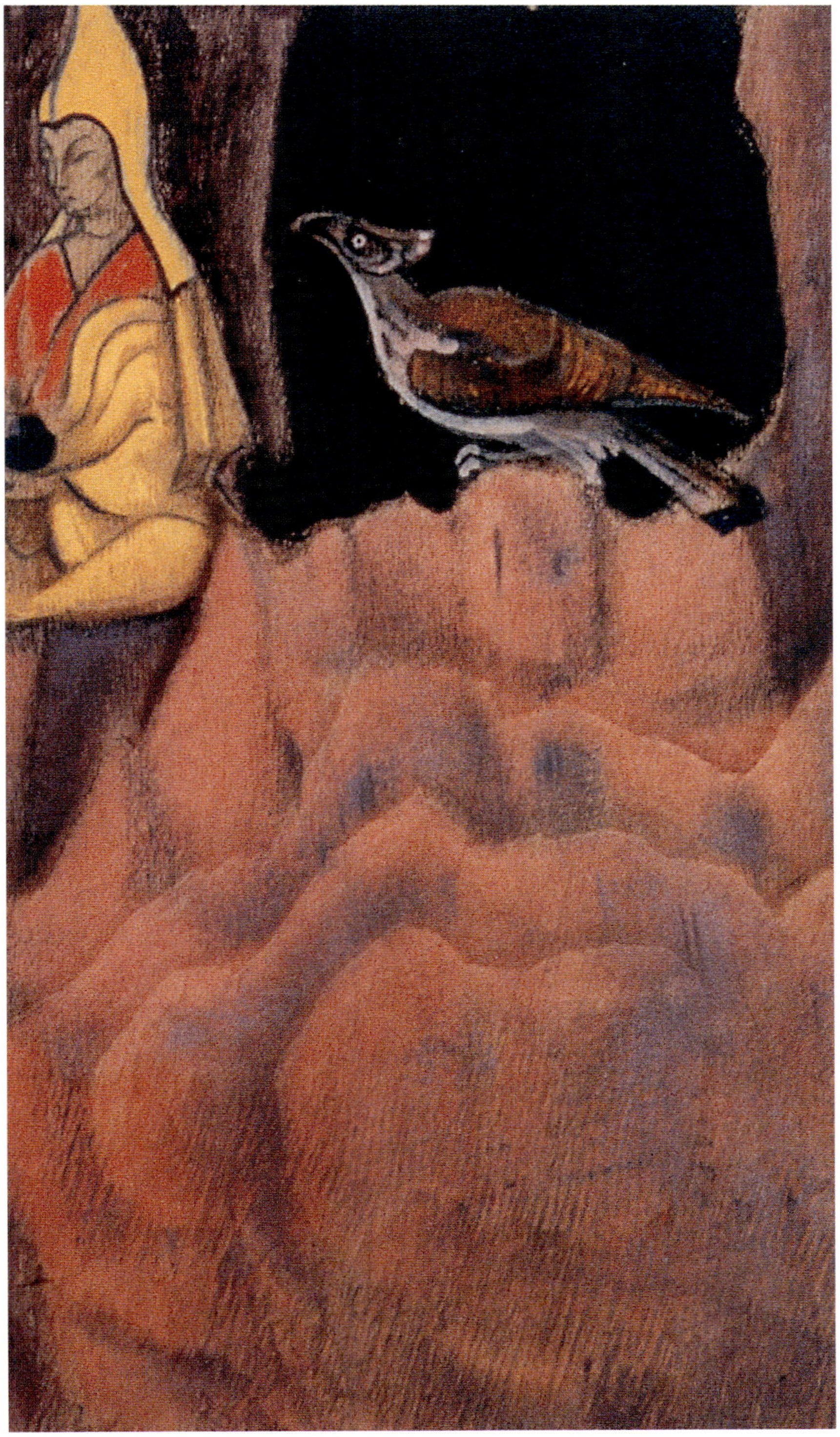

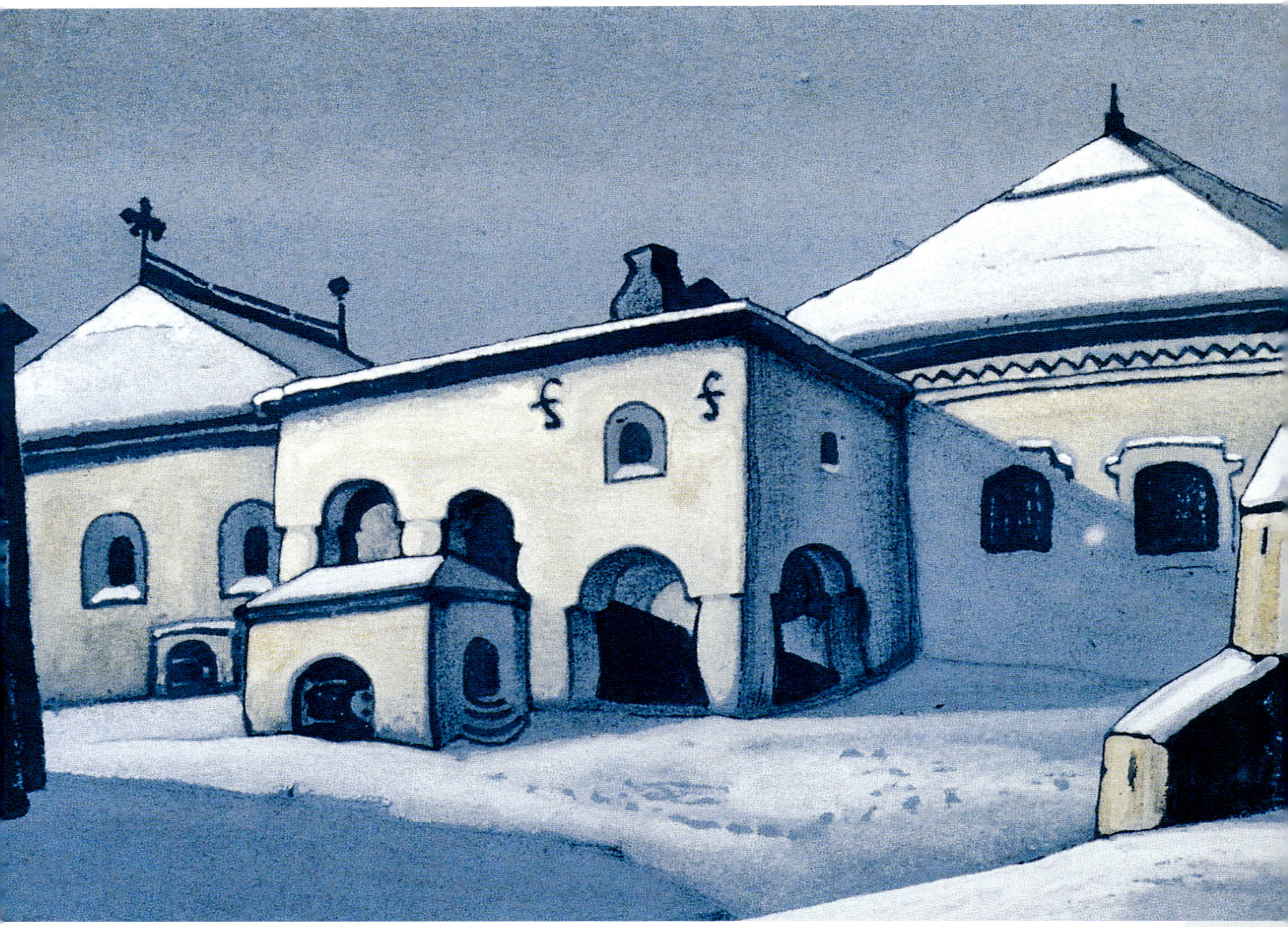

Old Church, ca. 1927

Tempera on cardboard, 52.7 x 37 cm.
Nicholas Roerich Museum, New York

16

Old Church

The old church in this painting, with Russian style eaves and recessed arches, Roerich saw in Mongolia when his expedition stayed there in 1927. It is a subtle study of neutrals with whitewashed walls, snow-encrusted ground and wintery sky, all turned a variety of greys and ochres by the sun. In the midst of the Asian buildings the artist painted at this time – Buddhist monasteries, fortresses and mountain dwellings – it is interesting to find an example that recalls so clearly his Architectural series in Russia at the beginning of the century. Now, however, he has replaced the Gauguin method of applying large patches of pigment with a more even spread of colour. His early series had favoured the use of oil and fairly close views of specific features. (59) In this period, he prefers tempera, due in part to the exigencies of travel, and his expeditionary state of mind prompt a longer view of the subject.

From their preparations in Sikkim during 1924 to the middle of 1928, Roerich and his entourage encircled Central Asia, passing through Kashmir and moving northeast along the old caravan route to Ladak. From there in September 1925 they travelled on to Chinese Turkestan, visiting Khotan and Urumchi, which they left in May 1926, detouring to Moscow. Sina Fosdick, then married to Maurice Lichtmann, sailed with her husband from New York to meet the Roerichs in June 1926. They met in the Russian capital so that, as she later clarified, Roerich could 'get permission to explore the Altai mountain regions in Siberia,' adding 'we worked hard for two weeks to get the necessary papers.' (60) Her trip had other urgent purposes:

The expedition had lost a great deal of equipment, and my husband and I were taking out new supplies. There was also much to discuss regarding the institutions in America. (61)

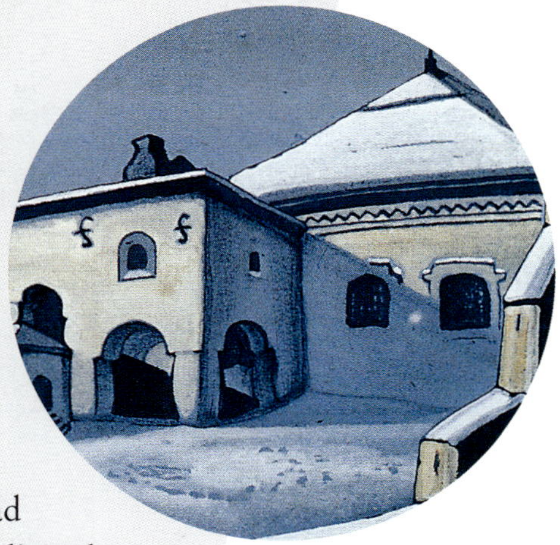

The Roerichs and Lichtmanns went by the Trans-Siberian Railway to the Soviet city of Omsk and then 'by steamer along the Siberian rivers and finally by horse into the mountains,' with Roerich painting, sketching and collecting data en route.(62)

By August 1926 the Roerichs had gone on to Urga, the capital of Mongolia, where the artist began sketching for the *Old Church*, a site which must have been poignant, though he could not have known that he had seen Russia for the last time.

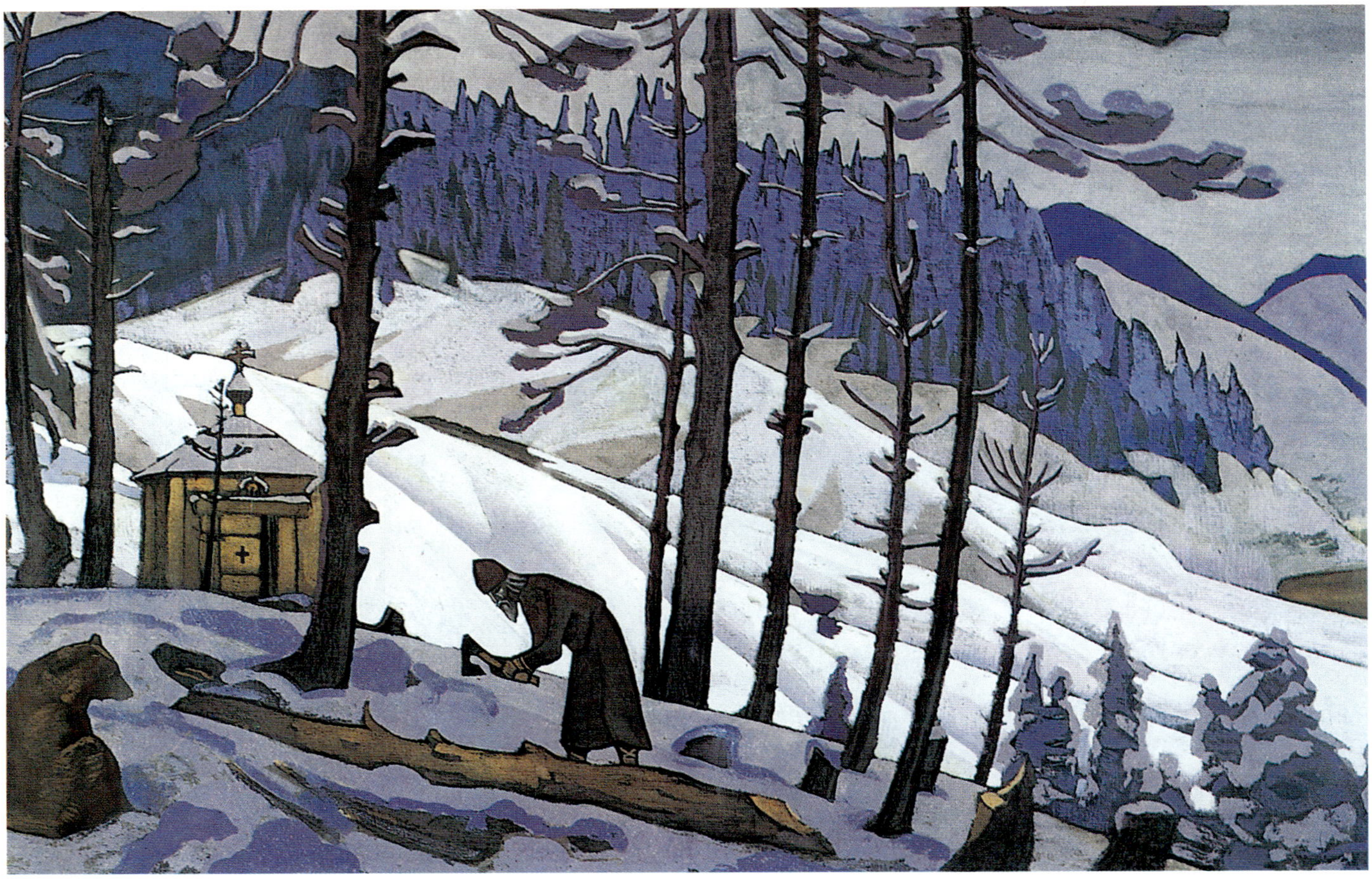

Sergius the Builder, 1925

Tempera on canvas, 73.6 x 117 cm.
Bolling Collection, Miami, Florida

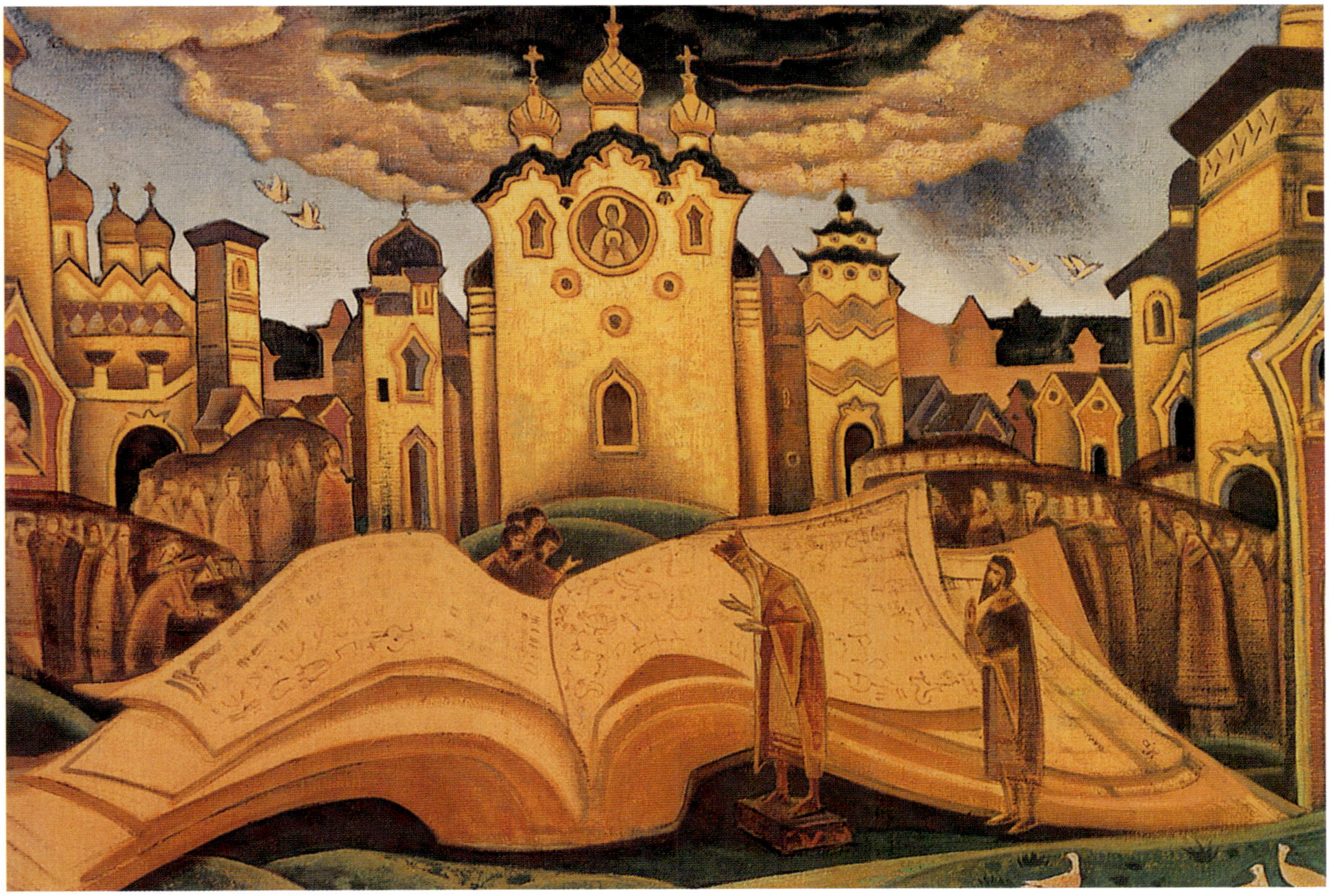

The Book of Doves, 1922

Tempera on canvas, 75 x 101.6 cm.
Museum of Oriental Art, Moscow

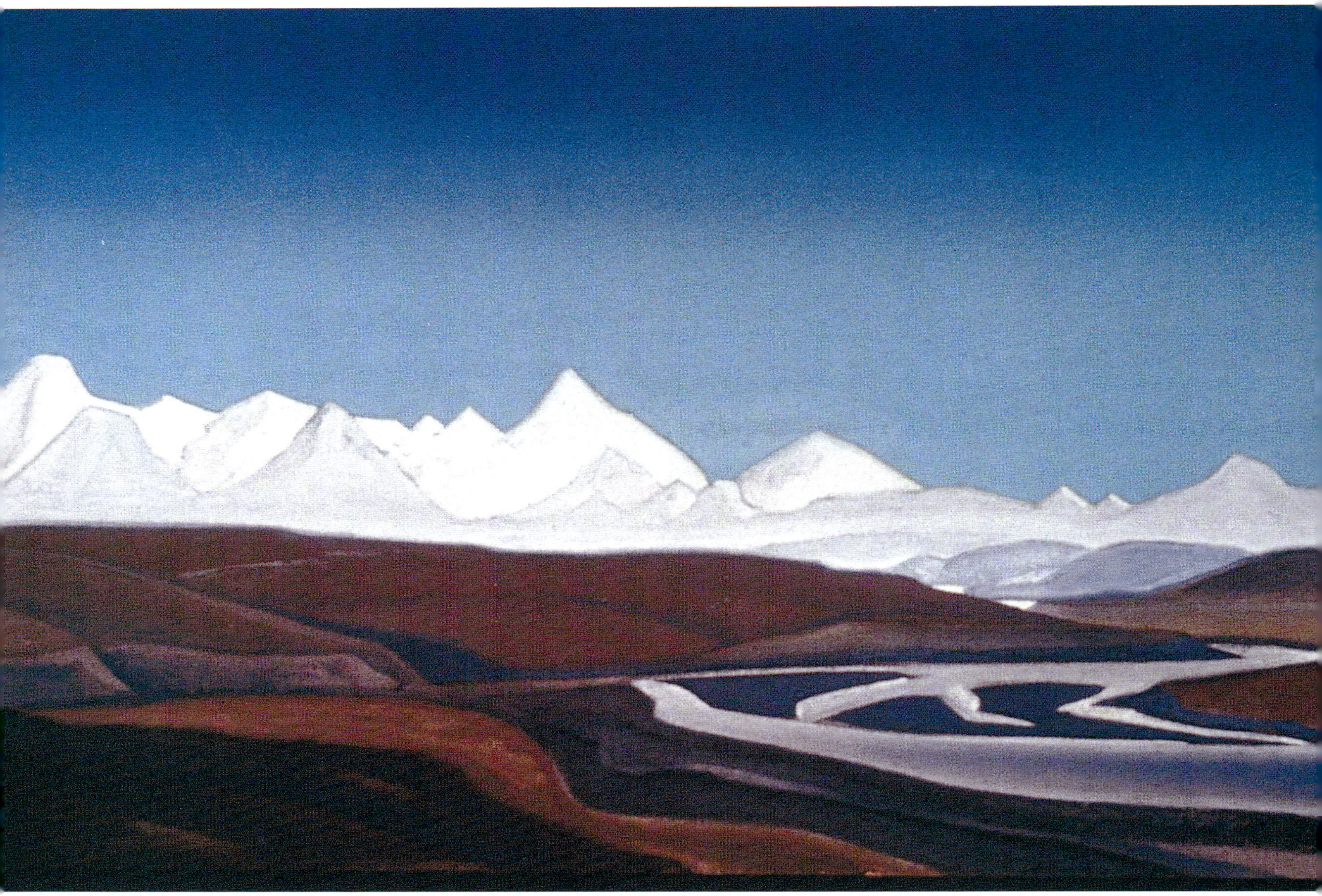

The greatest & holiest of Thang-La, 1928/29

Tempera on canvas, 97.1 x 61.6 cm.
Nicholas Roerich Museum, New York

17 The greatest & holiest of Thang-La

Roerich's panorama of glacial peaks in the Thang-La Range sets up a series of dramatic contrasts. The brilliance of the icy mountains is highlighted by the dark plateau, which is broken up by geometrical fragments of bluish grey, no doubt the salt lakes of the area. The artist devotes two-thirds of the canvas to the vast sky, rendered in a clear blue that accentuates the white of the snowy summits, making their circular formation appear to be lit from an unseen source at the centre. During the expedition George Roerich recorded a local legend of the view his father painted:

The Pass of Thang-La is believed to be the abode of some thirty-three gods or heavenly denizens, and our Mongols and Tibetans said that it was an auspicious sign that we were crossing the pass on an exceptionally fine day. There is a firm belief among the caravaneers of Tibet, that whenever

an undesirable person comes into Tibet, a scornful wind blows over the pass and the unlucky travelers freeze on the icy slopes of the mountain. (63)

Years later, whenever Sina Fosdick showed this painting at the Nicholas Roerich Museum, she recited a similar tale the artist had told her:

As a caravan approaches the lofty peaks, the guide stops and announces, 'I am not permitted to take you further.' Naturally, the people in the caravan ask him why not, and he answers, 'If you are destined to reach this place, you do not need my help. If you are not meant to get there, no one can take you.'(64)

Bringing further supplies from America, she had rejoined the expedition at Urga, when it was 'wintering in Mongolia in 1927 before crossing the Gobi Desert to reach Tibet.' (65) The Roerichs procured Dodge touring cars from Mongolian authorities to facilitate desert travel when they left Urga in

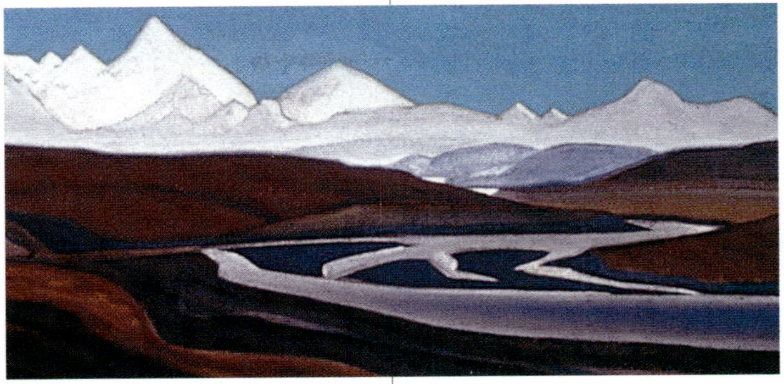

April. A week later arid conditions forced them to change the method of transport to camels. They moved thus through the Gobi, spending June and July in the higher mountain valleys, where they acquired horses and other pack animals for an August departure to Tibet. In October they reached Thang-La and, having survived a treacherous winter in Tibet, they travelled through Ladak to return to base at Talai-Pho-Brang near Darjeeling in May 1928.

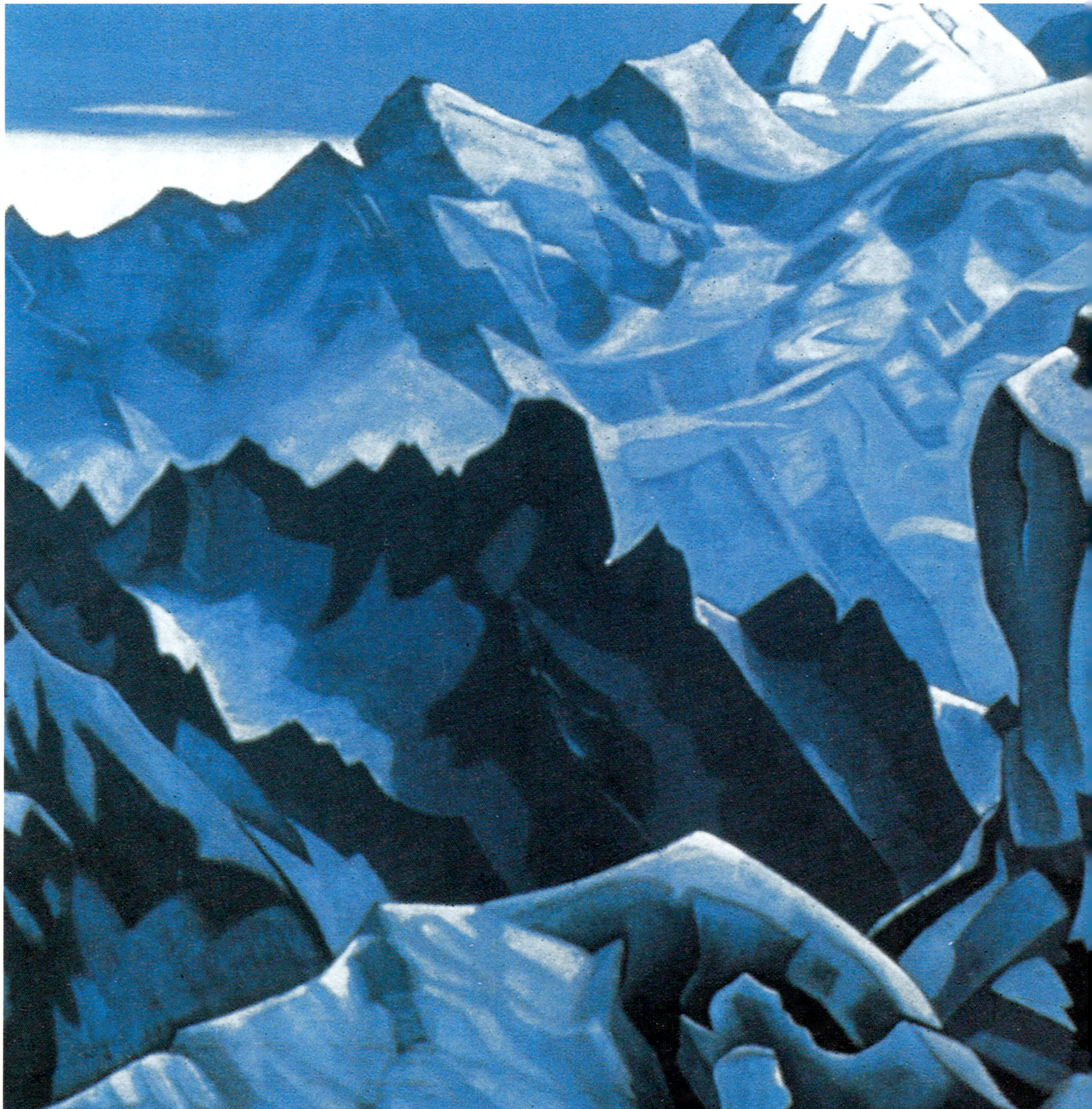

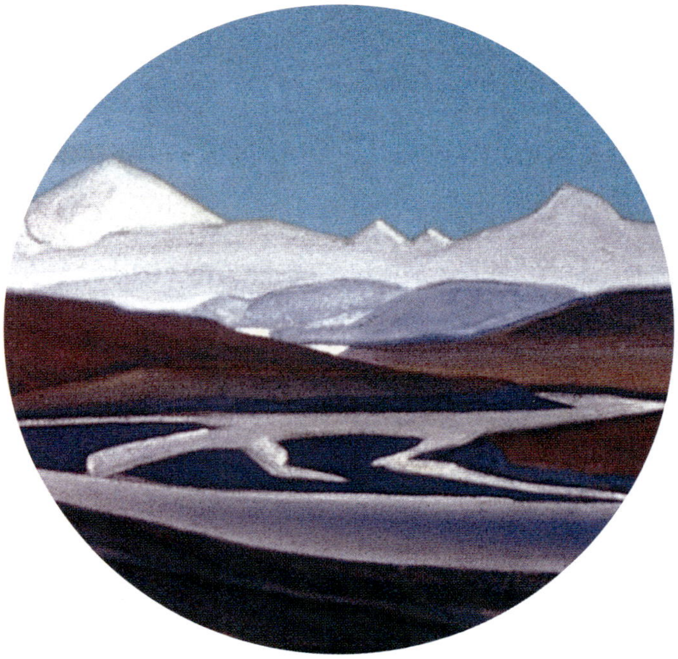

The greatest and holiest of Thang-La, detail

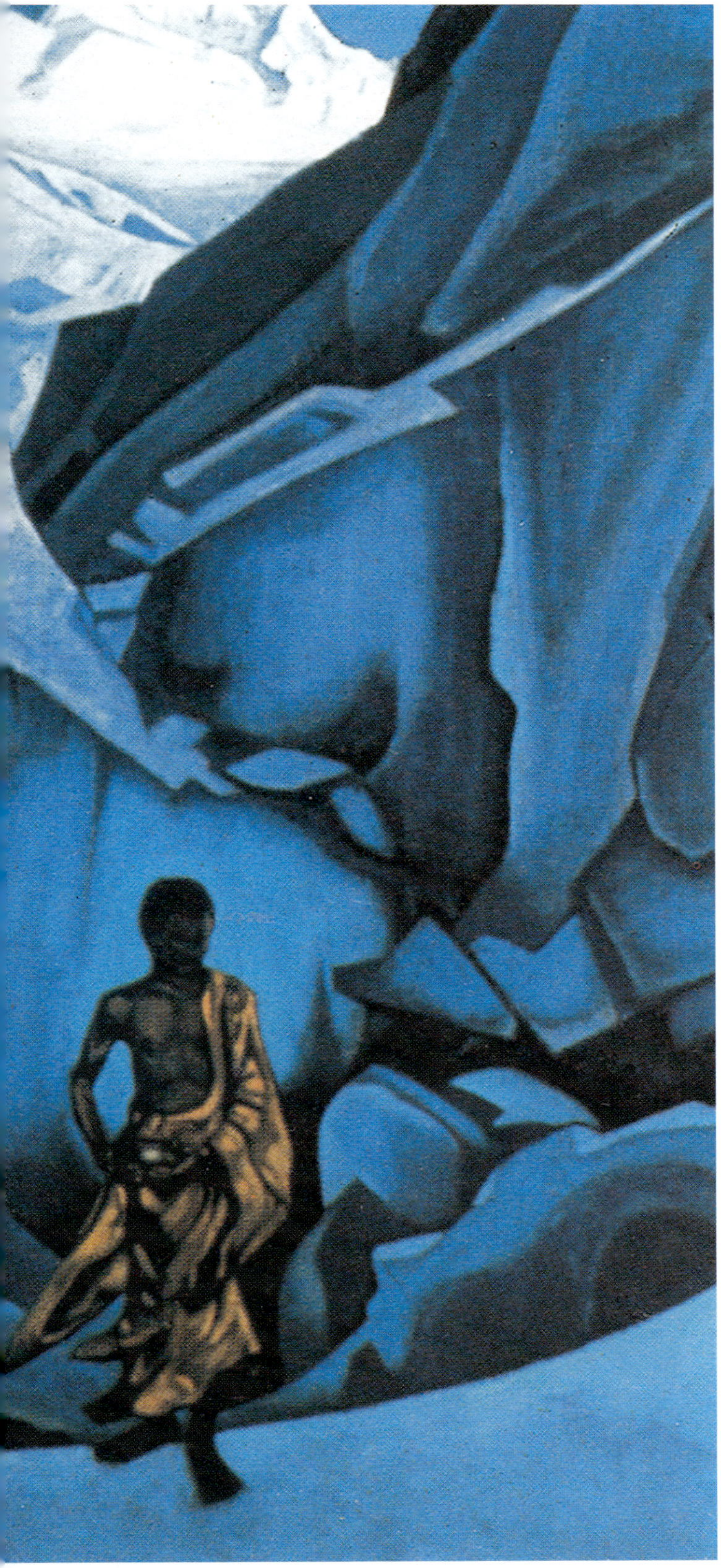

Kanchenjunga (variante), 1927
Nicholas Roerich Museum, New York

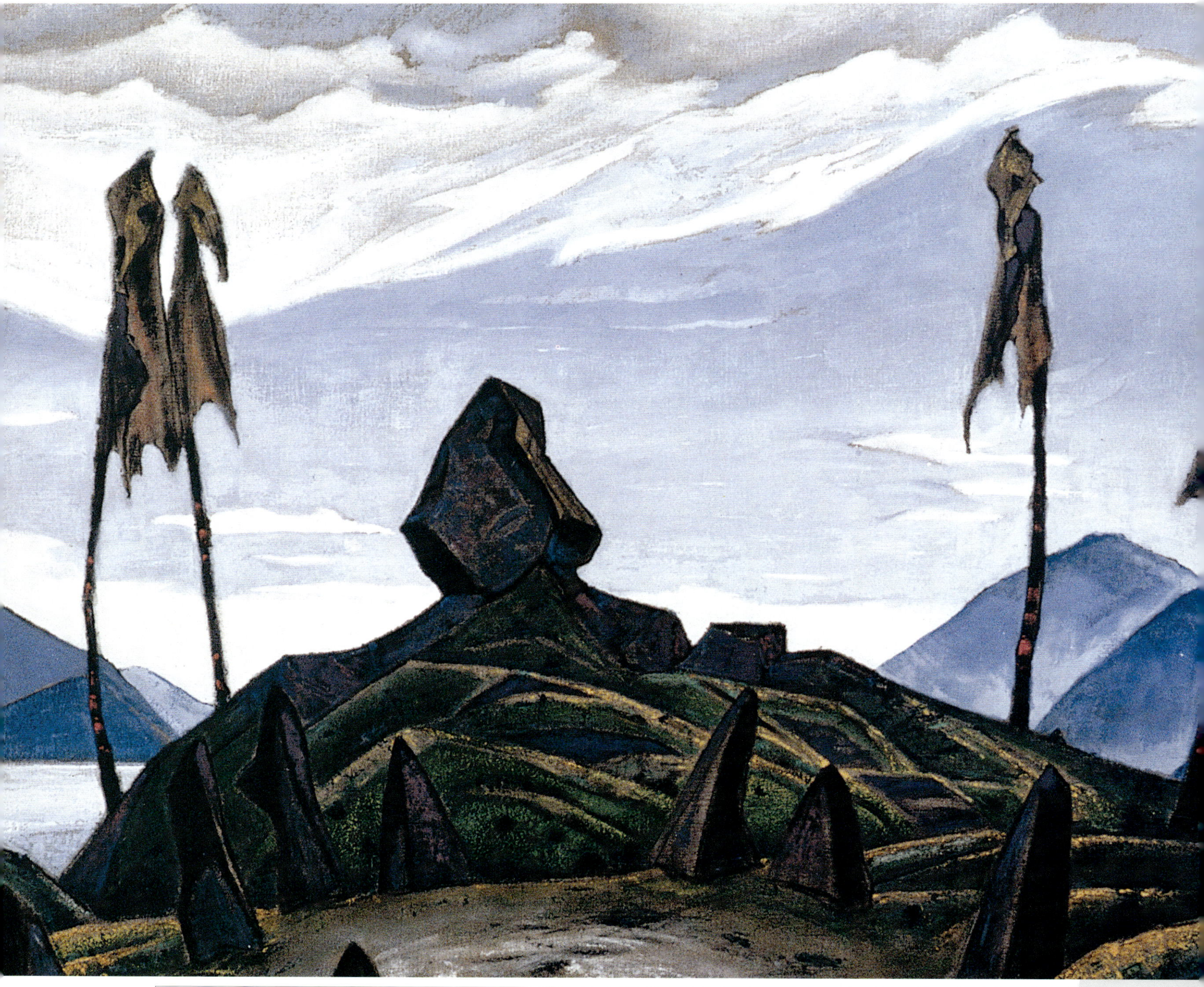

Sketch for the curtain, Le Sacre du Printemps, 1929

Tempera on canvas, 127 x 75 cm.
Nicholas Roerich Museum, New York

Sketch for *Curtain, Le Sacre du Printemps*

18

The conductor Leopold Stokowski organized the American premiere of *Le Sacre du Printemps* around Roerich's return from the Central Asian expedition. Stokowsky reminded the public that the ballet was created by Igor Stravinsky and Roerich and announced to the press that 'Roerich is now back from Tibet and is in New York,' emphasizing the larger world view of the new staging over the original:

Although the creators of this work . . . are both Russians, we are not aiming to make this production of the work essentially Russian, because we feel that the ideas and feelings it expresses are universal. (66)

When Roerich prepared the scenario and designs for the legendary first version of *Le Sacre* in 1913, he drew upon studies of the ancient Slavs that were so key to his art in that period. (67) In the interim he had travelled widely throughout Europe, the United States and Asia, and quite naturally his interest in archaic civilizations expanded to encompass the cultural archetypes he encountered, particularly in the American Southwest and the Trans-Himalayas. Stokowski reflected this direction in Roerich's work when he said in an interview about their current Sacre that 'many tribes of Indians in this country have similar ritualistic ceremonies every spring, and the same is true of many Asiatic countries.' (68)

This decor design shows a circle of pointed stones in front of a dark green hill. It is sculpted by rock and capped with a large boulder which seems to have a kneeling figure carved into its side. Tall poles surmounted by animal skulls and skins ring the stone circle. A grey lake and steep blue mountains can be seen beyond the ritual site. The sky, painted in broad washes of white and pale lilac, like the background generally, reflects the artist's recent peregrinations on the roof of the world.

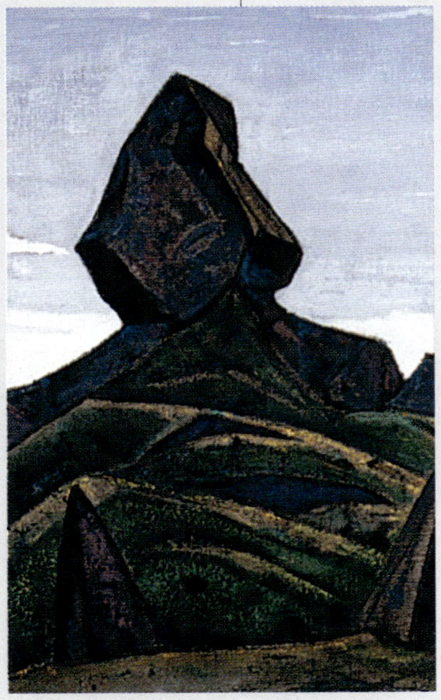

The 1913 Sacre had Roerich's two landscapes of the Russian north – one for day and one for night – their austerity matched by Nijinsky's ritual dance. Diaghilev revived the work in 1920 with choreography by Leonide Massine, and it became less primitive, despite the exclusive use of Roerich's nocturnal set with its ceremonial stones and skulls. Massine also created the 1930 production with its return to ritual and with Roerich's choice of Martha Graham as the soloist for the sacred dance. (69)

Sketch for the curtain,
Le Sacre du Printemps, detail

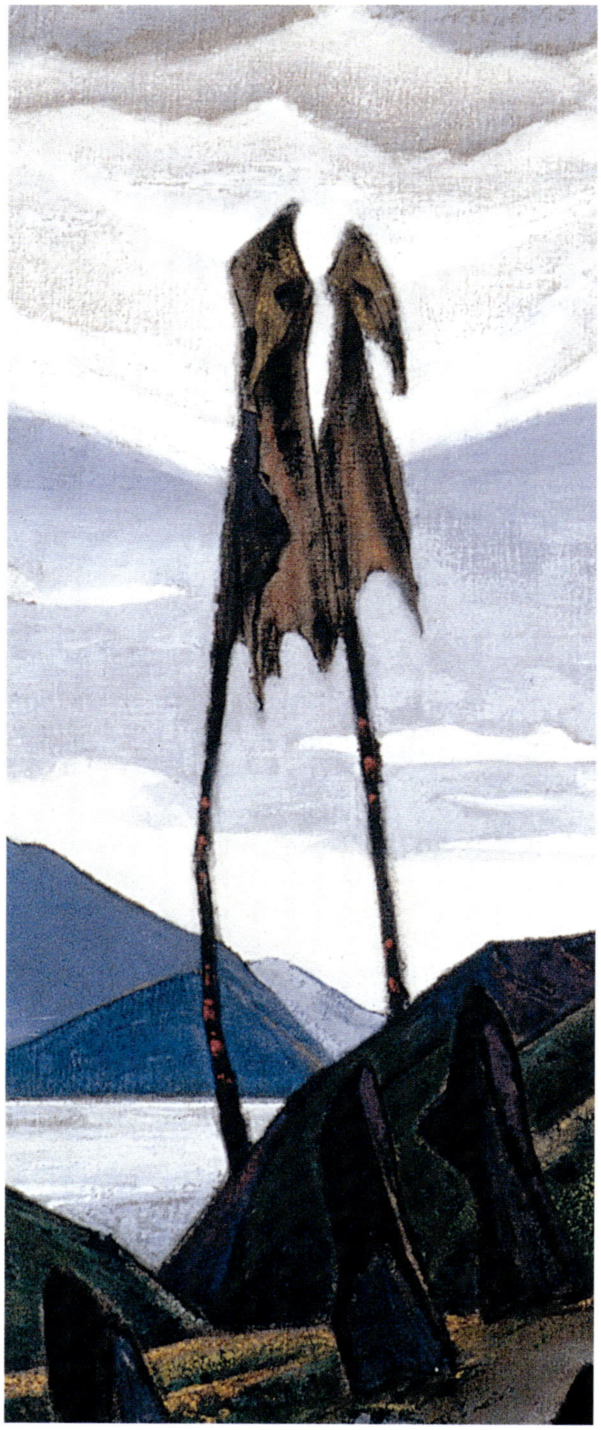

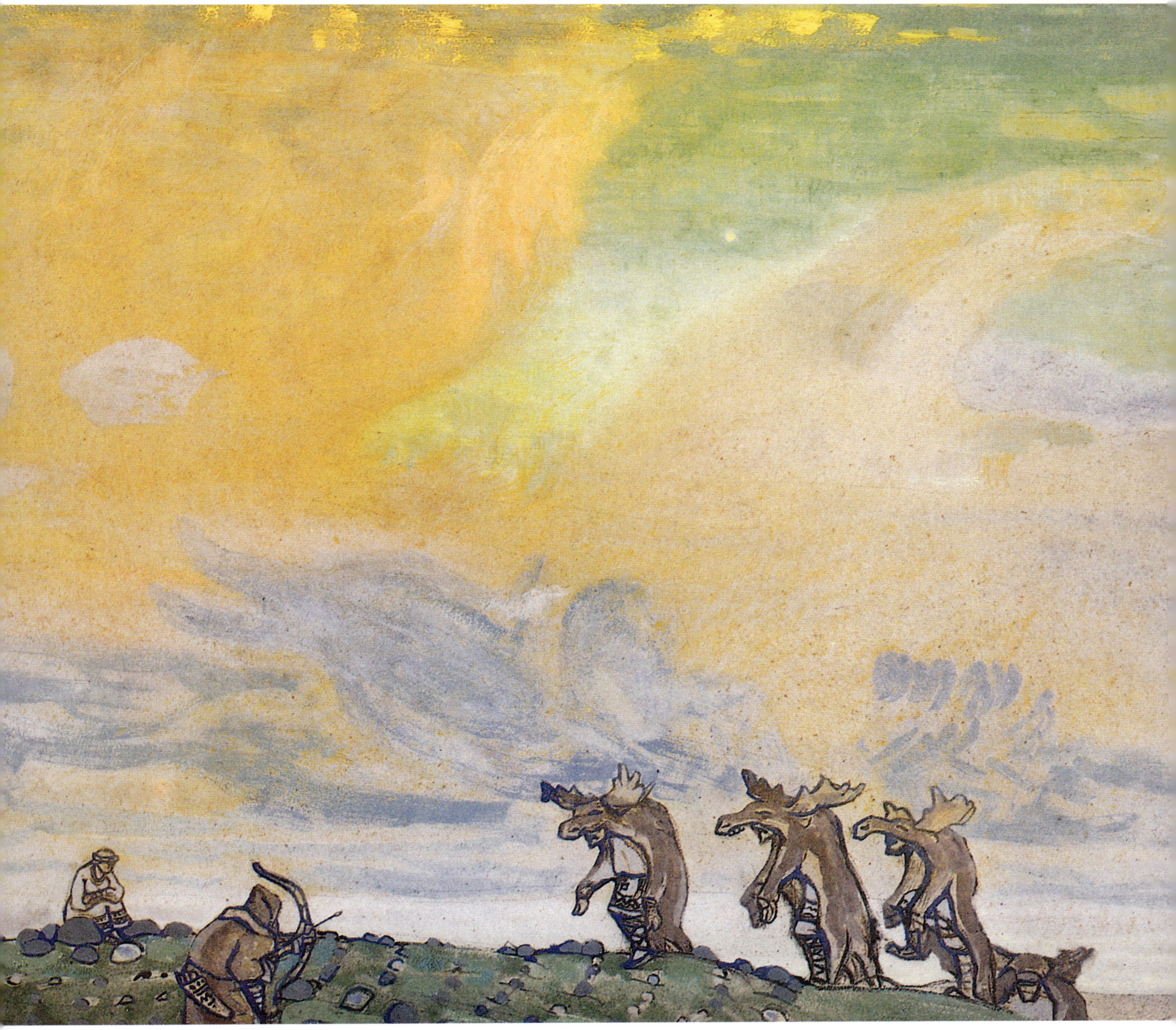

The Great Sacrifice, 1910

Originally intended as the backdrop for Act II of Le Sacre du Printemps, this sketch eventually became the design for the entr'acte curtain.
Tempera on canvas, 73,6 x 81,3 cm.
Bolling Collection, Miami, Florida

The host of Gessar Khan, 1931

Tempera on canvas, 140 x 94 cm.
Nicholas Roerich Museum, New York

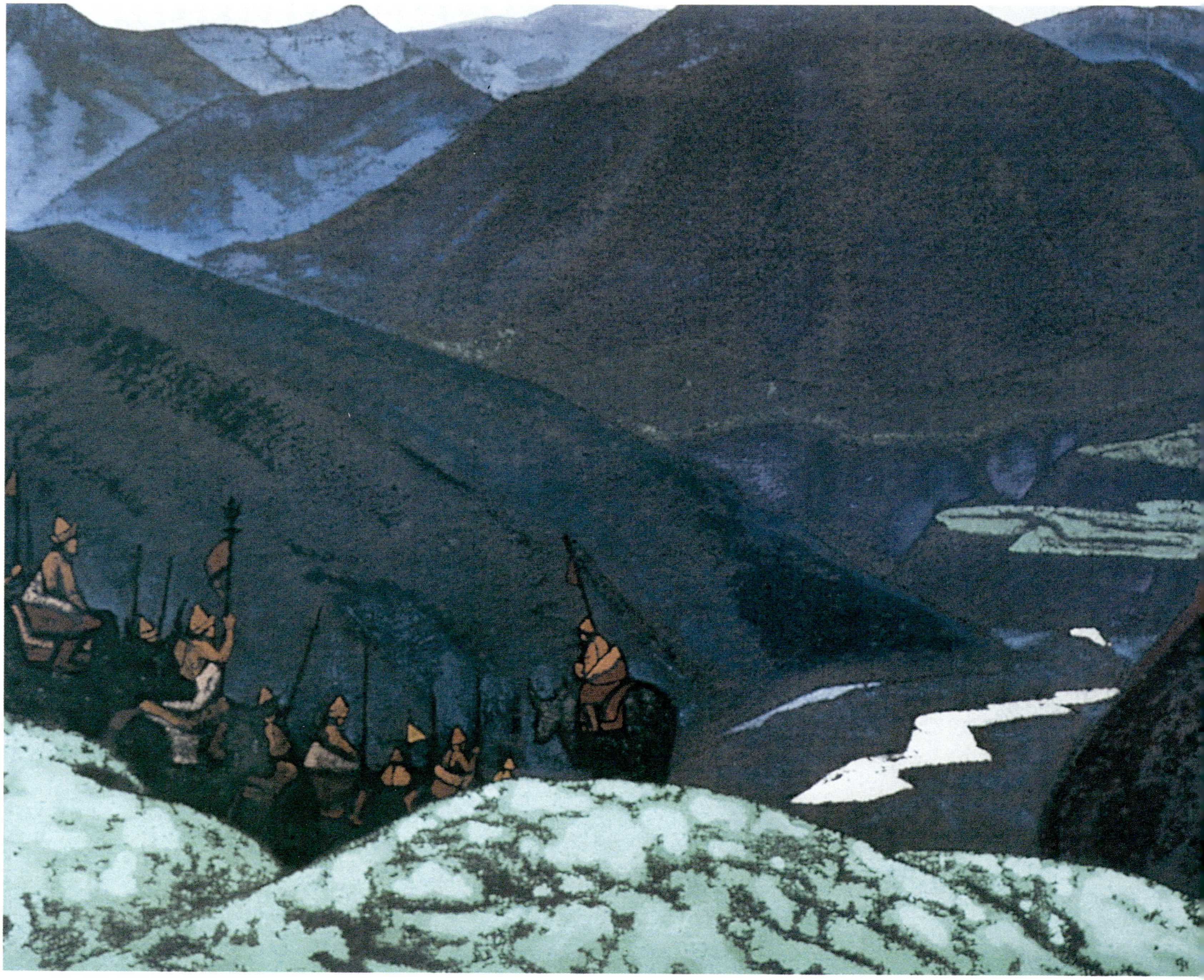

19

The host of Gessar Khan

The epic poem about Gessar Khan has been called the *Iliad of Central Asia.* (70) It describes the adventures of an eleventh century warrior, who over time accrued the accolades of a popular hero fighting for the good of the common man. The voluminous Gessariad, which exists in Mongolian, Chinese, Buryat and Tibetan languages, was studied in various versions by members of Roerich's expedition, and the artist treated this subject in several other paintings, among them: *The Saga of Gessar (1926)* and two paintings entitled *The Sword of Gessar* (1932 and 1943) (71).

In *The Host of Gessar Khan* Roerich depicts a band of the hero's followers descending an ice-covered slope, all of them mounted on buffaloes and armed with lances. The leader, possibly Gessar himself, surveys them from higher ground as they pass him in tight formation on the bottom left corner of the canvas. The rest of the painting is devoted to the terrain that challenges them. Forbidding as these massive and sombre mountains are, the grouping of warriors and their weapons suggest that human opponents pose a greater danger. Between the icy white of the foreground and grim purple behind them, the men provide a warm contrast, bundled up in brown and ochre garments and unified by their pennants. The dark palette and the arrangement of figures relate more to the Slavic works of Roerich's early career – like *The Campaign (1899)* and *The Patrol (1905)* – than to his recent Asian paintings with their brilliant colours and single figures isolated in immense settings.(72)

Shortly after the expedition, writing about the legendary Gessar, Roerich quoted the chronicler of Tibetan culture, Alexandra David-Neel, who was particularly interested in the Buddhist concept of the hero's return to earth in the future:

> Gessar Khan is a hero whose next incarnation will take place in northern Shambhala where he will unite with his associates and leaders who followed him in his previous life. They will reincarnate in Shambhala to which they will be attracted by the mysterious power of their ruler or by those mysterious voices which are only heard by the initiate. (73)

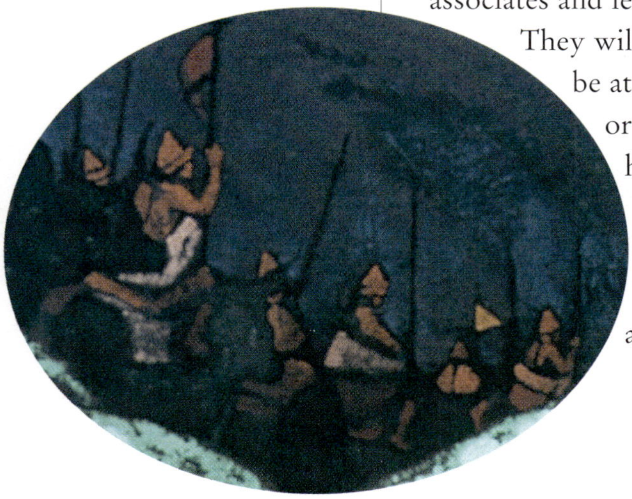

The arrow is an attribute of Gessar and a sign of his expected return. Roerich's bright arrow shapes in the middle ground signal such associations in this canvas.

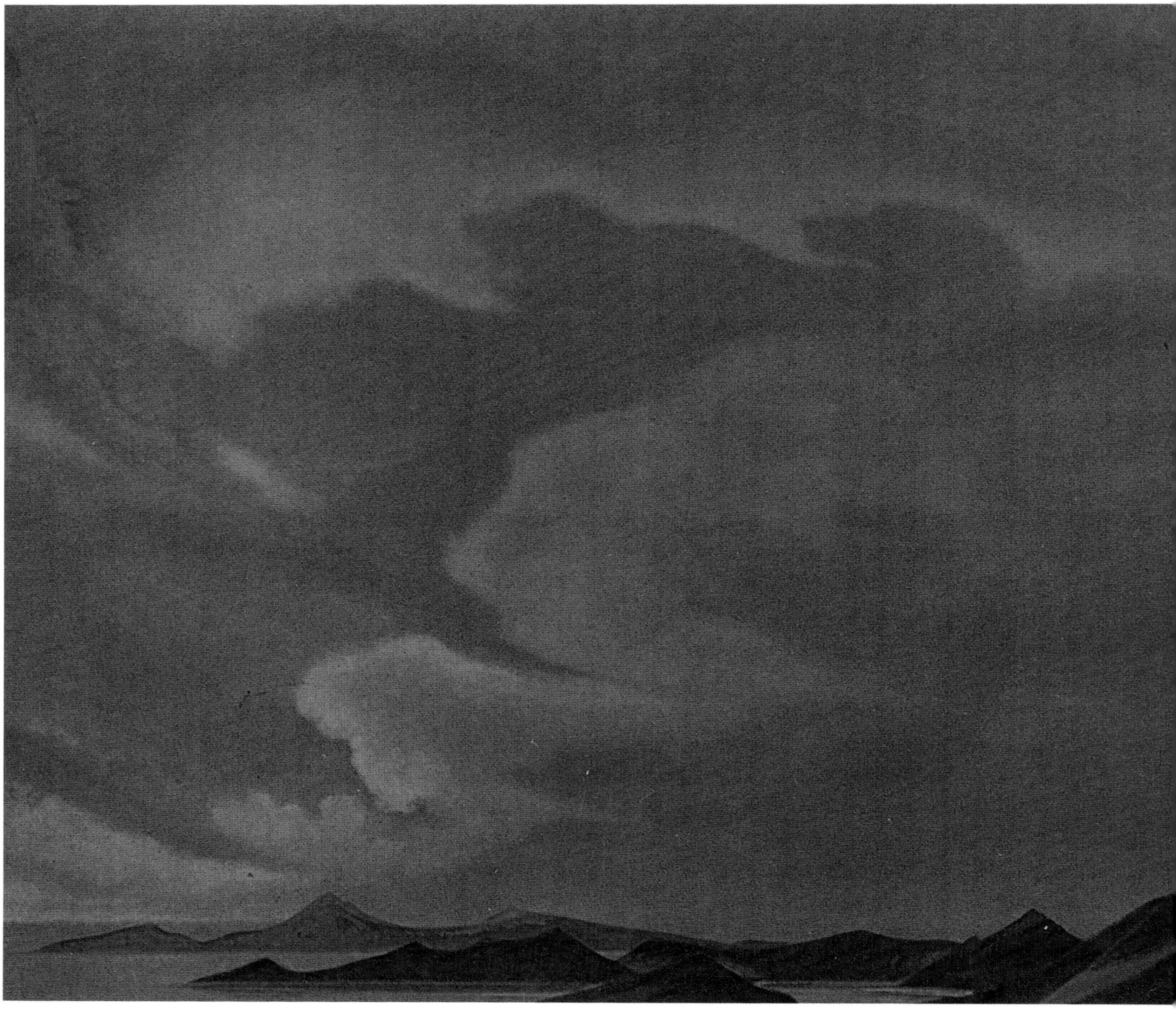

'The epic poem about Gessar Khan has

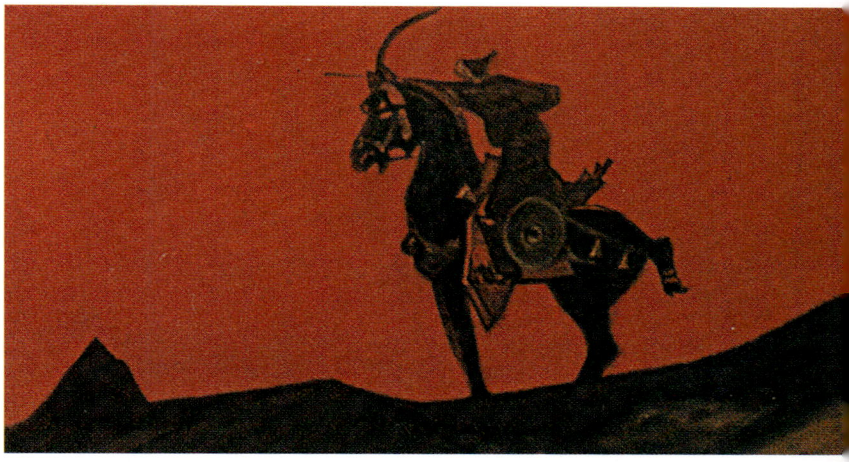

The Host of Gessar Khan, detail

Gessar Khan, 1941

Tempera on canvas, 62 x 126 cm.
Memorial flat of Yuri Roerich, Moscow

been called the Iliad of Central Asia.'

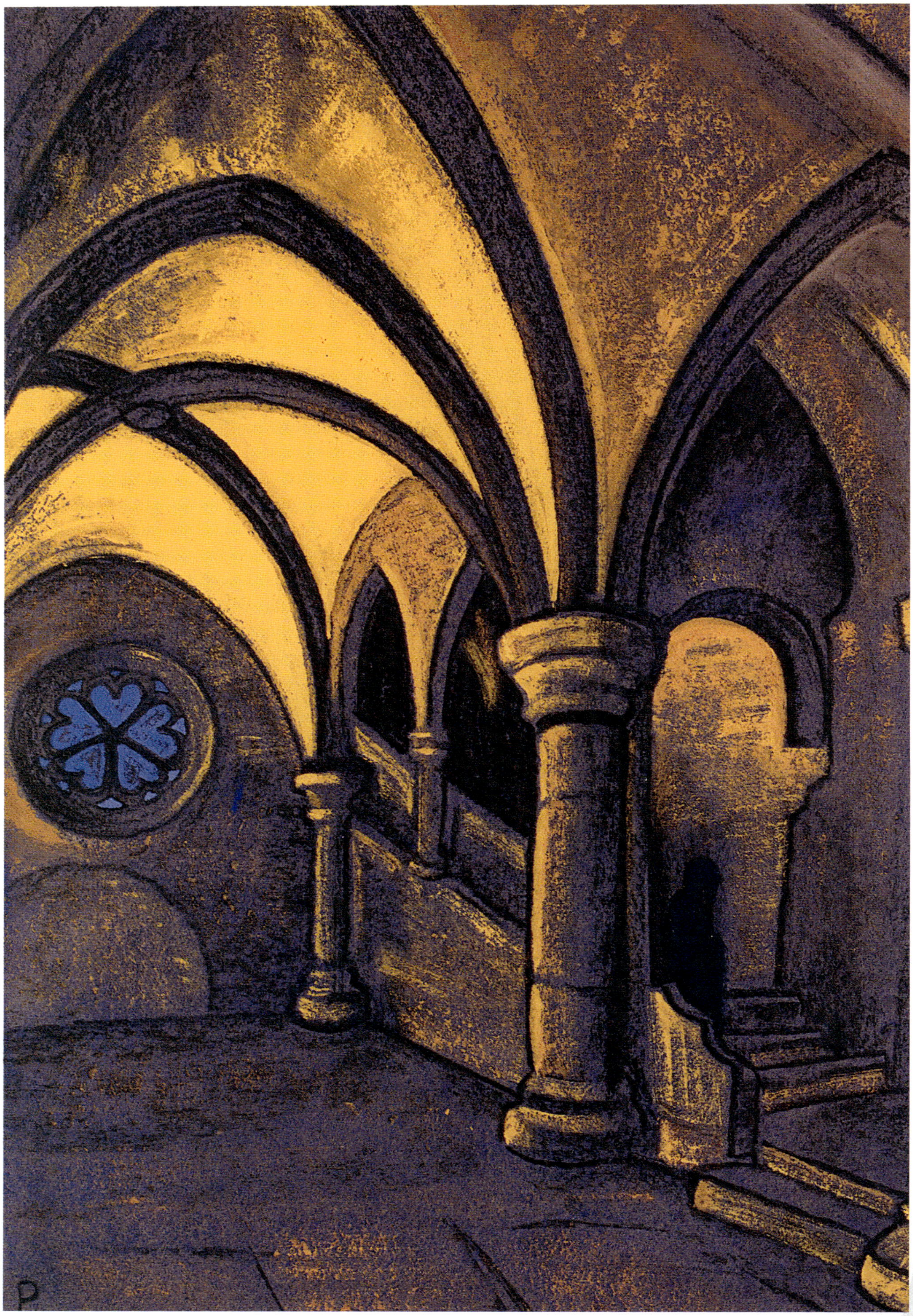

20

Maleine's Chamber

After his 1929 designs for the American production of *Le Sacre du Printemps,* Roerich was not involved in theatre for over a decade. Yet in the early nineteen thirties he reflected on his work for the Symbolist dramas of Maurice Maeterlinck, as in this painting, *Maleine's Chamber.* Though executed in Roerich's standard media for stage work – tempera on card – it was neither commissioned nor realized by a theatre. It may have been motivated by the 1931 conference for his international peace pact, convened in Bruges, where he had once met the Belgian playwright. (74)

In *Princess Maleine* Maeterlinck created a Shakespearean tragedy about a murderous and demented queen who victimizes the princess. Roerich had designed fourteen sets for Moscow's Svobodna (Free) Theatre in 1913, but they were never realized due to lack of funds. He conceived ominous entrances: receding arches in the castle gate, empty stairways and dungeon passages.(75) But this chamber for the princess, with its vaulted ceiling, is full of golden light, intensified by the blue of the circular window. Every detail expresses the purity and radiance of the princess.

Before the 1931 Bruges conference Roerich noted what an appropriate location this ancient city provided, possessing the kind of architectural monuments the pact was to protect. He said its chimes had inspired him and the composer who scored Maeterlinck's work, Maurice Steinberg: 'I am often reminded of the music of the opera, Princess Maleine, dedicated to me and based on the beneficent harmony of the bells of old Bruges.' (76) Reporting that Maeterlinck 'has responded most cordially to our pact,' Roerich reminisced: 'I heard that he very much approved of my sketches for *Princess Maleine, Sister Beatrice, Pelléas* and *Mélisande and The Blind,*' and added that those for Princess Maleine were 'scattered in many museums – Stockholm, Helsinki, Moscow, New York.' (77) Parmenia Migel Ekstrom, whose mother was US delegate, attended the second Belgian conference:

I can remember, when I was seventeen, going to Bruges in Belgium, to attend the Roerich Pact and Banner of Peace Conference in 1932. We arrived a day late and everything was finished, but they reconvened the conference so that my mother could take part. (78)

Maleine's Chamber, ca. 1931

Tempera on cardboard,
30 x 44.5 cm.
Nicholas Roerich Museum,
New York

'Every detail expresses...

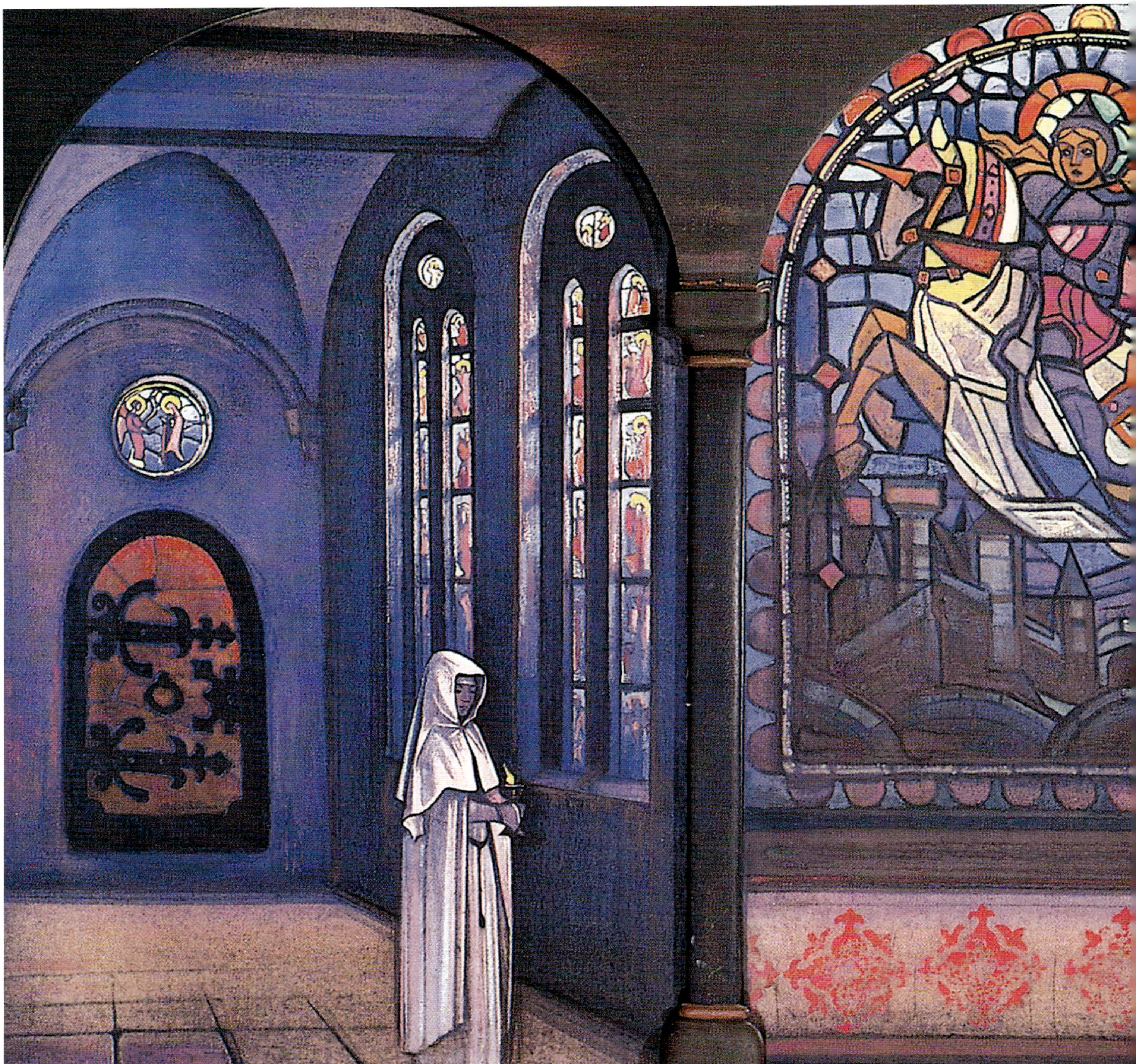

purity and radiance'.

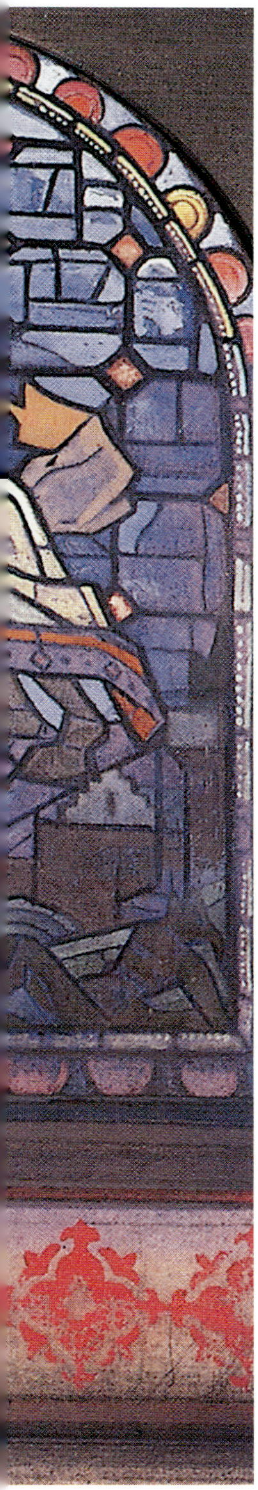

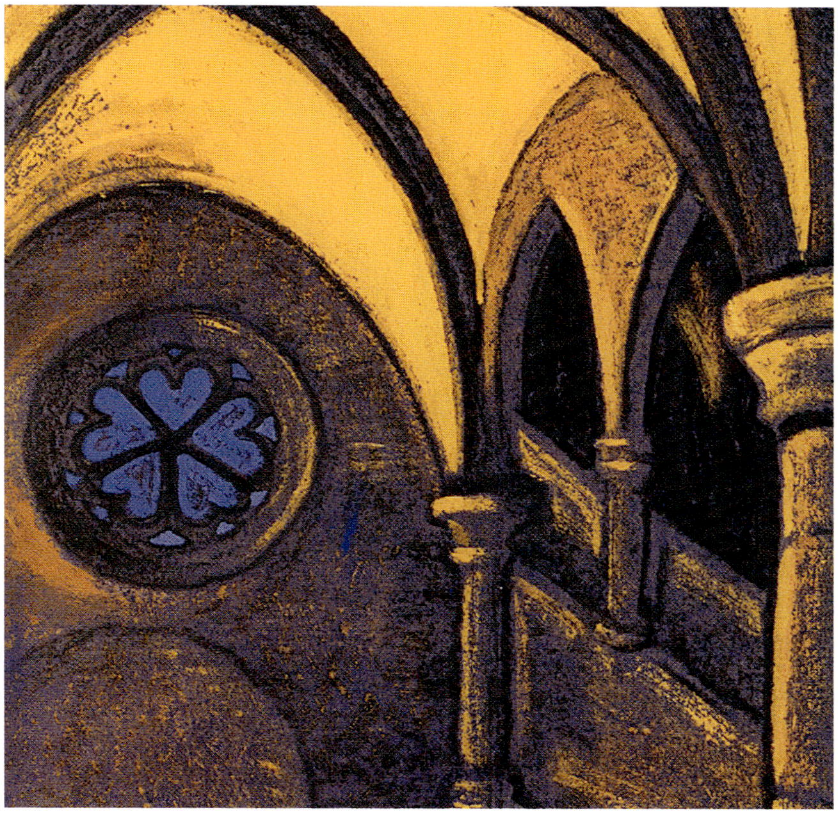

Maleine's Chamber, detail

Glory to the Hero, 1933

Tempera on canvas, 84 x 100 cm.
Nicholas Roerich Museum, New York

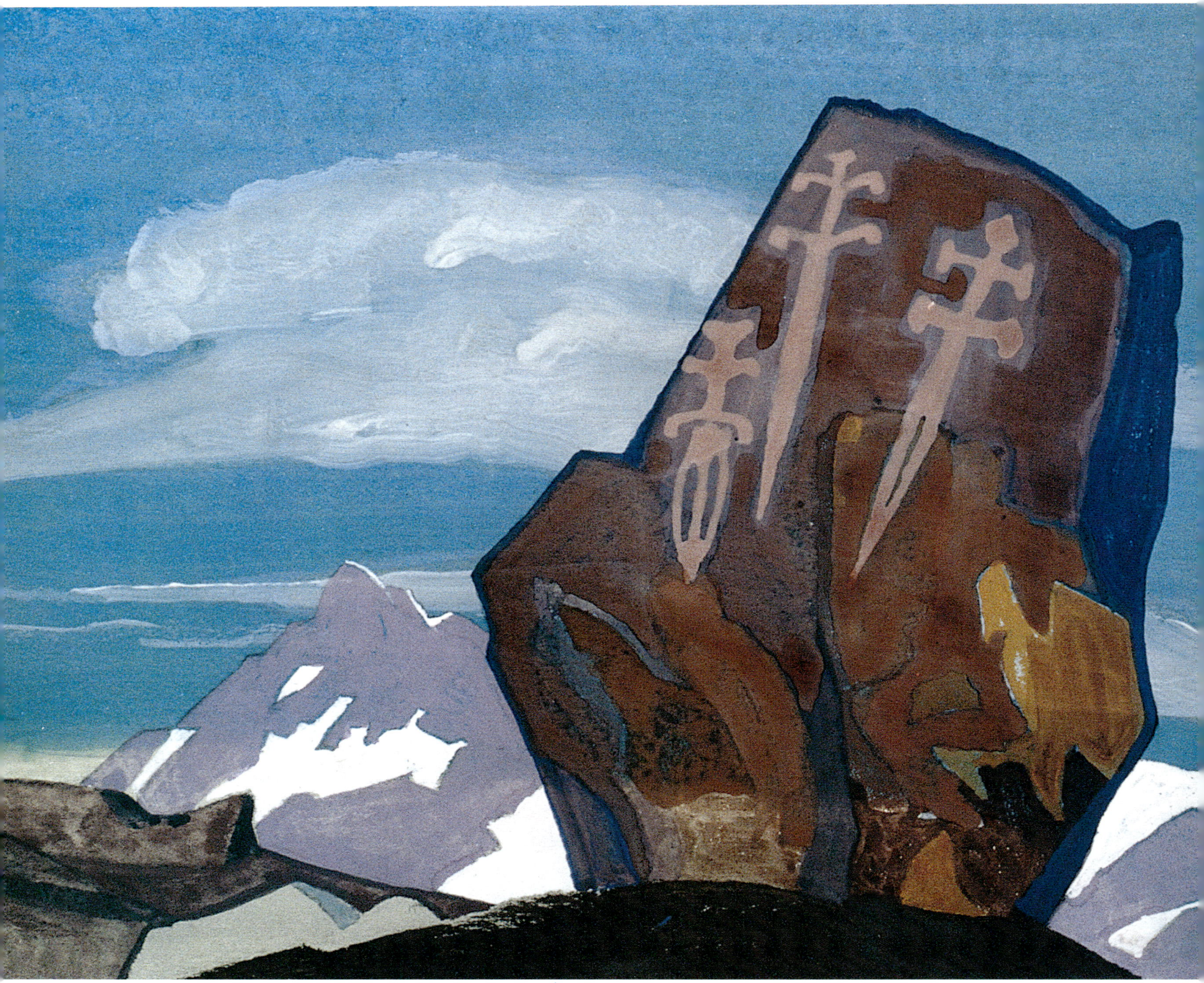

The Three Glaives, 1932

Tempera on cardboard, 36.8 x 27 cm.
Nicholas Roerich Museum, New York

21

The Three Glaives

The painting provides a close view of a large boulder carved with three glaives or archaic swords, each one with a different style of blade and hilt. Behind the boulder is a jagged brown ridge and a crevice with melting ice. In the further distance is a tall range of lilac mountains with residual snow on some of the peaks and slopes. The palette is warm, implying the approach of spring, with a soft blue sky and diaphanous clouds. Roerich executed this small canvas at Naggar in the Kulu Valley of north India, where he and his family established their home after the Central Asian expedition. It is a scene from his great journey, according to Sina Fosdick, who passed on Roerich's reminiscences of this mysterious stone seen in southern Tibet. To the people of that region, Roerich had told her:

> The swords represented the ancient prediction of three great wars that mankind might have to endure. Two of them would devastate the earth, but the third, if it should happen, would mark the end of humanity. (79)

She called *The Three Glaives* a prophetic painting, and it is clear that although the artist was outside Europe, he was acutely aware of the tensions developing there and the threat of hostilities among the major nations.

Given the fresh tones of the canvas, its brightness and sense of hope, Roerich can hardly be said to have created a doomsday painting. The apparent discrepancy between subject and treatment must be intentional from the hand of an artist so concerned about the state of the world. It was during this period that he had started his campaign, the *Roerich Pact* and *Banner of Peace,* which called for the protection of cultural artefacts during times of war. (80) It seems fair to conclude that he had faith in mans' ability to avert the ultimate disaster.

Further study of the painting reveals animal forms that may convey the idea of an inherent power guarding human destiny. At the base of the boulder are suggested several birds ready to defend and, in the sky, vaporous beasts race to meet the challenge. A larger variant of this work is also in the collection of the Nicholas Roerich Museum. Enigmatic stones incised with symbols had fascinated the artist since the time of his monumental canvas, *Treasure of the Angels,* of 1905. (81)

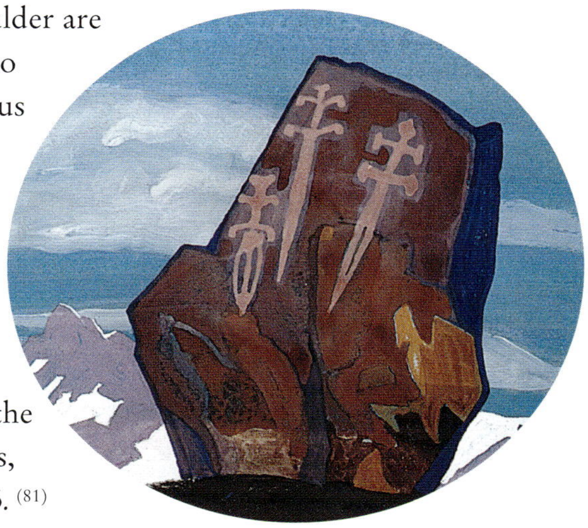

'Given the fresh tones of the canvas, its brightness and sense of hope, Roerich can hardly be said to have created a doomsday painting.'

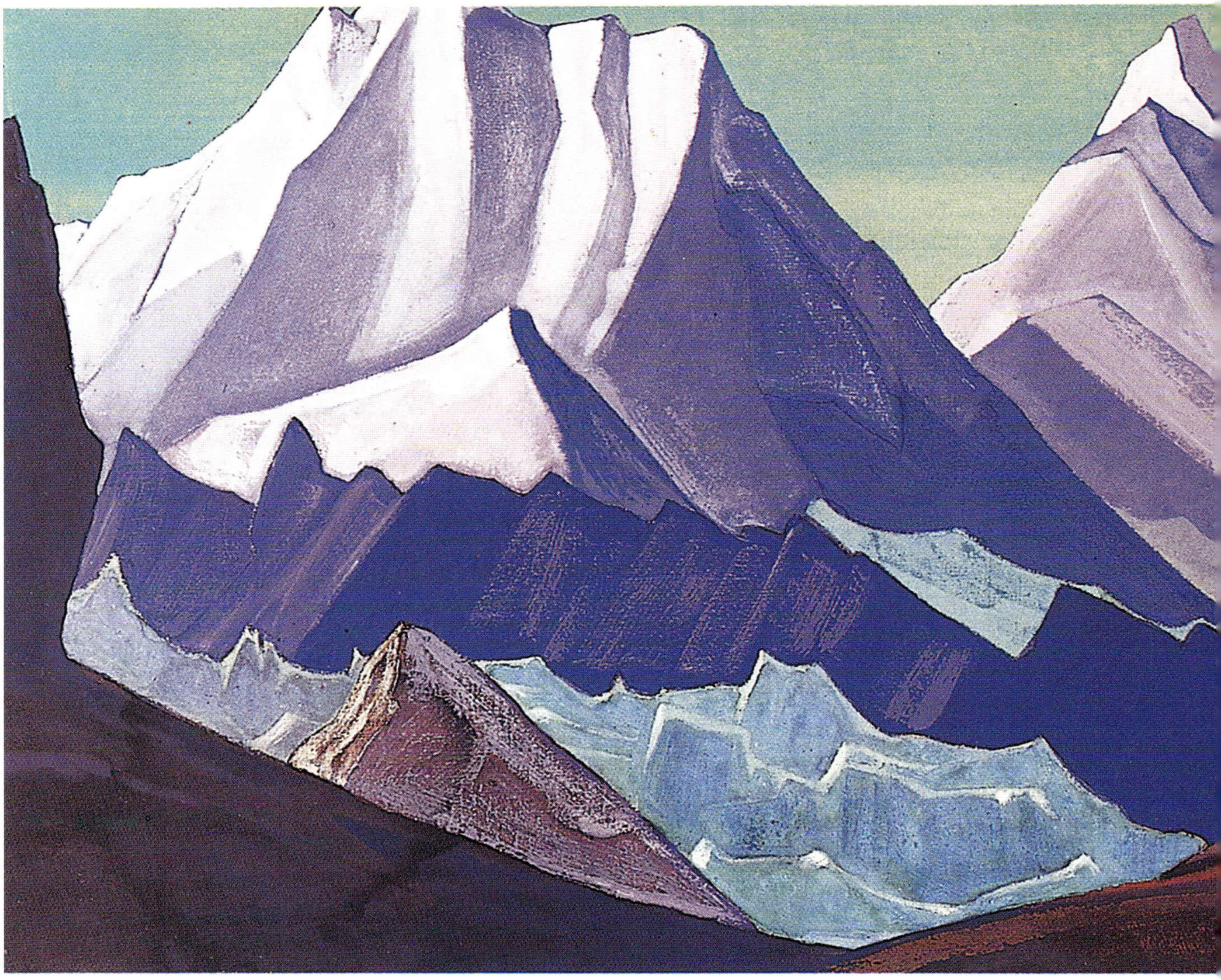

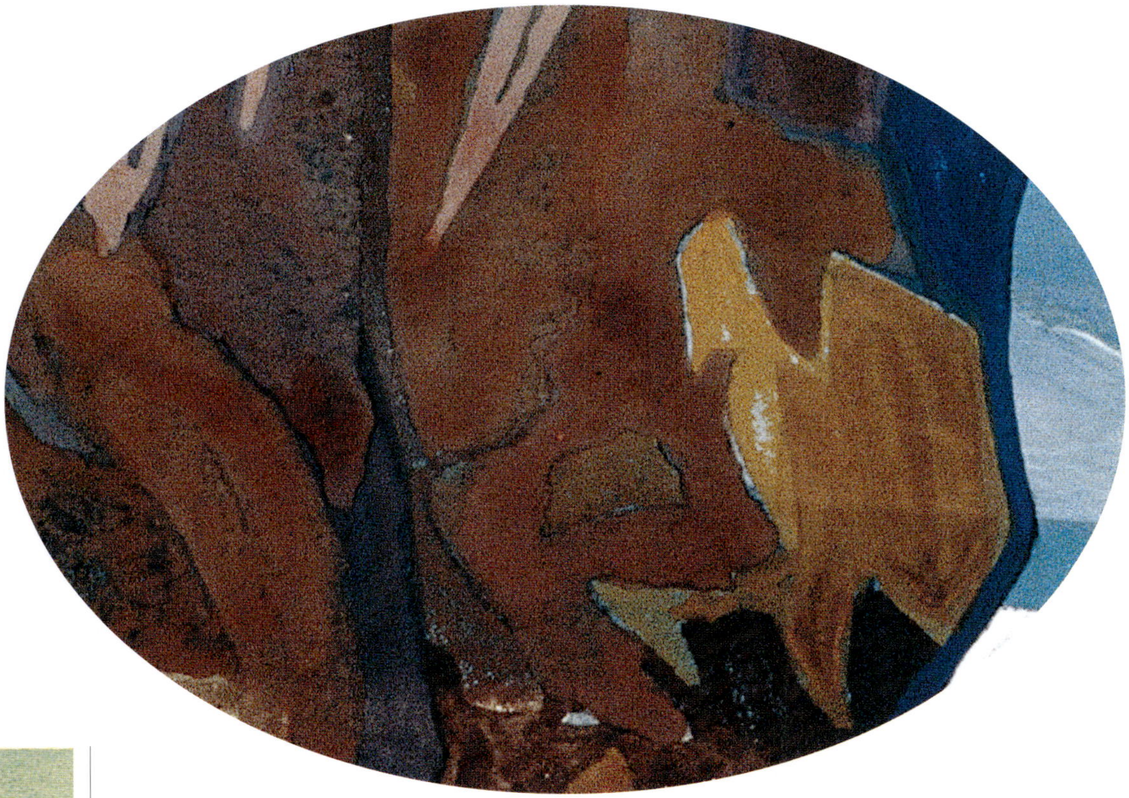

The Three Glaives, detail

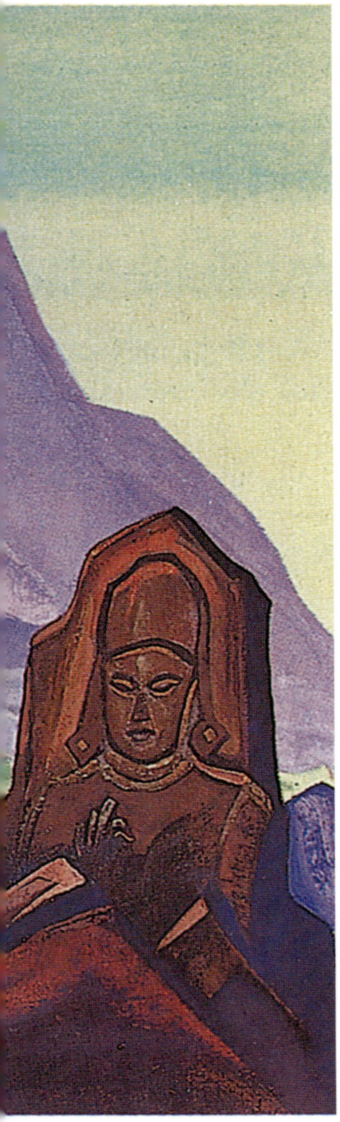

Maitreya, 1932

Tempera on canvas, 48.2 x 81.2 cm.
Museum of Oriental Art, Moscow

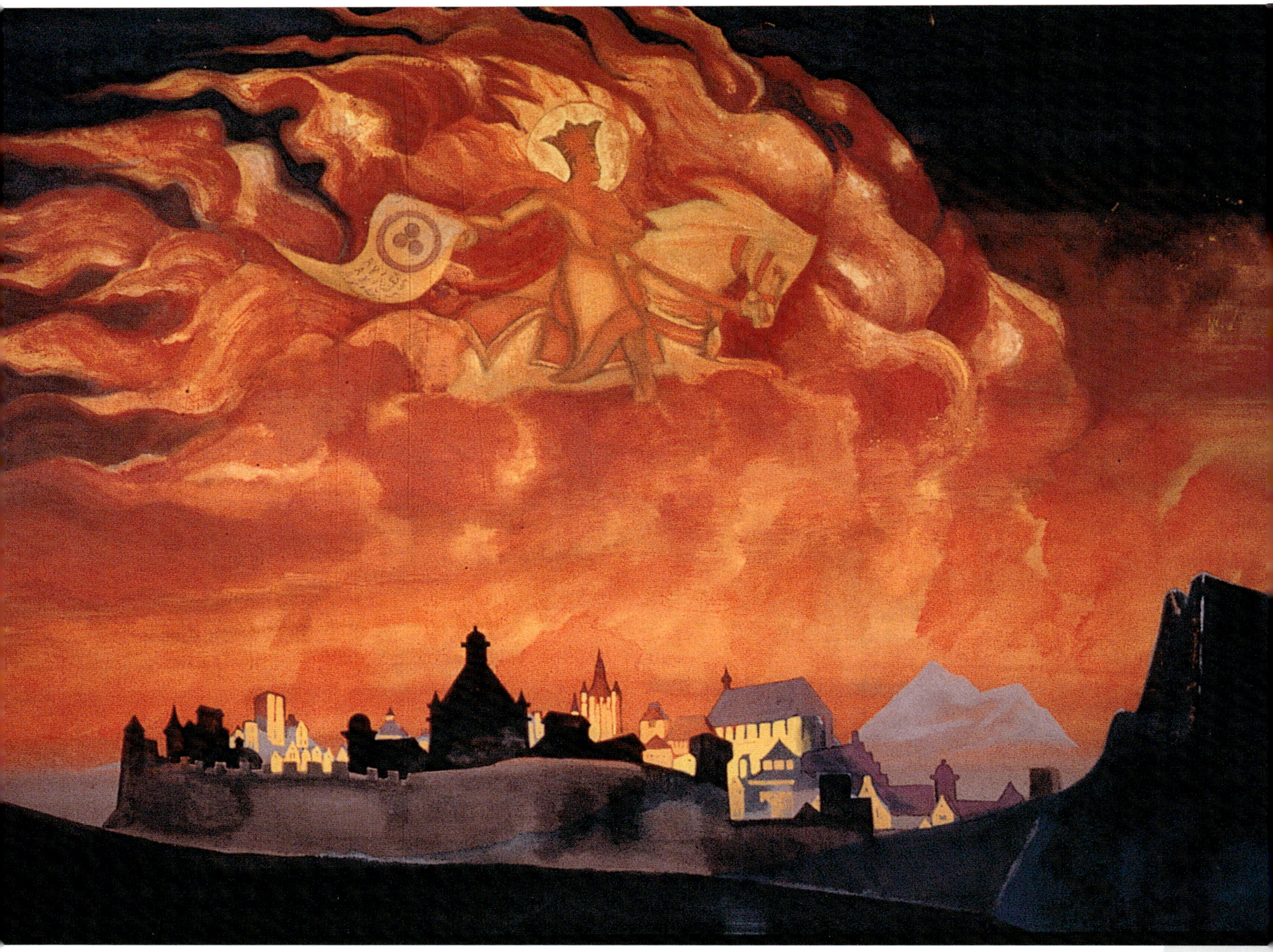

St Sophia - The Almighty's Wisdom, 1932

Tempera on canvas, 152 x 107 cm.
Nicholas Roerich Museum, New York

22 *St Sophia, The Almighty's Wisdom*

The year Roerich did this painting saw the consolidation of forces which, by the end of the decade, would erupt into World War II. In Germany the Nazis became the largest single party in the Reichstag, leading to Adolf Hitler's election the next year as chancellor with special dictatorial powers. Also in 1932 the British Union of Fascists was founded, as right wing movements grew throughout Europe. Meanwhile, in the United States, the liberal-minded Franklin D Roosevelt, who would become leader of the Allied powers during the war, began his first term as president.

At this critical time Roerich created the cautionary work, *St Sophia – The Almighty's Wisdom.* A rider on a white horse arcs through the sky in a cloud of flames so brilliant they illuminate facades in the city below. The varied national styles of architecture indicate that, rather than being a specific geographical location, this city is a synthesis of cultures endangered by the anticipated conflict. Wearing a three- pointed crown surrounded by a halo, the rider is an image of Sophia, not a female saint but an aspect of the Trinity. Roerich uses this most philosophical of Christian principles to symbolize the role of wisdom in counteracting the momentum of war. The rider carries the Banner of Peace with its ring enclosing three circles, which represent art, science and religion within the sphere of culture. [82] By articulating the need to protect what has been achieved in these fields – the treasures of human creativity – Roerich believed that man could offset the root causes of global conflict.

In this painting the artist seems to have created a companion piece to Arnold Böcklin's *La Guerre* from 1896, which shows four mythological figures as the horsemen of the apocalypse, riding through the smoke over a burning city. [83] While Böcklin focuses on destruction and the terrors of war, Roerich proposes acts and attitudes of prevention, depicting a messenger of peace over an international city as yet unharmed. Svetoslav Roerich confirmed that his father admired the work of Arnold Böcklin, the leading Swiss painter of the nineteenth century and a major Symbolist. [84] Having lived through World War I, and perhaps bearing in mind such prophecies as the Tibetan glaives, Roerich wished to use his art and his altruistic institutions as an antidote to those forces moving the world toward war in the thirties.

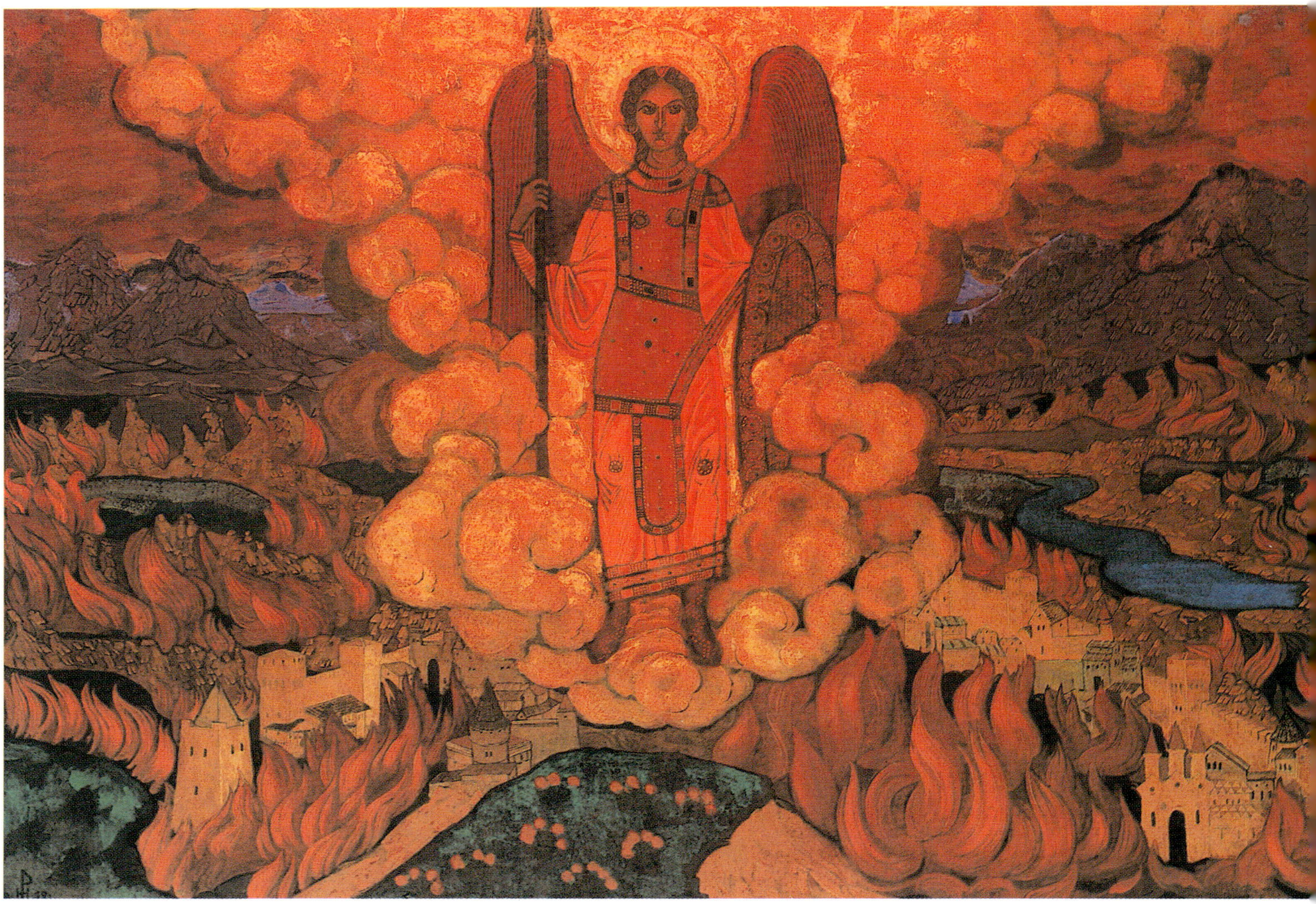

The Last Angel, 1912

Tempera on board, 52 x 99 cm.
Nicholas Roerich Museum, New York

St Sophia, The Almighty's Wisdom, detail

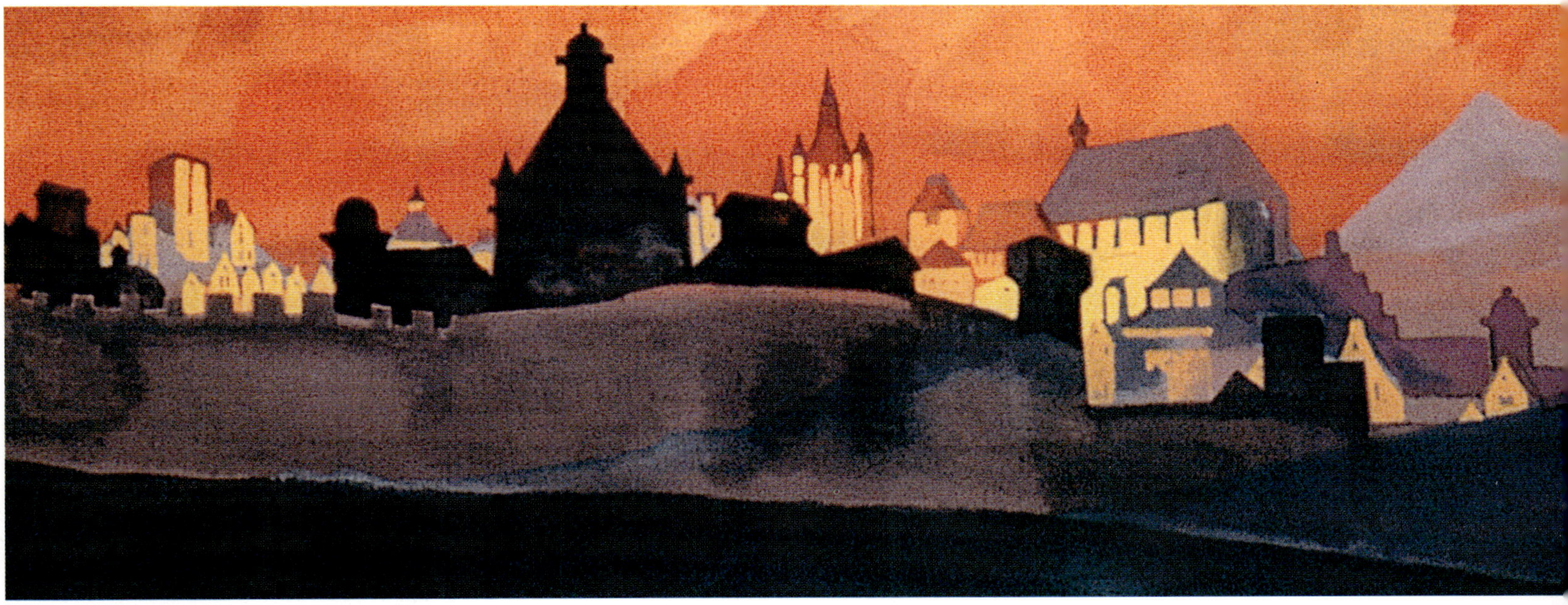

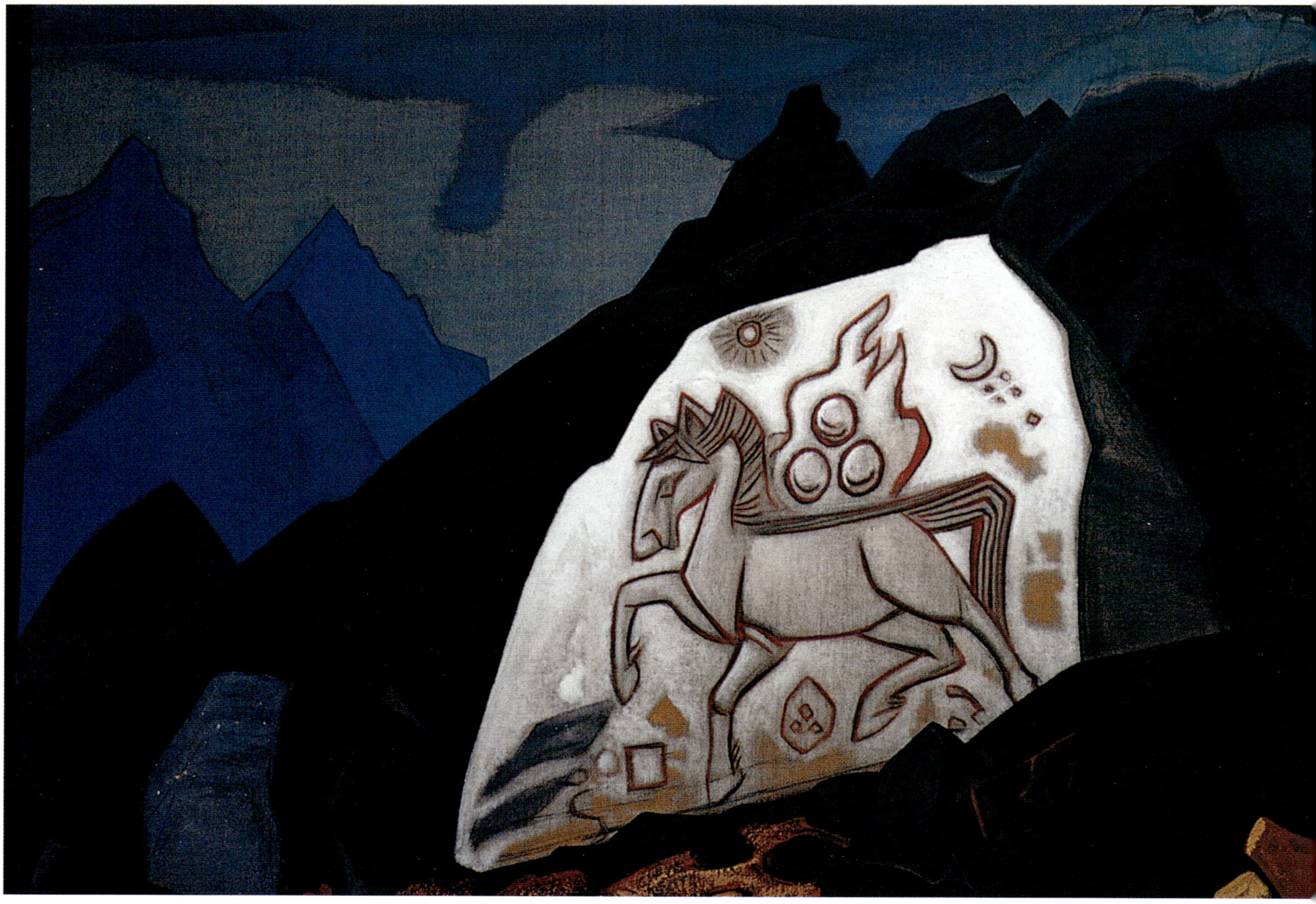

The White Stone, 1933

Tempera on canvas, 105.4 x 82.5 cm.
Nicholas Roerich Museum, New York

23 The White Stone

The painting features a large white boulder emblazoned with symbols: a moving horse bears on its back a sacred flame, which contains three globes. Around the horse are signs associated with transmutation – the sun, the moon with a cluster of stars, a circle, a square, serpentine lines, large green leaves and a six-sided shield with three diamonds. The background is a mountainscape in cool colours. Beneath the foreground boulder, inscribed with the Tibetan mantram *Om Mani Padme Hum,* the rocks seem to be on fire. *The White Stone* is alternatively called *Sign of Chintamani.* Another canvas, *Treasure of the World – Chintamani,* painted by the artist in 1924 on arrival in India, shows the horse with a flaming casket, said to contain a stone. (85)

The concept of Chintamani was documented by Helena Roerich in one of her published letters, which states that 'the east especially is full of legends about this gift, 'a stone fragment with beneficent powers. (86) Further details relate quite specifically to her husband's paintings. 'The white horse, Erdeni Mori, of Tibet and Mongolia,' she explains, 'carries Chintamani (the treasure of the world).' The stone is traditionally kept in a thirteenth century casket 'said to have been made from leather which had been in the possession of Solomon himself,' and 'many alchemic symbols are inscribed upon the leather,' similar perhaps to those in *The White Stone.*

The three globes recall the Banner of Peace emblem of Roerich's pact, for which he and his supporters campaigned from 1929, organizing committees in countries as disparate as France and Manchuria and setting up international conferences in Belgium, Uruquay and the United States. The pact was signed by 29 nations at the White House in Washington on Pan-American Day, 15 April, 1935, in the presence of President Roosevelt, who declared: 'This treaty possesses a spiritual significance far deeper than the text of the instrument itself.' (87) The Roerich Pact and Banner of Peace 'is really educational,' Svetoslav Roerich affirmed:

Father never thought that any kind of pact, or any kind of paper, could really limit mankind and safeguard its cultural treasures. It is educative to bring people slowly to a realization of the value of the world's works of art – the greater achievements, the better aspirations of mankind. (88)

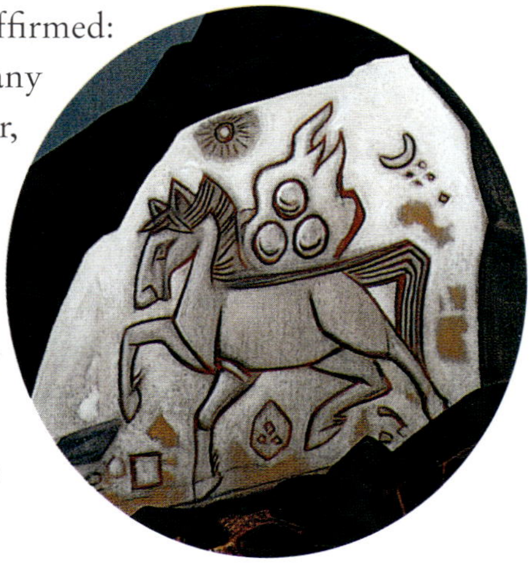

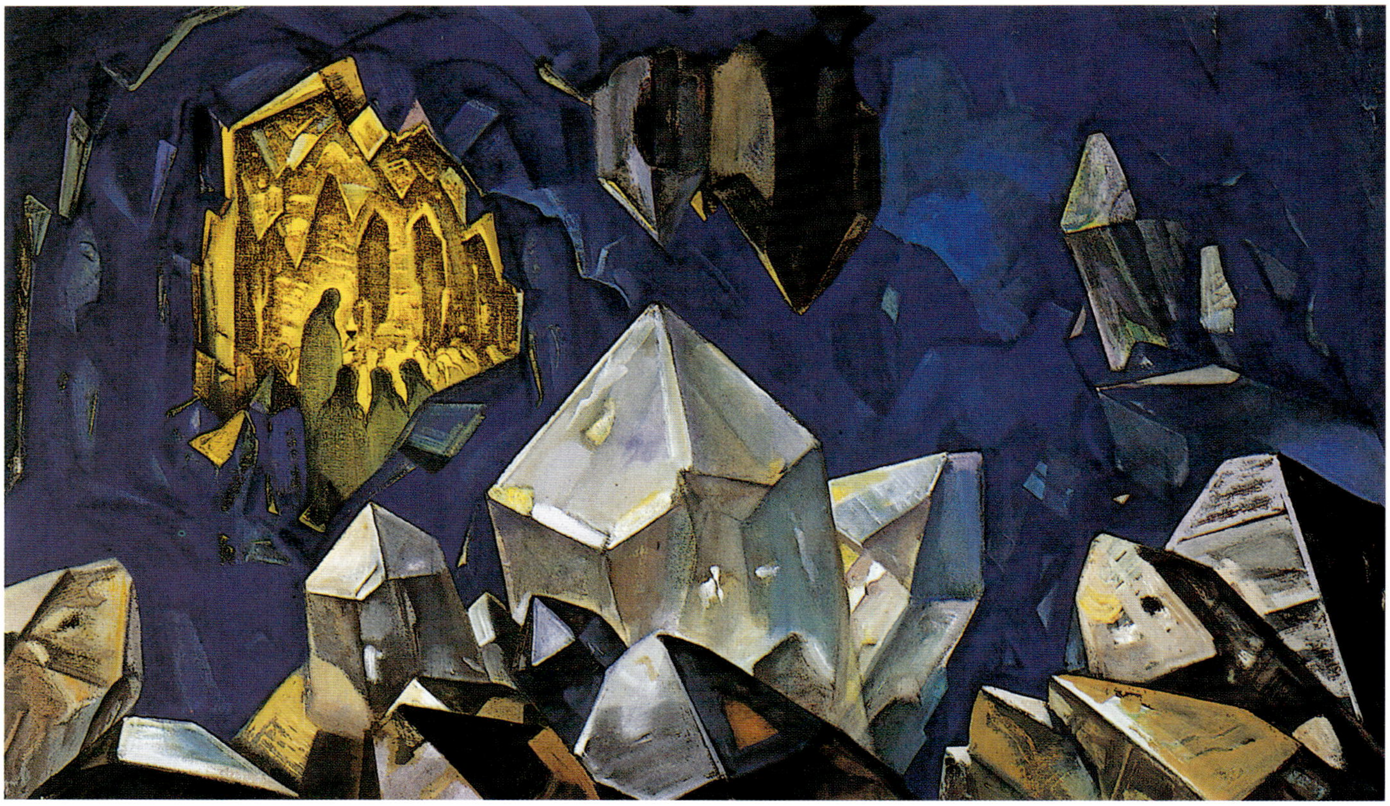

Treasure of the Mountain

Tempera on canvas, 73.6 x 117 cm.
Nicholas Roerich Museum, New York

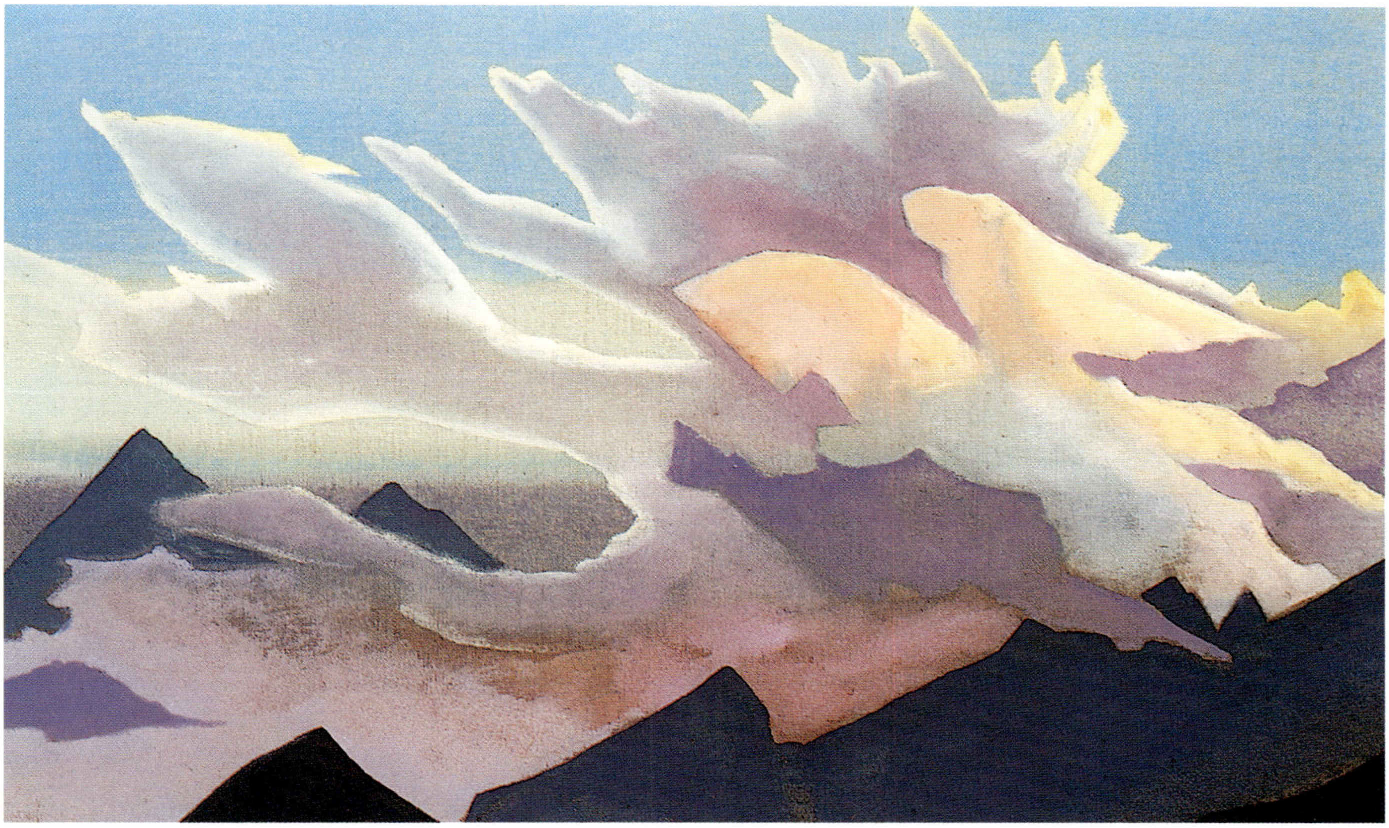

Warrior of Light, 1933

Tempera on canvas, 48.2 x 78.7 cm.
Stibbe Collection, Greenwich, Connecticut

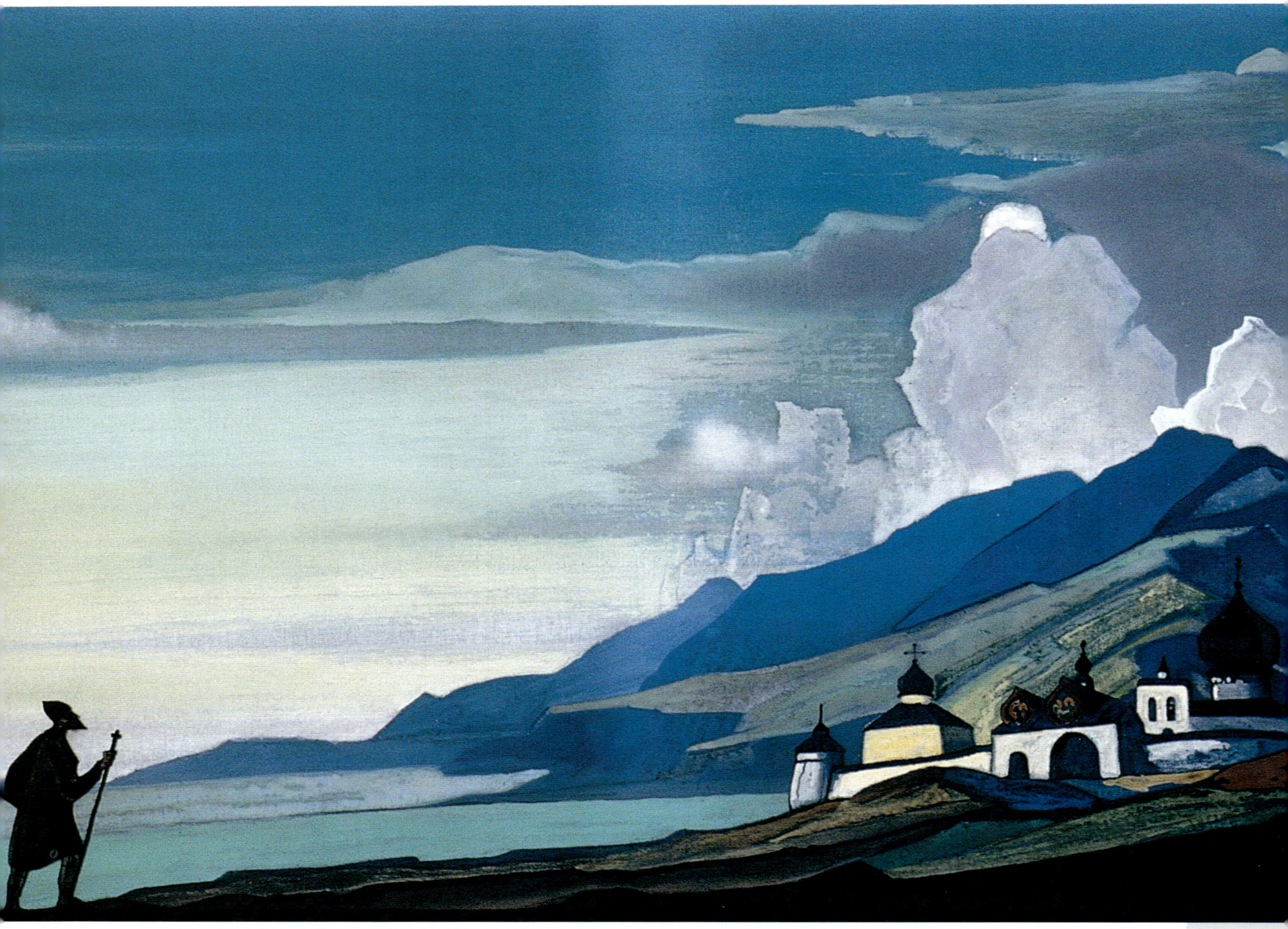

Wanderer from the Resplendent City, 1933

Tempera on canvas, 97 x 62 cm.
Nicholas Roerich Museum, New York

24 *Wanderer from the Resplendent City*

A traveller with a pack and a staff surmounted by a cross walks along the shoreline toward a monastery. The tilt of his head, accentuated by the sharp angles of his hat and beard, indicate that his line of vision has risen above the cupolas and distant hills to the towering white clouds. The rapt attention signalled by his posture suggests the clouds convey a vision to him, perhaps some revelation from his pilgrimage. A diminutive figure, he is seen in silhouette against the horizontal bands of colour – soft greens, yellows and blues – that give the landscape a sense of boundless space. The composition encourages the viewer to wonder how far this man has journeyed and to speculate on what he has experienced.

Sina Fosdick, referring to her conversations with the artist, said that 'the wanderer, who has been to the resplendent city, has come back to tell everyone about it,' and she observed, pensively, that 'his profile resembles Professor Roerich.' (89) This painting draws upon the cultural archetype of the wanderer, which Chloe Obolensky illustrates in her book, *The Russian Empire*, with a photograph from around 1870. His hat, beard, bag and stick are the accoutrements which identify the wanderer in this canvas and in many works of art and literature. Commenting on the photograph, Obolensky summarizes the archetypal tradition:

> A striking feature of Russia's religious life, which stemmed from the Middle Ages and survived even the 1917 Revolution, were the pilgrims who walked from shrine to shrine within the country or journeyed to distant holy places, such as Palestine or Mount Athos. The Church housed them in special hostels and blessed them as they set out on their way. (90)

Some wanderers came from the ranks of the Old Believers. Excommunicated in the seventeenth century for rejecting Archbishop Nikon's return to Greek liturgy, the Old Believers became a Christian sect outside Orthodoxy. Many migrated to the Altai mountains in Siberia. During the Central Asian expedition, a lama spoke to Roerich about the resplendent city that stimulated certain of their pilgrimages: 'I can tell you how, from distant Altai, many Old Believers went to seek for the so-called Belavodye (White Waters) and never returned.' (91) But Roerich came back to tell the tale.

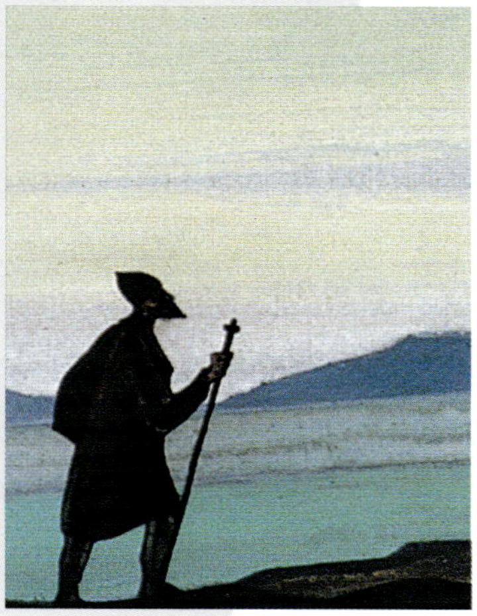

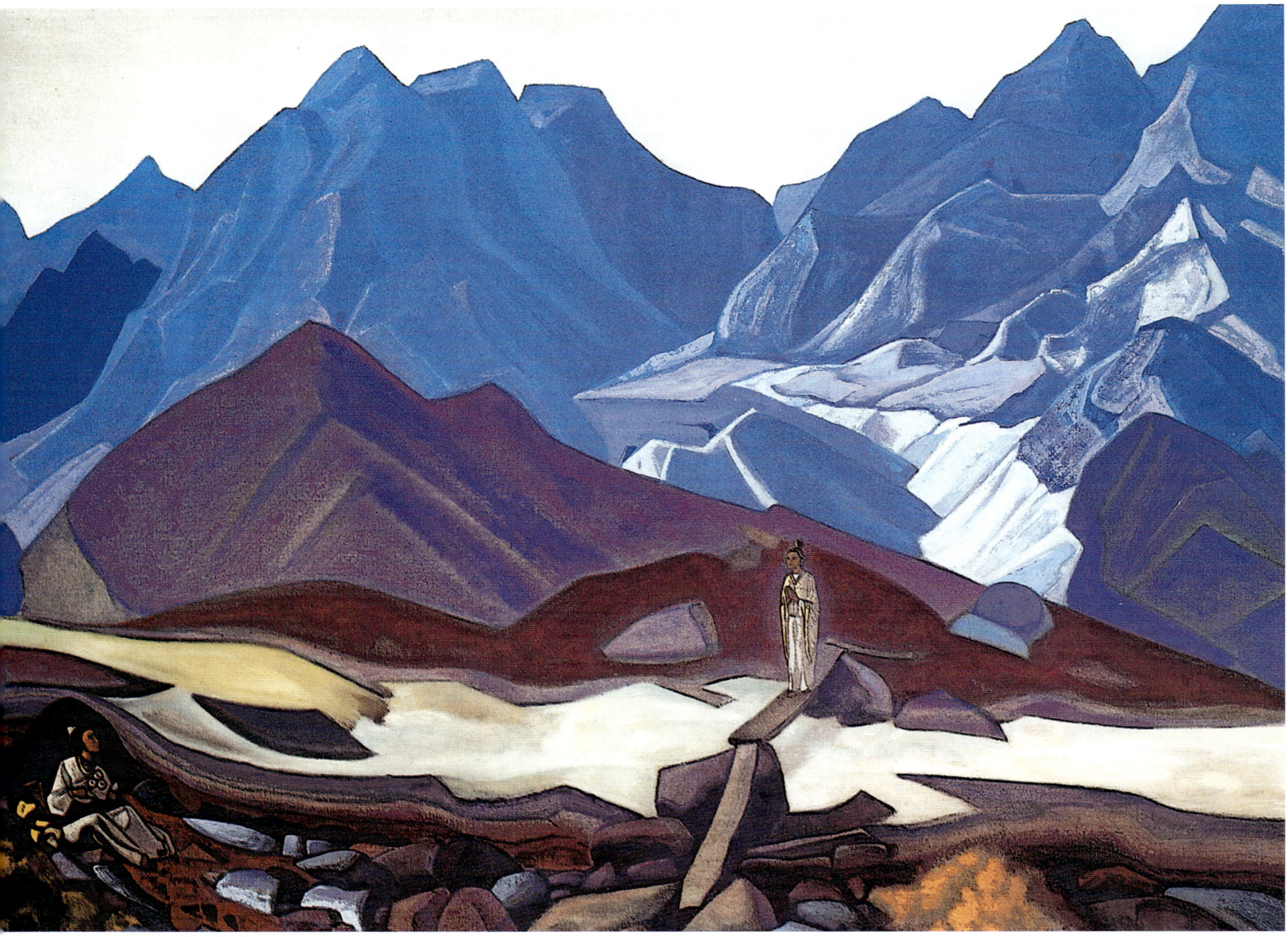

From Beyond, 1936

Tempera on canvas, 104 x 134.6 cm.
Nicholas Roerich Museum, New York

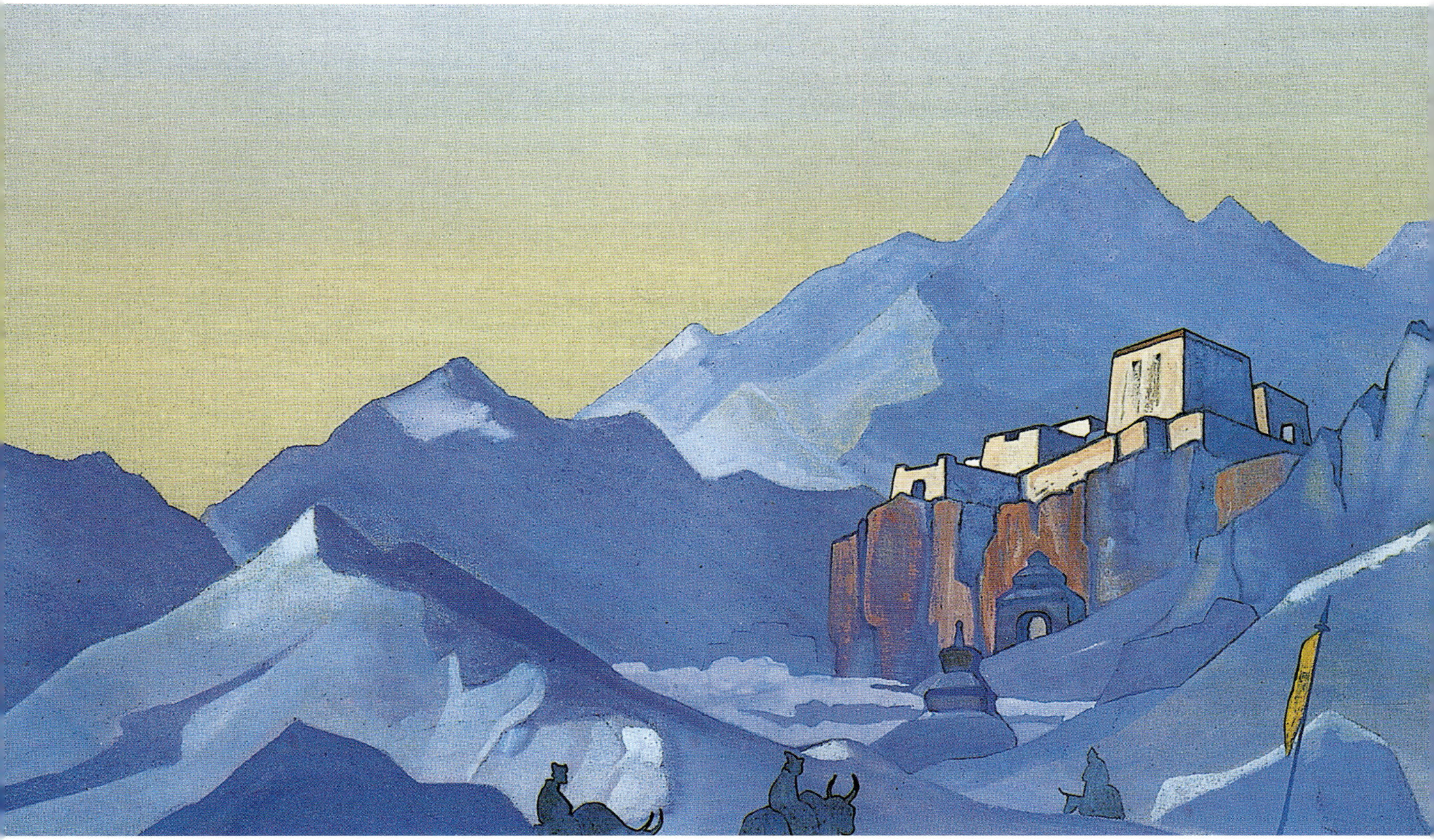

Path to Kailas, 1932

Tempera on canvas, 46.2 x 79.3 cm.
Nicholas Roerich Museum, New York

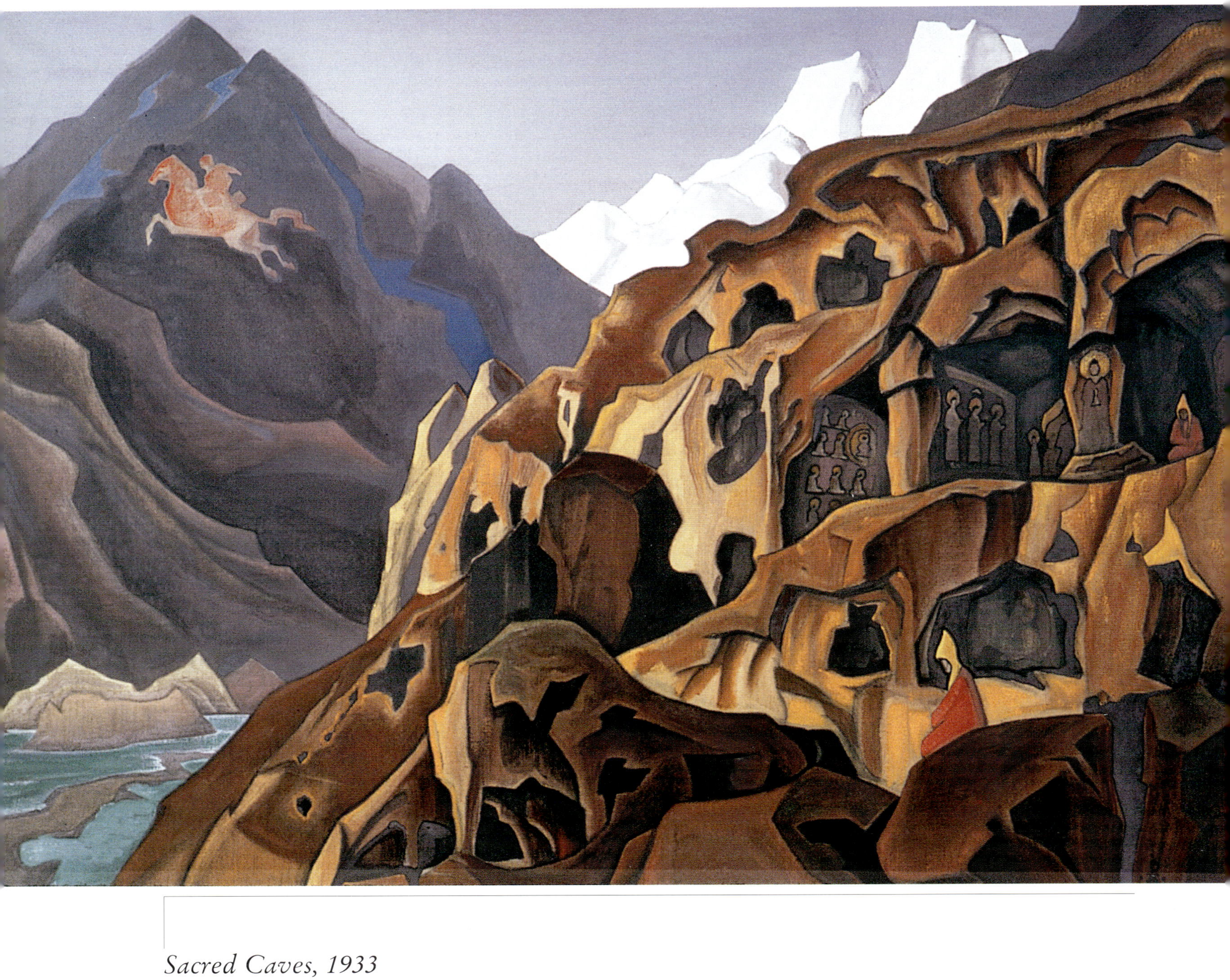

Sacred Caves, 1933

Tempera on canvas, 153 x 107 cm.
Nicholas Roerich Museum, New York

25 *Sacred Caves*

During his expedition Roerich recorded in his journal the experience of coming upon painted caves near Khotan in October 1925 and Kashgar in March 1926. Very high up in the sandy rocks, something is silhouetted. We have no doubt that these are openings of old Buddhist caves. And so it is. Some of them are outlined very high and the entrances to them are crumbled. But three caves are on a low slope. (92)

The condition of the cave frescoes documented not only the ravages of nature but also the cultural conflicts of the region, when Buddhism was superceded by Islam:

The ceilings and the walls are pretty well gone. Of course it is the Moslems who have destroyed the images they hate. Near the ground a little below are still seen the remnants of ornaments, covered over with Turki inscriptions. (93)

In this March journal entry Roerich also mentions that 'the caves face the east,' and he imagines the outlook for the Buddhists who meditated there: 'Before the eyes of the hermits spread the broad mountain view – a good and beautiful place.' (94)

Both entries describe features which appear in two paintings on the subject: *The Power of the Caves,* dated 1925, one of seven canvases in his *Signs of Maitrey,* a series which Roerich presented to cultural officials when he was in Moscow in 1926; and this later variant *Sacred Caves,* which he painted in his studio at Naggar in the Kulu Valley. (95) The composition of the two paintings is almost identical. Lamas in yellow hats and red robes are meditating in front of the caves. The terraced rock face of the mountain and the rugged cave entrances are thrown into relief by the morning sun. On the distant mountainside is the figure of a horse and rider, red in the 1925 painting and white in the one from 1933. This image is used in various Asian religions to signify the coming of an avatar, a new spiritual teacher for mankind. Buddhists use the name, Maitreya, Hindus, the Kalki Avatar; Muslims, the Imam Mahdi. Svetoslav Roerich, discussing his father's multicultural approach and understanding of comparative religion, said that, to him, Buddhism 'was most important, but at the same time every philosophy had a place in his thinking.' (96)

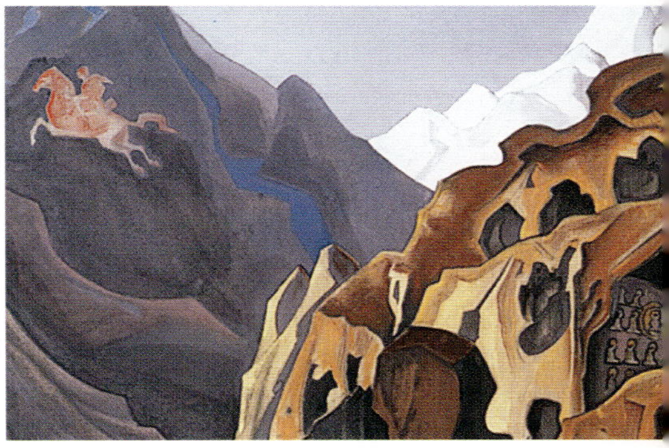

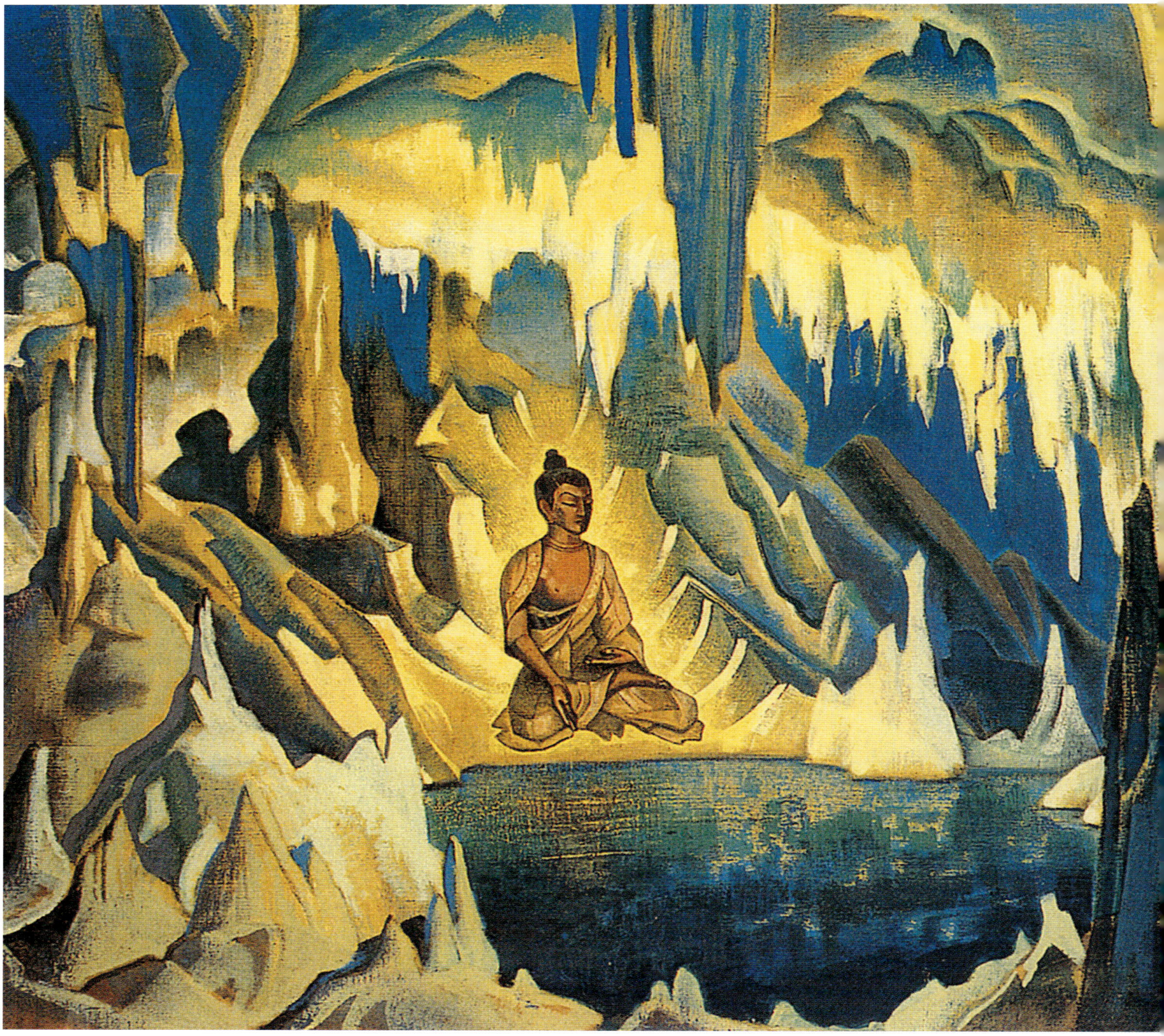

Buddha the Conqueror, 1925

Tempera on cardboard.
Nicholas Roerich Museum, New York

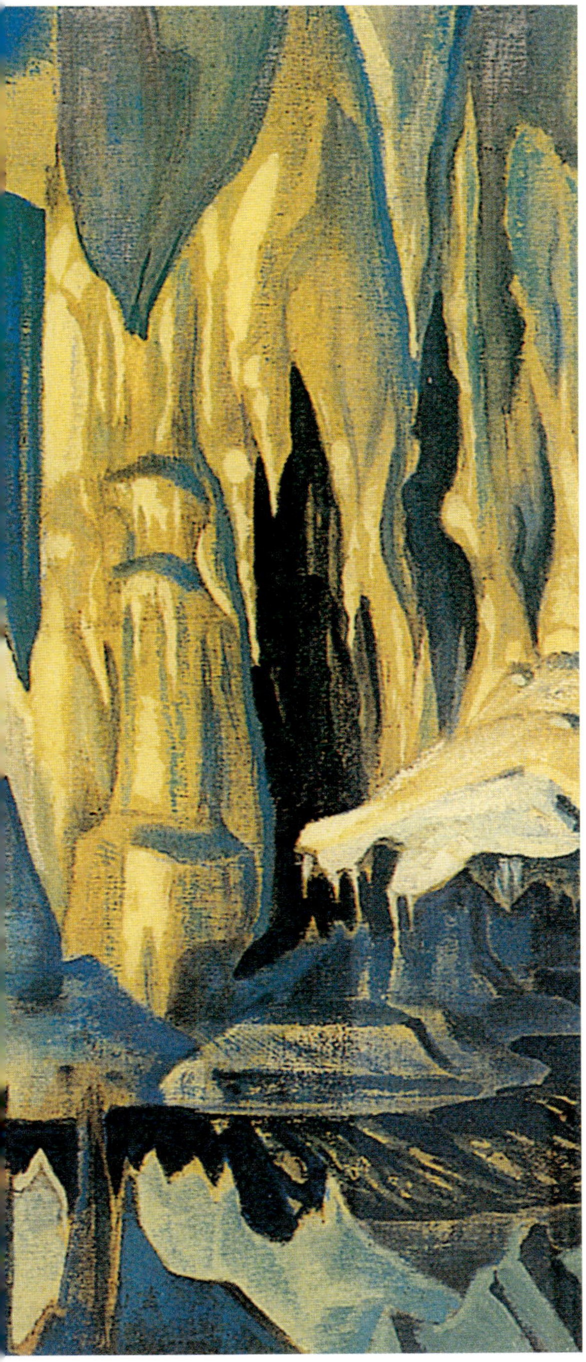

'During his expedition Roerich recorded in his journal the experience of coming upon painted caves.'

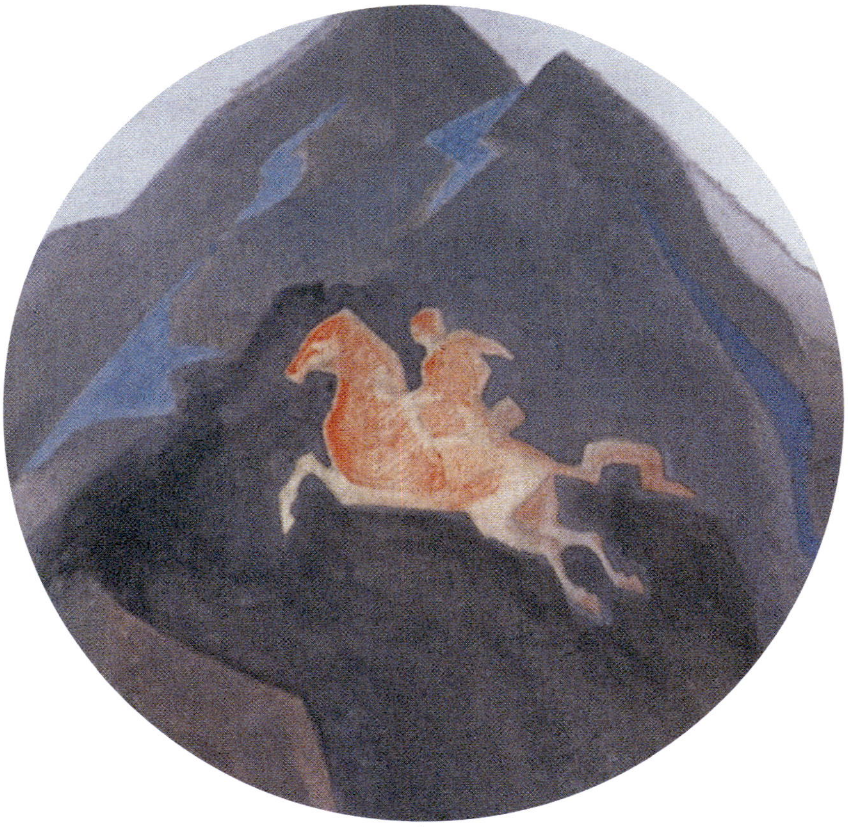

Sacred Caves, detail

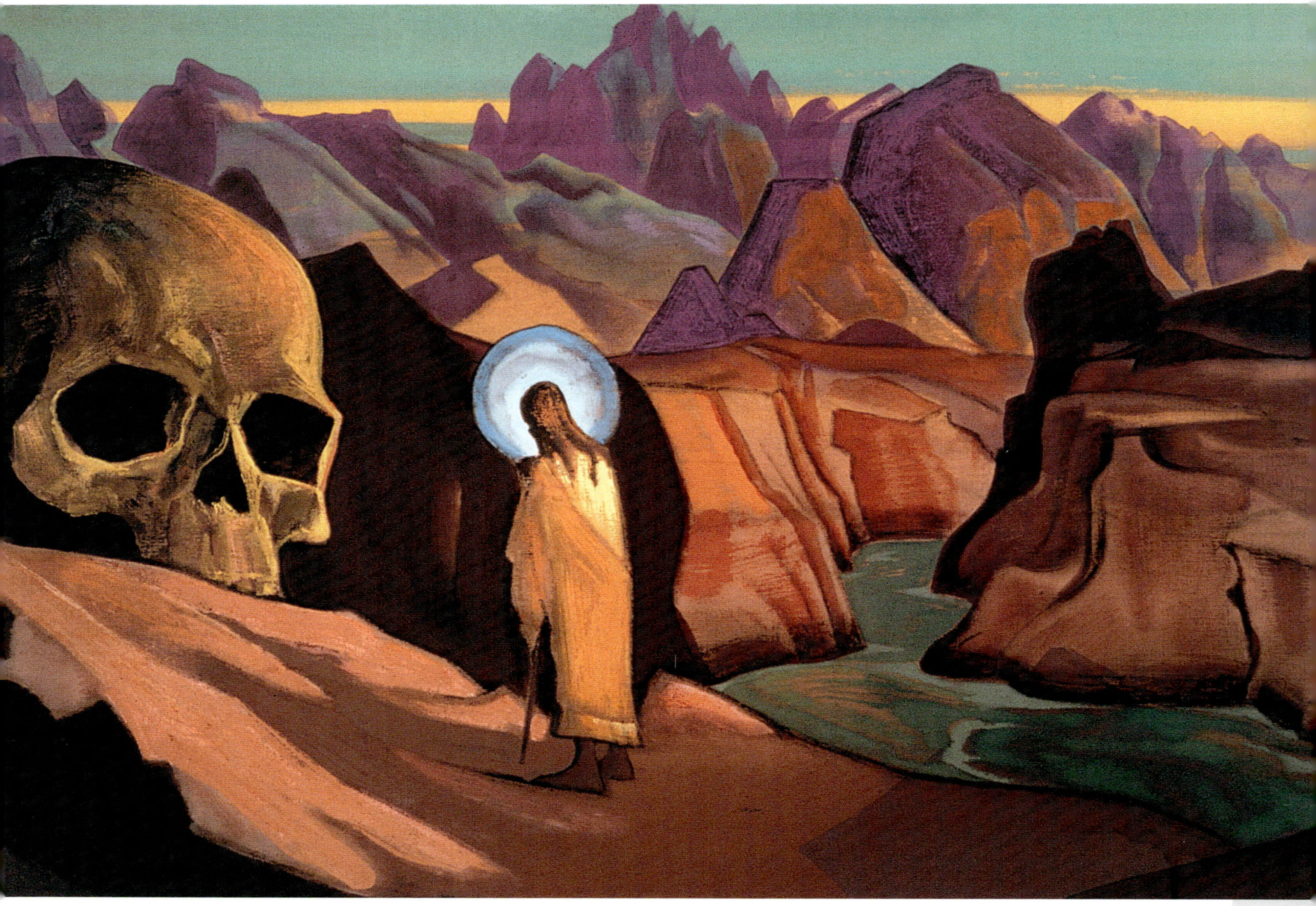

Issa and the Skull of the Giant, 1933

Tempera on canvas, 120.6 x 76.2 cm.
Nicholas Roerich Museum, New York

26 *Issa and the Skull of the Giant*

In *Tradition and the Individual Talent*, T S Eliot defined the modern idea of cultural legacy, arguing that master artists do not just use the past but authenticate it through transformation of its resources in the present. [97] Svetoslav Roerich made the same point about his father's integration of artistic influences. Among the French painters Roerich valued, apart from Gauguin, were Gustave Moreau, in whose studio the artist had hoped to enroll in 1900; Fernand Cormon, with whom he did study; and Pierre Puvis de Chavannes, whom Roerich listed among his key teachers, along with Kuindzhi and Cormon. Another specific inspiration was the Symbolist painting of Odilon Redon, which Roerich admired, as his son explained, for its decorative and evocative qualities. [98] Roerich shared with Redon and many artists of their time a high regard for the Japanese print, particularly its dramatic composition and mystery.

A convention of art in Japan, sometimes disconcerting to western eyes, is disproportionate imagery. For example, nineteenth century artist Katsushika Hokusai contrasted mortals with supernaturals rendered as huge disembodied heads, as in *The Murdered Kasane Appears to the Monk Yuten* and *The Sea Monk*. [99] Roerich recast this convention to convey the magnitude of certain spiritual figures. *Dream of the Orient* (1920) shows a massive head meditating over a landscape; *Padma Sambhava* (1924) and *Dorje the Daring One* (1940) use similar distortions. (100)

In *Issa and the Skull of the Giant* Roerich portrays Jesus Christ in the standard iconography of long dark hair, white robe, halo and staff, but the setting is Central Asian. Christ stands before a skull the size of a boulder – an allegory for the remains of a great teaching he must restore to mankind. In 1925 Roerich recorded legends of Jesus after the crucifixion teaching in the east where he was known as Issa:

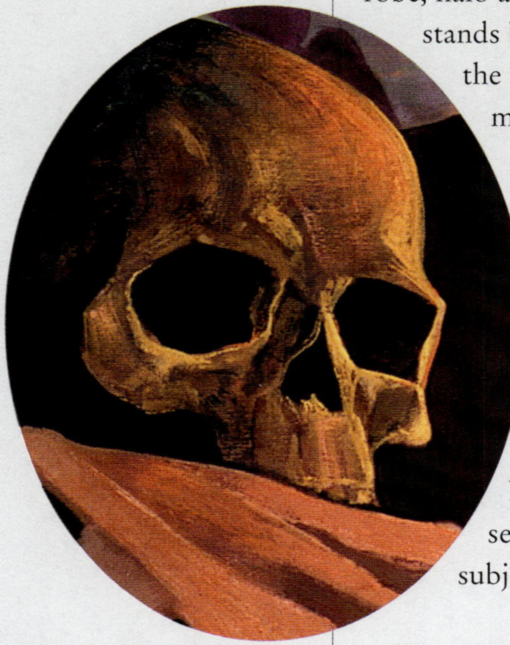

> One might wonder what relation Moslems, Hindus or Buddhists have with Issa. But it is still more significant to see how vital are great ideas and how they penetrate even the most remote places. Never may one discover the source of such legends. But even if they originated from ancient Nestorian Apocrypha at present it is instructive to see the widespread and deep consideration paid to the subject. [101]

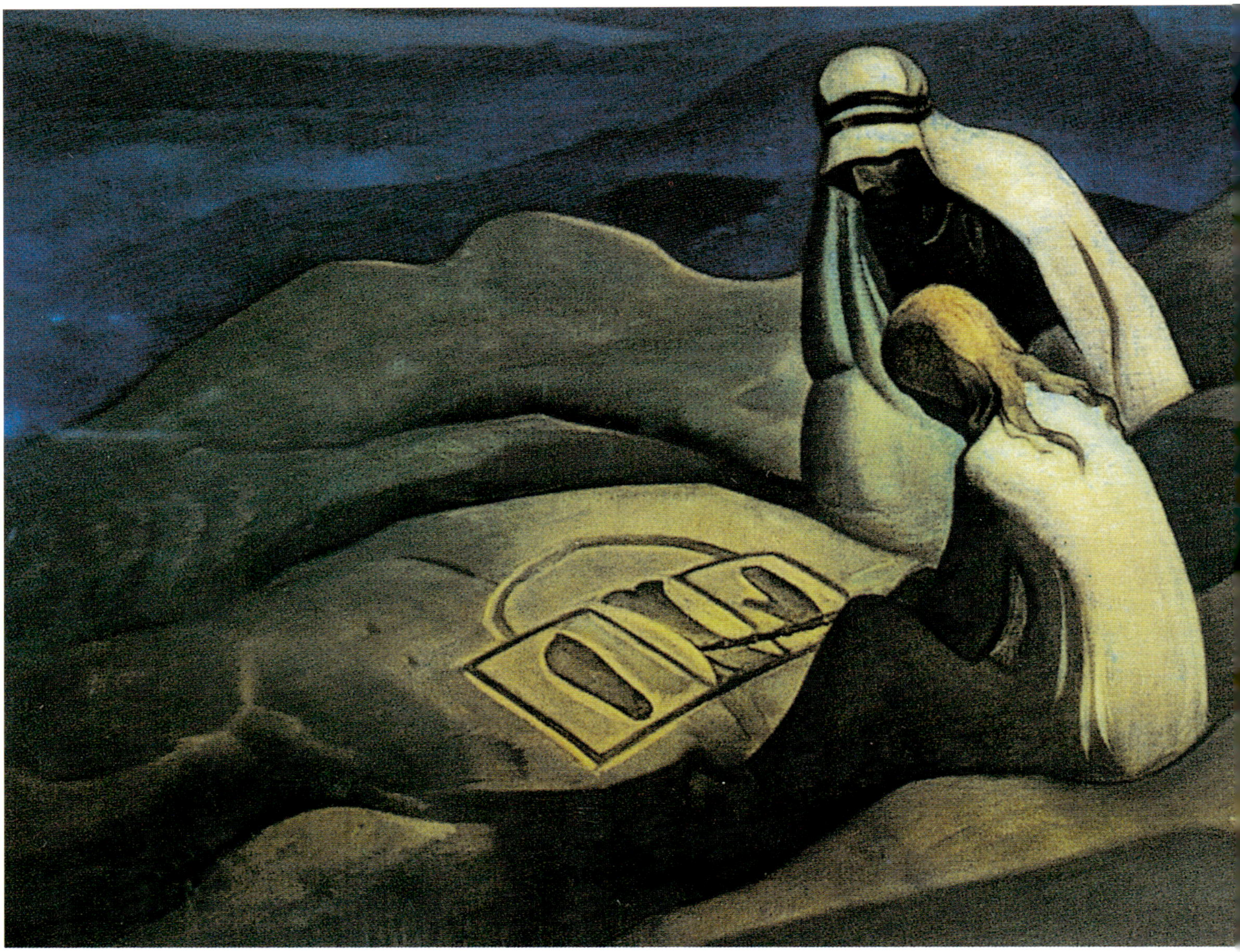

Signs of Christ

Nicholas Roerich Museum, New York

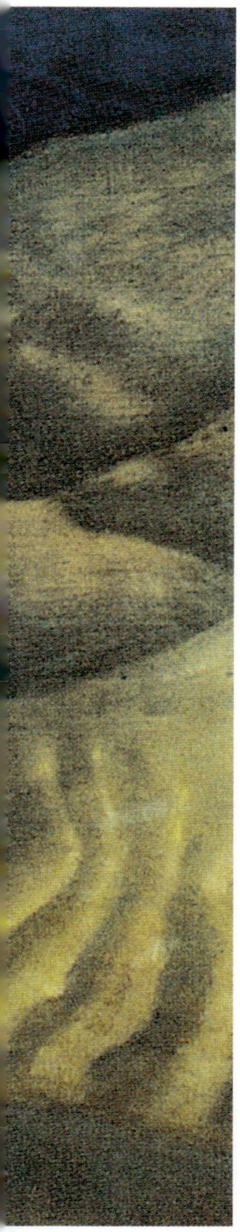

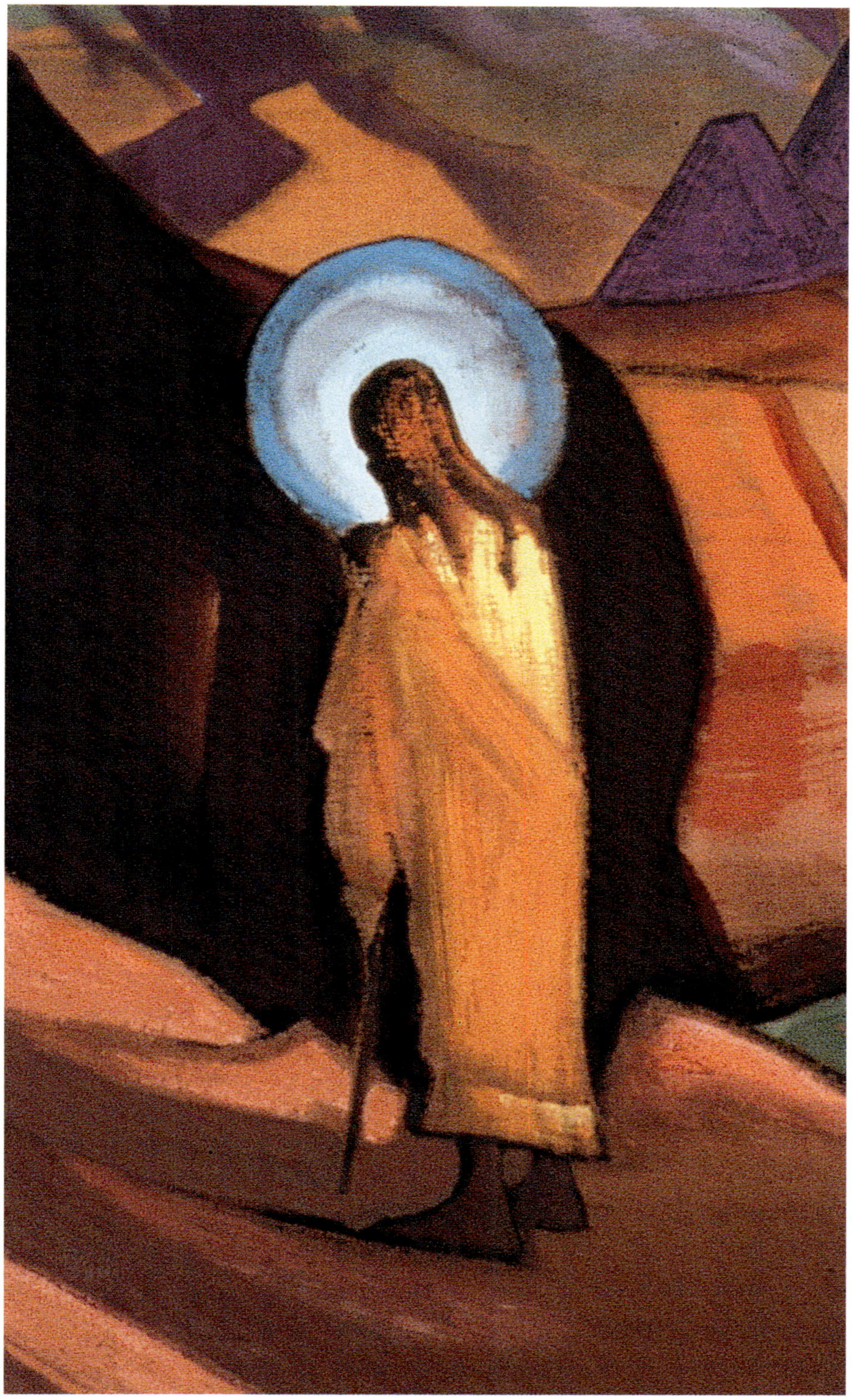

Issa and the Skull of the Giant, detail

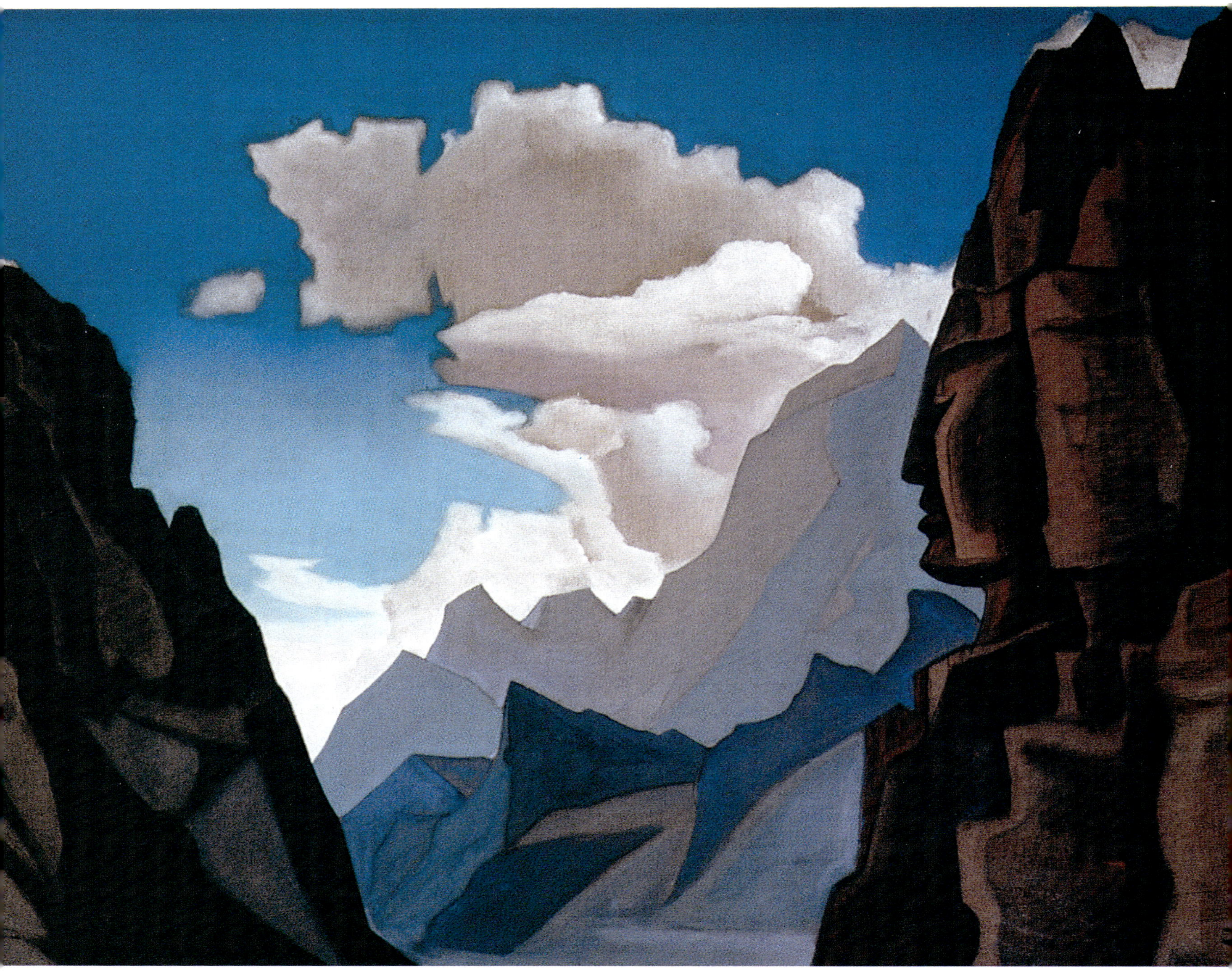

Great Spirit of the Himalayas, 1934

Tempera on canvas, 105.4 x 86.4 cm.
Nicholas Roerich Museum, New York

27 *Great Spirit of the Himalayas*

Roerich had several approaches to mountainscapes. At home in the Kulu Valley he was surrounded by the Himalayas and could paint directly from nature. Also, after the expedition, he had sketches and photographs which helped him depict from memory mountain regions he had visited. But, as a Symbolist, he rendered many subjects from his imagination, including mountains which did not exist except as configurations of his inner life. This last approach is exemplified by *The Great Spirit of the Himalayas,* a tribute to Buddhism. The canvas counterposes two steep mountains, their sharply faceted sides highlighted by white clouds and the blue of distant peaks and sky. The mountain on the right suggests a lama in a pointed hat, with the sun casting red and yellow light on his profile. The mountain on the left reveals another face, this one upside down, a black-hatted sorcerer. Roerich may be illustrating the struggle he witnessed in Tibet between Buddhism and the old Bon-po:

In addition to the . . . Red-Cap sect of Padma Sambhava, and many other branches, the Bon-po or Black Faith, is also spread considerably in Tibet. . . . The Bon-po say that the Buddhists are their enemies. . . . ceremonials are conducted in a way precisely contrary to those of the Buddhists. The sign of the Swastika is represented in an inverted direction. The processions in the temple walk away from the sun. [102]

Later in 1934, the year he did this imagined mountainscape, the artist had occasion to practice yet another approach, the portrait of a particular mountain, in a new location.

The United States Department of Agriculture invited Roerich to lead an expedition to Manchuria and Mongolia in search of drought resistant plants to alleviate the dust bowl conditions of the American midwest, one of the crises of the great Depression. En route the artist had to make arrangements with officials in Japan. While there he portrayed Fujiyama in several canvases, capturing the unique yet ever changing identity of this celebrated mountain. Svetoslav Roerich remarked on the tradition of mountain portraiture, comparing his father with the Japanese artist he most esteemed, 'Hokusai, who painted numerous views of Fujiyama, trying to bring out the various moods and aspects, which he felt he had seen in it.' [103]

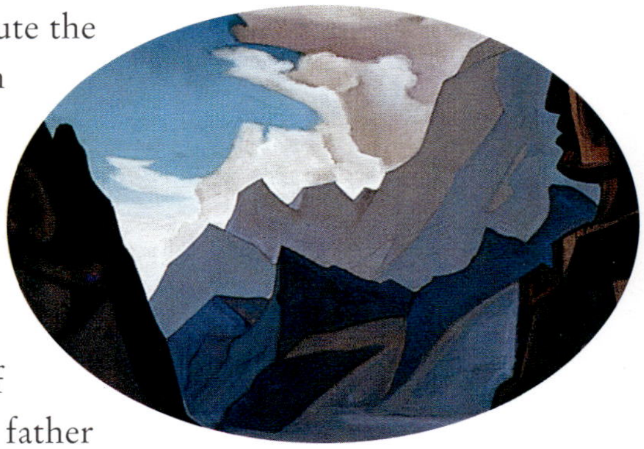

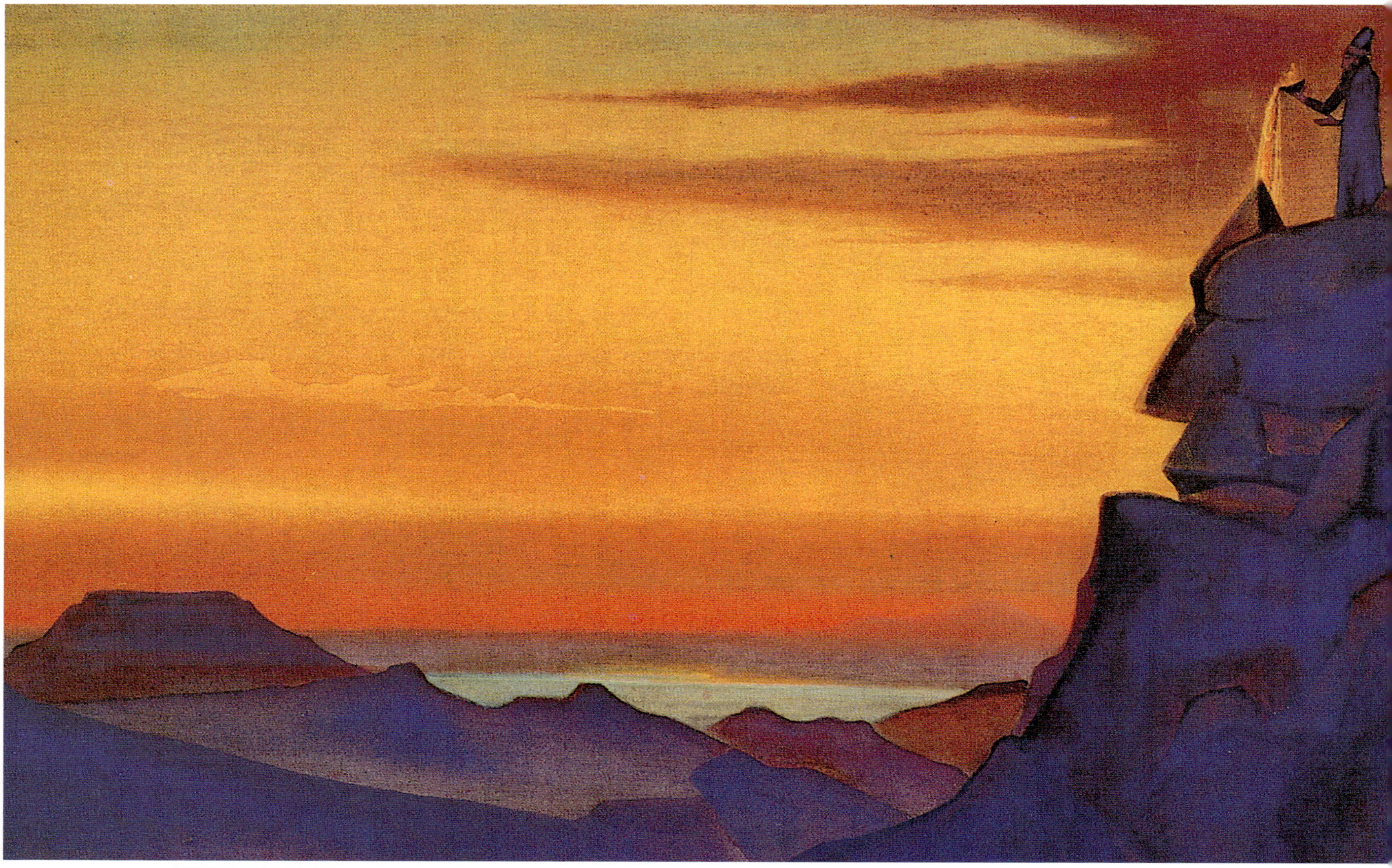

Zoroaster, 1931

Tempera on canvas, 73,6 x 117 cm.
Svetoslav Roerich Collection, Bangalore, India

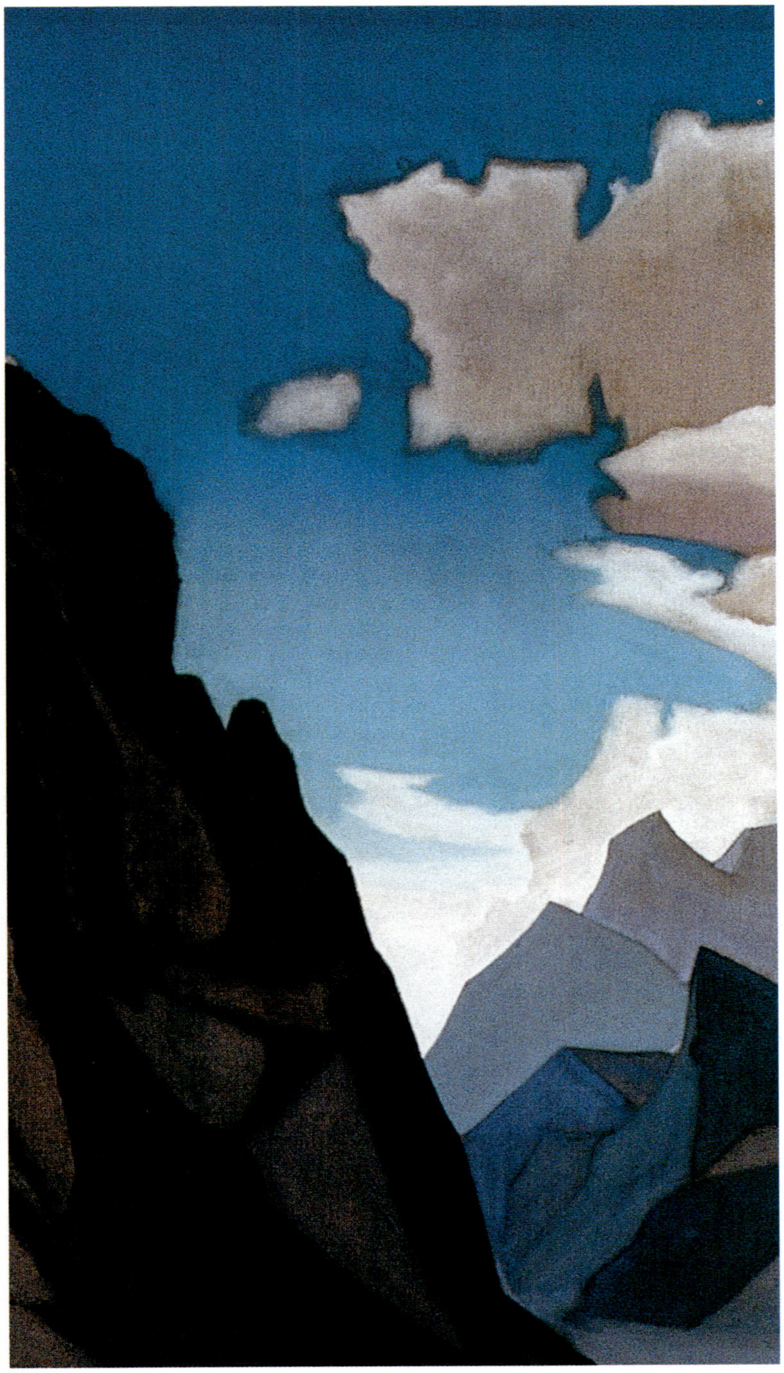

Great Spirit of the Himalayas, detail

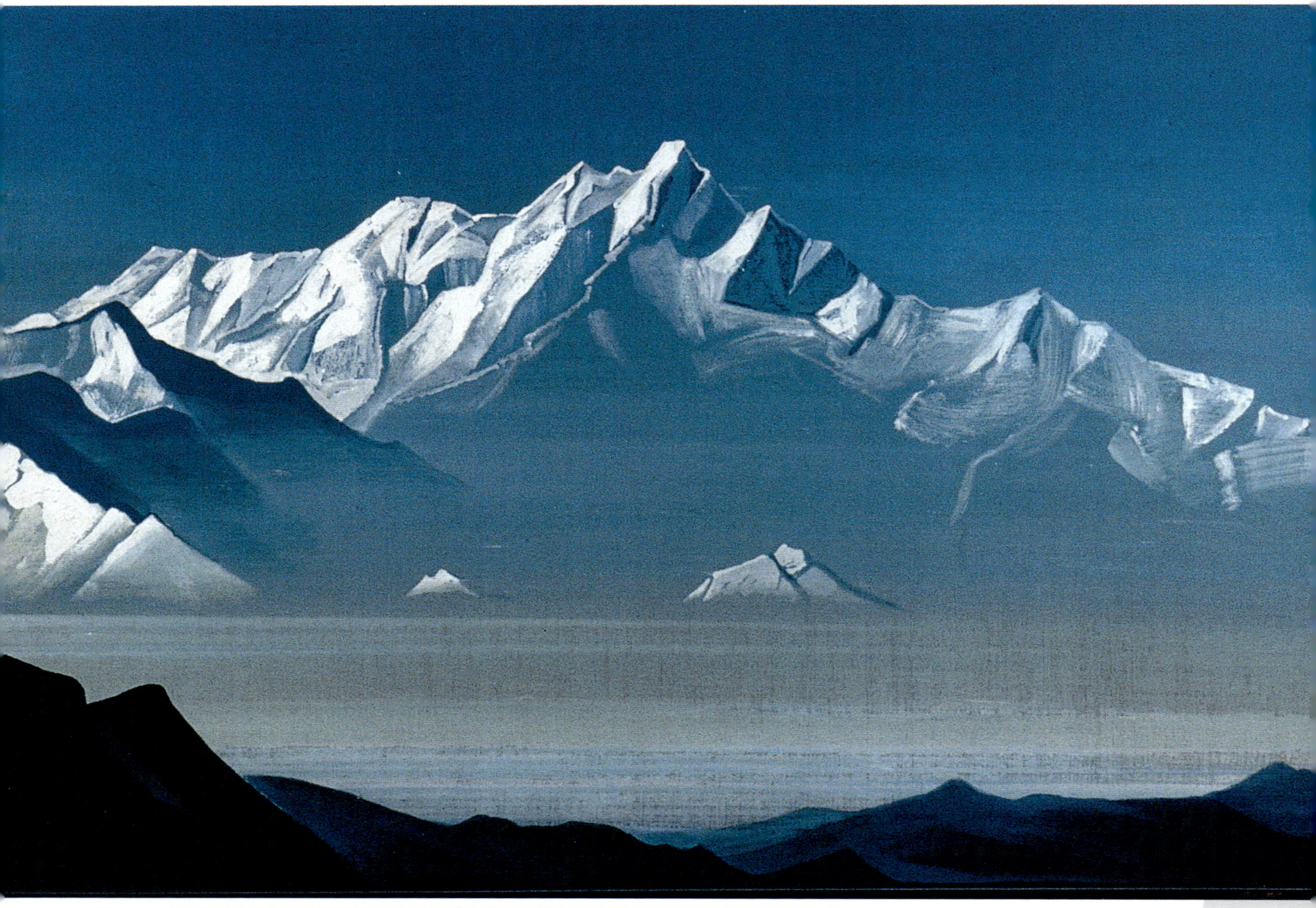

Mount of the Five Treasures, 1930's

Tempera on canvas, 78.7 x 46.4 cm.
Nicholas Roerich Museum, New York

28 *Mount of the Five Treasures*

When he first arrived in north India, Roerich observed that 'the view of Darjeeling itself disappoints you,' and asked with a touch of irony, 'is it necessary to seek the Himalayas in order to find merely a corner of Switzerland?' (104) He had, of course, painted the Alps in Chamonix and St Moritz some months earlier, treating them in terse, simply coloured compositions that paralleled those of his Swiss contemporary, the Symbolist Ferdinand Hodler, Böcklin's key rival. Svetoslav Roerich said that his own painterly 'approach to the mountain,' like his 'father's and Hodler's was first the structural aspect, then the harmony of colour – the wonderful interplay of light and shade.' (105) But Roerich had not been in India long before the Himalayas emboldened him, prompting sharper lines, stronger colours and more dramatic viewpoints. Although in his various paintings of Kanchenjunga he continued to use the horizontal aspect that he and Hodler had favoured, Roerich discovered an ambience of another order, in which geographical and spiritual reality are fused.

In Roerich's writings about Kanchenjunga he chronicled the rich culture associated with this mountain, how in Sikkim there are dances for 'the great day of homage to Kanchenjunga,' how inside the mountain there are 'subterranean passages' that lead to 'the stone door which has never been opened,' and how beyond the mountain are ritual sites 'of the great sun cult' and of Agni, 'the sign of fire.' (106) He also stated that the four syllables of the name Kan-chen-ju-nga mean 'five treasures of the great snow,' referring not to valuables of a material nature but to the knowledge behind the closed door which will some day 'nourish all mankind.' (107)

Mount of the Five Treasures is a majestic portrait of Kanchenjunga presented in five bands of luminous colour. First, in the foreground, are dark blue foothills, their contours defined by fine edges of light. Second, there is the rising mist in pale blue streaked by the sun. Third, in the middle distance, are the lower jutting peaks in grey and white shaded by blue. Fourth, the icy facets of Kanchenjunga blaze in light made ever more brilliant by the fifth band, the saturated blue of the sky. This monument, so alive in his imagination since the gravure of his childhood home, seems to have liberated the artist, setting him on a new trajectory toward pure painting.

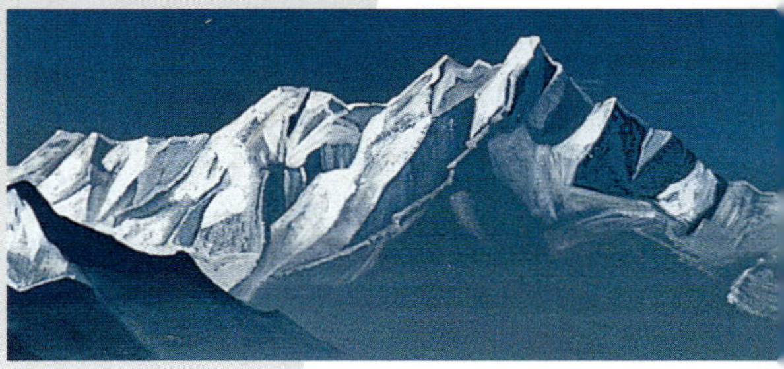

Kanchenjunga, 1944

Nicholas Roerich Museum, New York

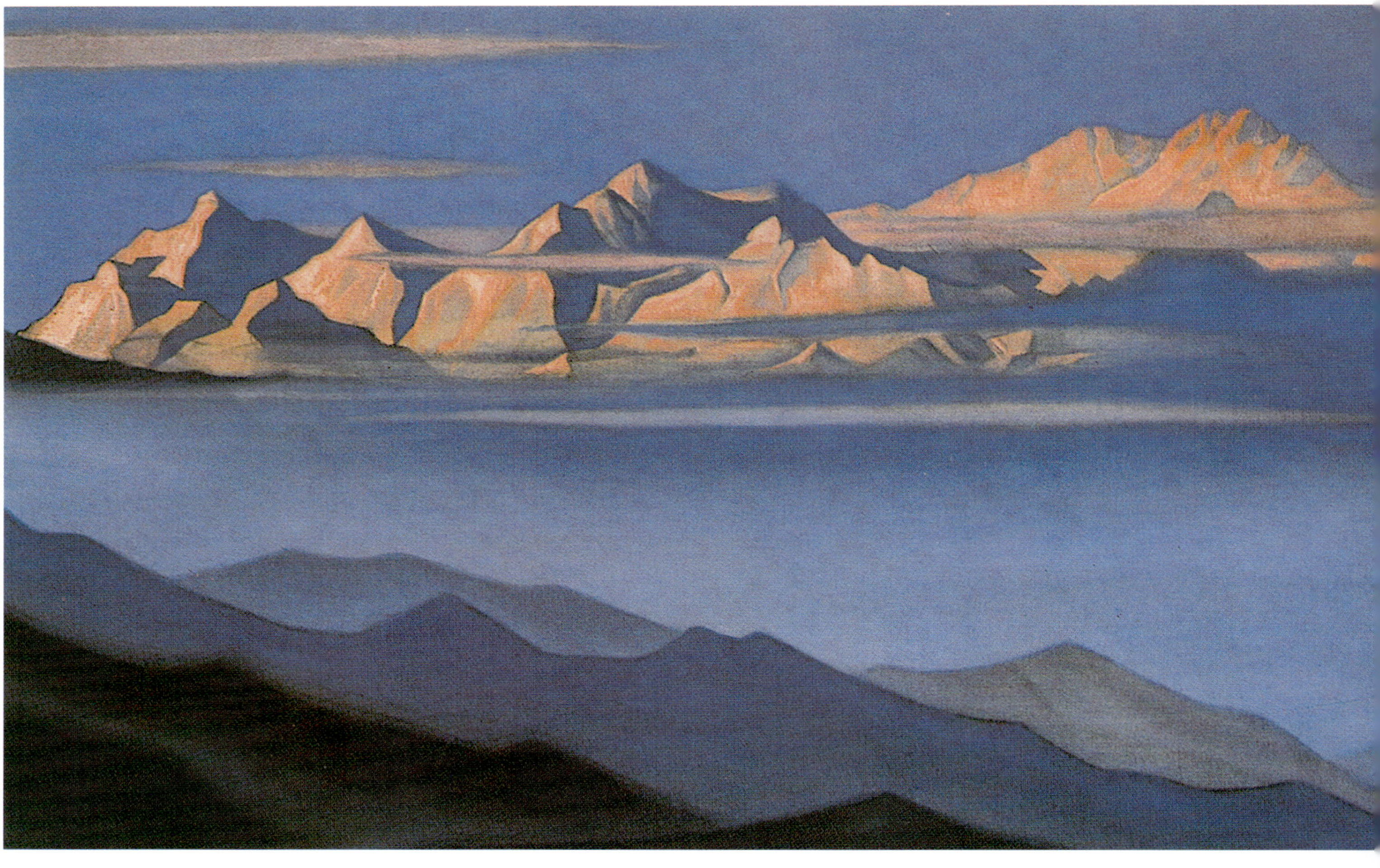

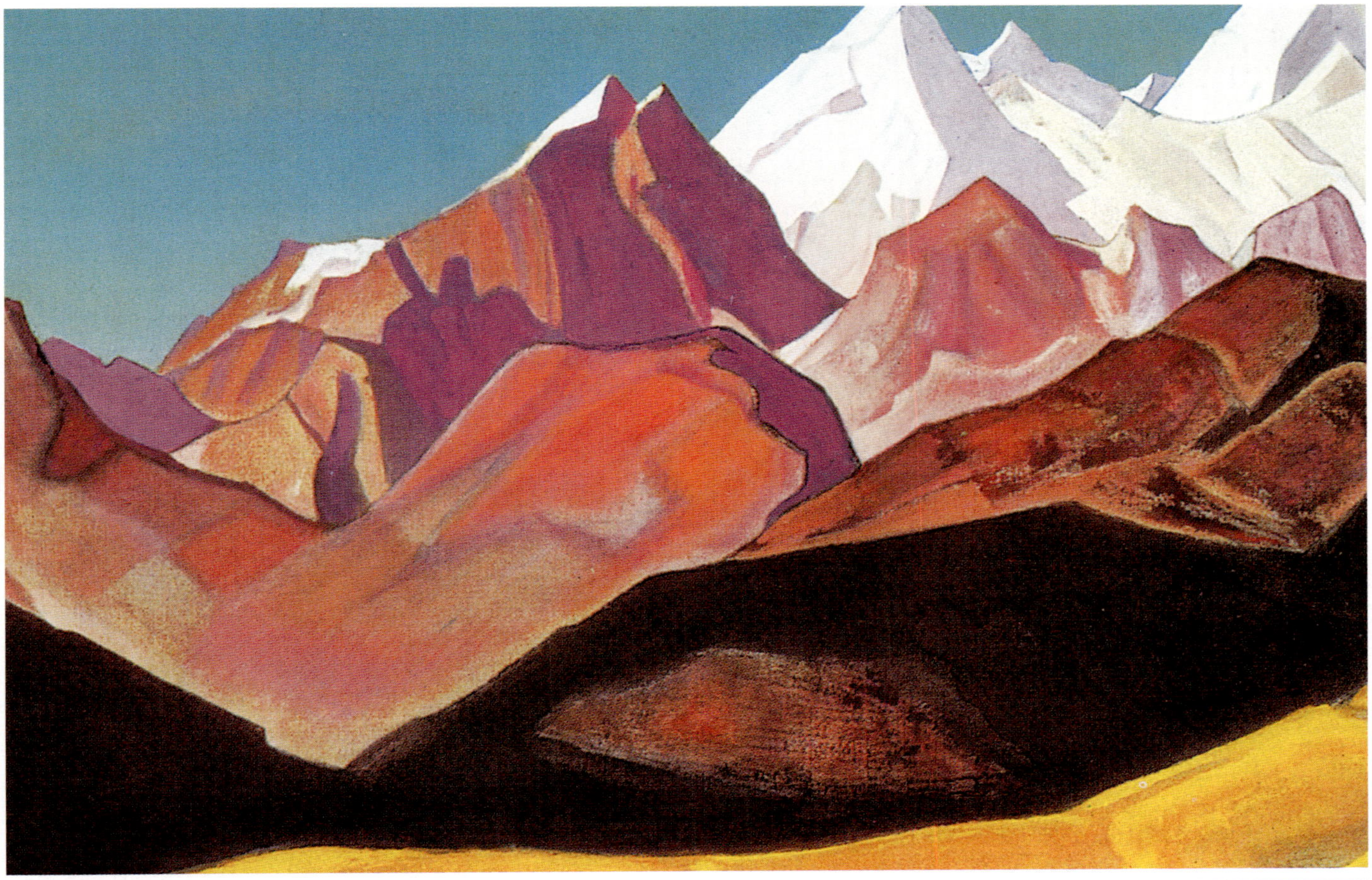

Himalaya, white mountains

Nicholas Roerich Museum, New York

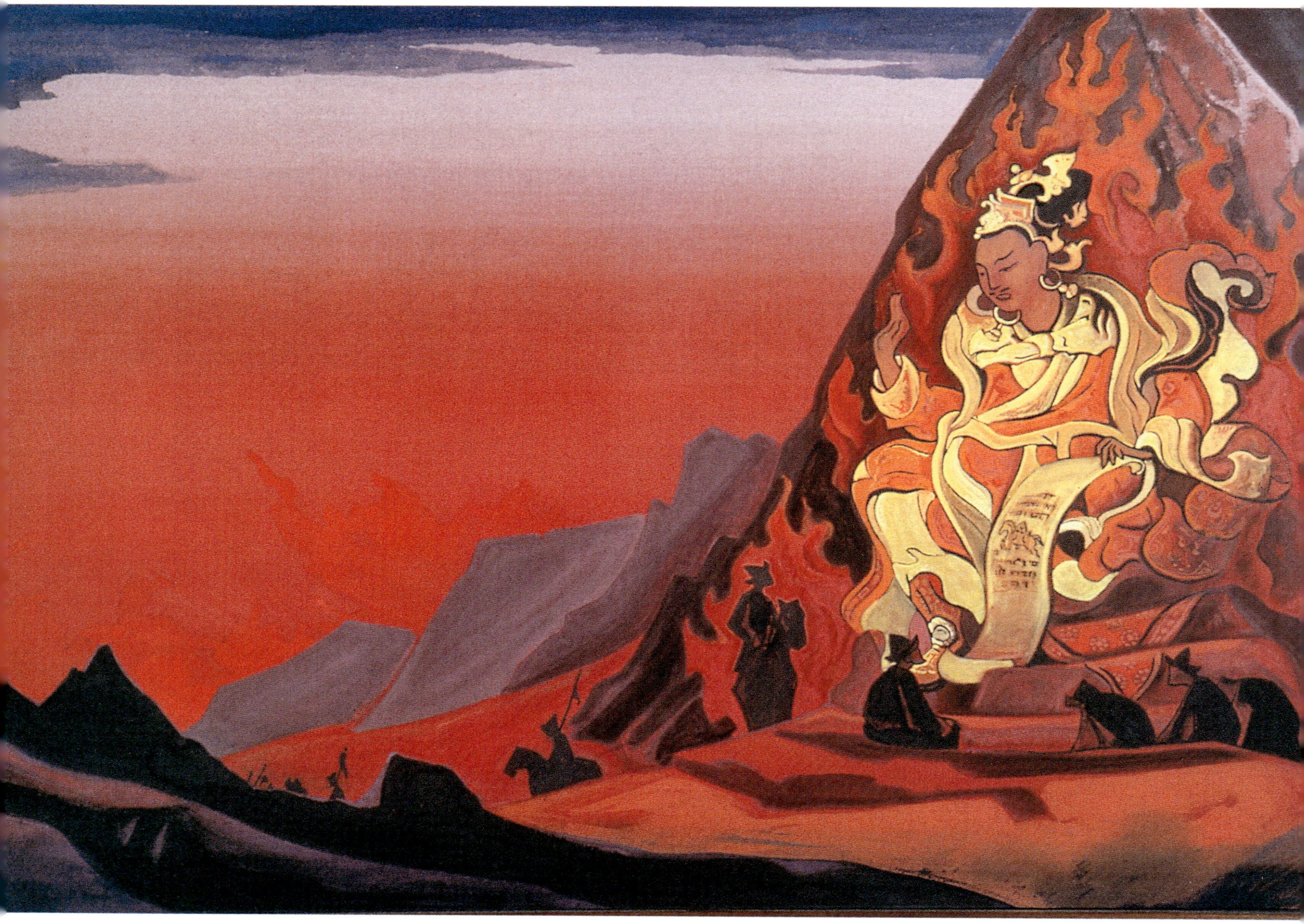

Command of Rigden Djapo, 1930's

Tempera on canvas, 99 x 63.5 cm.
Nicholas Roerich Museum, New York

29 *Command of Rigden Djapo*

The painting concerns the Tibetan tradition of Rigden Djapo, the ruler of the legendary kingdom of Shambhala. He is represented as an enormous figure in golden robe and headdress, enthroned on a carpeted dias and surrounded by red flames. A rich contrast to the dark mountain behind them, the figure and the flames are conceived in the stylized manner of Tibetan religious art. The rest of the canvas shows the messengers of the ruler, some in attendance and some departing on horseback with lances and pennants. They are silhouetted against the mountainscape, which is suffused with sunset orange and pink. In the book *Shambhala* Roerich transcribed his conversation with a lama which elucidates the imagery of this canvas: It is related how the blessed Rigden Djapo manifests himself, to give commands to his messengers; how on the black rock, on the way to Ladak, the mighty ruler appears. And from all directions, the messenger-riders appear in deep reverence to listen; and in full speed they rush to fulfil what is ordained by the great wisdom.(108)

Rigden Djapo is often associated with the manifestation of Buddha known as Maitreya. He is typically portrayed in a seated posture with the right foot touching the ground, which indicates that he is approaching mankind as the new teacher. Roerich also depicts him in a characteristic mudra, the right hand raised in the sign of safeguarding. (109) The left holds the scroll of the future with the symbol of Chintamani, the treasure of the world, borne by the mythic horse of Central Asia.

Command of Rigden Djapo draws upon the conventions of tanka painting, the sacred icons of Tibet, which Roerich adapts to contemporary purpose, much as he did with Russian Orthodox art in his early career. As a rule tankas are constructed with a disproportionately large hierarchical figure in the centre of a schematized cosmology. This painting presents an asymmetrical composition, the central figure at the right, leaving the left of the canvas empty enough to suggest the distance the messengers must travel. This momentous appearance of Rigden Djapo takes place, not in a diagram of the cosmos, but in a particular locale. The artist thus communicates the immediacy of such legends in the popular life of the east he encountered. (107)

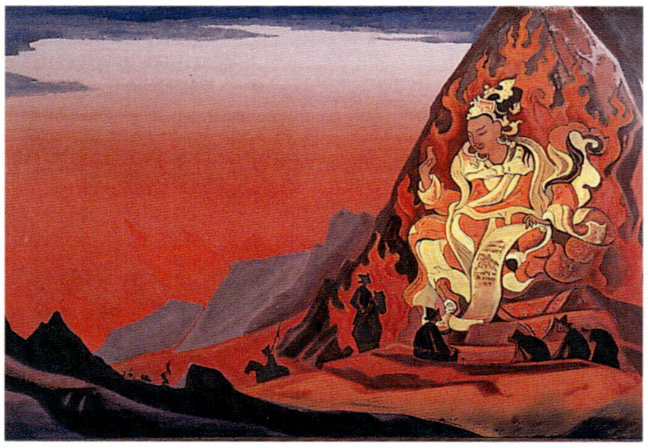

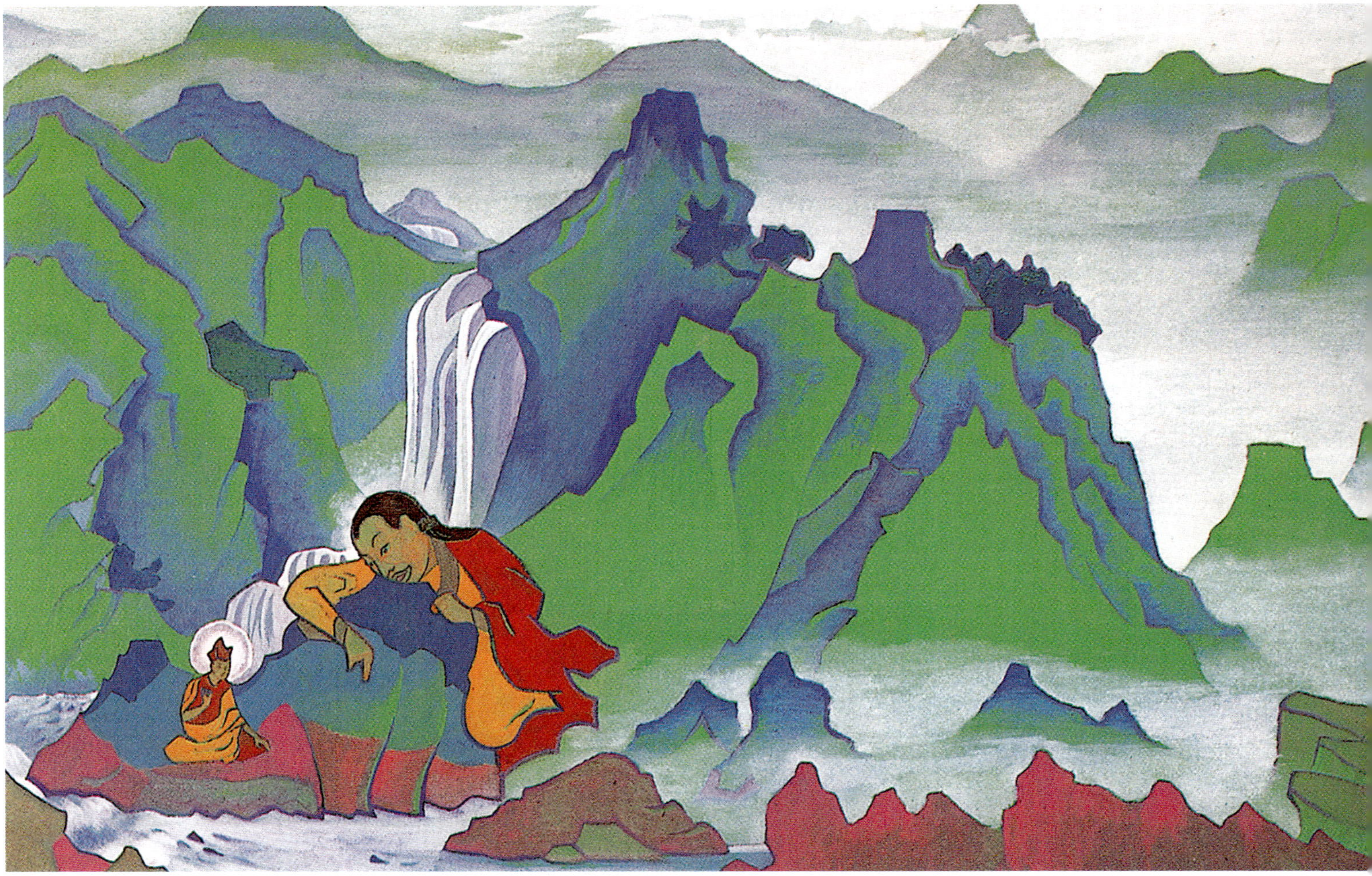

Padma Sambhava, 1924

Tempera on canvas, 73.6 x 117 cm.
Nicholas Roerich Museum, New York

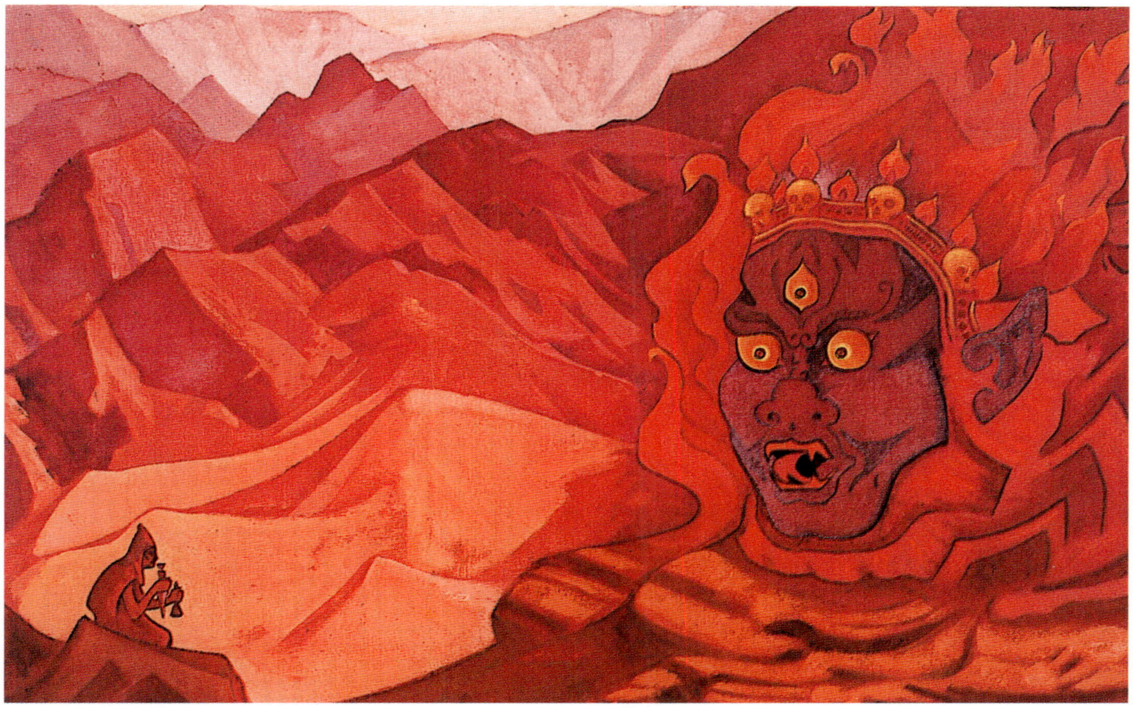

Dorje the Daring One, 1925

Tempera on canvas, 75 x 117 cm.
Nicholas Roerich Museum, New York

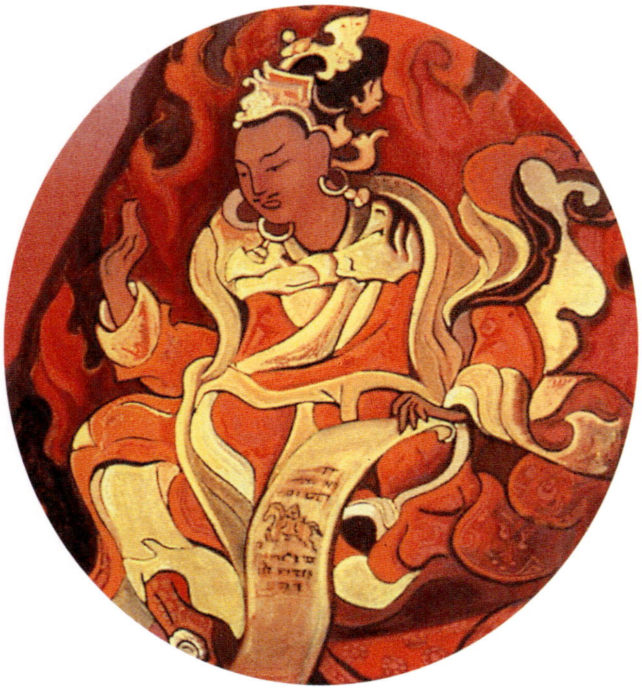

Command of Rigden Djapo, detail

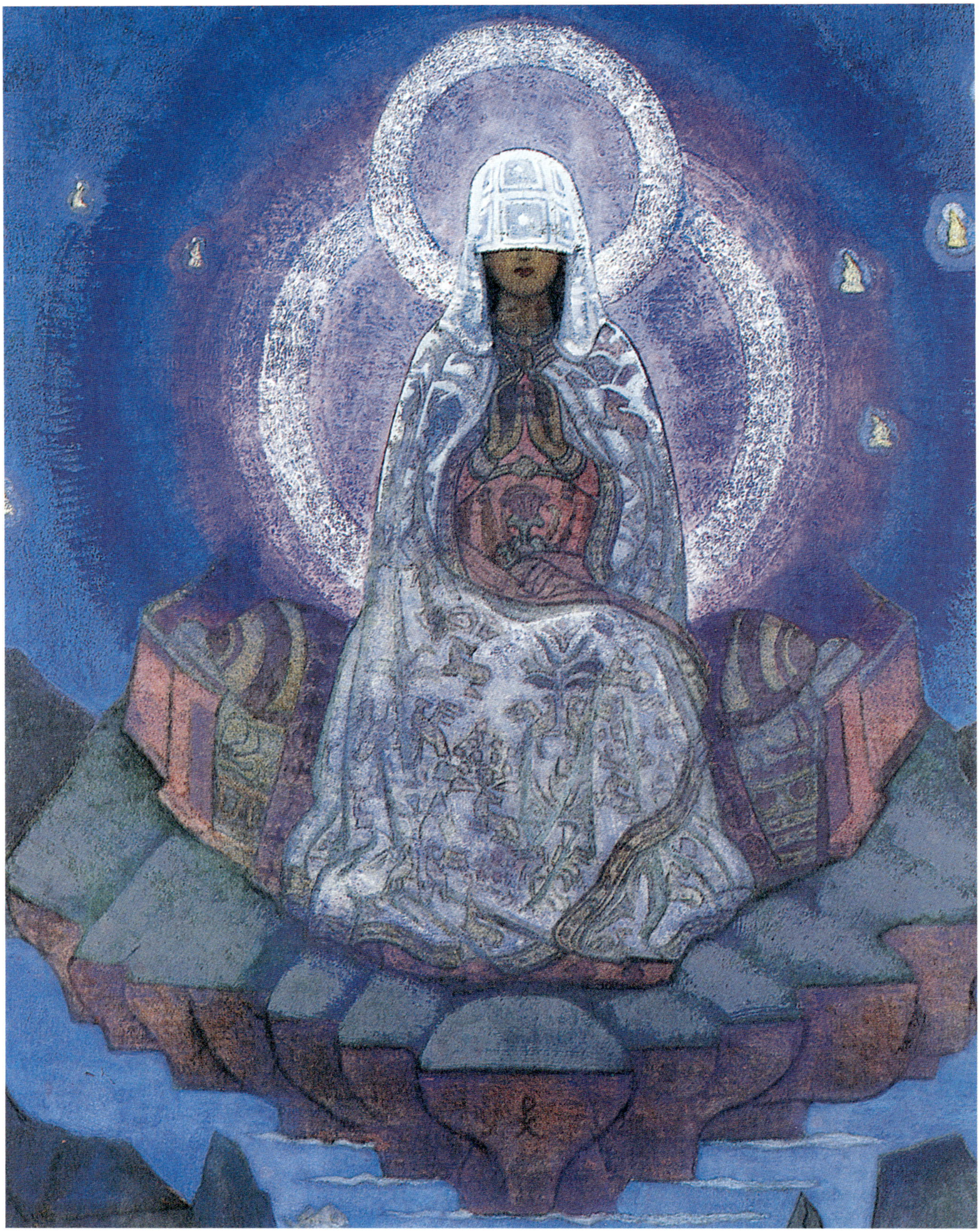

Mother of the World, 1930's

Tempera on canvas, 72.4 x 103.5 cm.
Nicholas Roerich Museum, New York

30

Mother of the World

Nicholas and Helena Roerich, born and educated in the Christian tradition, widened their perspective during the early years of their marriage in Russia, by studying the contemporary Hindu teachings of Sri Ramakrishna and Swami Vivekananda, on the one hand, and, on the other, Buddhism and Helena Blavatsky's Theosophy. (110) Such knowledge informed Roerich's depiction of archetypes from the many cultures he traversed, east and west. And it was the foundation of Madame Roerich's writing in the system called Agni Yoga – by 1937 she had finished thirteen volumes – which emphasized the feminine principle in modern spirituality. (111)

The monumental fresco *Queen of Heaven,* which Roerich created for Princess Maria Tenisheva's Church of the Holy Spirit at Talashkino between 1911 and 1914, had already universalized the Orthodox madonna. Later he wrote and painted on the themes of female spiritual leadership and the manifestations of the divine matriarch:

To both east and west, the image of the great mother – womanhood – is the bridge of ultimate unification . . . . [the Orthodox Virgin] is but another facet of . . . . [the Chinese goddess] Kwan Yin. When the west exalts . . . the Italian madonna, and feels the deep penetration of the paintings of Duccio and Fra Angelico, we are reminded of the . . . [Tibetan female divinity] Dukkar . . . . The images of the Mother of the World . . . merge together in one conception [which] ordains that there should be, not division, but construction. (112)

Mother of the World updates conventions from Russian icons and Tibetan tankas. In this canvas and the first version from 1924, the artist enthrones the hieratic figure on an island of stone. The aureoles around her head and body are encircled by the blue of sky and sea. Roerich's early canvas illumined the firmament with the planet Venus and the constellations Orion and the Great Bear. This later work turns these heavenly bodies into auras around arhats or bodhisattvas. The protective veil preserves mysteries yet unknown to man. Like such Symbolists as Lucien Lévy- *Dhurmer in Silence* (1895) and Mikhail Vrubel in *The Swan Princess* (1900), Roerich often explored the enigmatic power of woman in secular as well as sacred roles. (113)

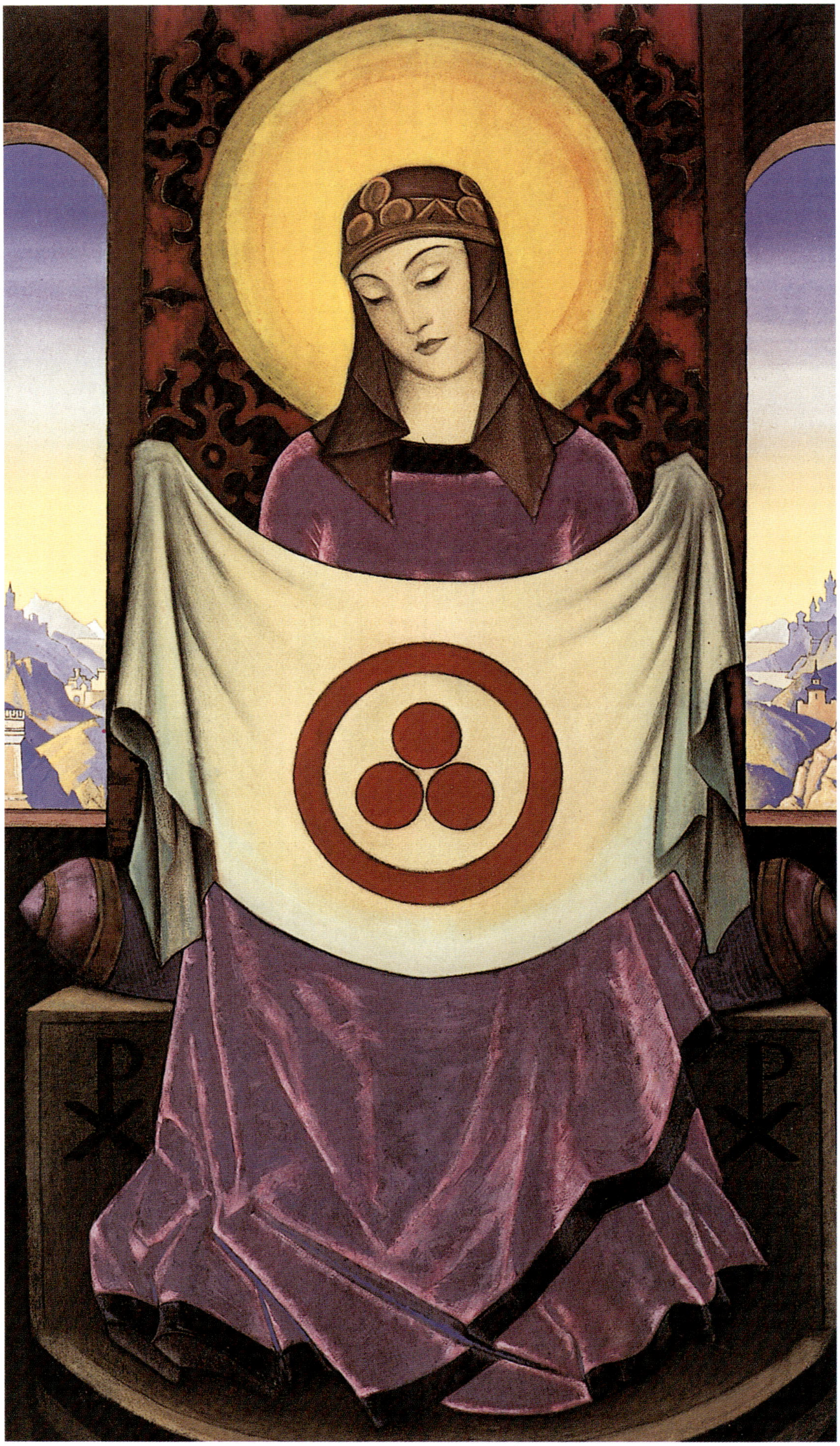

Madonna Oriflamma, 1932

Tempera on canvas, 173 x 100 cm. Nicholas Roerich Museum, New York

'Such knowledge informed Roerich's depiction of archetypes from the many cultures he traversed, east and west.'

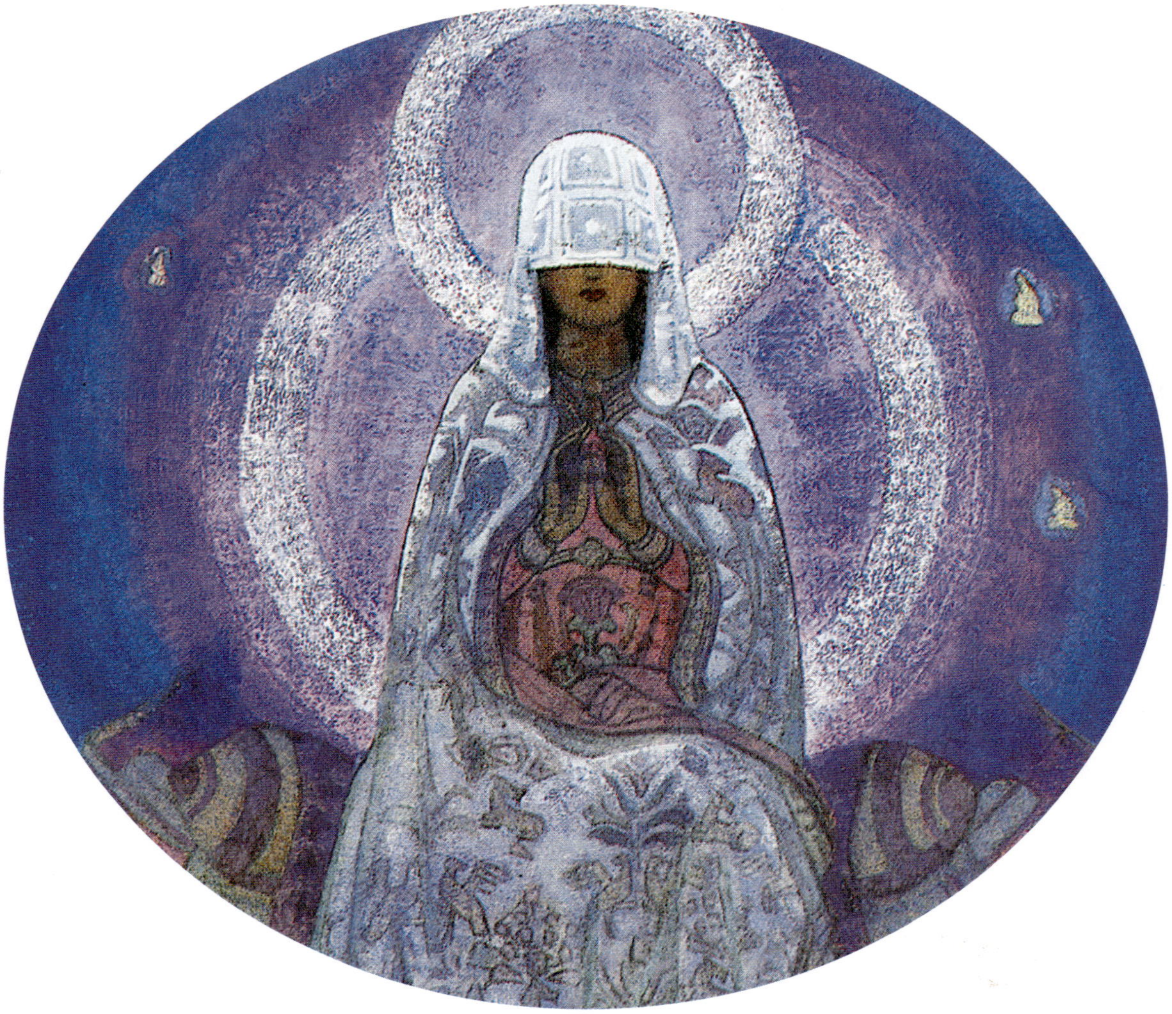

Mother of the World, detail

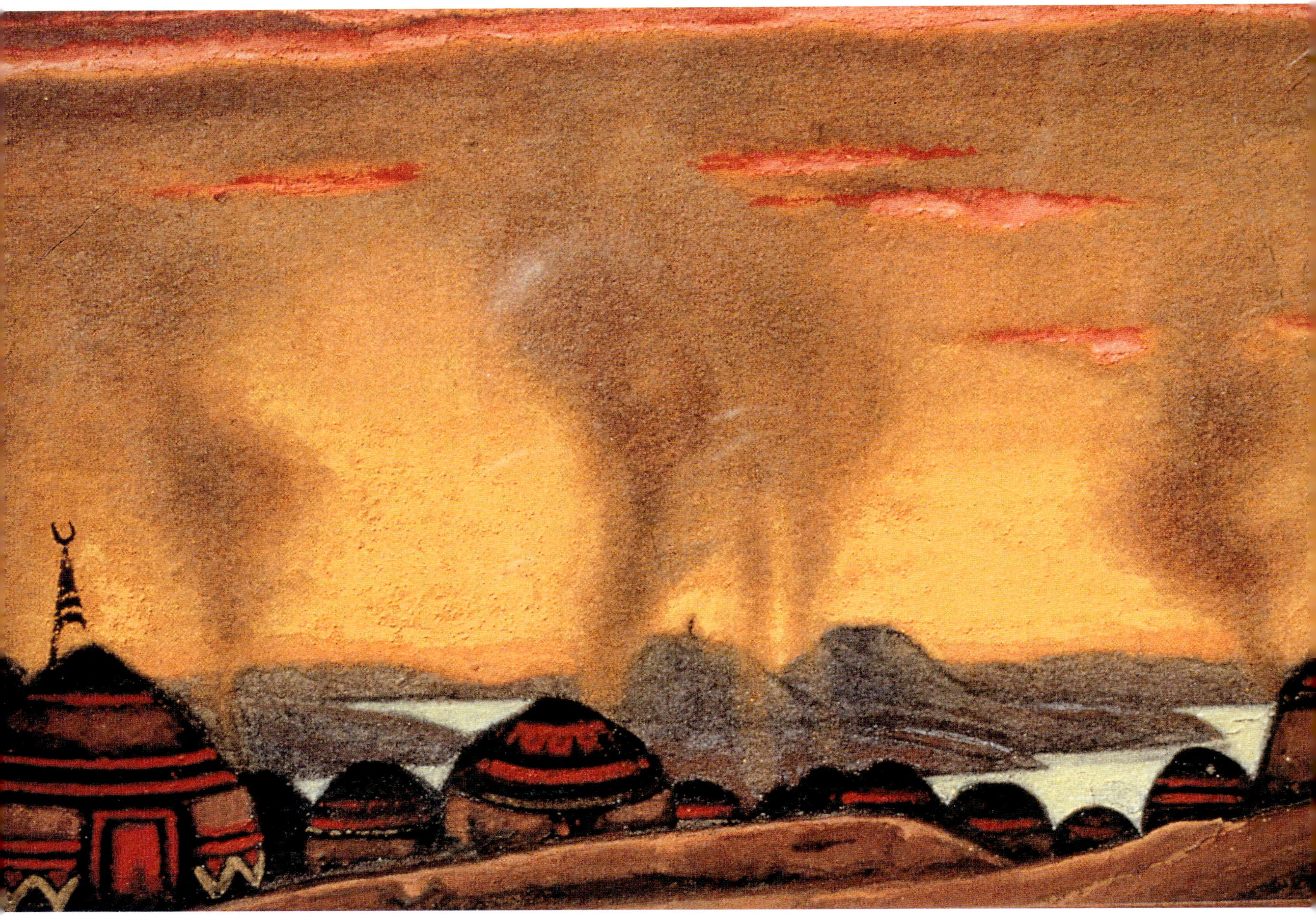

Polovtsian Camp, 1944

Tempera on cardboard, 50 x 35 cm.
Nicholas Roerich Museum, New York

31 *Polovtsian Camp*

Toward the end of World War II, Leonide Massine, who wished to stage a New York production of the ballet from Prince Igor, wrote to Roerich in India for sketches. The artist sent five costume maquettes and this decor design, *Polovtsian Camp.* His original work on the ballet, which Diaghilev presented in Paris in 1909, had marked Roerich's breakthrough as an international artist. (114) His name, with Léon Bakst and Alexander Benois, became synonymous with Ballets Russes design.

Both versions display rows of Polovtsi tents, or yurts, with smoke rising against a background of low hills and waterways. In 1909 the patterns on the yurts were freely painted in soft orange and terracotta, which contrasted subtly with an ochre sky. In 1944, however, the patterns are hard-edged and brightly coloured. The yurts stand out against an intense gold sky with high red clouds. In the original version, a pole with a simple pennant identified the camp, but in this sketch the standards are surmounted with ornate flags and emblems, including a Muslim crescent. Roerich's 1909 backdrop, in its evocative World of Art style, had transported Parisians to the boundless steppes of Central Asia. Since then the artist had travelled such terrain, and his 1944 design testifies to the extremes he observed both in nature and culture.

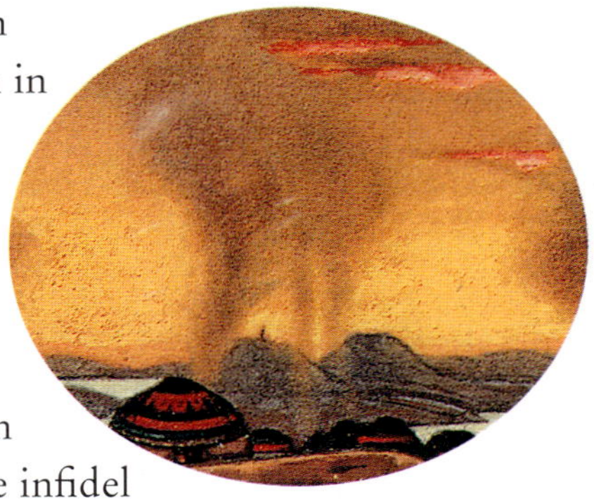

Two years before this commission from Massine, Roerich contemplated the plight of Russia in a canvas entitled *Prince Igor's Campaign.* It showed the medieval Russian prince and his Christian knights on their fateful march to fight the infidel Polovtsi. The scene is permeated with foreboding, the sun darkened by an eclipsing moon. Since autumn 1935, when Roerich returned from the US government expedition, he had isolated himself in Kulu. Helena Roerich called it a 'black year with seven eclipses,' even though the peace pact was signed that spring while her husband was on expedition, and the family flourished in all its creative ventures. (115) But things took a calamitous turn through a series of corrupt manoeuvres. The chairman of the Roerich Museum in New York seized the premises and all its assets in a takeover. A fabricated tax evasion charge prevented the artist from returning to defend everything he had built. (116) Receiving the news in Central Asia, Roerich, like Prince Igor on the steppes, confronted the collapse of his realm and reputation.

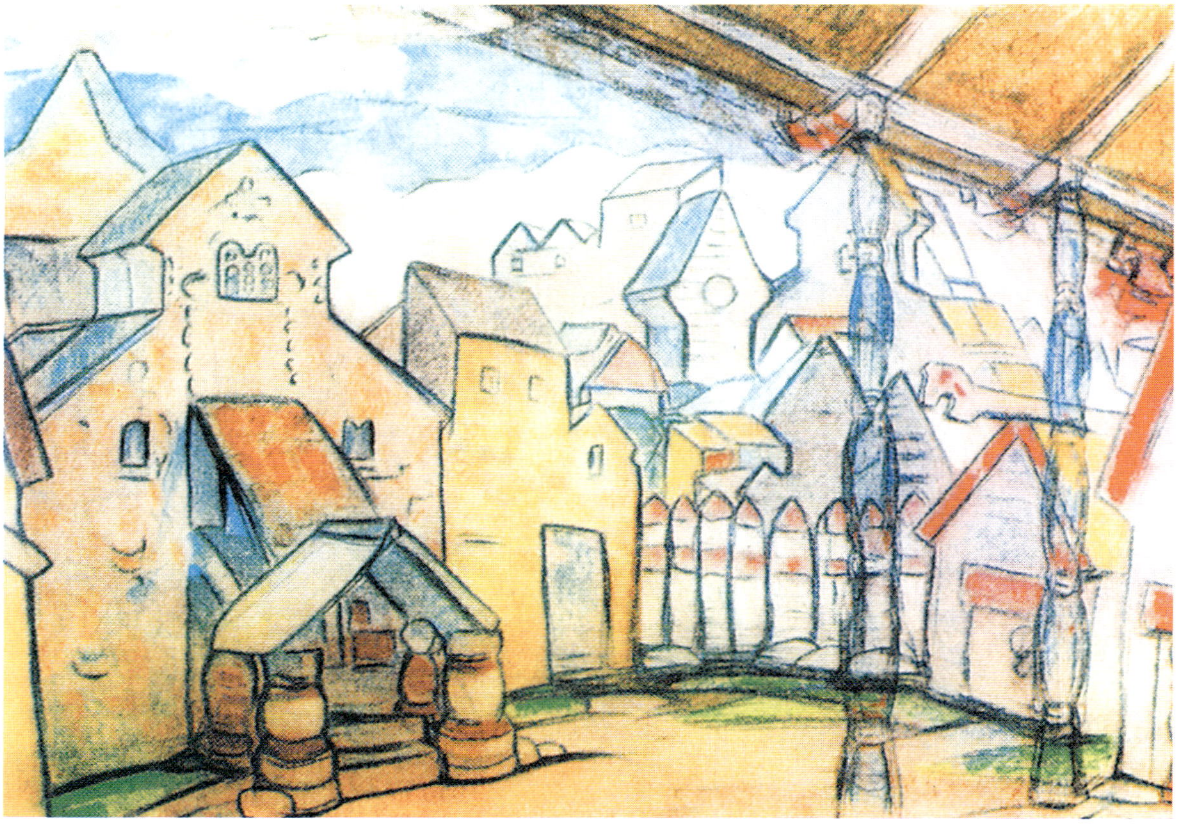

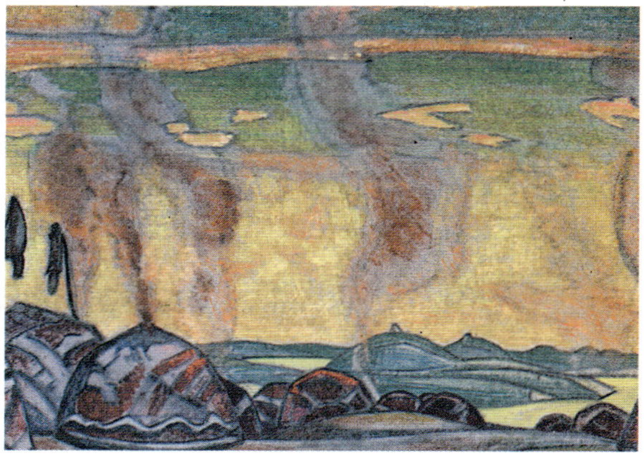

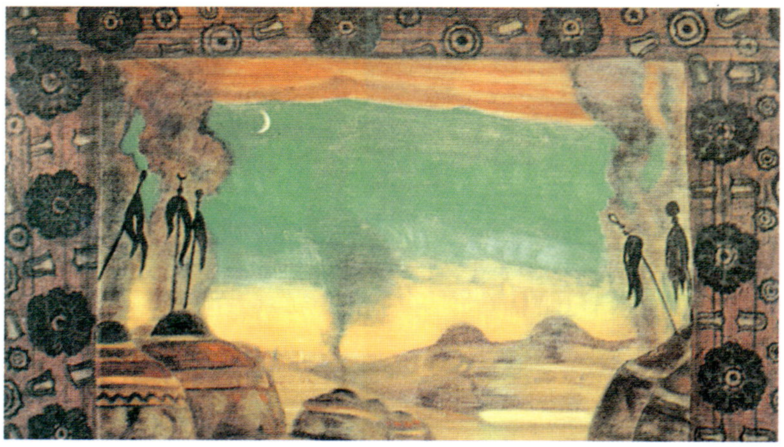

Three setting skteches for Prince Igor

Tempera and pastel on board

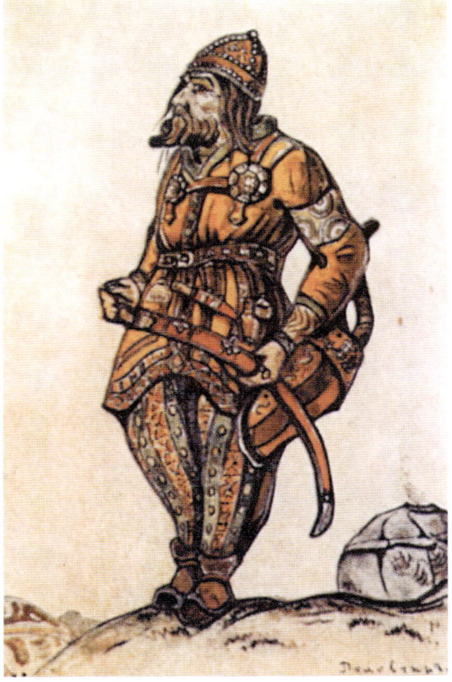

Two costume sketches for Prince Igor

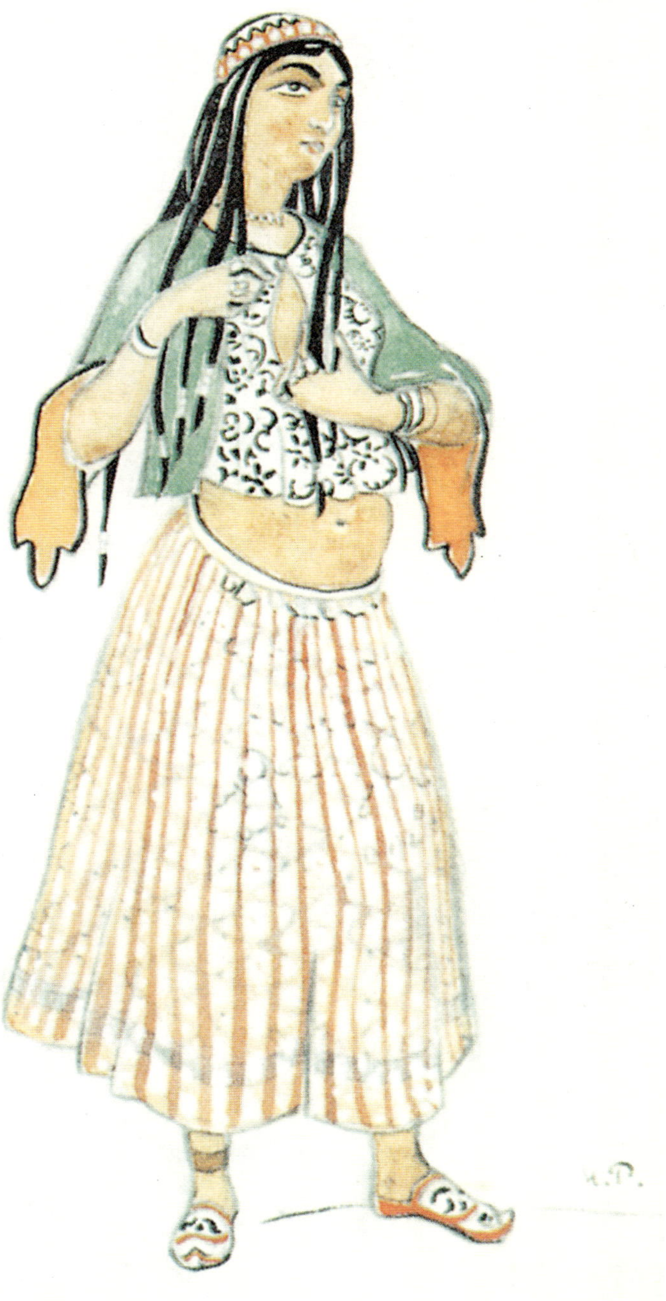

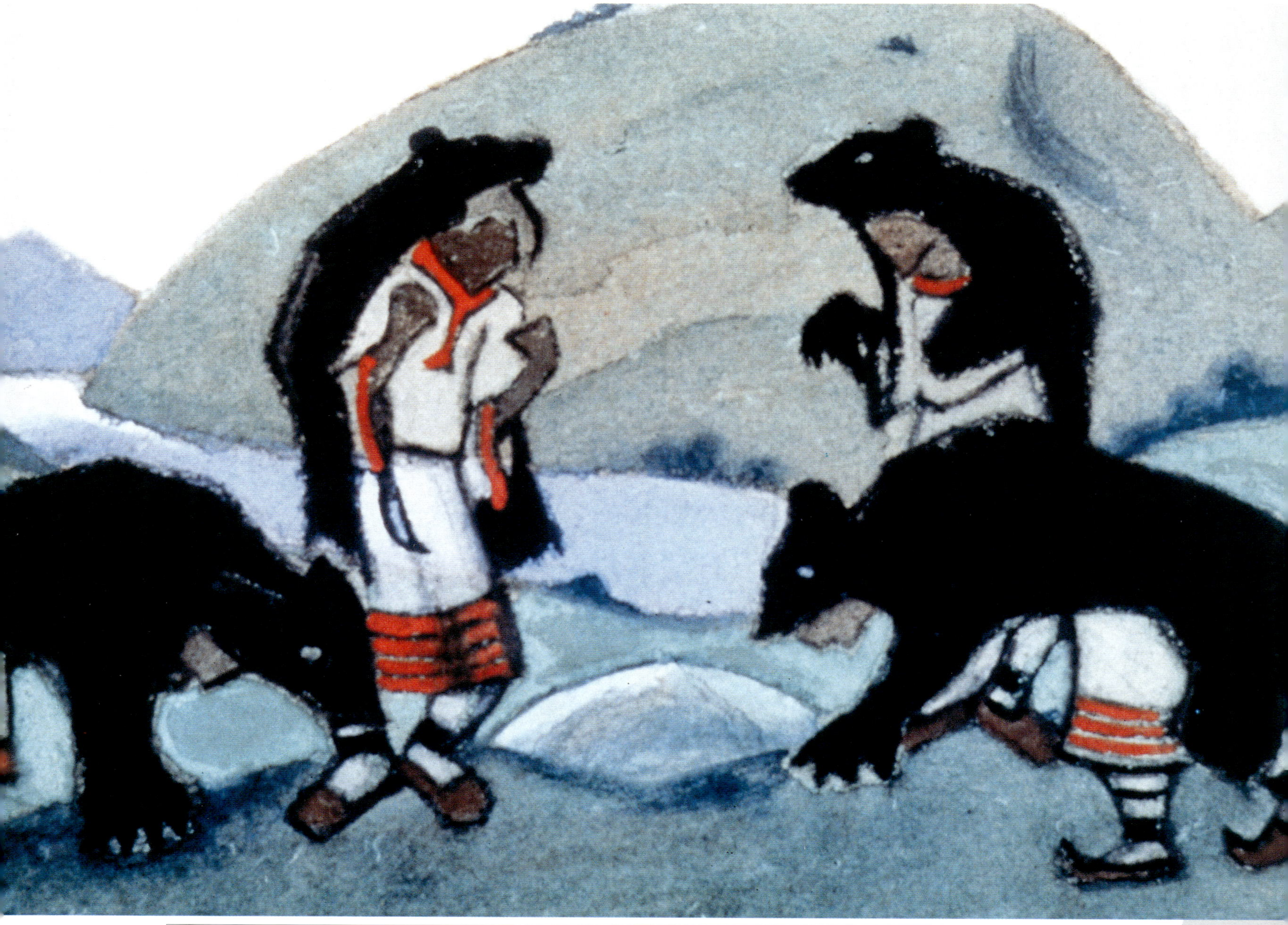

Dancers in Bearskins, 1944

Tempera on canvas, 50 x 35 cm.
Nicholas Roerich Museum, New York

32

Dancers in Bearskins

At the same time Massine requested the Prince Igor designs, he asked Roerich to do another version of *Le Sacre du Printemps.* The artist painted a decor sketch and four costume designs, including *Dancers in Bearskins.* In the 1913 *Sacre,* the Ancestors cloaked in animal furs were seen rising from the earth, an effect achieved by men emerging from trapdoors onto the Champs-Elysées stage. Dances that imitate animals are fundamental to archaic ceremonies throughout the world, and Roerich preserved this archetype in each of his Sacres. His travel journals recorded analogues to the rites he had studied of the ancient Slavs. The folk art of north India fascinated Roerich with its parallels to the Russia of his youth. His designs, like his costumes in this third version, are restricted to basic motifs and primary colours accented by black and brown. The decor adds Himalayan atmosphere to a northern Russian scene, and the costumes, no longer handpainted, are decorated with appliqué of layered fabric, a technique typical of the Indian regions that border on Tibet. (117)

Roerich was capable of living as an anchorite artist, and this final period of his life was closely circumscribed geographically. At last he stayed in one place to paint and write, completing many articles and the autobiographical collection, *My Life.* In these years his art evolved into what could be called ecstatic abstraction. Although he continued to make historical and mythological canvases, his creative urge was toward radical simplification, rendering the elemental form and colour of the Himalayas as a graph of spiritual ascent. Svetoslav Roerich, who kept these paintings, believed they were his father's finest work, a synthesis of all he had done. (118) Although Roerich did not go out into the world at this point, it came to him. He often communicated with international representatives of his peace pact and national leaders of India such as Jawaharlal Nehru in the troubled years leading to Independence and Partition.

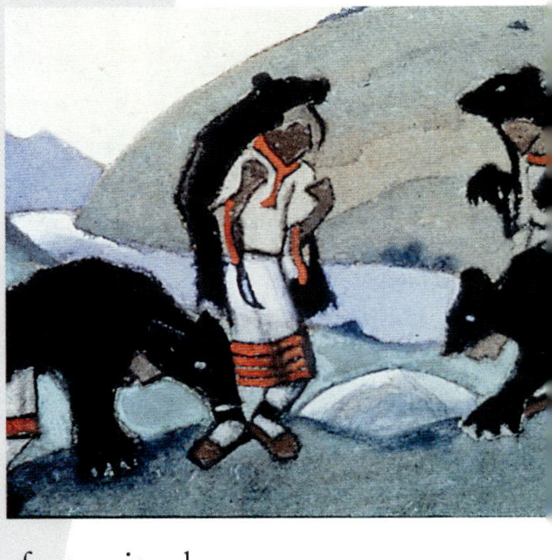

The artist died at the end of 1947, and the next year Nehru paid tribute to him at the opening of the commemorative exhibition in Delhi. Also in 1948 India signed and ratified the Roerich Pact. Although the 1944 designs for Prince Igor were never realized, Roerich's last Sacre was staged posthumously at La Scala, Milan, in 1948. His most famous work, this ballet about creativity and sacrifice was a perfect epitaph.

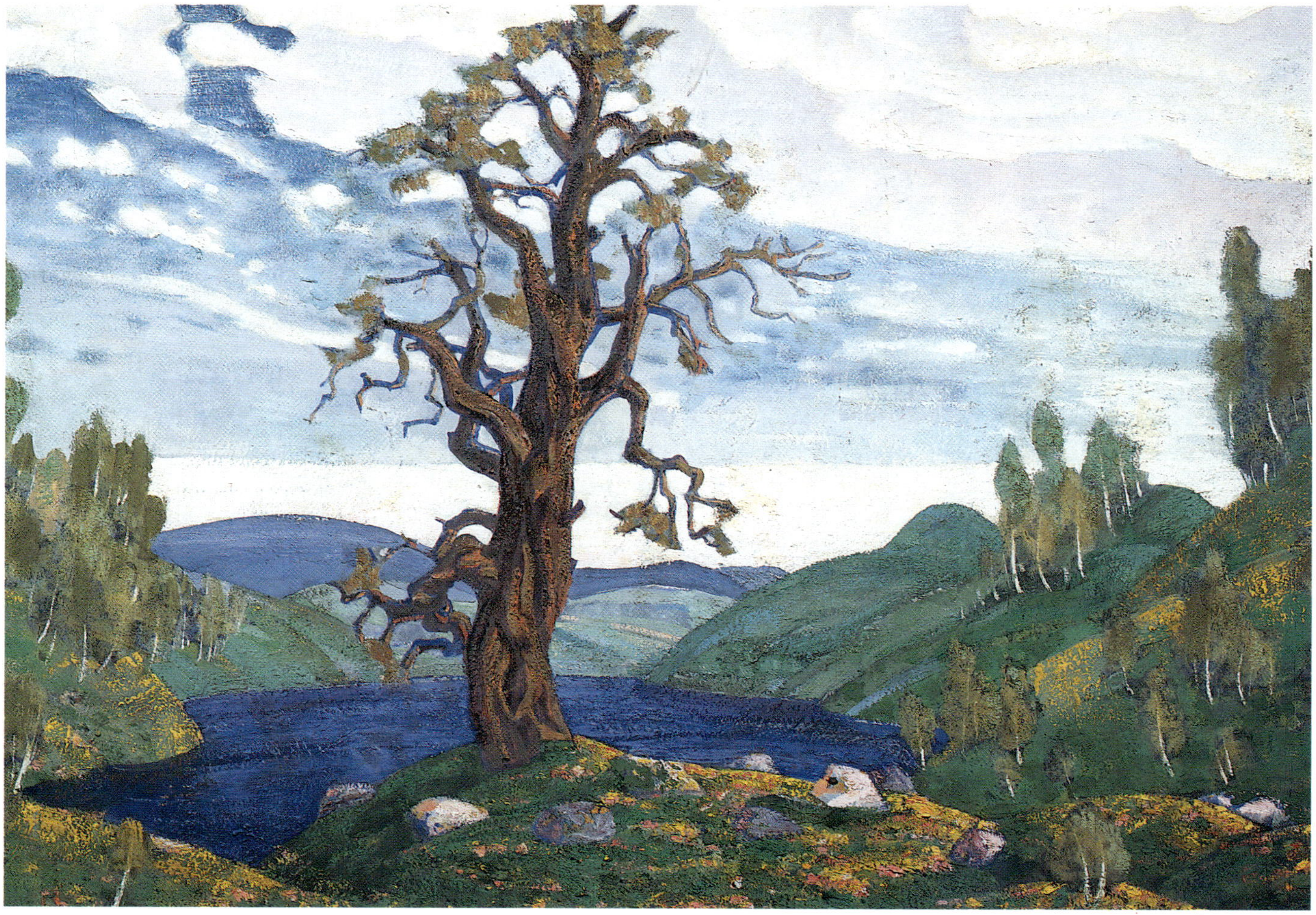

A kiss to the Earth, 1912

Sketch for Le Sacre du Printemps
Tempera on cardboad, 62 x 94 cm.
Russian Museum, Saint Petersburg

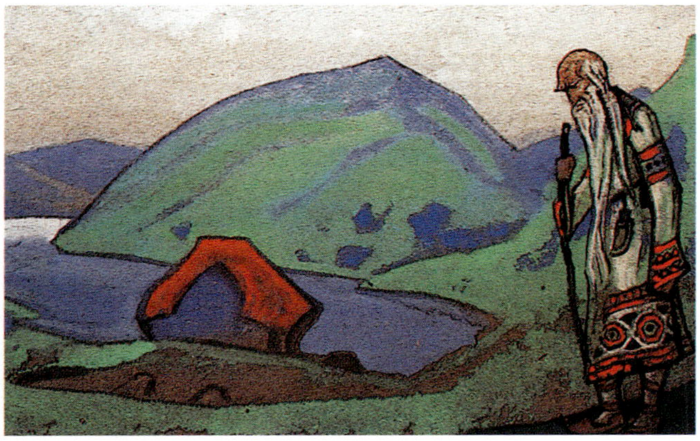

Astrologer

Costumes and set designs for Le Sacre du Printemps, 1944
Tempera on canvas, 35 x 50 cm.
Nicholas Roerich Museum, New York

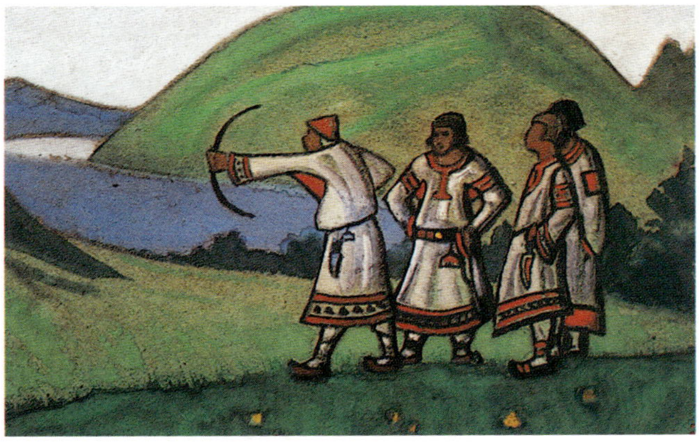

Warriors with bows

Costumes and set designs for Le Sacre du Printemps, 1944
Tempera on canvas, 35 x 50 cm.
Nicholas Roerich Museum, New York

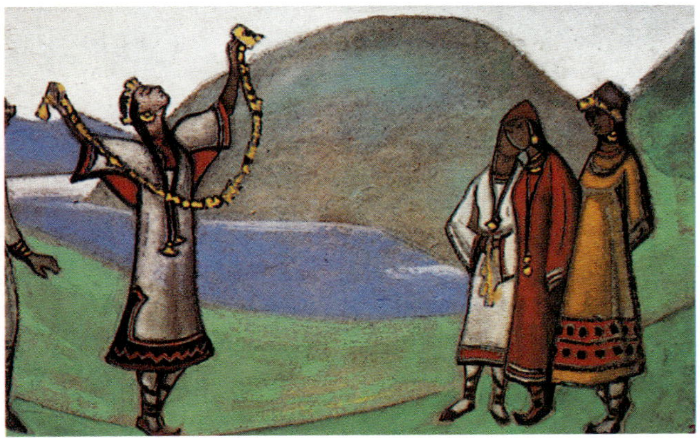

Maidens with Garlands

Costumes and set designs for Le Sacre du Printemps, 1944
Tempera on canvas, 35 x 50 cm.
Nicholas Roerich Museum, New York

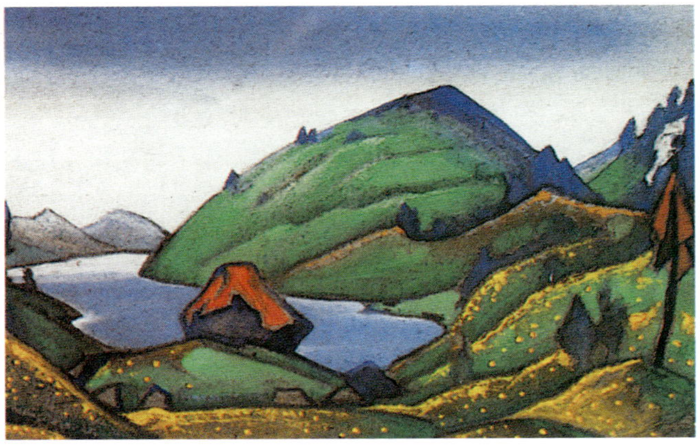

Set Design, Act I

Costumes and set designs for Le Sacre du Printemps, 1944
Tempera on canvas, 35 x 50 cm.
Nicholas Roerich Museum, New York

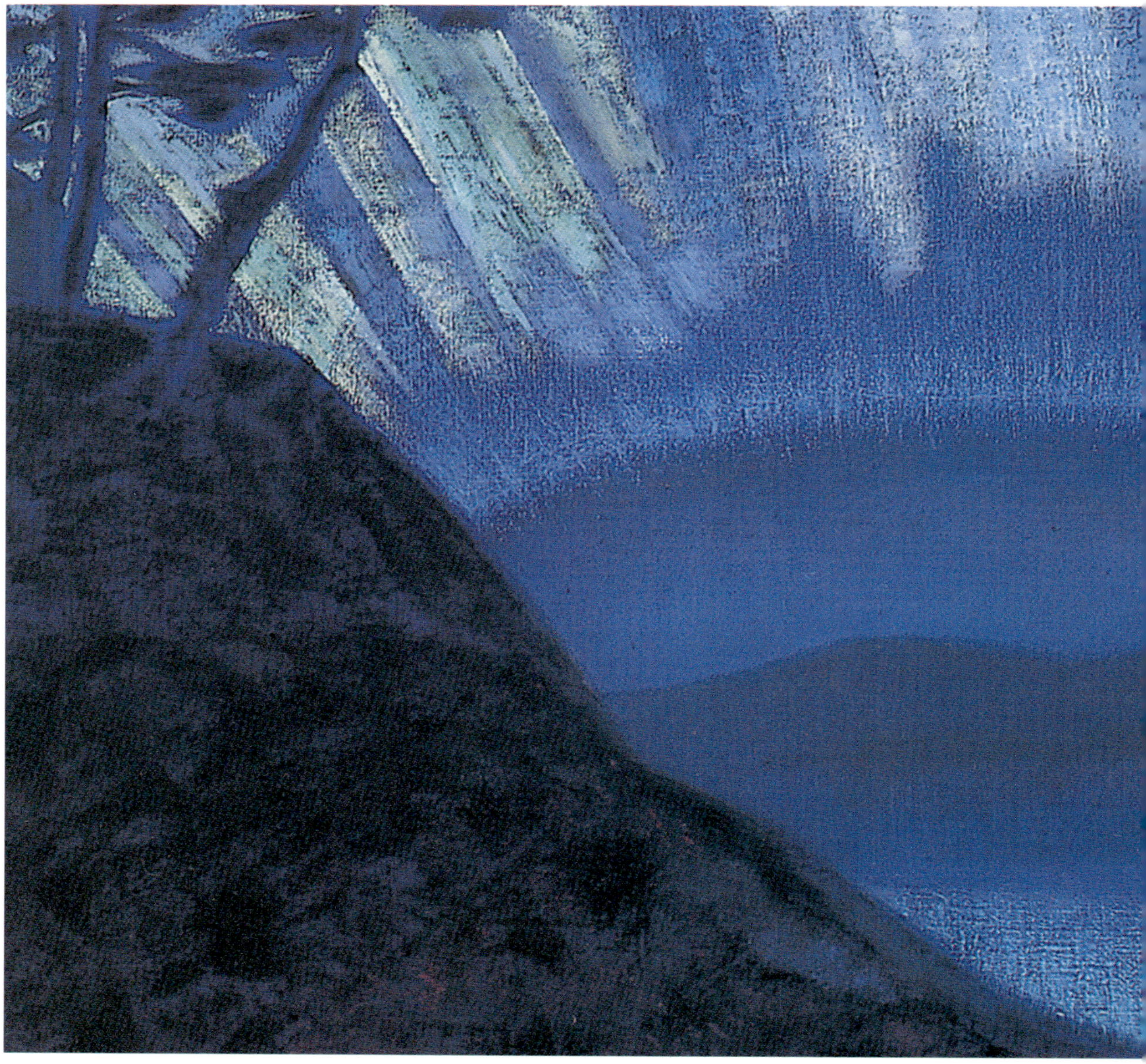

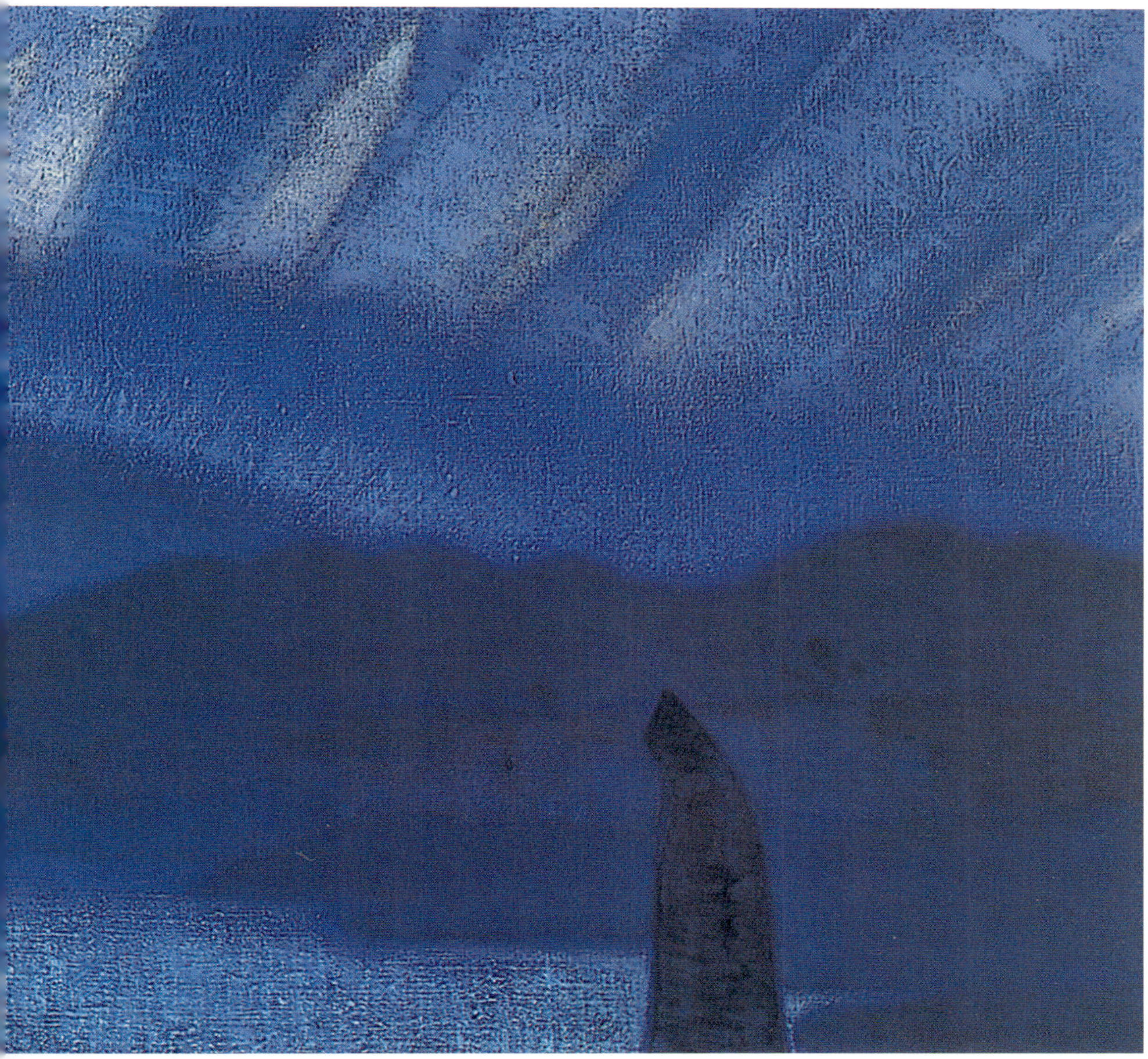

Bridge of Glory, 1923

Tempera on canvas, 82.5 x 163.8 cm.
Nicholas Roerich Museum, New York

Notes

* *(Capitalization has been standardized within quotations that appear in the text).*

** *(Russian titles have been translated and Russian publishers transliterated).*

1. Background on the ideological poles in the World of Art can be found in Beverly Whitney Kean, *All the Empty Palaces: The Merchant Patrons of Modern Art in Pre-Revolutionary Russia* (London: Barrie and Jenkins, 1983), pp 44-55, and general information in *The World of Art Movement in Early Twentieth Century Russia*, ed. Alexander Kamensky, trans. from Russian, Arthur Shkarosky-Raffe (Leningrad: Aurora Art Publishers, 1991).

2. *Spells of Russia*, catalogue of the Nicholas Roerich exhibition, Goupil Gallery (London: William Marchant, 1920).

3. Sina Fosdick, *Nicholas Roerich: A Brief Biography* (New York: Nicholas Roerich Museum, 1964).

4. Francis Grant, Interviews by the author (New York: November and December, 1982).

5. Extracts from the memoirs, *Diary Leaves: My Life*, are published in Russian in *N K Roerich: From his Literary Legacy*, ed. M T Kuzmina (Moscow: Iskusstvo, 1974).

6. Svetoslav Roerich, Interviews by the author (Bangalore, India: September and October, 1983).

7. *Building the Town* is reproduced in colour in the Russian text by Valentina P Knyzeva, *N. Roerich* (Moscow: Iskusstvo, 1968), plate 6.

8. *Princess in the Tower* is reproduced in colour in Sergei Golynets, *Ivan Bilibin*, trans. Glenys Ann Kozlov (London and Sydney: Pan Books, and Leningrad: Aurora Art Publishers, 1981), plate 15, and *Song of the Volga* in colour in Peg Weiss, *Kandinsky and Old Russia: The Artist as Ethnographer and Shaman* (New Haven and London: Yale Univeristy Press, 1995), plate 39.

9. The larger canvas in oil of *Building the Ships* is reproduced in colour in Jacqueline Decter with the Nicholas Roerich Museum, *Nicholas Roerich: The Life and Art of a Russian Master* (London: Thames and Hudson, 1989), p 56.

10. Examples are reproduced in monochrome in John E Bowlt, *The Silver Age: Russian Art of the Early Twentieth Century and the World of Art Group* (Newtonville, Massachusetts: Oriental Research Partners, 1982), plates after pp 76 and 195.

11. Sina Fosdick, Interviews by the author (New York: November, 1981 and October, November, December, 1982).

12. 'Spectacle,' *Adamant* (Paris: Presse Franco-Russe, 1923, and New York: Corona Mundi, 1924), p 49.

13. Svetoslav Roerich, Interviews.

14. The series is documented in *Roerich-Himalaya*, illustrated monograph with articles by Frances Grant, Mary Siegrist, George Grebenstchikoff, Ivan Narodny and Nicholas Roerich (New York: Brentano's, 1926), pp 192-193. Another work entitled *Elborus* is listed as part of *Pages from an Album* from 1933 in the Russian anthology, *N K Roerich: Life and Work* (Moscow: Izobrazitel'noe iskusstvo, 1978), p 290.

15. Svetoslav Roerich, Interviews.

16. *The Peak of Elborus in Sunlight* is reproduced in colour in the Russian text by V S Manin, *Arkhip Ivanovich Kuindzhi* (Leningrad: Khudozhnik USSR, 1987), plate 42.

17. *Conflagration* is reproduced in monochrome in the Russian text by E I Polyakova, *Nicholas Roerich* (Moscow: Iskusstvo, 1973), plate 35.

18. *Toledo* and *Laocoon* are reproduced in colour in Philip Troutman, *El Greco* (London: Spring Books, 1963), plates xxix and xxx.

19. This extract of Remizov's poem is included in the Russian text by Paul Belikov and Valentina Knyazeva, *Roerich* (Moscow: Molodaya Gvardiya, 1972), p 123.

20. Roerich's article was published in the Russian periodical, *Art and Artistic Industry*, Journal of the Society of the Encouragement of the Arts (St Petersburg: N° 9 and 10, June-July, 1899), pp 719-730, and in the Russian text of his *Complete Works* (Moscow: Sitin, 1914), pp 41-58.

21. *They Drag Them Along* is reproduced in colour in the Russian text by L V Korotkina, *Roerich in Petersburg-Petrograd* (Leningrad: Lenizdat, 1985), between pp 128-129.

22. Roerich's poetry was published in the Russian text, *Flowers of Morya* (Berlin: Slovo-Verlag, 1921). The collection was augmented in *Flame in Chalice*, trans. by Mary Siegrist (New York: Roerich Museum Press, 1930).

23. 'Spells of Finland,' *Realm of Light* (New York: Roerich Museum Press, 1931), p 151.

24. Gallen-Kallela's illustrations are presented in colour with the epic text as it was constructed from ancient Finnish runes by nineteenth century scholar, Elias Lönnrot, in *Kalevala*, ed., Aivi Gallen-Kallela, trans. from Finnish, W F Kirby (Helsinki: Werner Söderström Osakeyhtiö, 1985).

25. Daniel Aaron, Introduction to Henry Wadsworth Longfellow, *The Song of Hiawatha* (London: Everyman, J M Dent, 1993), pp xi-xii and xv.

26. The 1947 variant of *The Hidden Treasure* is reproduced in colour in Decter, *Nicholas Roerich*, pp 210-211.

27. The series is documented in *Roerich-Himalaya*, p 196.

28. *Wanderers* is included in *N K Roerich*, ed. Kuzmina, p 187.

29. The series is documented in *Roerich-Himalaya*, p 198.

30. Nina Selivanova, *The World of Roerich* (Paris: Presse Franco-Russe, 1923, and New York: Corona Mundi, 1923), p 87.

31. *Kedara Ragini* and *Todi Ragini* are reproduced in colour in Marguerite-Marie Deneck, *Indian Art* (London, New York, etc: Hamlyn, 1967), plates 38 and 39.

32. Photographs of the Nymph in motion are included in *Nijinsky: Prélude : l'Après-Midi d'un Faune*, ed. Jean-Michel Nectoux, trans. from French, Vendôme Press (Paris: Editions Adam Biro, 1989, and London: Thames and Hudson, 1990).

33. Sina Fosdick, Interviews.

34. Vasnetsov's designs for *Snegurochka* are reproduced in colour in V Shanina, *Victor Vasnetsov*, trans. V Friedman (Leningrad: Aurora Art Publishers, 1979), plates 65-75.

35. *And We Open the Gates* in the larger tempera version is reproduced in colour in Decter, p 122.

36. Svetoslav Roerich, Interviews.

37. The complete series is reproduced in monochrome in *Roerich*, ed. Corona Mundi, (New York: Corona Mundi, 1924), pp 41-46. *And We Do Not Fear* as well as *And We See* are reproduced in colour in Decter, pp 124-126.

38. *Leaves of Morya's Garden*, Vol I (The Call), the first volume in the Agni Yoga Series, was published first in Russian (Paris: Presse Franco-Russe, 1924), and in English, trans. Sina Fosdick (New York: Agni Yoga Society, 1924).

39. Frances Grant, Interviews.

40. Christian Brinton, *The Nicholas Roerich Exhibition* (New York: Redfield, Kendrick, Odell, 1920).

41. Manin, *Kuindzhi*, plates 20, 21 and 42.

42. Roerich's masterpiece of theatrical design is discussed in this text on pp 38 and 66. The posture is particularly suggestive of Nijinsky's choreography for the Chosen One in the climactic 'Sacrificial Dance,' as preserved in the drawings of Valentine Gross-Hugo, which are correlated with the music in Millicent Hodson, *Nijinsky's Crime Against Grace: Reconstruction Score of the Original Choreography for Le Sacre du Printemps* (New York: Pendragon Press, 1996) pp 166-169.

43. Richard Buckle, *Diaghilev* (New York: Atheneum, 1980), p 145.

44. Quoted in Buckle, *ibid*.

45. The Pskov paintings are documented in *Roerich-Himalaya*, p 188.

46. Parmenia Migel Ekstrom, Interviews with the author (New York: October and November, 1982). The show of Roerich designs took place at the Cordier and Ekstrom Gallery, New York, during November and December, 1974. The catalogue, introduced by Parmenia Migel Ekstrom, was entitled *Nicolas Roerich-Decors and Costumes for Diaghilev Ballet Russes and Russian Operas* (New York : Cordier and Ekstrom, 1925).

47. Nicholas Roerich, *Altai-Himalaya*, intro. by Claude Bragdon (London: Jarrolds, 1929), p 14.

48. George N Roerich, *Trails to Inmost Asia: Five Years of Exploration with the Roerich Central Asian Expedition* (New Haven: Yale University Press, and London: Humphrey Milford with Oxford University Press, 1931), p xii.

49. Svetoslav Roerich, Interviews.

50. Sina Fosdick, Interviews.

51. Roerich, *Altai-Himalaya*, p 15.

52. The seven other paintings, which are documented and reproduced in monochrome, unless otherwise indicated, in *Roerich-Himalaya*, are *Higher Than the Mountains,*

Fire Blossom (colour), *He Who Hastens, She Who Leads, Pearl of Searching* (colour), *Book of Wisdom and White and Heavenly* (colour), pp 9-11, 21, 71, 81, 109, 129, 164 and 183

53. George N Roerich, *Tibetan Paintings* (Paris: Libraire Orientaliste, Paul Geuthner, 1925).

54. George N Roerich, Author's Note, *Trails to Inmost* Asia, p xi.

55. *Ibid.*

56. Alexandra David-Neel, *Initiations and Initiates in Tibet*, trans. Fred Rothwell (London: Rider, 1931), p 211 and note 2.

57. *Leaves of Morya's Garden* (Vol I, The Call), p 23.

58. Sina Fosdick, Interviews.

59. Examples of the *Architectural* series are reproduced in colour in Decter, pp 58-60 and Knyazeva, plates 7 and 8.

60. Sina Fosdick, Interviews.

61. *Ibid.*

62. *Ibid.*

63. George N Roerich, *Trails to Inmost Asia*, p 290.

64. Sina Fosdick, Interviews.

65. *Ibid.*

66. Leopold Stokowski quoted in 'Producing Stravinsky's Ballet,' *New York Times* (23 March, 1930), p. IX-9.

67. *Ibid.*

68. *Ibid.*

69. Roerich's choice of Graham as the *Sacre* soloist was communicated to the author in several conversations, notably with Eleanor King, who danced in the Stokowski production and spoke about her experience during the Dance Critics conference, *The Rite of Spring at Seventy-Five* (New York Public Library at Lincoln Center, 5-7 November, 1987).

70. Belikov and Knyazeva, *Roerich*, pp 187-188.

71. *The Saga of Gessar* is reproduced in monochrome in Nicholas Roerich, *Himalayas: Abode of Light* (Bombay: Narlanda, and London: David Marlowe, 1947), p 89. It is related to the painting, *Whispers of the Desert* from the *Maitreya* series, 1925-1926, reproduced in monochrome in Polyakova, *Nicholas Roerich*, plate 45. The 1932 version of *The Sword of Gessar* is reproduced in colour in the bilingual text compiled and introduced by L Korotkina, *Nikolay Roerich* (Leningrad: Aurora Art Publishers, 1976), plate 15, and the 1943 version is documented in *N K Roerich: Life and Work*, p 300.

72. *The Campaign* is reproduced in monochrome in Korotkina, *Roerich in Petersburg-Petrograd*, between pp 96 and 97, and *The Patrol* in colour in Kuzmina, *N K Roerich,* plate 6.

73. Quoted by Roerich in *Heart of Asia* (New York: Roerich Museum Press, 1930), pp 114-115.

74. Sina Fosdick, Interviews.

75. A dungeon design for the 1913 *Princess Maleine* is reproduced in monochrome in Sergei Ernst's Russian text, *Nicholas Roerich* (Petersburg: Sv Evgenii, 1918), plate 45, together with some of his easel paintings from 1915-1916 on the theme, plates 6, 10 and 11.

76. 'Peace Pact Conference in Bruges,' *Realm of Light* (New York: Roerich Museum Press, 1931), p 107.

77. '*Encounters*' (1940) is included in *N K Roerich*, ed. Kuzmina, p 192.

78. Parmenia Migel Ekstrom, Interviews.

79. Sina Fosdick, Interviews.

80. 'Aims and History,' *The Roerich Pact and Banner of Peace* (New York: The Roerich Pact and Banner of Peace Committee, 1947), pp 5-17.

81. *Treasure of the Angels* is reproduced in colour in Kenneth Archer, 'A Russian Apocalypse Rediscovered,' *Sotheby's Preview* (London: October, 1998), p 30.

82. Banner of Peace Symbol, *The Roerich Pact*, pp 31-32.

83. *La Guerre* is reproduced in colour in Jean Cassou, *The Concise Encyclopedia of Symbolism*, trans. Susie Saunders (Paris: Editions Aimery Somogy, 1979, and London: Omega, 1984), p 58.

84. Svetoslav Roerich, Interviews

85. *Treasure of the World – Chintamani* is reproduced in colour in *Roerich- Himalaya*, p. 31, where it is simply titled *Treasure of the World*.

86. *Letters of Helena Roerich* (Vol II, 1935-1939), originally published in Russian (Riga: Latvian Roerich Society, 1940), trans. V L Dutko, (New York: Agni Yoga Society, 1967), p 73.

87. 'Call to World Unity,' *The Roerich Pact*, p 3.

88. Svetoslav Roerich, Interviews.

89. Sina Fosdick, Interviews.

90. Chloe Obolensky, *The Russian Empire: A Portrait in Photographs*, intro. by Max Hayward (New York : Random House, 1979), p 189.

91. 'Shambhala, The Resplendent' (1928) in *Shambhala* (New York: Frederick A Stokes, 1930), p 15.

92. *Altai-Himalaya*, p 236.

93. *Ibid.*

94. *Ibid.*

95. *The Power of the Caves* is reproduced in colour in *N K Roerich: Life and Work*, plate 35, and the *Maitreya* series is documented on p 284.

96. Svetoslav Roerich, Interviews.

97. The essay is included in T. S. Eliot, *The Sacred Wood, Essays on Poetry and Criticism* (London: Faber and Faber, 1920, paperback edition, 1997), p 41.

98. Svetoslav Roerich, Interviews.

99. *The Murdered Kasane Appears to the Monk Yuten* and *The Sea Monk* are reproduced in monochrome in Siegfried Wichmann, *Japonisme: The Japanese Influence on Western art since 1858*, originally published in German, trans. by Mary Whittall etc (Herrsching: Schuler Verlagsgesellschaft, 1980, and London: Thames and Hudson, 1981), plates 715 and 717. The influence of Hokusai on Redon in terms of disproportion is evident in plates 726-729.

100. *Dream of the Orient* is reproduced in monochrome in *Roerich*, ed. Corona Mundi, plate 32, and *Padma Sambhava* and *Dorje the Daring One* in colour in Decter, p 155.

101. *Altai-Himalaya*, pp 89-90.

102. *Heart of Asia*, pp 83-84.

103. Svetoslav Roerich, Interviews.

104. *Altai-Himalaya,* p 13.

105. Svetoslav Roerich, Interviews.

106. 'Treasures of the Snows' in *Himalayas – Abode of Light*, pp 19, 21 and 25.

107. 'Frontiers of Shambhala' in *ibid.*, p 120.

108. 'Shambhala, The Resplendent' in *Shambhala*, p 12.

109. James Hall, *Illustrated Dictionary of Symbols in Eastern and Western Art* (London: John Murray, 1994) p 131-133.

110. Helena Roerich's early interest in Ramakrishna and Vivekananda is documented in her *Letters* (Vol II, 1935-1939), p 277, as is her reading of post-Blavatskian Theosophical literature while she was residing in the United States. In her later years she translated Blavatsky's major work, *The Secret Doctrine* from the original English into Russian. In 1926 she wrote and privately printed *Foundations of Buddhism*, which was translated into English and published posthumously (New York: Agni Yoga Society, 1971).

111. She did a second volume of *Leaves of Morya's Garden* (Illumination), published in 1925, and then completed the following: *New Era Community*, 1926; *Agni Yoga*, 1929; *Infinity* (Vols I and II), 1930; *Hierarchy*, 1931; *Heart*, 1932; *Fiery World* (Vols I, II and III), 1933, 1934 and 1935; *Aum*, 1936; and *Brotherhood*, 1937. In 1938 she went on to do four volumes of *Supermundane*, two volumes of which have been translated into English (New York: Agni Yoga Society, 1994 and 1995).

112. *Himavat: Diary Leaves* (Allahabad: Kitabistan, 1946), p 286-287.

113. *Silence* is reproduced in monochrome in Philippe Jullian, *The Symbolists*, originally published in French, trans. by Mary Anne Stevens (Oxford: Phaidon, 1973), plate 63, and *The Swan-Princess* in colour in Cassou, *The Concise Encyclopedia of Symbolism*, p 147.

114. Buckle describes Roerich's designs for the Paris production of Prince Igor in *Diaghilev*, p 142.

115. *Letters of Helena Roerich* (Vol II, 1935-1939), pp 76-77.

116. Frances Grant, Sina Fosdick, Svetoslav Roerich, Interviews.

117. Kenneth Archer and Millicent Hodson, The Northern Spring of Roerich's Several Sacres, trans. by Olivier Cautrès, *Hommage à Léonide Massine*, Programme de L'Opéra de Nice, (23, 25, 30 and 31 December, 1994), pp 40-46, and republished in *The Beacon* (New York: Vol LVII, No 8, March-April, 1996), pp 16-20.

118. Svetoslav Roerich, Interviews.

Selected Bibliography

(Russian titles have been translated and Russian publishers transliterated).

Archer, Kenneth. *'A Russian Apocalypse Rediscovered,' Sotheby's Preview,* London: October, 1998, 30

______________. Interviews with Parmenia Migel Ekstrom. New York: October and November, 1982. (unpublished)

______________. Interviews with Sina Fosdick. New York: November, 1981 and October, November, December, 1982. (unpublished)

______________. Interviews with Francis Grant. New York: November and December, 1982. (unpublished)

______________. Interviews with Svetoslav Roerich. Bangalore, India: September and October, 1983. (unpublished)

______________ and Millicent Hodson. 'The Northern Spring of Roerich's Several Sacres.' Trans. into French by Olivier Cautrès. *Hommage à Léonide Massine, Programme de L'Opéra de Nice,* (23, 25, 30 and 31 December, 1994), 40-46. Republished in English. *The Beacon* (New York: Vol LVII, N^O 8, March-April, 1996), 16-20.

Art and Artistic Industry. Journal of the Society of the Encouragement of the Arts. (Russian) St Petersburg: N^OS 9 and 10, June-July, 1899, 719-730.

Belikov, Paul and Valentina Knyazeva. *Roerich.* (Russian) Moscow: Molodaya Gvardiya, 1972.

Blavatsky, H P. *The Secret Doctrine* (Vols I. and II.) London, New York, Adyar: The Theosophical Publishing Company, 1888. Facsimile edition of original. Los Angeles: The Theosophy Company, 1964.

Bowlt, John E. *The Silver Age: Russian Art of the Early Twentieth Century and the World of Art Group.* Newtonville, Massachusetts: Oriental Research Partners, 1982.

Brinton, Christian. *The Nicholas Roerich Exhibition.* New York: Redfield, Kendrick, Odell, 1920.

Buckle, Richard. *Diaghilev.* New York: Atheneum, 1980.

Cassou, Jean. *The Concise Encyclopedia of Symbolism.* Paris: Editions Aimery Somogy, 1979. Trans. from French by Susie Saunders. London: Omega, 1984.

David-Neel, Alexandra. *Initiations and Initiates in Tibet.* Trans. from French by Fred Rothwell. London: Rider, 1931.

Dector, Jacqueline, with the Nicholas Roerich Museum. Nicholas Roerich: *The Life and Art of a Russian Master.* London: Thames and Hudson, 1989.

Deneck, Marguerite-Marie. *Indian Art.* London, New York, etc: Hamlyn, 1967.

Eliot, T S. *The Sacred Wood, Essays on Poetry and Criticism.* London: Faber and Faber, 1920, paperback edition, 1997.

Ernst, Sergei. *Nicholas Roerich.* (Russian) Petersburg: Sv Evgenii, 1918.

Fosdick, Sina. *Nicholas Roerich: A Brief Biography.* New York: Nicholas Roerich Museum, 1964.

Golynets, Sergei. *Ivan Bilibin.* Trans. from Russian by Glenys Ann Kozlov. London and Sydney: Pan Books, and Leningrad: Aurora Art Publishers, 1981.

Hall, James. *Illustrated Dictionary of Symbols in Eastern and Western Art.* London: John Murray, 1994.

Hodson, Millicent. *Nijinsky's Crime Against Grace: Reconstruction Score of the Original Choreography for Le Sacre du Printemps.* New York: Pendragon Press,1996.

Jullian, Philippe. *The Symbolists.* Trans. from French by Mary Anne Stevens.Oxford: Phaidon, 1973.

Kalevala. Text constructed by Elias Lönnrot. Edition illustrated by Akseli Gallen-Kallela. Aivi Gallen-Kallela (ed.). Trans. from the Finnish by W F Kirby. Helsinki: Werner Söderström Osakeyhtiö, 1985.

Kamensky, Alexander (ed.). *The World of Art Movement in Early Twentieth Century Russia.* Trans. from Russian by Arthur Shkarosky-Raffe. Leningrad: Aurora Art Publishers, 1991.

Kean, Beverly Whitney. *All the Empty Palaces: The Merchant Patrons of Modern Art in Pre-Revolutionary Russia.* London: Barrie and Jenkins, 1983.

Knyazeva, Valentina P. *Roerich.* (Russian) Moscow: Iskusstvo, 1968.

Korotkina, *L V. Roerich in Petersburg-Petrograd.* (Russian) Leningrad: Lenizdat,1985.

Kuzmina, M T (ed.). *N K Roerich: From his Literary Legacy.* (Russian) Moscow: Iskusstvo, 1974.

Longfellow, Henry Wadsworth. *The Song of Hiawatha.* Intr. by Daniel Aaron. London: Everyman, J M Dent, 1993.

Manin, V S. *Arkhip Ivanovich Kuindzhi.* (Russian) Leningrad: Khudozhnik USSR, 1987.

Nectoux, Jean-Michel (ed.). *Nijinsky: Prélude à l'Après-Midi d'un Faune.* Paris: Editions Adam Biro, 1939. Trans. from French by Vendôme Press. London: Thames and Hudson, 1990.

Nicholas Roerich, *Decors and costumes for Diaghilev's Ballets Russes and Russian Operas.* Intro by Parmenia Migel Ekstrom. New York : Cordier and Ekstrom, 1974.

Nikolay Roerich. (Russian and English) Intro. by L Korotkina. Leningrad: Aurora Art Publishers, 1976.

N K Roerich: Life and Work. (Russian) Moscow: Izobrazitel'noe iskusstvo, 1978.

Obolensky, Chloe. *The Russian Empire: A Portrait in Photographs.* Intro. by Max Hayward. New York: Random House, 1979.

Polyakova, E I. *Nicholas Roerich.* (Russian) Moscow: Iskusstvo, 1973.

'Producing Stravinsky's Ballet,' *New York Times*, 23 March, 1930, IX-9.

The Rite of Spring at Seventy-Five. The Dance Critics Confrence. New York Public Library at Lincoln Center, 5-7 November, 1987.

Roerich. Corona Mundi (ed.). New York: Corona Mundi, 1924.

Roerich, George N. *Tibetan Paintings.* Paris: Libraire Orientaliste, Paul Geuthner,1925.

______________. *Trails to Inmost Asia: Five Years of Exploration with the Roerich Central Asian Expedition.* New Haven: Yale University Press, and London: Humphrey Milford with Oxford University Press, 1931.

Roerich, Helena (ed. and amanuensis). Agni Yoga Series (13 Vols). Trans. from Russian by Sina Fosdick. New York: Agni Yoga Society, 1924-37. *Leaves of Morya's Garden*, Vol I (*The Call*), 1924; and Vol II (*Illumination*) 1925; *New Era Community*, 1926; *Agni Yoga*, 1929; *Infinity* (Vols I and II), 1930; *Hierarchy*, 1931; *Heart*, 1932; *Fiery World* (Vols I, II and III), 1933, 1934 and 1935; Aum, 1936; and *Brotherhood*, 1937.

______________. (ed. and amanuensis). Agni Yoga Series (4 Vols). *Supermundane*, 1938. Trans. from Russian. Agni Yoga Society, New York. (Vols I and II) 1994 and 1995.

______________. *Foundations of Buddhism.* Privately printed in Russian, 1926. Trans. into English. New York: Agni Yoga Society, 1971.

______________. *Letters* (Vol I, 1929-1938 and Vol II, 1935-1939). Riga: Latvian Roerich Society, 1935 and 1940. Trans. from Russian by V L Dutko. New York: Agni Yoga Society, 1954 and 1967

Roerich-Himalaya. New York: Brentano's, 1926.

Roerich, Nicholas. *Adamant.* Paris: Presse Franco-Russe, 1923, and New York: Corona Mundi, 1924.

______________. *Altai-Himalaya.* Intro. by Claude Bragdon. London: Jarrolds,1929.

______________. *Complete Works*, Vol I. (Russian) Moscow: Sitin, 1914.

______________. *Flowers of Morya.* (Russian) Berlin: Slovo-Verlag, 1921. Augmented and republished as *Flame in Chalice.* Translated from Russian by Mary Siegrist. New York: Roerich Museum Press, 1930

______________. *Heart of Asia.* New York: Roerich Museum Press, 1930.

______________. *Himalayas: Abode of Light.* Bombay: Narlanda, and London: David Marlowe, 1947.

______________. *Himavat: Diary Leaves.* Allahabad: Kitabistan, 1946.

______________ *Realm of Light.* New York: Roerich Museum Press, 1931.

______________ *Shambhala.* New York: Frederick A Stokes, 1930.

The Roerich Pact and Banner of Peace. New York: The Roerich Pact Committee, 1947.

Selivanova, Nina. *The World of Roerich.* Paris: Presse Franco-Russe and New York: Corona Mundi, 1923.

Shanina, V. *Victor Vasnetsov.* Trans. from Russian by V Friedman. Leningrad: Aurora Art Publishers, 1979.

Spells of Russia. Catalogue of the Nicholas Roerich exhibition, Goupil Gallery. London: William Marchant, 1920.

Troutman, Philip. *El Greco.* London: Spring Books, 1963.

Weiss, Peg. *Kandinsky and Old Russia: The Artist as Ethnographer and Shaman.* New Haven and London: Yale University Press, 1995.

Wichmann, Siegfried. *Japonisme: The Japanese Influence on Western art since 1858.* Herrsching: Schuler Verlagsgesellschaft, 1980. Trans. from German by Mary Whittall etc. London: Thames and Hudson, 1981.

Picture list

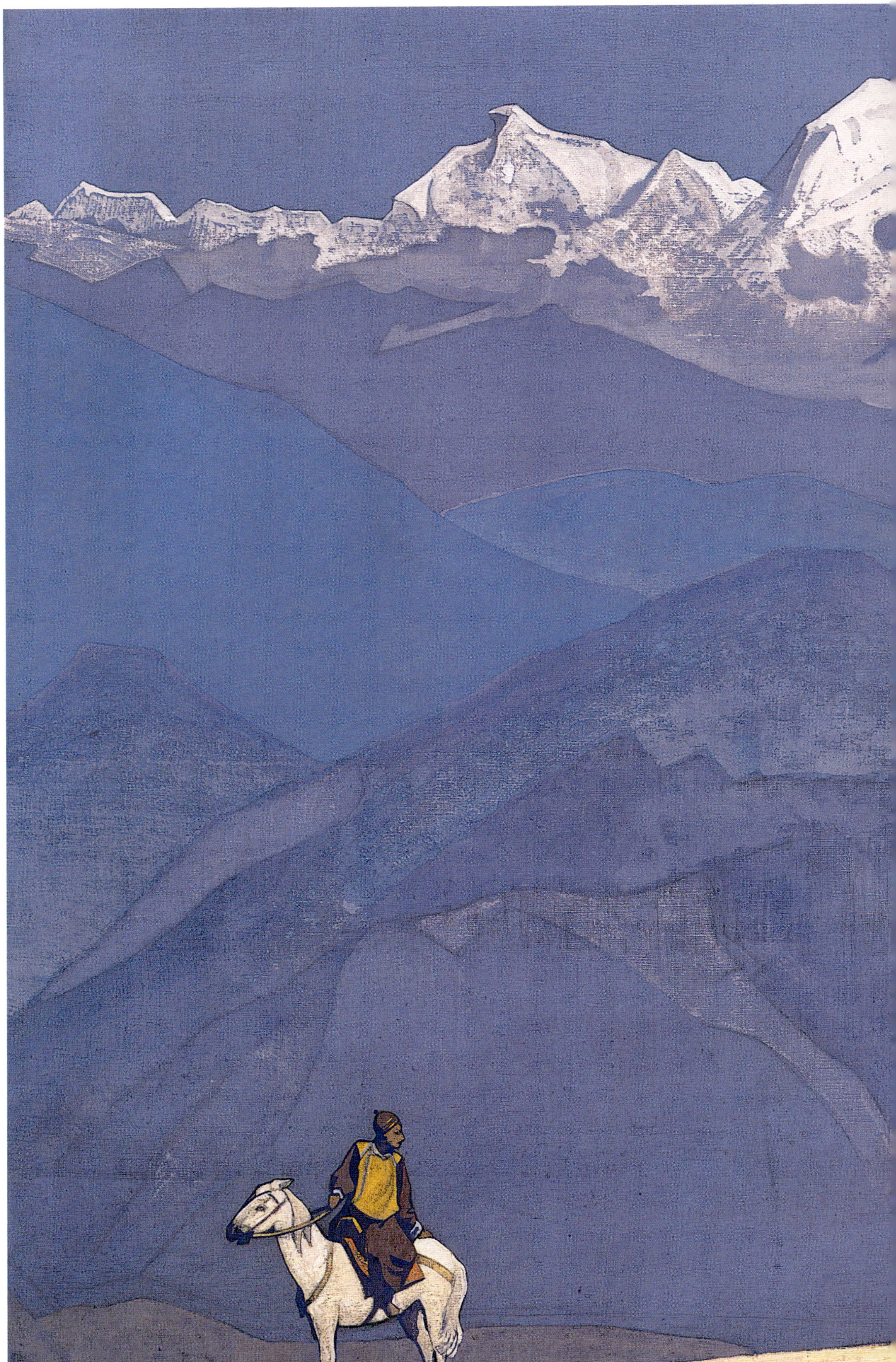

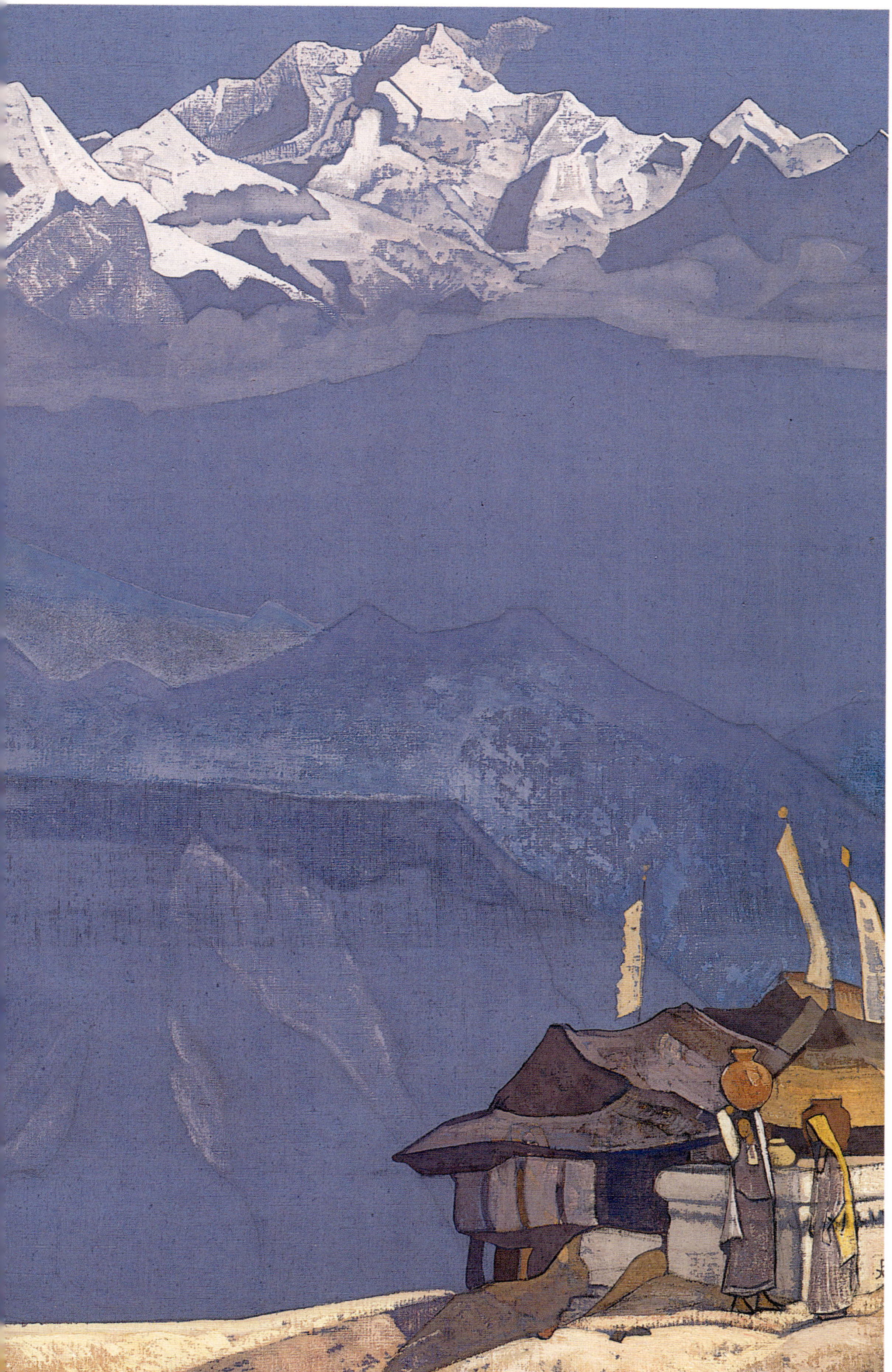

Remember, 1924

Tempera on canvas,
127 x 91.4 cm.
Nicholas Roerich
Museum, New York